At the commencement of World War II, the Navy and the Army—woefully lacking small ships able to ply shallow, reef-infested South and Southwest Pacific waters, which were necessary to support island ground combat—initially acquired whatever was available in ports, harbors, and backwaters to meet their needs. These vessels included schooners, ancient ferry boats, luggers, fishing trawlers, tuna boats, tugs, launches, lighters, surf boats, ketches, yachts, and yawls. The services took whatever craft they could get—some barely seaworthy—as the urgency of need did not permit discrimination in what was purchased or chartered. Gen. Douglas MacArthur, needing his own Navy to support leapfrog operations up the New Guinea coast, found his vessels in Australia and New Zealand, and the Navy its small ships and craft in America. These "Pacific island hoppers" were later supplemented with other small vessels newly constructed in American boat and shipyards. Among them were sixty Navy wooden-hulled 103-foot small coastal transports, hundreds of Army freight-supply ships and large tugs, and lesser numbers of coastal tankers and harbor tugs. The Army ships—most of steel construction, a few of wood—were manned by Coast Guard, Merchant Marine, or Army crews. The islands hoppers worked mostly with amphibious forces, but also supported PT boat squadrons, and as "maids of all duties" engaged in a variety of operations. Periodic combat with Japanese planes off the New Guinea coast and in the Solomon Islands transitioned to frequent battles with conventional and kamikaze aircraft and suicide Q-boats during the Philippine Islands Campaign. Significant numbers of the island hoppers earned battle stars, and crewmen awards for valor including the Navy Cross, the Silver Star and the Bronze Star medals. Following the war, the Navy acquired some of the Army ships; many served in the Korean War and a few in Vietnam. Three of the former freight-supply ships were employed for intelligence gathering; the most famous, USS Pueblo, was captured by North Korea. Others led interesting careers under civilian ownership; one was run aground while engaged in drug smuggling in the Caribbean, and another served as a "radio pirate" off England, broadcasting BBC-banned rock and roll music over the airwaves in 1966.

MacArthur and Halsey's "Pacific Island Hoppers"

Also by David D. Bruhn

Ready to Answer All Bells

Wooden Ships and Iron Men: The U.S. Navy's Ocean Minesweepers, 1953–1994

Wooden Ships and Iron Men: The U.S. Navy's Coastal and Motor Minesweepers, 1941–1953

Wooden Ships and Iron Men: The U.S. Navy's Coastal and Inshore Minesweepers, and the Minecraft That Served in Vietnam, 1953–1976

MacArthur and Halsey's "Pacific Island Hoppers"

The Forgotten Fleet of World War II

David D. Bruhn

HERITAGE BOOKS
2014

HERITAGE BOOKS
AN IMPRINT OF HERITAGE BOOKS, INC.

Books, CDs, and more—Worldwide

For our listing of thousands of titles see our website
at
www.HeritageBooks.com

Published 2014 by
HERITAGE BOOKS, INC.
Publishing Division
5810 Ruatan Street
Berwyn Heights, Md. 20740

Copyright © 2014 Cdr. David D. Bruhn, USN (Retired)

Heritage Books by the author:

MacArthur and Halsey's "Pacific Island Hoppers:" The Forgotten Fleet of World War II

Wooden Ships and Iron Men: The U.S. Navy's Ocean Minesweepers, 1953–1994

Wooden Ships and Iron Men: The U.S. Navy's Coastal and Motor Minesweepers, 1941–1953

Wooden Ships and Iron Men: The U.S. Navy's Coastal and Inshore Minesweepers, and the Minecraft that Served in Vietnam, 1953–1976

All rights reserved. No part of this book may be reproduced or transmitted in any form or by any means, electronic or mechanical, including photocopying, recording or by any information storage and retrieval system without written permission from the author, except for the inclusion of brief quotations in a review.

International Standard Book Numbers
Paperbound: 978-0-7884-5541-4
Clothbound: 978-0-7884-9098-9

To the veterans, men and women, of World War II

Contents

Foreword by Kemper Goffigon III xiii
Preface. xvii
Acknowledgments. xxix
1 Condition "Very Red". 1
2 Papua, New Guinea, and the "Catboat Flotilla". 15
3 The Army and Navy "Pacific Island Hoppers". 25
4 Search for Enemy Spies and Coast Watchers. 37
5 New Georgia Campaign. 49
6 Voyage to Australia and Initial Operations 67
7 Capture of Lae and Finschhafen 81
8 Coastal Transports Sunk and Damaged at Arawe, New Britain 95
9 Support for PT Boats and the Treasury Islands Landings 111
10 JFK Rescues Marine Paratroopers on Choiseul Island. 123
11 Assault and Capture of Tarawa 129
12 Army/Navy Support for Allied Coast Watchers 137
13 Through the Bismarcks. 143
14 Capture and Occupation of Guam 155
15 Support for Motor Torpedo Boat Squadrons. 161
16 Leyte and Mindoro Landings. 165
17 Lingayen Gulf Landings 203
18 Suicide Boat Attacks at Nasugbu, Luzon 219
19 Assault and Occupation of Okinawa. 229
20 Borneo Campaign of 1945 241
21 Final U.S. Naval Battle of World War II 251
Postscript 259
Appendix A: Battle Stars Earned During World War II. 267
Appendix B: Army Freight (F) and Freight-Supply (FS) Ships. 271
Appendix C: Army Harbor Tugs. 283
Appendix D: Navy Small Coastal Transports 285
Appendix E: Award Citations for Final U.S. Naval Battle 291
Appendix F: Navy Unit Awards. 295
Bibliography. 299
Notes. 303
Index 337
About the Author 367

Photos

Preface: *APc-15* under way during builder's trials off Camden, Maine xx
3-1: Drawing of *APc-1* with a camouflage paint scheme 33
3-2: *APc-68* as HMS *FT-25* under way near East Boothbay, Maine 35
4-1: *APc-29* at anchor off Guadalcanal Island 43
5-1: *APc-38* under way in San Francisco Bay near builder's yard 63
6-1: *APc-17* during launching at Camden, Maine, builder's yard 68
8-1: *Enemy Strike from Rabaul* (painting by Richard DeRosset) 94
8-2: Kemper Goffigon III, commanding officer of *APc-15* 107
10-1: John F. Kennedy's *PT-59* (painting by Richard DeRosset) 122
14-1: *APc-46* at anchor off Guadalcanal Island 160
15-1: *FS-175* of the 2nd Engineer Special Brigade 163
16-1: *F-15* of the 2nd Engineer Special Brigade 170
16-2: Former *LT-455* as USNS *T-ATA-240* 181
16-3: Former *Y-87* as Navy fuel oil barge *YO-242* 188
16-4: *ST-381* of the 2nd Engineer Special Brigade 190
19-1: *APc-42* moored at Guiuan, Samar, Philippine Islands 238
Postscript-1: *APc-9* arriving at San Francisco Bay 260
Postscript-2: *Brule* on the Bassac River, Republic of Vietnam 262
Postscript-3: *Olga Patricia* off the coast of England 264

Maps

1-1: Solomon Islands 2
1-2: Papua, New Guinea 3
1-3: Guadalcanal and Tulagi, Solomon Islands 4
2-1: Manila Bay area of Luzon, Philippine Islands. 17
4-1: Vitiaz and Dampier Straits 40
4-2: Russell Islands, Solomons 46
5-1: New Georgia Islands, Solomons. 51
6-1: New Caledonia Island 71
6-2: Australia. 73
9-1: Treasury Islands, Solomons. 116
10-1: Bougainville, Solomon Islands 124
11-1: Gilbert Islands, Central Pacific. 130
11-2: Allied route from the Gilberts to Japan. 132
11-3: Tarawa Atoll, Gilbert Islands. 133
12-1: Santa Cruz Islands, Solomons. 138
12-2: New Hebrides Islands, South Pacific 139
13-1: Admiralty Islands, Bismarck Archipelago. 146
13-2: Hollandia, New Guinea 149
14-1: Marianas Islands, Central Pacific. 157
14-2: Guam, Marianas Islands 158
15-1: Morotai Island, Dutch East Indies 164
16-1: Leyte Gulf, Leyte Island, Philippines 166
16-2: Philippine Islands. 169
17-1: Lingayen Gulf, Luzon Island, Philippines. 208
19-1: Okinawa, Ryukyu Islands 236
20-1: Borneo Island 243
21-1: Shanghai, China 252

Foreword

David Bruhn has produced a book that should sit proudly in the bookcase of many Americans. It is a story of the forgotten fleet of World War II, the "Pacific Island Hoppers." These included the APc coastal transports, PT boats, sub-chasers, minesweepers, and other small craft including the wooden 36-foot Higgins boats, which ferried out troops to hostile beaches during many of the amphibious landings in the Pacific theater of war. The amphibious operations along the Papua and New Guinea coasts included both sea-to-shore, and shore-to-shore ("leap frogging") craft movements. The Army operated its own freight-supply ships, tugs and coastal tankers. The Navy's small ships and craft were manned by Navy or Coast Guard personnel and the Army's "island hoppers" by Coast Guardsmen, Merchant Mariners, and in a few cases by Soldiers.

The important contribution of these unsung vessels to the Pacific War effort is vividly told by the author. Many of these small ships and craft were exposed almost daily to Japanese gunfire and aircraft attacks. Typhoons and storms were a constant menace, and in the New Guinea area the energy-sapping heat was accompanied by high humidity resulting from frequent torrential rains. Daily showers were common, and on some days there was a downpour nearly every hour.

As the commanding officer of the USS *APc-15*, my ship was employed as a command and navigation ship to guide landing craft to enemy beaches during amphibious landings. Our other duties included hauling troops, ammunition, cargo, mail and supplies to established beachheads. The ship's complement was three officers and twenty-seven enlisted men; all were reservists and few had any sea experience prior to the war. We had a chief motor machinist's mate who was regular Navy but he got so seasick on the *APc-15* that he had to be transferred off the ship. The senior enlisted was a chief boatswain's mate in his 40s, with prior service and who had been called back. The assignment of officers aboard was by official orders from the Bureau of Naval Personnel. After receiving my officer's commission, I had served aboard the coastal minesweeper USS *Kingbird* (AMc-56)—a former Gloucester fishing vessel, the *Governor Saltonstall*—out of Boston, and I accordingly had a little more experience and was senior to the other two officers aboard the *APc-15*.

The safety of a ship's crew and its morale is important, particularly in wartime. Thus, a commanding officer may sometimes purposely choose not to "follow the book." As we made our way across the Pacific via Bora Bora, the Fijian Islands, Pago Pago, New Caledonia, and an independent ship transit across the Coral Sea to Brisbane, Australia, many of my crew were on the lookout in each port for additional weapons to augment the four 20mm guns on board the *APc-15*. The Navy Washington D.C. bureaucracy and the naval architect it employed to design the ship had their ideas regarding what constituted self-defense for small coastal transports, and the men going to war had their own ideas about adequate armament—the basic philosophy being "more firepower is better." So, while I should have censured the men who "commandeered" machine guns from rear area shore bases, I was actually pleased with the ingenuity and resourcefulness they exhibited in looking out after our ship. I also bent the rules while the *APc-15* was at Cairns, Australia, for three and a half to four months undergoing repairs following the fight off New Britain against a flight of Japanese dive-bombers and fighter aircraft.

Although only a small community, Cairns hosted an excellent marine railway for hauling out damaged vessels for repair. The locals were very friendly, and we made friends with the proprietor of a hotel close to where the ship was dry-docked. I traded Navy rations for whisky and beer; not officially allowed. However, the Aussies got a chance to eat something besides lamb and the officers and the men enjoyed the spirits, although truthfully the whisky was not a good whisky and the beer was always warm.

Regarding the action off New Britain that is depicted on the book cover and adequately described herein, I will only add that it was over in two or three minutes, sufficient time for the *APc-15* to be lost or saved. We tragically lost good men that day and many others were injured, but our losses would have been much greater but for the collective heroic actions of the officers and men, of which I am very proud.

It is my pleasure to salute David Bruhn for his excellent story of courage and heroism by the small ships and their crews, both my

APc-15 and hundreds of other vessels. The personnel that manned and fought these little fellows were a courageous and valiant group. The book provides the public a long overdue tale of the small ships' contributions to victory in the Pacific, and is a deserved tribute to their personnel, who went in harm's way more often than you can imagine.

Kemper Goffigon III
Former Commanding Officer, USS *APc-15* (1943–1944)
20 November 2013

Preface

> During World War II the U.S. Army owned and operated a fleet of 111,006 vessels—more than the Navy. While most of these were small craft, 1,665 were ocean-going ships over 1,000 tons. These included transports, supply ships, repair, and spare parts vessels. At the height of World War II, 244 of these ships were manned for the Army by the Coast Guard. Unlike the Navy and Coast Guard which preserves the logs of its ships and honors their memory, the Army tended to view its vessels with the emotional attachment rendered a truck or any other piece of equipment; an inanimate object to be discarded and written off once it has served its purpose. As a result, these Army vessels have come to be known as "The Forgotten Fleet of World War II."
>
> U.S. Coast Guard Historian's Office observation, September 2004[1]

MACARTHUR'S NAVY

The above quote aptly describes the perspective of Army leadership during World War II, which valued ships, and tugs and other small vessels towing barges, only for their ability to deliver men and materials to beachheads, or hastily constructed ports in forward areas. This is not surprising, given that soldiers—who are primarily concerned with ground combat—tend to view ships as a means of transportation, or to provide them food, ammunition, and other materials ashore. Gen. Douglas MacArthur well understood, however, like Gen. George Washington had during the Revolutionary War, the relationship of a strong navy to the success of an army. Washington stated in 1781 "Without a decisive naval force we can do nothing definitive, and with it, everything honorable and glorious."

MacArthur had neither ships nor shipping when he established headquarters in Australia in April 1942, following his evacuation from the Philippines, and began to plan his Papua, New Guinea Campaign. Moreover, he could expect little help from the U.S. Navy's

Pacific Fleet. It faced superior Japanese forces, was itself short of ships and, as is well known, there was no love lost between the general and the fleet commander, Adm. Chester Nimitz. In order to support his planned "leapfrog" operations—amphibious landings designed to bypass Japanese strongholds as Allied troops progressed up the New Guinea coast along the road back to the Philippines—MacArthur created his own navy. A majority of this flotilla was comprised of small ships and craft referred to as "island hoppers," because when not plying shallow, reef-infested uncharted coastal waters, they worked intra-island waters of the same description.

STOPGAP FORCES

MacArthur sent representatives to Australia and New Zealand to find vessels to deliver his troops, supplies, and combat materials along the Papua, New Guinea, coastlines, and to take away army casualties and bodies of soldiers killed in combat. This ramshackle fleet of trawlers, schooners, luggers, and ketches—termed the "Catboat Flotilla"— was operated by young boys and elderly men deemed unfit for military service by the Australian government. The next type of "island hoppers" to report for duty in the South and Southwest Pacific were Yard Patrol Craft (YPs) ordered to these theaters by the U.S. Navy. In anticipation of war, the Navy had begun in 1941 to procure fishing vessels, yachts, whalers, tugs, and other type ships and craft—basically anything that floated, and which could be fitted with machine guns and ideally depth charges—for duty as patrol vessels off America's east, west, and gulf coasts. Although initially assigned to the commandants of Naval Districts, some of the larger, more seaworthy YPs—former San Diego tuna clippers and Massachusetts fishing trawlers—were dispatched to the Pacific. The Army was also procuring trawlers, tow boats, purse seiners, and sailing schooners. After being refitted for war service, they were designated "Freight and Passenger Vessel (Small)" or TP. Some of the Army TPs, like Navy YPs, were sent to the Pacific.

The Catboat Flotilla, YPs, and TPs were "stopgap forces," which by necessity supported combat operations until America's shipyards could, after fulfilling higher priority requirements for aircraft carriers, cruisers, destroyers and other combatants, build small cargo ships. The first purposefully-built small ships to serve as "island hoppers" were sixty-nine Navy wooden-hulled small coastal transports. Intended to be 103-foot minesweepers, the design and construction of more capable 136-foot Yard Minesweepers resulted in Navy discussion about the possibility of "raider transports," probably for use in the South Pacific. Within a few days, the classification Coastal Transport, Small (APc) was created on 22 April 1942.

NAVY SMALL COASTAL TRANSPORTS

Twenty-two of the small coastal transports—APcs 1 through 22—were based at Milne Bay, New Guinea after their arrival in Australia in May 1943, twenty-eight—APcs 23 through 50—were assigned to Guadalcanal in the Solomon Islands, and the remaining ten ships—APcs *95, 96, 98, 101–103,* and *108–111*—serving in the Pacific were at Noumea; Efate Island; Espiritu Santo, New Hebrides; Funa Futi, Ellice Islands; and, Honolulu, Hawaii. Assignments of some ships changed over the course of the war as operational requirements dictated.

The modestly designed and equipped 103-foot wooden ships were propelled by a single diesel engine, and armed with four 20mm anti-aircraft guns. Enterprising commanding officers and their crews, however, typically acquired machine guns to augment their armament, because, as noted by the captain of a sub-chaser in reference to encounters with Japanese planes "volume of fire power is all important." The *APc-15* was particularly proficient at "obtaining" additional guns, which helped enable her to survive a withering attack by a flight of 20-25 enemy aircraft off New Britain. During that grim fight, everyone aboard, except the commanding officer and three men on the bridge and one man in the engine room, were assigned as gunners, loaders, or another gun crew position for the ship's four 20mm guns, four .50-caliber and two .30-caliber machine guns—resulting in ten barrels blazing away, which saved the diminutive *APc–15.*

The ship's captain, Kemper Goffigon III, was, like a majority of his peers, a young man; 24–26 years of age while in command. A graduate of the University of Virginia, he received his officer's commission via the V7 program, a twelve-week course of instruction conducted at the U.S. Naval Academy at Annapolis, Maryland. Following twenty months of combat duty in the Southwest Pacific, Goffigon received orders in December 1944 transferring him to Norfolk, Virginia. Soon after reporting for duty to the naval station, he took command of the yard patrol craft *YP-61,* a 98-foot former Coast Guard cutter, USCGC *Dallas,* constructed in 1925 by the Defoe Boat & Motor Works of Detroit, Michigan. (The author's book *Battle Stars for the Cactus Navy* is

USS *APc-15* under way during builder's trials off Camden, Maine, on 6 October 1942. She is carrying two 20mm guns on the bridge, part of the original design for the class. Two additional 20mm single gun mounts were added, one on a platform on the bow and one on the after end of the superstructure. There were also aboard this ship off Arawe, New Britain, an additional four .50-caliber and two .30-caliber machine guns. (U.S. Navy photo # 19-N-38017, now in the collections of the US National Archives RG-19-LCM: http://www.navsource.org/archives/09/23/092301502.jpg)

devoted to the service of the Navy's some seven hundred Yard Patrol Craft (YP) and Patrol Yachts (PY/PYc) of World War II.) Goffigon continued to serve as the ship's captain until September 1945, when following Japan's surrender he was discharged from the Navy. He entered the University of Virginia, Law School in 1946 and earned his law degree in 1948.

OPERATIONS ALONG THE NEW GUINEA COAST AND IN THE SOLOMONS

> *Let there be built great ships which can cast upon a beach, in any weather, large numbers of the heaviest tanks.*
>
> Winston Churchill, 1940 Memo to War Department

Much of the service of the small coastal transports assigned to APc Flotilla 5 at Guadalcanal and APc Flotilla 7 at Milne Bay involved serving as "navigation and guide ships" for groups of LCTs (tank landing craft) during amphibious operations. American shipyards churned out hundreds of these amphibious assault ships—developed initially by the British Royal Navy and designed for landing tanks on beachheads—for the U.S. Navy during the war.

In addition to working with the amphibious forces, the small wooden cargo ships, being "maids of all duties," did whatever was asked of them. In the Solomons, APcs transported U.S. and Fijian troops charged with searching islands for enemy spies and coast watchers, embarked hydrographic parties to survey critical uncharted waters, and hauled shiploads of palm thatches to Guadalcanal. The thatches were used for camouflage over "hideaways," sanctuaries in coves or near river banks designed to shield small vessels from the view of Japanese fighter aircraft and dive-bombers during frequent air raids. It was necessary to obtain thatches from other islands, as the palms on Guadalcanal had been decimated by gunfire and bombs. The island waters charted included those of Pavuvu, which Army staff officers—believing the small, uninhabited island to be a tropical paradise, after viewing it during a flyover—had selected for use as a rest camp for soldiers and Marines. The troops sent there did not, however, relish the experience. The island was home to muddy tidal swamps; covered with a thick mat of smelly, rotten coconut goo; and hosted legions of land crabs. A Marine wryly observed the only benefit time spent on Pavuvu offered was, due to the universally-hated conditions, as a means for replacements to bond with hardened combat veterans before they went into battle together. One of the most interesting APc assignments was that of the *APc-46*. She arrived off Guam the day American troops stormed the Japanese-held island to serve as an improvised seaplane base; refueling and rearming Catalinas.

Small, coastal transports in New Guinea transported amphibious scouts—the precursors of Navy SEALs—charged with carrying out beach reconnaissance before amphibious landings, and APcs in both the Solomons and New Guinea supported motor torpedo boat squadrons. This assistance took the form of delivering food, fuel, water, ammunition, torpedoes, spare parts, and other materials to forward operating areas, and serving as base communications ships there until relieved by a sister ship bringing resupply.

It was not my intention to highlight John F. Kennedy's short albeit action-packed service in the South Pacific, but I found in my research that his duty aboard the motor torpedo boats *PT-109* and *PT-59* was intertwined with other themes of this book. Following his passage from San Francisco across the Pacific aboard the transport ship USS *Rochambeau* (AP-63) and subsequent transfer to the USS *LST-449* at Espiritu Santo, Hebrides, Kennedy was embarked aboard the tank landing ship off Guadalcanal on 7 April 1943 when Adm. Isoroku Yamamoto—the architect of the attack on Pearl Harbor—launched Operation I-GO. This operation was a counter-offensive in which an armada of aircraft attacked Allied ships, aircraft, and bases in the southeast Solomon Islands and New Guinea. This action is described in Chapter One, titled "Condition Very Red." Kennedy disembarked at Tulagi, across the New Georgia Sound from Guadalcanal, a week later, and took command of the *PT-109* on 23 April 1943. Much has been written about the loss of his boat, due to a collision with the Japanese destroyer *Amagiri* the night of 1-2 August 1943, and of Kennedy's efforts to get his crew ashore and care for the men, for which he earned the Navy and Marine Corps medal. Since the details of this event are so well know there is no discussion of it herein. There is a short chapter describing the heroic actions of the *PT-59*, which Kennedy took command of in September 1943, and of a second motor torpedo boat, the *PT-236*, in extracting U.S. Marines—trapped and pinned down by enemy fire at the mouth of the Warrior River—off Choiseul Island the night of 2 November. Following this action, Kennedy was involved in "barge busting," combat operations against Japanese self-propelled and heavily armed barges transporting enemy soldiers and supplies. Before, on 18 November, a doctor directed Kennedy—who was both physically and mental exhausted and had lost twenty-five pounds—to go to the hospital at Tulagi. That same day he gave up his command of *PT-59* to Ens. John N. Mitchell (who would be United States District Attorney under President Richard M. Nixon) and left the Solomons on 21 December 1943.[2]

DUTY IN THE EASTERN, CENTRAL, AND SOUTH PACIFIC

The other ten APcs that served in the Pacific also had diverse tasking. Two of the ships were assigned duty with Service Squadron 2 in Hawaii transporting personnel and cargo between bases in the islands. Another two were based with a small number of other ships at Funa Futi, Ellice Islands to form mobile Service Squadron 4, created to support the invasion of Tarawa Atoll in the Gilbert Islands. The remaining six APcs were assigned to Noumea, New Caledonia, for duty with

Service Squadron, South Pacific Force. An APc at Noumea underwent conversion for duty as a refrigeration ship before assignment to Efate Island, New Hebrides, as the relief for the only ship of the United States Navy to be named for the nymph Echo. The war service of the two-masted scow *Echo* was the basis for a Hollywood comedy war film released in 1960, titled *The Wackiest Ship in the Army*, starring Jack Lemmon, Ricky Nelson, and Chips Rafferty. The plot involved a secret mission to deliver an Australian coast watcher to a location only a shallow-draft vessel could reach, and the ship's encounter with Japanese forces and role in helping to win the Battle of the Bismarck Sea. In actuality, the scow *Echo* supported Australian coast watchers, rescued many downed American aircraft crews, and is thought to have helped track down two Japanese submarines, in addition to her more mundane cargo ship duties.

Small coastal transports at Tarawa were dispatched to islands of the atoll to recruit native laborers for work on Betio Island on the southwest corner of Tarawa. In related operations, the ships brought thousands of bales of Pandanus thatch back to Tarawa for use by natives in the construction of living huts. The former Japanese base at Betio, which American forces had captured during the invasion of Tarawa, had been wrecked as a result of air strikes and fighting, and chaos, ruins, a litter of corpses and decaying food dumps extended over the entire 285 acres. Practically every square foot of the island had to be cleared and graded in order for the Seabees (Navy Construction Battalion personnel) to begin installations and improvements. A few months later, one of these small coastal transports rescued the crew of the Army freight ship *F-14* which had, while in passage across the Pacific, suffered a casualty to its reduction gears and then drifted for thirty days before the wind and seas finally deposited the incapacitated ship off Tabiteuea Island in the Gilberts. The word "rescue" might be misleading. When the *APc-108* located the 99-foot freighter anchored off a reef, her captain and the other Merchant Mariners assigned to the vessel with the exception of a five-man watch section maintained aboard, were living ashore in native villages.

THE ARMY'S FREIGHT-SUPPLY SHIPS, TUGS, AND COASTAL TANKERS

Requiring vast numbers of small ships to support its ground forces in the Southwest Pacific—and in other theaters of war—the Army contracted for the construction of hundreds of freight and freight-supply ships, hundreds of large and small tugs, and many fewer coastal tankers and harbor tugs. These vessels began to arrive in the Southwest Pacific, fresh from their builders' yards, in 1944. An urgent need for their service in support of combat operations on expanding fronts minimized time normally spent to "shake down" bright and shiny new ships to find any flaws and correct them before extended operations.

Some readers may be wondering whether the Navy manned some of the Army ships; if so, the answer is no. Under a Joint Chiefs of Staff agreement signed 14 March 1944, the Coast Guard was designated to crew certain types of small Army Transportation Corps vessels. These were large tugs (LT), freight vessels (F), freight-supply ships (FS), Army Marine Repair Ships (AMRS) and tankers (TY). Thus, Coast Guard crews manned many of the F, FS, and LT ships. The remaining ships were crewed by Merchant Mariners or by personnel of the Army Transport Service or Army Engineer Special Brigades.

ARMY AND NAVY ISLAND HOPPERS JOIN FOR PHILIPPINES CAMPAIGN

The strategy of Adm. William Halsey's South Pacific forces and Gen. Douglas MacArthur's Southwest Pacific forces—of which the units of APc Flotillas 5 and 7 were a part—was to move northwest up through the Solomon Islands and up the New Guinea coast, respectively, converge, and break through the Japanese-held Bismarck Archipelago. Allied control of the Vitiaz and Dampier Straits, sea passages between the southwest side of New Britain Island, a part of the Bismarck Archipelago, and New Guinea, was a necessary step along MacArthur's planned New Guinea-to-the-Philippines invasion route. After taking the Admiralty Islands in Spring 1944—thereby finally breaking the Bismarck Barrier—MacArthur's next objective was to leapfrog the Japanese garrison at Wewak, New Guinea, into Hollandia, and establish a new headquarters there. This operation too was successful, and from Hollandia, Allied forces including Army and Navy island hoppers staged for the Philippine Islands Campaign. The base there supported the impending landings on Leyte, and virtually everybody and everything en route to the Philippines campaign would pass through Hollandia.

ISLAND HOPPERS SUBJECT TO KAMIKAZE AND SUICIDE BOAT ATTACKS

The Battle of Leyte Gulf was fought in waters near the Philippine islands of Leyte and Samar from 23 to 26 October 1944, between U.S. and Australian forces and the Japanese Navy. It was the first battle in which Japanese aircraft carried out organized kamikaze attacks. The Japanese still had plenty of planes, as their aircraft factories were replacing the heavy losses suffered by the air groups of the Imperial Navy in the Battle of the Philippine Sea. The loss of experienced aviators was not so easy to overcome, since pilot training lagged behind aircraft production, and thus military leaders adopted the use of kamikaze aircraft. The Japanese Navy also accepted the idea of employing mini-submarines, suicide boats, and suicide divers ("human mines"). Many of the island hoppers encountered kamikaze as well as conventional plane attacks during heavy and persistent air raids in the Philippine Islands Campaign. One, the *FS-309*, survived an attack by a suicide Q boat while moored alongside the Wawa River Wharf at Nasugbu Bay, Luzon Island. Three Navy small coastal transports and thirty Army vessels collectively earned 38 battle stars during the campaign; a summary of these unit awards follow:

Leyte Operation
Navy Small Coastal Transport *APc-18*
Army Freight-Supply Ships *FS-167*, *FS-364*, and *FS-388*
Army Large Tugs *LT-20*, *LT-134*, *LT-229*, *LT-231*, *LT-454*, and *LT-637*
Army Coastal Tanker *Y-6*

Luzon Operation: Mindoro Landings
Army Large Tug *LT-1*
Army Small Tug *ST-381*
Army Harbor Tugs *TP-113* and *TP-129*
Army Coastal Tanker *Y-14*

Luzon Operation: Lingayen Gulf Landing
Navy Small Coastal Transports *APc-12* and *APc-16*
Army Freight-Supply Ships *FS-156*, *FS-171*, *FS-174*, *FS-254*, *FS-364*, and *FS-366*
Army Large Tugs *LT-229*, *LT-231*, and *LT-454*
Army Coastal Tankers *Y-6* and *Y-21*

Manila Bay Operations
   Army Freight-Supply Ships *FS-163*, *FS-168*, *FS-191*, *FS-352*, *FS-365*, *FS-387*, *FS-388* (two battle stars), and *FS-399*

Despite their significantly fewer numbers, the sixty Navy small coastal transports that served in the Pacific collectively garnered fifty battle stars during the war—a few more than the Army island hoppers. However, to be fair, the APcs arrived in the Pacific theater much earlier and thus had more opportunities to encounter enemy forces. The breakdown of Army small ship battle stars by vessel type are freight-supply ship: 24, large tug: 11, coastal tanker: 4, harbor tug: 2, freight & passenger vessel: 2, and small tug: one. A single freight and passenger vessel, the *FP-47*, MacArthur's Press Ship, received two stars. The *ST-381*, which spanning only 72 feet was the smallest vessel to receive a battle star and the only small tug, earned the respect of the escort commander of the convoy of which she was a part due to the intrepidness of her captain and crew; a combination of civilians, and soldiers of the 2nd Engineer Special Brigade. The Army ships typically only operated with Navy ships during convoy transits, during which Navy commanders were normally annoyed by the lack of adequate communications equipment aboard the Army vessels and their associated difficulties in executing signaled speed and course changes—let alone formation maneuvers. (A summary of the unit awards received by these Army and Navy ships, and names of their commanding officers if known, are provided in Appendix A.)

PARTICIPATION IN REMAINING BATTLES

Following the Philippine Islands Campaign, four small coastal transports earned battle stars for the assault and occupation of Okinawa, and four freight-supply ships and the *FP-47* battle stars at Borneo during the final major Allied campaign in the Southwest Pacific during World War II.

A short chapter is devoted to details of the final U.S. naval battle of the war, which was won off the China coast by a handful of Yanks—one Army captain, two Marine Corps officers, one Navy lieutenant, and four Navy enlisted—aboard two commandeered Chinese sailing junks. The Navy's first battle under sail since the Civil War days took place on 20 August 1945, five days after the Japanese armistice, during which eight Americans—whose duties had included training Chinese pirates as guerillas to fight the Japanese occupiers—bested a heavily armed Japanese army junk, killing forty-three Japanese, taking thirty-nine prisoner, and capturing the ship. Lt. Livingston "Swede" Swentzel, Jr., commander of the group, and Gunner's Mate Third James R. Reid, Jr. received the Navy Cross. Three others, Marine 2nd Lt. Stewart L. Pittman, Motor Machinist's Mate Second David A. Baker, and Gunner's Mate First William K. Barrett were awarded the Silver Star Medal for their heroism during the sea battle.

POST-WAR NAVAL SERVICE OF FORMER ARMY SHIPS

Following the war, the Navy disposed of the small coastal transports via transfer to allies or sale, but acquired forty-five of the rugged steel freight-supply ships between 1947 and 1966. Nine of these vessels received unit awards for combat duty in the Korean or Vietnam War, or for service as intelligence gathering ships. The most well-known being the USS *Pueblo* (AGER-2/ex *FS-344*); which North Korean naval forces captured on 23 January 1968. The former freight-supply ship most viewed by the public was the light cargo ship USS *Hewell* (AKL-14/ex *FS-391*). She garnered seven battle stars during the Korean War, but is best known as the fictitious Navy cargo ship *Reluctant* depicted in the 1955 American comedy-drama film *Mr. Roberts* which, filmed in Hawaii, stared Henry Fonda, James Cagney, William Powell, and Jack Lemmon. Other freight-supply ships also had interesting post–World War II service. Following her naval stint as USS *Deal* (AKL-2), the former *FS-263* operated in 1966 off the coast of England as a pirate radio station transmitting "Swinging Radio England" (SRE), initially as the motor vessel M.V. *Olga Patricia* and after a name change as the *Laissez Faire*. As depicted in the 2009 motion picture *Pirate Radio*, from aboard the ex-*Deal* and other ships located in international waters off England's east coast, rebellious disc jockeys were broadcasting rock 'n' roll music which, although spreading like wildfire in the United States, was all but banished from the British airwaves. The BBC owned all but one commercial TV network, and the broadcasting corporation favored a bland fare of news and information, light entertainments and children's programs. Most recently, the former freight-supply and "radio pirate" ship was employed as the fishing vessel *Earl J. Conrad, Jr.* out of Reedville, Virginia.

It is my hope that readers will enjoy the small portion of the history of the forgotten fleet contained in the pages of this book.

Acknowledgments

I am greatly indebted to renowned maritime artist Richard DeRosset for graciously allowing me to use a copy of his magnificent painting *Enemy Strike from Rabaul*, depicting the small coastal transport USS *APc-15* during a battle with a flight of Japanese dive-bombers and fighters, as the cover art for this book. Kemper Goffigon III, who received the Navy Cross for his heroic actions that day as the ship's commanding officer, provided me details about the battle off Arawe on the southwestern coast of New Britain. Frank J. Andruss Sr., curator of *The Mosquito Fleet Exhibit* and the author of several books about PT boats, shared his expert knowledge with the author and made available to DeRosset hundreds of photos related to the specific armament and equipment fitted in the *PT-59* and *PT-236*. These two motor torpedo boats, under the command of Lt. John F. Kennedy and Ens. William F. Crawford, rescued U.S. Marines pinned down by Japanese forces at the mouth of the Warrior River off Choiseul Island the evening of 2 November 1943. A chapter of the book is devoted to this little-known event, which Richard brilliantly captured on canvas in his *Salvation from the Sea*. A copy of this accurate and dramatic painting is also included herein. Finally, Jo-Ann Parks has once again created an eloquent book as a result of her discerning eye and prowess in design and typesetting.

1

Condition "Very Red"

> Estimated 40–50; No time to count; planes could be seen in nearly every direction however, and those diving in first were followed closely by others.
>
> Several planes were observed to fall during the attack and several more were observed gliding in a damaged condition after completing their dive. The necessity of looking for and shooting at new attackers prevented one from following the movements of any particular plane after it had ceased to become an immediate menace.
>
> USS *Conflict* (AM-85) Anti-Aircraft Action Report describing an attack on 7 April 1943 by a group of dive-bombers on shipping in Tulagi Harbor. An estimated 160 Japanese fighters and bombers attacked the Guadalcanal-Tulagi area that day.

By the spring of 1943, the Allies had pushed the Japanese out of the southern Solomon Islands, as witnessed by the enemy's evacuation of all its forces from Guadalcanal by 7 February 1943. The next undertaking was to push them out of the northern Solomons. Guadalcanal Island had been a pivotal piece of island real estate; one that both sides had wanted to control and to which they had committed large numbers of forces. Aircraft launched from the bitterly contested, and now American-controlled Henderson Field enabled Allied forces to expand their presence in the South Pacific while thwarting the Japanese thrust.[1]

Fleet Adm. Isoroku Yamamoto, commander-in-chief Combined Fleet, had tried earlier to engage and defeat the U.S. Pacific Fleet in decisive battles at Midway, Eastern Solomons, and Santa Cruz Island, and failed. Having lost Guadalcanal, he launched Operation I-GO, a counter-offensive in which an armada of aircraft attacked Allied ships,

Map 1-1

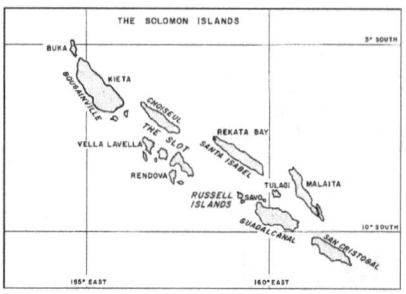

Guadalcanal in the Solomon Islands was a bitterly contested piece of real estate. Its capture by U.S. ground troops, supported by air and naval forces, after months of combat with Japanese on the island, preceded continued Allied movement northwestward up the enemy-held Solomons.
Source: http://www.ibiblio.org/hyperwar/USN/ACTC/img/actc-35.jpg

aircraft, and advanced bases in the southeast Solomon Islands and what today is known as New Guinea. New Guinea was then split into three areas: the Territory of New Guinea, the northeastern part of the island of New Guinea and surrounding islands; the Territory of Papua, the southeastern part of New Guinea; and, Dutch New Guinea, the western part of the island (later known as West Papua). The goal of the operation was to set back the Allies expected spring offensive and to give Japan time to prepare for defense of the Bismarcks Barrier. The Allies Papuan Campaign had concluded on 23 January 1943, after Australian and American troops moving up the Papua coast captured in succession Gona, Buna, and Sanananda, removing the threat of a planned enemy land attack on Port Moresby. Located on the southeastern coast of New Guinea, Japanese control of Port Moresby would have afforded them a staging point and air base only 340 miles from the Cape York Peninsula in Australia, from which to sever the sea lines of communications from America. Gen. Douglas MacArthur, supreme commander of Allied Forces in the Southwest Pacific Area, now needed to gain an overwater route through the enemy controlled Bismarck Archipelago—a group of islands off northeastern New Guinea—to continue along a New Guinea-Mindanao axis his promised return to the Philippines.[2]

In support of I-GO, four Japanese Imperial Navy Third Fleet carriers—the *Hiyo*, *Junyo*, *Zuiho*, and *Zuikaku*—contributed 96 fighters, 65 dive-bombers and a handful of torpedo planes to augment the land-based force of 86 fighters, 27 dive-bombers, 72 twin-engine bombers and some additional torpedo planes of the Eleventh Air Fleet. This powerful air armada was first concentrated 565 miles west-northwest of Guadalcanal at Rabaul, the largest Japanese military

Map 1-2

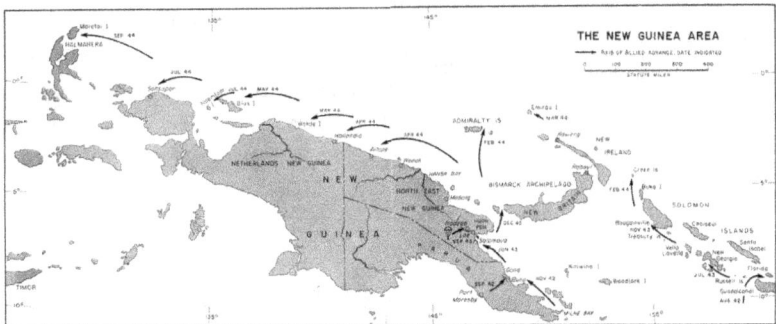

After defending Port Moresby, Papua, from a Japanese invasion, and establishing a base at Milne Bay, MacArthur's Australian and American forces advanced northwestward up the east coast of Papua, New Guinea along his road back to the Philippines. *Source:* http://www.history.army.mil/books/AMH/Map23-43.jpg

activity in the South Pacific. The medium bombers and fighters then relocated southward to airbases in the upper Solomons: at Kahili on the southern coast of Bougainville, at Buka Island near Bougainville, and at Ballale a small island south of Bougainville. At a little past noon on 7 April, a Bougainville coast watcher reported aircraft flying out of Buka; shortly thereafter came similar warnings of take-offs from Kahili and Ballale. While it is uncertain how many planes actually pressed home the ensuing attack—in what would be the largest and most damaging air attack of the year on shipping in the Guadalcanal-Tulagi area—observers in the New Georgia Group of the Solomon Islands counted 160 aircraft flying southeast from their bases.[3]

To meet this onslaught, 76 Allied fighter planes—36 Wildcats, 9 Corsairs, 6 Warhawks, 12 Lightnings and 13 Airacobras—launched from Henderson Field on Guadalcanal and stacked up in groups over Savo Island awaiting the Japanese. The temperature was 83 degrees, with high cumulous clouds and overcast, light winds from the south-southeast, and unlimited visibility. All but eighteen "Vals" and twenty-one "Zekes" of the Japanese planes belonged to the four carriers. Val and Zeke were Allied codenames for the Aichi D3A dive-bomber and Mitsubishi A6M Zero fighter aircraft, respectively. While Allied fighters engaged their counterparts in aerial combat, Vals slipped into "Iron Bottom Sound"—the southern portion of New Georgia Sound between Guadalcanal, Savo Island, and Florida Island—unopposed.

Map 1-3

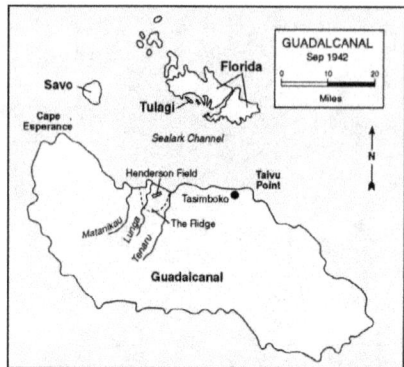

Tulagi, a small island nestled inside the bay of Florida Island, lay twenty miles across the New Georgia Sound. This waterway, which orientated along a northwest-southeast axis, ran between the Northern and Southern Solomon Islands, was commonly referred as "the Slot" by American servicemen.
Source: www.nps.gov/history/history/online_books/npswapa/extContent/usmc/pcn-190-003130-00/sec6.htm

The body of water was referred to thus by sailors, due to the large numbers of ships and aircraft sent to the bottom there during the recent Guadalcanal Campaign.[4]

Across the twenty-mile wide Sound, the submarine rescue ship *Ortolan* (ASR-5) lay off the north coast of Guadalcanal. At 1500, she sighted a large formation of 75-100 planes, twenty miles distant, approaching from the west. The main body initially split into four striking groups: one toward the task force of which she was a part, located to the north and west of Florida Island; a second toward the Tulagi area; a third toward Henderson Field; and a fourth toward a convoy of transport ships retiring down Lengo Channel. (Tulagi was nestled inside the bay of larger Florida Island, which both lay twenty miles across the New Georgia Sound, termed "the Slot," from Guadalcanal.) A separate group of planes approached the destroyer *Aaron Ward* (DD-483) and the tank landing ship, *LST-449*, she was escorting. As four of the planes remained overhead, the others attacked in pairs, sweeping down to dive bomb the warships, located off the northern coast of Guadalcanal near Berande Point proceeding eastward towards Lengo Channel.[5]

The first air attacks were, however, on ships in Tulagi Harbor. Present there were the former resplendent four-masted barkentine *Erskine M. Phelps*—which built in 1898, had been relegated to duty as a bunker barge (AON-147)—with the New Zealand minesweeper HMNZ *Moa* (T233) fueling alongside, the minesweeper *Conflict* (AM-85), oiler *Kanawha* (AO-1), and some thirty smaller vessels including a group of tank landing craft, LCTs *58, 62, 63, 156, 182, 322, 323,* and *369*. The action opened with 40 to 50 olive-brown colored, single-wing bombers diving down steeply and very fast, amidst antiaircraft fire from ships and two quads of 40mm guns on the heights of Tulagi, to release bombs. The *Moa* took a direct hit and sank in four minutes with the loss of five men missing and one officer and twelve men wounded. *Kanawha*, attacked off Songonangona Island at the entrance to Tulagi Harbor, suffered two direct bomb strikes that set her aflame and knocked her engines and fire rooms out of commission. As the planes pulled up out of their dives and leveled off, about twelve headed towards, unbeknownst to them, the location of the *Niagara* and the *Rail*, and others flew eastward.[6]

The 267-foot *Niagara* (AGP-1) was a former yacht, the *Hi-Esmaro*, converted to the Navy's first motor torpedo boat tender. She was moored starboard side to the bank of a small bay at Florida Island near the mouth of the Maliali River, with the minesweeper *Rail* (AM-26) made up outboard of her receiving water. The *Niagara*'s after action report described briefly the arrival of the enemy aircraft over Tulagi, and the ensuing attacks against shipping there, and the action involving the tender:

> At 1500 planes approached from the westward and were engaged by our planes over the Tulagi Area at about 12,000 feet. Dive bombers started peeling-off in a steep dive attacking ships in Tulagi Harbor. Bombs appeared to be released between 600 and 1,500 feet altitude. Planes pulled out of their dives between 75 and 200 feet altitude.
>
> Ten or twelve planes retired up the channel toward the NIAGARA sharp on the port bow at high speed and low altitude. All planes except one passed to port; that one passed just clearing the treetops and partially obscured to starboard. The planes came in two waves, distance between each plane of each wave varied from 300 to 1,000 yards.[7]

The aircraft were unaware of the presence of the two ships—due to foliage along the shore that obscured them from scrutiny—had expended their bombs, and were not prepared to strafe the two vessels. The *Niagara* took every plane streaking down her port side under fire with all eight of her 20mm guns. The combined barrage of gunfire from her and the *Rail* downed or damaged several bombers that crashed back in the woods or were streaming smoke as they withdrew. The action concluded at 1520 with the *Rail* having suffered some damage due to friendly fire. Eager to down the enemy, *Niagara*'s gunners had fired through the minesweeper's topside rigging, and shot away her boat boom, as well as the starboard forward guide for the mainmast and two high-frequency radio antennas.[8]

SMALL COASTAL TRANSPORT SHOOTS DOWN TWO ATTACKERS

The ships in the area had earlier received a "Condition Red" broadcast from Guadalcanal at about 1445 and a few minutes later, as large numbers of planes appeared over Tulagi and Savo Island off the northwest coast of Guadalcanal, and the water between them, an unprecedented "Condition Very Red." When an alarm signaled Condition Red, it meant that an enemy air raid was imminent. Adm. William F. Halsey, commander South Pacific Force, had directed the withdrawal of all Task Force 32 ships, along with Task Unit 36.1.3—comprised of destroyers *Farenholt* (DD-491) and *Woodworth* (DD-460), and oiler *Tappahannock* (AO-43)—and the *Kanawha* from Guadalcanal at the earliest practical time in anticipation of Japanese air attacks. Many ships had fled or were fleeing; others, whose departure had been delayed and smaller vessels too slow to attempt escape, awaited arrival of the enemy overhead.[9]

Among the ships still present at Tulagi that afternoon were a group of six recently built wooden-hulled "Small Coastal Transports." Following a lengthy Pacific crossing, the *APc-23, 24, 25, 26, 33,* and *34* had arrived at Guadalcanal a few days earlier on 29 March, and reported for duty to commander Landing Force Flotillas, South Pacific, Rear Adm. George H. Fort. The 103-foot stubby ships, whose complement was three officers and twenty-eight enlisted, were of austere construction. Today, Navy frigates and smaller ships driven by a single propeller are fitted with two propulsion engines, so that in the event of a casualty to one engine, the ship can still operate. Larger ships such as destroyers and cruisers have four engines driving two shafts, and carriers, nuclear reactors powering four shafts. The APcs were propelled by a single 400 hp diesel engine. For self-protection, the diminutive ships had four single 20mm anti-aircraft guns. These type weapons would prove to have little stopping power against enemy heavy aircraft and kamikaze attacks. However, they were effective at short ranges in which slower heavier-caliber guns had difficulty tracking a target. Skill of gunner's mates in manually training and elevating mounts was paramount for acquisition of high-speed aircraft. Some APcs also had two or more .30-caliber or .50-caliber machine guns but they were of little use against enemy planes. As might be expected, additional armament was greatly desired by the crews of ships going in harm's way, and machine guns found their way aboard by whatever means possible. A former commanding officer of one of these ships joked that he probably would have been court martialed by the Navy for the theft of guns, explaining "they knew who took them," had he not received an award for valor associated with the defense of his ship.[10]

The *APc-33*, commanded by Lt. James E. Locke, United States Naval Reserve, was making a portside approach to Sturgis Dock at Tulagi when a group of approximately thirty-five enemy dive-bombers, approaching over land from off her port bow, appeared suddenly less than five miles distant. He immediately ordered starboard rudder to open the shore and gain sea room to maneuver and try to evade planes making diving and strafing attacks. As a pair of Vals made a run on the wooden ship from her starboard side, her gunners opened at 1,000 yards with guns elevated from 70 to 85 degrees above the horizon and continued to fire at the aircraft until they had closed to 300 yards. Japanese carrier-based Val dive-bombers with a top speed of 239 miles per hour were a difficult target for shipboard gunners, and very deadly. In addition to carrying a single 550 lb. bomb or two 132 lb. ones, the aircraft were fitted with three 7.7mm machine guns, enabling concurrent bombing and strafing runs. The necessity of applying a large lead angle for such fast moving aircraft was emphasized in Navy training. The 20mm gunners aboard the *APc-33* had apparently learned this lesson well as, despite no previous combat experience, they shot down both aircraft. Hit in the forward part of the fuselage, the planes burst into flames directly overhead, and plunged into the water astern of the ship.[11]

RESCUE OF *KANAWHA* SURVIVORS

The fleet oiler *Kanawha* had similarly tried to escape the confines of Tulagi Harbor. However, while still in the narrow channel nearing the entrance, with little maneuvering room, five planes attacked her. Two dropped bombs hit the ship; one demolished her engine room causing a loss of power and fires aft, the other struck forward of her bridge, setting bunker oil aflame. With no means to fight the blaze except with buckets of water, which were ineffective, the commanding officer ordered the crew to abandon while there was still slight way on the ship, to preclude for survivors entering the water the hazard of burning oil on the surface. There were then no other vessels nearby for rescue work.[12]

Thereafter, several small vessels, including submarine chasers, coastal transports, tank landing craft, and the minesweeper *Conflict* proceeded to the *Kanawha* to fight the fire aboard her and pick up survivors. The minesweeper *Rail* approached the *APc-33*, which had recovered Lt. C. W. Brockway, the *Kanawha*'s first lieutenant and navigator, and fourteen of her crew, two seriously injured. At Brockway's request, the larger steel-hulled ship took him and eleven of the men off the *33* for transport alongside the *Kanawha* to determine if the fire aboard her could be brought under control. The flames were extinguished, but it was evident the oiler was sinking. Three ships made up to her—the *Rail* alongside to port, the fleet tug *Menominee* (AT-73) to starboard, and the net tender *Butternut* (YN-4) towing ahead—and, as she continued to draw more water, beached the *Kanawha* on the southeast point of Tulagi Island. The efforts to save her would be for naught. She slid off the reef at 0400 the following morning and sank in about twenty-five fathoms of water.[13]

AARON WARD SUNK; JFK ABOARD SHIP DAMAGED IN SAME ATTACK

The *Aaron Ward*, the first American warship to fire its guns in anger in World War II—the second shot from its No. 3 gun had sunk a Japanese Type-*A* midget submarine off the entrance to Pearl Harbor the morning of 7 December 1941—was also sunk by enemy aircraft. At 1512, as three planes dove out of clouds near the sun flying an attack profile, the destroyer's commanding officer ordered flank speed and her 40mm and 20mm guns opened. Ranges to the targets were inside 2,000 yards, allowing just seconds to bring down the aircraft. It was too little time; one bomb hit the after engine room, rupturing the ship's side and flooding the compartment. Two others landed abreast each fire room, and the explosions parted hull seams or blew holes in the sides, and both these compartments flooded as well. Three other planes dove on the destroyer, and bomb hits in the water close aboard to port aggravating the existing damage. The *Ortolan* took the *Aaron Ward* in tow, and fleet tug *Vireo* (AT-144) came alongside and began to pump water from her forward engine room. Despite the efforts to stem flooding aboard the destroyer, she sank while under tow to

Purvis Bay, Florida Island. In addition to the loss of their ship the survivors suffered twenty-seven shipmates killed and seven missing.[14]

Aboard the *LST-449*, whom the *Aaron Ward* had been ordered to screen and had joined off Togoma Point on the north coast of Guadalcanal, was Lt. (jg) John F. Kennedy, USN. After taking passage aboard the transport USS *Rochambeau* (AP-63) from San Francisco to Espiritu Santo, New Hebrides, he had boarded the tank landing ship there along with 170 soldiers and a few other naval officers bound for assignments in the Solomons for transit to Guadalcanal. The *LST-449* had arrived off Togoma Point at noon, and twenty minutes later received warning that condition red was in effect. Thereafter a boat came out with orders to form task unit 31.1.1 with the *Aaron Ward* and the *LST-446* and to retire in the direction of Espiritu. Neither of those ships were then in sight. The destroyer was sighted a few minutes later and joined at high speed. The *446* never rendezvoused with the *Aaron Ward* and *LST-449*.[15]

Nine Vals attacked the *LST-449* at 1509; a minute later two bombs landed in the water close aboard off the port and starboard quarters of the ship. The commanding officer dodged these, and four more near misses, by maneuvering with full right and left rudder. Lt. Carlton S. Livingston's vision was obstructed by a tank landing craft being carried on deck, necessitating his ordering the rudder put over when the bridge phone talker relayed to him a lookout reported a plane was diving. The ship was shaken severely by the bomb explosions, three off each side of the LST and all within seventy-five feet. The blast from the nearest one, which landed off the ship's port quarter, lifted the stern, causing the vessel to list to starboard about twenty degrees. The explosion also lifted and stove in the side of a 36-foot landing boat suspended from port davits, sprung bulkheads, and caused some machinery derangement.[16]

Her gunners expended 1,600 rounds of 20mm ammunition and 13 rounds of 3-inch/.50-caliber during the action. Despite jams on the No. 2 and No. 6 twenty-millimeter guns, and the first shell for the 3-inch gun failing to seat, two planes were shot down and were seen to crash in the water and a third was on fire and trailing smoke as it withdrew. When the attack had eased, the LST closed the *Aaron Ward*, from which smoke was emitting and red flames licking to offer assistance. Before she could reach her, the *Ortolan* made fast to the destroyer, whereupon the *LST-449* stood down Lunga Channel. She and the submarine chaser *SC-521* retired eastward towards Espiritu Santo, to avoid being in the Guadalcanal area in the event of another air strike there the following day. The LST put into Guadalcanal on 12 April and Tulagi across the Slot two days later. Kennedy disembarked there, reported to Motor Torpedo Boat Squadron Two, and took command of the *PT-109* on 23 April 1943.[17]

The officers and men of the *Aaron Ward*, *LST-449*, and *SC-521* received battle stars to affix to the Asiatic-Pacific campaign ribbons on their uniform blouses. Lieutenant Livingston saved the *LST-449*, and undoubtedly the lives of some of those aboard her, including possibly Kennedy's. In his endorsement of the after action report, Rear Adm. George H. Fort noted that Livingston had had little room for error in evading falling bombs, due to his ship's slow speed, which allowed little time to get out from under free-falling ordnance dropped by low flying planes:

> The Commanding Officer, U.S.S. LST 449 deserves great credit for his smart handling of his ship during this attack. Although his ship is capable of only ten (10) knots speed, he succeeded in avoiding six (6) bombs, and suffered only minor damage as a result of near misses.[18]

Ideally, gun crews could train their mounts on enemy aircraft and down them before they could dive bomb or strafe their target. This, however, was hard to do against fast moving, maneuvering planes, which is why small, slow vessels in particular sought to acquire machine guns—by whatever means possible—to augment their self-defense capabilities.

FINAL TALLY

In addition to sinking the destroyer *Aaron Ward*, the fleet oiler *Kanawha*, and the New Zealand minesweeper *Moa*, dive-bombing attacks damaged the cargo ship *Adhara*, the tank landing ship *LST-449* and the oil barge *Erskine M. Phelps*. United States Pacific Fleet "Operations in Pacific Ocean Areas, April 1943" summarized enemy losses thus:

> Of more than 160 enemy aircraft sighted over or en route to Guadalcanal-Tulagi area, our fighters report destroying 26 VF [fighters]

and 13 VB [bombers] at the loss of 1 pilot and 7 planes. In addition, ships report shooting down about 25 VB. There is probably some duplication in both ship and aircraft reports. From a study of location of crashes observed and planes sighted retiring, it is estimated that the total damage inflicted on the enemy from fighters and AA [anti-aircraft] fire was less than 25 planes.

Commander, Naval Base Fold [Tulagi] also expressed a conservative estimate of enemy losses in the Tulagi Harbor area, due also to a reluctance to double or triple-count planes hit by more than one ship or by Marine Corps artillery battery fire:

> No correct estimates of number of planes shot down can be given as reports from different vessels and [shore] gun positions vary widely. To date wreckage of three enemy planes have been found in this area; and it appears definite that four more were downed.

Shipboard fire may have accounted for additional enemy aircraft, beyond those found, as some damaged planes may have crashed out of sight in ocean waters or island jungles, while trying to make it safely back to their airfields.[19]

The six coastal transports apparently all emerged unscathed from the air raid. Although information is scarce regarding the actions of the *APc-23* and *APc-25*, they too, like the *APc-33*, received battle stars. Summary information about the diminutive ships, which had just arrived at Guadalcanal, ending a three-month voyage from San Pedro, California via stops at Pearl Harbor; Tutuila, Samoa; Viti Levu, Fiji; Noumea, New Caledonia; and Espiritu Santo, New Hebrides, as well as the names of their commanding officers follows:

Ship	Length in Feet	Disp. Tons	Year Built	Commanding Officer
Built at Fulton Shipyard, Antioch, California				
APc-23	103	147	1942	Lt. Dennis Mann, USNR
APc-24	103	147	1942	Lt. Bernard F. Seligman, USNR
APc-25	103	147	1942	Lt. John D. Cartano, USNR
APc-26	103	147	1942	Lt. (jg) James B. Dunigan, USNR
Built at Anderson & Cristofani, San Francisco, California				
APc-33	103	147	1942	Lt. James E. Locke, USNR
APc-34	103	147	1942	Lt. (jg) H. B. Palmer, USNR

Chapter 1
STALEMATE

> *Everyone knew there "could be only one Yamamoto and nobody could take his place." His loss "dealt an almost unbearable blow to the morale of all the military forces."*
>
> Vice Adm. Shigeru Fukudome, Fleet Adm. Isoroku Yamamoto's chief of staff, commenting on the death of the Japanese admiral responsible for the December 7th attack on Pearl Harbor, who was shot down over Buin Island, Solomon Islands, by an American P38 Lightning fighter aircraft on 18 April 1943[20]

The 7 April 1943 air raid on the Guadalcanal-Tulagi area temporarily brought Allied naval surface operations to a standstill. All shipping was withdrawn to the south, and a proposed surface ship bombardment of enemy airfields at Vila and Munda in the New Georgia Island Group by Rear Adm. Robert Giffen's Task Force 18 was cancelled. For nearly ten days, Allied operations focused generally on the immediate defense of existing positions. Overall, there was little change in the Allied and Japanese positions. The enemy had demonstrated mobility of air power by the attack on 7 April, followed by immediate withdrawal of the attack group; however, overall, Japanese air operations remained essentially defensive. It thus appeared that until Allied forces could impose a sufficiently heavy rate of attrition to weaken enemy strength, the current stalemate broken occasionally by sudden strikes in force would continue.[21]

A degradation in Japanese leadership occurred on 18 April 1943, when Adm. Isoroku Yamamoto was gathered to his ancestors. The commander in chief Combined Fleet had planned to tour Japanese bases in the Solomons and New Guinea to inspect air units participating in the I-GO operation and to boost morale following the dispiriting Japanese loss of Guadalcanal. He and staff members had boarded two "Bettys" at Rabaul that morning at 0800 and accompanied by six "Zeros" took off for Buin airfield, on the southern coast of Bougainville near Kahili village. Just as the escorts withdrew and the bombers prepared to land, one of a flight of four P38 Lightning fighter aircraft—termed the "Killer Section"—launched from Henderson Field shot down the aircraft carrying Yamamoto and a second fighter of the 339th Fighter Squadron disposed of the other bomber. The other twelve P38s of the group were there to fly top cover.[22]

After an encoded message advising the commanders of Base Unit No. 1, the 11th Air Flotilla, and the 26th Air Flotilla of Yamamoto's itinerary, as well as the number and types of planes that would transport and accompany him, was intercepted and deciphered by U.S. naval intelligence, the information was passed to Washington, D.C. American President Franklin D. Roosevelt ordered Secretary of the Navy Frank Knox to "get Yamamoto." Knox then instructed Adm. Chester W. Nimitz of Roosevelt's direction who, after consulting Adm. William F. Halsey, Jr., commander, South Pacific, authorized the mission. The details of Yamamoto's death were hushed up. The *New York Times* of 21 May 1943 reported:

> Admiral Isoroku Yamamoto, commander in chief of the combined Japanese Fleet, who reportedly boasted he would dictate peace terms to the United States from a seat in the White House, was killed during April "while engaged in combat with the enemy" aboard a warplane, Japanese Imperial Headquarters announced in a communiqué broadcast domestically this morning by the Tokyo radio.

"Gosh," said President Roosevelt upon hearing the news.[23]

2

Papua, New Guinea, and the "Catboat Flotilla"

> *In early 1942, there was considerable rivalry between General MacArthur and the U.S. Navy and there was little co-operation between the two areas of command. The net result was that there were no U.S. Navy ships, landing craft or Marines available in 1942 for operations in New Guinea. . . . So, in mid-1942, a straggle of non-descript wooden fishing trawlers, a gaggle of sailing craft, a few rusty freighters and some plywood landing craft, sailed north through the Great Barrier Reef of Australia. Some struck boldly across the Coral Sea to Port Moresby and Milne Bay in New Guinea. . . . Reckless courage and a great disregard for the odds and hardships played a great part in the success of the U.S. Army Small Ships, plus a complete lack of knowledge of all the dangers and difficulties that lay ahead for them.*
>
> Excerpts from an address to members of The Royal United Services Institution of New South Wales on 25 January 2005 by Capt. Ernest A. Flint, who served as a boy in the "Catboat Flotilla"[1]

The story of the "Pacific island hoppers" starts with the evacuation of Gen. Douglas MacArthur, the commander of the U.S. Army Forces in the Far East, from the Philippines to Australia, and the beginning of his subsequent drive through New Guinea on the road back to the Philippines. In addition to the devastating attack by carrier aircraft on Pearl Harbor on 7 December 1941, Japanese planes also attacked on 8 December (the 7th in Pearl Harbor) American bases on Guam, Wake Island, and in the Philippines. That same day, the Japanese 14th Army landed on Batan Island (not to be confused with the Bataan Peninsula) off the north coast of Luzon in the Philippines. Other landings two days later on Camiguin Island in northern Mindanao, and at Vigan,

Aparri, and Gonzaga in northern Luzon launched the enemy's Philippines Campaign.²

During the ensuing days and weeks, Adm. Thomas Hart's Asiatic Fleet was forced to evacuate the Cavite Naval Base at Sangley Point on the southeastern shore of Manila Bay, and flee southward, and MacArthur's army to withdraw from Manila, which lay eight miles to the northeast on the eastern shore. On 22 February 1942, President Franklin D. Roosevelt ordered MacArthur to proceed from the Philippines to Australia and establish a new headquarters. American and Filipino forces were then trying desperately to hold the Bataan Peninsula, which formed the northern boundary of the entrance to Manila Bay, and nearby Corregidor Island that divided the opening into two channels. Lt. John D. Bulkeley's Motor Torpedo Boat Squadron 3—*PT-32, PT-34, PT-35,* and *PT-41*—transported MacArthur as well as his family and members of his staff, and Rear Adm. Francis W. Rockwell and his staff, to Mindanao on 11 March, from whence B-17s flew them to Australia. Following a rearguard campaign, Lt. Gen. Jonathon M. Wainwright surrendered Corregidor and Manila Bay Forts and all the armed forces in the Philippines to the Japanese six weeks later. A bitter pill to swallow, and intended to prevent further effusion of blood, this action followed an epic struggle by Filipino and American soldiers to withstand for more than three months the constant and grueling fire of a superior enemy. Besieged on land and blockaded by sea, cut off from all sources of help in the Philippines and in America, the intrepid fighters had endured all that they could.³

Two weeks after MacArthur's arrival in Australia on 17 March, the Joint Chiefs of Staff ordered the Pacific divided into two commands, the Pacific Ocean Areas under Adm. Chester W. Nimitz and the Southwest Pacific Area under Lt. Gen. MacArthur. The Australian Government nominated MacArthur for the post of Supreme Commander in a proposed new Allied command, the Southwest Pacific Area (SWPA), and within a month the unified command was established under MacArthur. The Joint Chiefs directed him to hold the key military regions of Australia as bases for a future offensive, and to check the Japanese southward advance by destroying enemy shipping, aircraft, and bases in the Netherlands East Indies, New Guinea, and the Solomon Islands. Pending completion of formal arrangements, steps were taken to integrate the United States and Australian forces. The Australian Army was reorganized and regrouped, with more

Map 2-1

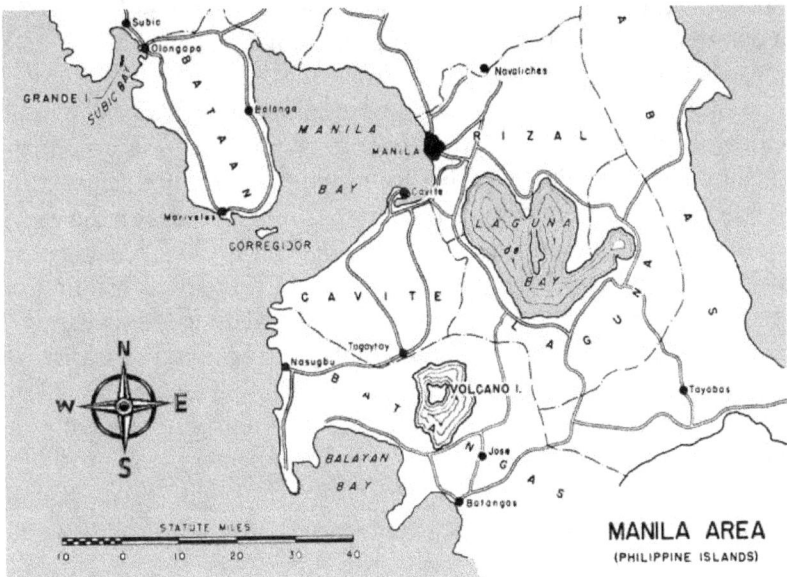

Manila Bay area of Luzon Island, Philippine Islands.
Source: http://www.ibiblio.org/hyperwar/USN/Building_Bases/maps/bases2-p391.jpg

emphasis given to training new recruits, the combined Australian and United States air forces were placed under the command of Lt. Gen. George H. Brett, USAAF, and Vice Adm. Herbert F. Leary, USN, assumed command of the naval forces.[4]

Upon constitution of the SWPA on 18 April 1942, MacArthur initially established his general headquarters at Melbourne, before transferring it three months later to Brisbane. The immediate problem confronting him was the defense of Australia. The forces available were wholly inadequate to cover such an extensive coastline against an expected invasion. Five thousand Japanese troops of the elite jungle-trained South Seas Detachment had stormed ashore at Rabaul in the Australian Territory of New Guinea on 23 January 1942, and quickly overwhelmed the small Australian garrison. The Japanese then began to develop Rabaul into a major base for further military operations in the Southwest Pacific area. MacArthur felt strongly that passive defense was strategically unsound, and decided to move the bulk of his forces forward more than a thousand miles to Port Moresby and force the Japanese to fight on his terms across the barrier of the Owen Stanley Range. These great mountains, nearly 14,000 feet high with large peaks and deep gorges, formed a natural barrier which ran the entire length of eastern New Guinea. Passage along the Kokoda Trail, a one-man-wide foot trail through dense jungle was the only feasible means of crossing the range.[5]

These geographical challenges were compounded by problems of climate and health. Penetrating, energy-sapping heat was accompanied by high humidity resulting from frequent torrential rains totaling as much as 300 inches per year. At the lower altitudes on the westward side of the mountains, there were swollen streams, reeking nipa palm woodlands and mangrove swamps, and dense mud. Millions of insects abounded, and clouds of mosquitoes, flies, leeches, chiggers, ants, fleas, and other parasites pestered man night and day. Disease was an unrelenting foe; malaria took a heavy toll, dengue fever was common, and deadly blackwater fever, though not so prevalent, was no less an adversary. Bacillary and amoebic dysentery were possibilities, tropical ulcers were easily formed from the slightest scratch, and hard to heal, and scrub typhus, ringworm, hookworm, and yaws all awaited careless soldiers.[6]

Despite these conditions, Japanese forces under Gen. Tomitaro Horii had advanced by late summer to within thirty-two kilometers of Port Moresby when ordered by Imperial General Headquarters to retract. Horii had suffered heavy casualties to Australian forces, his troops were exhausted, and he had outpaced his supply lines. More importantly, on Guadalcanal, an effort by Japanese forces to recapture Henderson Field on 14 September had been sounded defeated by the opposing U.S. Marines with a high number of casualties inflicted on the Japanese. After news of the defeat reached Japan, the top generals decided they could not support concurrent battle fronts on both New Guinea and Guadalcanal, and directed Horii to withdraw.[7]

Having abandoned the effort to reach Port Moresby over land, the only feasible approach by which the enemy could invade Australia was via a sea route through Milne Bay at the eastern tip of New Guinea. While Horii had attacked southward, other Japanese forces had captured the towns of Lae and Salamaua on the north coast of New Guinea, and established bases. Although temporarily halted in their advance toward Australia, the Japanese still controlled all the chains of islands across its northern sea approaches, with the single exception of southeastern New Guinea. The enemy also held the initiative as to the point of attack. Command of the sea enabled the Japanese to concentrate on a particular objective and overwhelm the defenders with superior forces. The Allies continued to strengthen Port Moresby as a land and air base. Located on the southeastern coast of the Papuan Peninsula, protected on the north by the Owen Stanley Range and flanked on the east by Milne Bay, it was well placed strategically except for its vulnerability to amphibious assault—which the Battle of the Coral Sea fought in early May 1942 had prevented.[8]

BATTLE OF CORAL SEA SAVES PORT MORESBY

In a grandiose scheme, Imperial General Headquarters had planned to first seize Tulagi in the Solomons and Port Moresby in Papua to secure mastery of the skies over the Coral Sea. The Combined Fleet would then move to the north Pacific to annihilate the United States Pacific Fleet, while capturing Midway and the Western Aleutian Islands. These victories would enable the Japanese to establish a ribbon defense, anchored at Attu, Midway, Wake, and the Marshall and Gilbert Islands. This effort, had it not been thwarted by the loss of three Japanese carriers, as well as large numbers of aircraft at Midway, would have been followed by invasion of New Caledonia and the Fijian and Samoan Islands to isolate Australia.[9]

The U.S. Navy lost the carrier *Lexington* (CV-2) on 8 May. However, a day earlier, planes from the "Lady Lex" and carrier *Yorktown* (CV-5) had put the Japanese carrier *Shoho* down in a mere ten minutes, prompting the signal "Scratch one flattop!" from the *Lexington*'s dive-bomber commander. The loss of the *Shoho*, which had been assigned to screen the Port Moresby Invasion force, so dispirited Vice Adm. Shigeyoshi Inouye he ordered the force, instead of proceeding through Jomard Passage in the Louisiades southeast of New Guinea and capturing Port Moresby, to remain a safe distance north of the archipelago. Fearful about risking a dozen transports aboard which was a sizable army—protected now only by heavy cruisers—south of Papua without air cover, he then ordered the group to withdraw to Rabaul. Though the Japanese could claim a tactical victory, the Battle of the Coral Sea was an operational and strategic defeat for them. The action by the U.S. Navy was particularly heartening to the Service and American people, coming on the heels of the loss of the Philippines to the enemy on 6 May 1942.[10]

THE "CATBOAT FLOTILLA"

Following this introduction of preceding events in the Pacific War, and of the relationship and linkage between MacArthur's efforts in Papua and New Guinea and Halsey's in the Solomons, an introduction of the "island hoppers" is in order. Both commanders needed small vessels to operate in shallow, often uncharted or poorly charted reef-infested waters in support of combat forces ashore. Prior to the construction and arrival in the theater of steel landing craft in spring 1943, they utilized whatever type small craft they could obtain; MacArthur acquiring his from Australia and New Zealand and Halsey from the United States.

Throughout the first half of 1942, a fleet of Australian-based Army cargo ships regularly sailed from ports on the east coast of Australia to deliver equipment, and supplies to support the troops at Port Moresby. That port was the main northern terminal up until the Japanese advance across the Owen Stanley Mountains was stopped. MacArthur had ordered in June the secret construction of an air, land, and naval base at Gili Gili, a village on Milne Bay, about 250 miles to the east-southeast of Port Moresby. When combat moved in November 1942 to the Japanese-held Buna-Gona area on the northeastern coast of Papua, Milne Bay became the main terminal. Cargo destined for water movement to Buna-Gona was transferred at Milne Bay to small boats and carried up along southeast New Guinea to Oro Bay. The 211-mile-long-coast from Milne Bay to Oro Bay had never been accurately charted. The most recent charts were dated 1895, and additional new coral formations, which grew rapidly in warm tropical waters, had formed since then. The area was thus considered by Army Col. Thomas B. Wilson, chief of Transportation, as the most dangerous coastline in the world. Australian vessels avoided this route before the war, sailing instead by way of Rabaul to ports on the north coast. Until as late as March 1943, U.S. Navy ships also prudently used the prewar route. As the Allies pushed up the northern coast of New Guinea, small vessels sailed beyond Oro Bay and Buna-Gona to Biak and Sansaport, and thence Morotai.[11]

Operations off New Guinea and neighboring islands required small vessels of shallow draft, able to navigate among coral reefs and close to land in shallow waters. The New Guinea ports in existence at the beginning of the war had only rudimentary facilities, and U.S. military forces found it necessary to construct other ports in mangrove swamps fringed with coral sand. Large oceangoing ships did not venture in 1942 up the coast northwest of Milne Bay. Cargo and troops were transferred at Port Moresby or Milne Bay to trawlers, schooners, luggers, and ketches, which hid in rivers and coves during the day to elude attack by Japanese float planes, and crept up the coast at night through uncharted waters to discharge their cargos. The vessels marked reefs encountered with empty oil drums and kept observations and depth soundings for subsequent use by the Royal Australian Navy in preparing charts. Perversely, reefs hazardous to safe navigation, gave protection from submarines. Larger vessels began to work the north coast of New Guinea in 1943, increasing to about 350 by mid-year the numbers of ships and craft of 500 tons or less employed in this service.[12]

Although they sailed under the American flag, the assortment of small ships and craft were of British-registry and crewed by very young and very old Australians. The Australian Government allowed the U.S. Army to recruit men and boys who were either too young or too old, or medically unfit for service in the Australian Military Forces. They ranged from age 15 to over 70 years in age. Among the older members were veterans of World War I and old hands in New Guinea's days of exploration, as well as men with only one arm and, in one or two cases, one leg. The Grace Building on the corner of York and King Street in Sydney was used by the Army's Small Ships Section, Transportation Service, for administrative offices and most hiring of crewmen was done there. Recruiting on a small scale was also carried out at Brisbane and Townsville. These Australians (civilian maritime employees) were supplied gratuitously with mosquito nets, helmets, gas masks, meat cans and other equipment before leaving Australia. After January 1943, employees in the combat zone were permitted to purchase clothing and tobacco by authorizing a deduction from their pay. They were forbidden to wear insignia on U.S. Army clothing and were required to wear arm bands to distinguish them from privates.[13]

In October 1942, all craft controlled by the U.S. Army's Small Ships Division were ordered to Milne Bay for service in delivering troops to and supplying the Buna-Gona region. The Australian crews rigged sails when engines broke down, and made emergency repairs when hulls were punctured by bullets or jagged coral. The 301st Coast Artillery Transport Detachment, formed at Fort McDowell, California "for the primary purpose of supplying trained gun crews for this Small Ship operation," arrived in Australia in April 1942; and on more than one occasion gun crews shot down attacking aircraft. By mid-February 1943, the Catboat Flotilla had lost three trawlers, one auxiliary schooner, and one auxiliary ketch. Arriving at one's destination was only half the problem. A trawler drawing only six feet of water could rarely get nearer to shore than fifty yards. This necessitated transferring cargo or personnel to native canoes or fishing trawlers. The latter would make the beach at the fastest speed possible from tired engines. The U.S. 32nd and 41st Infantry Divisions were landed in this fashion.[14]

During much of 1942, this fleet of small craft consisted entirely of vessels scoured from ports and harbors along Australia's coasts and in New Zealand: schooners, ancient ferry boats, luggers, rusty trawlers, tugs, launches, lighters, surf boats, ketches, yachts, and yawls. The Army's Small Ships Section took whatever craft it could get as the urgency of its needs did not permit discrimination or selection in what it purchased or chartered. Thus this disparate group, unofficially designated the "Catboat Flotilla," likely formed as motley a collection of seagoing craft as was every exposed to enemy gunfire. Number 10 Walsh Bay, in Sydney, became the Small Ships' victualing wharf where craft that had been purchased, leased, or commandeered were provisioned, fuelled, and fitted out, and then armed with .30- or .50-caliber machine guns, some of World War I vintage. One vessel was equipped with a light cannon its crew believed was more of a threat to them than to the Japanese. MacArthur reported on 9 September 1942 that the Section was "combing every river and harbor of this area for harbor lighters, trawlers and other small craft which are so necessary if we are ever to conduct successful campaigns from island to island in this area." As of 1 November, the Army Small Ships Section had 120 vessels on hand:

trawlers:	29	cabin cruisers:	8	tugboats:	4	motorships:	15
speed boats:	5	luggers:	2	towboats:	13	steamers:	5
auxiliary cutters:	1	ketches:	12	power lighters:	5	dummy barges:	1
motor launches:	11	harbor boats:	4	trawler hulls:	1	schooners:	4[15]

By 15 December 1942, the Section had acquired 195 craft with a total cargo capacity of more than 20,000 deadweight tons, in addition to 201 barges and landing craft. The latter were probably surf boats, and all 201 units presumably of local Australian construction.

MacArthur reported to the Army on 5 February 1943 that a thorough search of Australia and New Zealand had exhausted the supply of available vessels, and that it was, accordingly, no longer possible to charter or purchase serviceable craft locally. By 30 June 1943, the small ship fleet included 310 craft from Australian owners. More than half of the vessels were trawlers (51), motor tenders (62), and flat-topped wooden barges (46).[16]

A program for Australian-constructed craft for the U.S. Army had begun in September 1942. The Small Ships Section handled the program through the Australian Shipbuilding Board, which made contracts with shipbuilding firms. The construction was confined mainly to hulls. Engines, navigational equipment, and auxiliary machinery were supplied from the United States and installed by Australian builders. Vessel production was generally hampered by a shortage of labor, and by delays in acquisition of lumber and steel. The U.S. Army recognized in late 1942 that neither the Australian craft acquired from private owners, nor the craft constructed locally would meet all the requirements in the theater. The deficiency had to be filled by vessels acquired or constructed in the United States. In summer 1943 the first LSTs (tank landing ships), LCTs (tank landing craft), LCMs (mechanized landing craft), and DUKWs (amphibious trucks) arrived to reinforce the Catboat Flotilla. A flotilla of twenty-two Navy small coastal transports was based in Australia around that same period to serve the Southwest Pacific Area. In New Guinea itself, an express cargo service, consisting of Army F (99-foot) and FS (170-180 foot) vessels was established in July 1944. Its mission was to ensure rapid movement of high-priority cargo between New Guinea bases.[17]

3

The Army and Navy "Pacific Island Hoppers"

> *I don't know what the hell this "logistics" is that [Gen. George C.] Marshall is always talking about, but I want some of it!*
>
> Fleet Adm. Ernest J. King, USN, to a staff officer in 1942

THE ARMY'S TP VESSELS, "F SHIPS," LARGE TUGS, AND COASTAL TANKERS

Early in the war, the U.S. Army, like the U.S. Navy, took whatever it could get in the United States to meet its needs, including fishing vessels, ferry boats, yachts, and smaller pleasure craft. The vessels were given designations for administrative purposes, which generally fit the function anticipated, often determined by general size. The trawlers, tow boats, purse seiners, and sailing schooners acquired by the Army were designated "TP" for Small Freight and Passenger Vessels. The Army assigned to larger merchant vessels it acquired and refitted for war service, and for the new construction freight and cargo vessels it requisitioned from American boat and shipyards, F, FP, or FS designations. The FP vessels were reclassified FS during World War II. Beginning in 1943, the Army began taking delivery of Harbor Tugs, Large Tugs, and Coastal Tankers as well. A summary of these vessels follows:

Designation/General Description		Size and/or Type Vessel(s)
TP	Freight and Passenger Vessel (Small): Private vessels of under 100 feet in length refitted for wartime service	trawlers, tow boats, purse seiners, and sailing schooners
TP	Harbor Tug: Diesel-powered harbor tugs built in 1944	96-foot, wood
F	Cargo Vessel	99 or 102 feet in length, steel
FP	Freight and Passenger Vessel (Large): Vessels built for Army, plus private vessels refitted for wartime service	114-foot, wood, and various sizes for the other vessels
FS	Freight-Supply Vessel: Vessels built for Army, plus merchant ships converted for wartime service	114 (former FP vessels), 140, 148, 176, or 180 feet, wood or steel, and various sizes for the converted merchant ships
LT	Large Tug	94 to 149 feet, wood or steel
Y	Coastal Tankers	162 or 182 feet, steel[1]

For the purposes of this book, we will consider the vessels of the Australian Catboat Flotilla, the Navy's Small Coastal Transports (APc) and Yard Patrol Craft (YP)—former San Diego tuna clippers and Massachusetts fishing trawlers—and Army vessels listed above to be "island hoppers." The Navy's APcs and YPs in the South and Southwest Pacific were assigned to the Third and Seventh Fleets, respectively. The Army vessels under the control of MacArthur never formed a single fleet. Ships belonging to different organizations might be found in a single port of the Southwest Pacific, and conflicts regarding their operations were resolved in theater by MacArthur's general headquarters and in Washington, D.C. by the Joint Chiefs of Staff and the Combined Chiefs of Staff. Due to a dearth of available records it is near impossible to determine with exactness the composition of the Army fleet in the Southwest Pacific Area at a given time. This is because, unlike the Navy and Coast Guard which revered their ships, the Army viewed the vessels much as they would trucks.[2]

THE CATBOAT FLOTILLA AND ARMY TP VESSELS

The vessels of the Australian Catboat Flotilla, the Navy's YPs, and the Army's TP vessels were "stopgap forces" used to deliver soldiers, fuel, ammunition, food and supplies to combat areas in the Solomon Islands and along the New Guinea coasts. Eventually, new construction ships built in America's boat and shipyards for military service, such as the Army's freight-supply ships, tugs, and coastal tankers arrived in theater to supplement or replace the converted civilian craft. The following TP (small freight and passenger) vessels were assigned to the Army Small Ships Section in the Southwest Pacific. They represent only a portion of the TP vessels that served in the region during the war because other Army commands including the Sixth Army, had some allocated to them as well.

TP-102 (S-750)	TP-109 (S-679)	TP-112 (S-765)
TP-117 (S-864)	TP-109	TP-119 (S-996)
TP-121 (S-975)	TP-129 (S-863)	TP-130 (S-870)
TP-140	TP-242 (S-487, *San Jose*)	TP-243 (S-486, *Bennehaven*)
TP-244 (S-508, *Ardito*)	TP-245 (S-485, *San Giovanni*)	TP-246 (S-551, *Sea Tern*)

Five of the above fifteen vessels were former purse seiners. Three from Monterey, California, the *Ardito*, *San Jose*, and *San Giovanni*, were taken by U.S. Government representatives within a week of the Japanese attack on Pearl Harbor. In 1944, the Army took delivery of forty-three new 96-foot, diesel-powered, wooden harbor tugs, which it also designated TP; TP *97-131, 133-134, 224-225,* and *229-232*. These craft was produced at four small yards in California—Ackerman Boat, and Peyton Co., Newport Beach; Clyde W. Wood, Stockton; and Wilmington Boat Works, Wilmington—and four in Washington, all located in Tacoma—Pacific Boatbuilding, Peterson Boatbuilding Company, Petrich Shipbuilding, and Puget Sound Boatbuilding. Two of these harbor tugs, *TP-113* and *TP-129*, would later earn battle stars at Mindoro, Luzon during the Philippine Islands Campaign.[3]

PUGET SOUND FISHING VESSELS TAKEN FOR ARMY USE

Of course some people were unhappy about losing the vessels by which they made their living to the Army, particularly if they felt such action was unwarranted or unjust. An article published in the *Pacific Fisherman* in April, 1944, titled "Fish Boats Seized on Eve of Season," reported:

> Fish production was dealt a blow in March when War Shipping Administration set about requisitioning a group of Pacific fishing vessels just as they were readying for the fishing season.
>
> Twenty craft were reported marked for acquisition by the governmental agency. Half were to be halibut vessels of the 60' class and the balance Puget Sound-type salmon purse seiners, preference being shown for vessels which had not been trawling during the off-season.

"Captain Salset was given six hours to get his personal property off the *Ethel S.*," the first craft taken, while *Tacoma*, *Bergen*, and *Alrita* together with others of the class were reported under pre-requisition survey. The article further stated:

> Best information indicated that the vessels were being taken to satisfy requirements of the Army Transportation Service, which expects to use them in inter-island transport work in the South Pacific, where reefs and shallow water limit vessel size.

The article highlighted that a few weeks earlier the Coordinator of Fisheries, who was also the Secretary of the Interior, had castigated American fishermen for not having produced a larger volume of fish, and it closed with a biting critique:

> Federal vacillation and caprice, as exemplified in these last minute seizures of 20 vessels, has more to do with limiting the production of food than has any selfishness on the part of the fishermen. These men are loyal to the core, and willing to surrender their vessels where necessary; but they bitterly resent having to give up their property as the fishing season is opening, and at the behest of a federal agency which could easily have constructed vessels to meet its needs.

In addition to craft taken for duty in the Southwest Pacific, the Army acquired fishing and other type vessels in 1944-45 to serve in Alaskan waters as a part of a newly formed group titled the "Sea Rescue Group, Army Air Force, Alaska Division." One of these vessels was the *TP-92*, the former *Lone Wolf*. The purpose of this group was to rescue flyers that had crash landed off the Alaskan coast, events which in the absence of any help meant almost certain death from exposure to the elements.[4]

OTHER ARMY SMALL SHIPS SECTION VESSELS

In addition to TP vessels, there were also "F Ships," Large Tugs (LT), and Coastal Tankers (Y) assigned to the U.S. Army Small Ships Section in the Southwest Pacific. The below listing does not include the bulk of the Catboat Flotilla and other type ships of the U.S. Army Transport Service assigned to the Army Small Ships Section. It also represents only a portion of the fleet of F, FS, LT, and Y ships that served in the South and Southwest Pacific, as many of these vessels were assigned directly to the Sixth Army and to other Army and Navy commands.

F-73	F-95	F-96	F-117	F-119	F-122	F-126	F-129
F-130	FS-1	FS-27	FS-47	FS-143	FS-172	FS-195	FS-258
FS-267	FS-390	FS-528	LT-20	LT-125	LT-129	LT-133	LT-140
LT-219	LT-226	LT-348	LT-451	LT-530	LT-644	LT-645	LT-784
Y-3	Y-4	Y-5	Y-7	Y-11	Y-13	Y-15	Y-18
Y-19	Y-20	Y-21					

DELIVERY OF AMERICAN-BUILT VESSELS TO THE SOUTHWEST PACIFIC

Two hundred ninety-two TP, F, FS, LT, and Y vessels of the U.S. Army Transport Service, which include those of the Army Small Ships Section, served in the Southwest Pacific Theater during the war. Information about the delivery dates and hull numbers of these vessels follows:

TP Vessels (33 vessels)	Ship Length/ Designation	Date of Requisition	Units Delivered	Inclusive Dates of Delivery
Purse Seiner	Various/TP	10 May 43	5	23 Feb 44–Apr 44
Note: Likely the former *Ardito, Bennehaven, San Giovanni, San Jose,* and *Sea Tern*.				
Harbor Tug	96 feet/TP	10 May 43	5	23 Oct 44–15 Mar 45
Harbor Tug	96 feet/TP	13 Sep 43	23	5 Aug 44–27 Dec 44
Note: TP-97, 101-106, 108-110, 112-121, 124-125, 128-131 (two of the twenty-eight harbor tugs delivered are not accounted for in these hull numbers).				
Sailing Schooner	100 feet/TP		1	6 Dec 44
Sailing Schooner	100 feet/TP		2	4 Dec 44–20 Dec 44
Note: Likely three of the four former salmon schooners *Alrita, Bergen, Ethel S.,* and *Tacoma*, acquired by the Army.				

F Vessels (29 freight vessels)	Ship Length/ Designation	Date of Requisition	Units Delivered	Inclusive Dates of Delivery
Freight Vessel (F *1-3, 5-12, 14-16, 73-76, 92-96, 115-116, 121-122, 126, 128*)	99 feet/F		29	1943–1945

FS Vessels (166 freight-supply vessels)	Ship Length/ Designation	Date of Requisition	Units Delivered	Inclusive Dates of Delivery
Freight-Supply Vessel, Wood	114 feet/ FS-47		1	Jan 44
Freight-Supply Vessel, Steel (FS *141-160*)	170 feet/FS	1 Sep 43	20	23 May 44–16 Sep 44
Freight-Supply Vessel, Steel (FS *253-258, 260-280, 282-287, 309-312, 314-319, 343-356, 361-367, 371-374, 383-397, 404-408, 524-529, 546-550*)	176 feet/FS	1 Sep 43	99	13 Jul 44–Aug 45

FS Vessels (166 freight-supply vessels), continued	Ship Length/ Designation	Date of Requisition	Units Delivered	Inclusive Dates of Delivery
Freight-Supply Vessel, Steel (FS 162-179, 180-187, 190-203, 222-226)	180 feet/FS	1 Sep 43	46	11 Aug 44–Jul 45

LT Vessels (33 large tugs)	Ship Length/ Designation	Date of Requisition	Units Delivered	Inclusive Dates of Delivery
Large Tug, Steel	111 feet/LT	29 Nov 43	1	1 Aug 44
Large Tug, Steel	111 feet/LT	9 Nov 42	2	23 Mar 44–Apr 44
Large Tug, Steel	123 feet/LT	9 Nov 42	4	29 May 44–6 Aug 44
Large Tug, Steel	123 feet/LT	29 Nov 43	4	1 Aug 44–12 Oct 44
Large Tug, Steel	123 feet/LT	5 Jul 44	14	13 Apr 45–Sep 45
Large Tug, Steel	142 feet/LT	29 Nov 43	1	12 Oct 44
Large Tug, Steel	143 feet/LT	9 Nov 42	1	9 Sep 44
Large Tug, Steel	143 feet/LT	29 Nov 43	6	22 Aug 44–27 Dec 44

Y Vessels (31 coastal tankers)	Ship Length/ Designation	Date of Requisition	Units Delivered	Inclusive Dates of Delivery
Coastal Tanker, Steel	162 feet/Y	9 Nov 42	7	Aug 43–19 Jan 44
Coastal Tanker, Steel	162 feet/Y	5 Mar 44	4	25 Oct 44–18 Apr 45
Note: Y 13-15, 18-21, 35, 44-46				
coastal tanker, steel (Y 3-11)	180 feet/Y		9	1 Nov 43–1 Apr 44
Coastal Tanker, Steel	180 feet/Y	5 Mar 44	2	9 Feb 45–4 Mar 45
Coastal Tanker, Steel	180 feet/Y	2 Apr 44	9	25 Jul 45–Aug 45

Note: Y-53, 56, 58-59, 93, 100-101, 103, 108-109 (one of the twenty 180-foot vessels delivered is not accounted for in these hull numbers)

Total number of vessels: 292[5]

Coast Guard crews manned many of the FS ships, large tugs, and coastal tankers. The remaining vessels were crewed by Merchant Mariners or by personnel of the Army Transport Service or Army Engineer Special Brigades. Summary information about the characteristics of the freight vessels, freight and supply vessels, and harbor tugs, and the identify of commanding officers, if known, are provided in Appendices B and C.

It could be argued that the coastal tankers (Y) and harbor (TP) and large tugs (LT) were not truly island hoppers as much of their service was related to harbor craft duty. However, representatives of each ship types garnered battle stars, as did one Army small tug, the ST-381. Their stories are included in chapters describing the liberation of the Philippine Islands, during which the Army pressed into duty just about anything that floated to support combat operations.

LEGACY OF THE "SPLINTER FLEET"

Thousands of wooden vessels served in the U.S. Navy during World War II. This armada, which some fleet sailors derisively termed the "splinter fleet," was comprised initially of former civilian and commercially-owned yachts and fishing vessels, and later newly constructed wooden-hulled ships—such as PT boats, sub-chasers, and minesweepers—purposely designed for Navy tasks.

Well before the Japanese attack on Pearl Harbor on 7 December 1941, the U.S. Navy recognized that as the drumbeats of war drew ever nearer it required large numbers of ships than it could not quickly obtain. As such, representatives scoured the hundreds of ports, harbors and waterfronts along America's east, west, and gulf coasts, and Great Lakes, and acquired pretty much anything that would float and was large enough to be fitted with machine guns, and ideally depth charges, for use as patrol yachts (PY/PYc) or patrol vessels (YP). Some boats obtained from the fishing fleets, mostly purse seiners, were used as coastal (AMc) minesweepers or smaller base (AMb) minesweepers, the idea being, if they can pull nets, they can stream (pull) sweep gear. These some 800 vessels, many of which served throughout the entire war, helped to alleviate the great shortfall of ships. However, as soon as possible the Navy requisitioned the construction of large numbers of wooden vessels purposely designed for specific tasks or missions. These ships and craft included the small coastal transports (APc), that are the subject of this book, as well as the famous motor torpedo (PT) boats, well-known submarine chasers (SC), and the motor ("yard") minesweepers (YMS) and other types of fleet and district craft.

The construction of so many wooden vessels was due in part to President Franklin D. Roosevelt, an avid yachtsman. While Assistant Secretary of the Navy during World War I, he recognized that America's large shipyards were building warships and merchant vessels but that countless smaller boatyards were not directly involved in the nation's war effort. He knew that some of these yards had been building armed motor launches and patrol boats for Britain, France, and Russia, and that suitable small warships, made of wood to get around the steel shortage, could be mass-produced quickly and cheaply in these boatyards as a stopgap measure until larger ships became available.

The result was a group of 110-foot wooden submarine chasers, mockingly referred to as the "splinter fleet" by sailors of the traditional iron-ship Navy.[6]

THE NAVY'S SMALL COASTAL TRANSPORTS

When the United States entered World War II, Navy requirements for ships and craft greatly exceeded the existing capacity of boat and shipyards across America. This trend continued for some time, even as the nation's output increased dramatically due to increasing requirements associated with expanding war fronts. The result was that often the most pressing requirements determined what type ships came off the ways, and when, and resulted in the reclassification of some vessels already in service.

Interwar mobilization plans had called for wartime needs for coastal minesweepers to be met by taking craft from the fishing fleet. However, recognizing in 1941 that fleet requirements for coastal minesweepers would soon exceed the availability of fishing vessels that could be procured and converted to perform minesweeping duties, the Navy authorized construction of 70 *Accentor*-class ships. On 30 November 1941, Capt. Schuyler N. Pyne and naval architect Sidney Peters of the Bureau of Ships drew up preliminary requirements and sketch plans for a 97-foot, wooden-hulled, single propulsion diesel engine craft designed for 10-knot inshore operations. Built in boat- and shipyards along the eastern seaboard and California coast, the first of the *Accentors* was commissioned on 3 June 1941 and the last on 14 November 1942.[7]

On 19 January 1942 the Chief of Naval Operations (CNO) directed the construction of another fifty ships of this type, AMc 150-199. The Navy was then building a new, larger type of minesweeper, the 136-foot Motor ("Yard") Minesweeper, which had greater capabilities than the AMc class ships. In pursuit of improvements to the 97-foot coastal minesweeper, the Bureau of Ships issued specifications in February 1942 for a modified design for AMc 150-199 that would increase the ships' length to 103 feet and incorporate other changes. This process was interrupted on 13 April 1942 when the CNO directed that the fifty ships be constructed as "raider transports, AP," probably for use in the South Pacific. Within days the Navy's District Craft Development Board suggested three possible uses for the vessels, for which the category Coastal Transport, Small (APc) was created on 22 April 1942:

- transportation of 2 officers and 74 men (possibly a raiding party) for a maximum at sea duration of 24 hours
- transportation of 2 officers, 50 men, and a cargo of 1,500 cubic feet for 24 hours
- carry a cargo of 4,000 cubic feet (17 tons) and no passengers on a voyage of 2,500 miles

The planned AMc 150-199 thus became the APc 1-50 and the Navy, having decided to employ the ships primarily for the transportation of cargo, added a 2-ton capacity boom on the foremast serving an 8-foot by 7-foot hatch to the forward compartment. Since Pacific island hopping would require "longer legs" than did coastal minesweeping, fuel and water storage capacity was increased to extend the ships' range to 2,500 miles. The British, impressed by the ship design, ordered fifty of the small coastal transports on 6 June 1942. Two months later the Vice Chief of Naval Operations (VCNO) directed construction of an addition fifteen ships for a planned total of 115 APcs.[8]

Photo 3-1

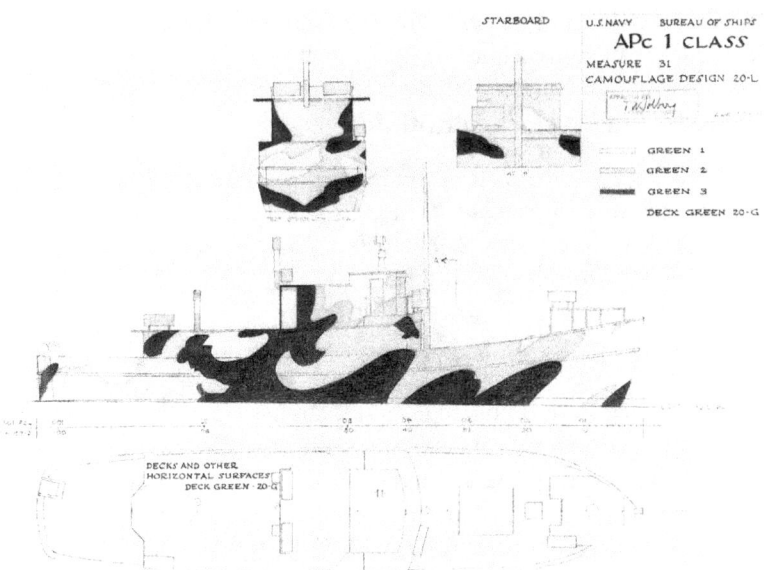

Drawing of the USS *APc-1* prepared by the Navy Bureau of Ships for a camouflage scheme intended for small coastal transports.
(Official U.S. Navy photograph, now in the collections of the U.S. National Archives: http://www.navsource.org/archives/09/23/092300101.jpg)

Meanwhile, the construction of a new type of amphibious craft (Landing Craft Infantry, Large) had begun and after it became apparent that the LCI(L)s were more suitable than APcs for use as troop carriers, the VCNO cancelled the fifteen APcs specified in his August directive. The cancellations were spread among contracts placed in late August and early September 1942, with initially all the planned ships between *APc-51* and *APc-115* that would now be constructed allocated to the British. Ultimately, the U.S. retained twenty-three of the fifty coastal transports earmarked for Great Britain. The U.S. Navy received nineteen of the ships—in addition to the fifty built for its use—and the remaining four were transferred under "Lend Lease" to Greece and Ecuador.[9]

Thus, sixty-nine wooden-hulled cargo ships sailed from builders' yards to join the U.S. Navy. Nine—*APc-86* through *APc-94*—all constructed by famed yacht builder Herreshoff Manufacturing of Bristol, Rhode Island, were assigned to the Atlantic Fleet. These ships were soon relegated to use as ferries for local naval facilities and were eventually disarmed, placed out of commission, and put in an "in service" status, with reduced crews, as district craft. The war service of the remaining sixty APcs that served in the South, Southwest, and Central Pacific was much different.[10]

AMERICA'S LEND LEASE PROGRAM

> *The United States should loan what articles were needed, as a man would loan his garden hose to help his neighbor put out a fire without reference to payment, but with the expectation that the hose itself would be returned.*
>
> Franklin D. Roosevelt, 17 December 1941

Lend Lease legislation enacted on 11 March 1941 authorized the U.S government to abandon its existing policy of neutrality and embark on an all-out military and naval defense program by issuing orders to private firms and by constructing new government plants. A further stipulation was that America would lend or lease to Great Britain as much of its war material production as could be spared. As a result of the fifteen cancelled small coastal transports, hull numbers APc 80-84, 99-100, 104-107, and 112-115 were not used, and the thirty vessels allocated to the Royal Navy were assigned British pendant numbers *FT-1* through *FT-30*. The planned transfer of *FT-15*, *24*, and *28* to Great Britain was later rescinded, and these three vessels went to Greece as the RHS *Lechovon*, RHS *Anchialos*, and RHS *Distomon*, respectively. In a separate action, Ecuador received the *APc-85* as the *Cinco De Junio*:

Original Designation	Allied Recipient	Allied Country's Designation or Name
APc-51, 52, 53, 54, 55, 56	United Kingdom	HMS *FT-1, 2, 3, 4, 5, 6*
APc-57	United Kingdom	HMS *FT-20*
APc-58, 59, 60, 61	United Kingdom	HMS *FT-7, 8, 9, 10*
APc-62, 63, 64	United Kingdom	HMS *FT-21, 22, 23*
APc-65, 66	United Kingdom	HMS *FT-11, 12*
APc-67	Greece	RHS *Lechovon*
APc-68, 69, 70	United Kingdom	HMS *FT-25, 26, 27*
APc-71, 72	United Kingdom	HMS *FT-13, 14*
APc-73	Greece	RHS *Anchialos*
APc-74	United Kingdom	HMS *FT-29*
APc-75	Greece	RHS *Distomon*
APc-76, 77, 78, 79	United Kingdom	HMS *FT-16, 17, 18, 19*
APc-85	Ecuador	BAE *Cinco De Junio*
APc-97	United Kingdom	HMS *FT-30*[11]

Photo 3-2

HMS FT-25 near East Boothbay, Maine on 7 September 1943. Built as *APc-68*, she was turned over to the British following construction under Lend-Lease. (Official U.S. Navy photograph # 19-N-51363, now in the collections of the U.S. National Archives RG-19-LCM: www.navsource.org/archives/09/23/092306801.jpg)

ARRIVAL IN THE PACIFIC THEATER

The first of the APcs that would serve in the Pacific arrived at Guadalcanal on 29 March 1943, joining a number of former San Diego tuna clippers and Massachusetts fishing trawlers which the Navy had dispatched to the theater for duty as small supply ships. These yard patrol craft were from among hundreds of former private or commercially-owned yachts, fishing vessels, whalers, ex-Prohibition era Coast Guard cutters, and basically anything else of sufficient size to be fitted with machine guns, which the Navy purchased, leased, or chartered for service in the American and Pacific Theaters. My book *Battle Stars for the Cactus Navy* is devoted to the service of these vessels, the Navy's patrol yachts (PY/PYc) and yard patrol craft (YP) of World War II. Details about the small coastal transports, including the names of commanding officers, are available in Appendix D.[12]

4

Search for Enemy Spies and Coast Watchers

> *As soon as practical after your arrival at Guadalcanal, search for and destroy or capture enemy spies and coast watchers on San Cristobal and adjacent islands, Ulawa Island, and in the Marau Sound area of Guadalcanal Island.*
>
> Order given Rear Adm. George H. Fort, commander Landing Craft Flotillas, by Rear Adm. Richmond K. Turner, commander Amphibious Force, Third Fleet on 31 May 1943[1]

ONGOING OPERATIONS IN THE SOLOMON ISLANDS

The Japanese evacuated all of its troops from Guadalcanal in early 1943, following a series of defeats to U.S. forces, but continued to strengthen their positions in the upper Solomons and to carry out air raids and submarine attacks on shipping in the southern islands. The Guadalcanal Campaign had been spurred by the Japanese occupation of Tulagi, a small island nestled in a bay at Florida Island opposite Guadalcanal, on 3 May 1942. Japan wanted an air field in the Solomons from which its land-based bombers could provide air cover for the advance of Imperial land forces to Port Moresby, the site of an Allied base. The thousands of troops based there were the Allies' last line of defense before Australia. Having found Tulagi fit only for a seaplane base, on 5 July 1942 Japanese forces landed on Guadalcanal, twenty miles across the New Georgia Sound from Tulagi, and began the rapid construction of Lunga Point Airfield from which the empire's planes could menace the shipping lanes to Australia.[2]

In an effort to prevent that eventuality and gain control of the Solomons, 11,000 members of the 1st Marine Division landed at

Guadalcanal on 7 August, and captured the airstrip at Lunga Point, as well as the Japanese encampment at Kukum on the west side of Lunga Point the following day. That same afternoon, after fierce fighting, Marines discharged at Tulagi took the Japanese-held island, as well as the smaller islands of Gavutu and Tanambogo. The captured airstrip on Guadalcanal was renamed Henderson Field, and its occupation and use by Allied forces temporarily halted Japanese expansion in the South Pacific. The significance of American control of the island—from which the Allies could expand their presence in the South Pacific while thwarting the Japanese thrust—was not lost on the enemy. Guadalcanal became a pivotal piece of island real estate, one that both sides wanted to control and to which they were willing to commit large numbers of forces.[3]

The Japanese made several attempts to retake Henderson Field between August and November 1942. The naval and land battles, and the smaller skirmishes and raids of the Guadalcanal Campaign culminated in the naval battle of Guadalcanal fought between 12 and 15 November. The battle was the last Japanese attempt to land enough troops to retake Henderson Field, but it was unsuccessful. The inability of the Japanese to capture Henderson Field doomed their effort on Guadalcanal, and they evacuated their remaining forces by 7 February 1943, conceding the island to the Allies. The importance of the Guadalcanal Campaign was summarized by Adm. Halsey, commander, South Pacific Force and South Pacific Area:

> Before Guadalcanal the enemy advanced at his pleasure—after Guadalcanal he retreated at ours.[4]

Following completion of the Japanese evacuation from Guadalcanal, there was a lull in the fighting in the Solomon Islands, as both sides wanted a breather. This interlude did not last long as Halsey's admonition "Keep pushing the Japs around" epitomized the prevailing attitude. The Americans had the advantage in quality of aircraft, and sometimes in numbers as well, while the Japanese had superior position. The only Allied airbase was Henderson Field on Guadalcanal, augmented by a fighter strip at Aola Bay and in the Russell Islands to the northwest. The Japanese had Rabaul and, progressing southwest through the Solomons toward Guadalcanal, facilities at Buka, Kahili, Vila, Munda, and Rekata Bay. The latter served only seaplanes.

Bombers were able to stage at Rabaul or Bougainville Island for raids on Tulagi-Guadalcanal, refuel en route, strike their targets, and return to Rabaul beyond the range of fliers from Henderson Field.[5]

On 15 March 1943, under a new Navy convention of identifying Atlantic fleets with even numbers and those in the Pacific with odd ones, the South Pacific Force under Halsey became the Third Fleet, and the Naval Forces Southwest Pacific under Vice Adm. Arthur S. Carpender became the Seventh Fleet. Both had the objective of breaking the Bismarck Islands Barrier, after first sweeping the Japanese out of the Solomon Islands. Allied control of the Vitiaz and Dampier Straits, sea passages between the southwest side of New Britain Island—a part of the Bismarck Archipelago—and New Guinea, was a necessary step along MacArthur's planned New Guinea-to-the-Philippines invasion route. Thus, as MacArthur's land forces continued to fight their way up the southeast coast of New Guinea to the Huon Peninsula opposite the straits, Halsey's forces planned to move northwestward through the Solomons. Top military brass determined that such progress would need to begin with the capture and occupation of the New Georgia Islands in the central Solomons.[6]

The New Georgia group, which lay 200 miles to the northwest of Guadalcanal, extended in a northwesterly-southeasterly direction for a distance of 150 miles. Most of the islands were mountainous and of volcanic origin, and there were lagoons off some formed by barrier islands and coral reefs. As early as August 1942 there had been reports of Japanese activity in this area. The enemy had used hideouts and dispersal anchorages as staging points for ferrying troops and supplies to Guadalcanal. Later, after their failure to gain command of the air over Guadalcanal, the Japanese had begun to construct an air base near Munda Point on the southwest coast of New Georgia Island. The location was almost immune from invasion from the sea as there were only two approaches to Munda Point; one from the north through Diamond Narrows, a deep but very narrow channel; the other from the west across Munda Bar, where water depth was a mere two fathoms. Shortly before completion of the Munda airfield on 29 December 1942, construction was begun on a second air base, twenty-five miles to the northwest near the mouth of the Vila River on the southern tip of Kolombangara Island. Further north in the Solomons, there was an airfield at the south end of Vella Lavella Island, five airfields

Chapter 4

Map 4-1

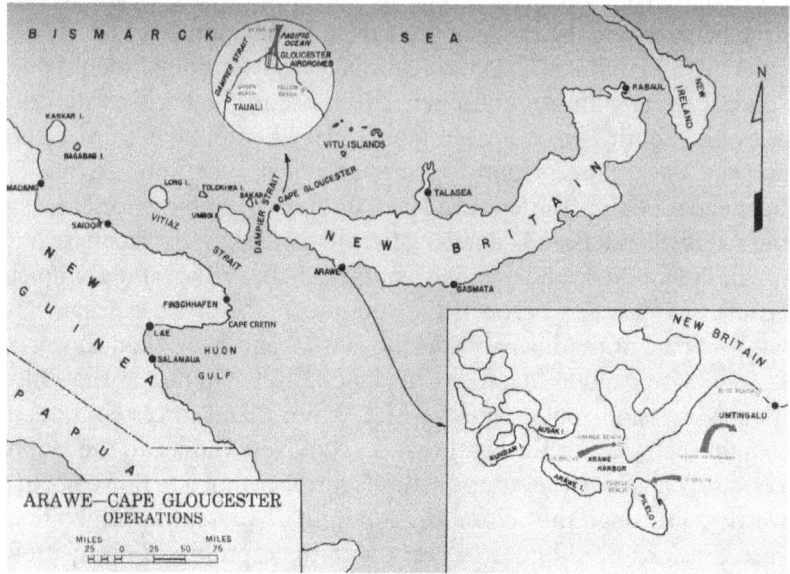

ARAWE—CAPE GLOUCESTER OPERATIONS

Vitiaz and Dampier Straits: Allied control of these sea passages between New Britain Island—a part of the Bismarck Archipelago—and New Guinea was a critical step along the planned New Guinea-to-the-Philippines invasion route. The most powerful Japanese base in the South Pacific was located at Rabaul on northeastern tip of New Britain.
Source: www.lib.utexas.edu/maps/historical/engineers_v1_1947/arawe_cape_gloucester_1947.jpg

on Bougainville Island, Ballale Island airfield in the Shortland Islands south of Bougainville Island, and another airfield on Buka Island just north of Bougainville Island. All were backed up by five airfields around Rabaul, 375 miles northwest of Munda.[7]

Following preliminary bombing of Munda and occupation of the Russell Islands by the Allies for use as a motor torpedo boat base, airstrip, and staging point for the planned advance into New Georgia, the final offensive to clear the Japanese from the New Georgia area was to open on 30 June 1943. In preparation for the offensive, termed Operation TOENAILS, Rear Adm. George H. Fort, commander Landing Craft Flotillas, relocated to Guadalcanal—where a large part of his expeditionary forces were gathering—from his administrative headquarters at Noumea, New Caledonia, 840 miles to the southward. After arriving at Camp Crocodile on Koli Point at Guadalcanal on 1 June, he immediately established an operational headquarters and began preparations for the New Georgia offensive. One of his first actions was to carry out orders from Rear Adm. Richmond K. Turner—who commanded the amphibious forces of the Third Fleet, of which his landing craft flotillas were a part—to search for and eliminate any infiltrators on nearby islands. There were indications that the Japanese had spies and coast watchers with radios on San Cristobal and adjacent islands, Ulawa Island, and in the Marau Sound areas of Guadalcanal. To assist in this endeavor, the commanding general U.S. Army Fourteenth Corps, Maj. Gen. Oscar W. Griswold, was to provide about 150 Fijian troops for the purpose of finding and destroying enemy agents in those areas. The islands, under the Resident Commissioner, British Solomon Islands, were expected to have in them a few British officials and native police.[8]

SMALL COASTAL TRANSPORTS CONTINUE TO ARRIVE IN THEATER

On 27 May 1943, a group of five small coastal transports—APcs *27, 28, 29, 30,* and *31*—arrived at Guadalcanal from Noumea, New Caledonia, followed by a separate group of four—APcs *32, 35, 36,* and *37* the next day. Upon reaching Guadalcanal after a long Pacific crossing, operational control of the vessels passed to commander, Naval Bases, Solomons, Capt. William M. Quigley, USN. The nine small coastal transports joined six sister ships—APcs *23, 24, 25, 26, 33,* and *34*—which, having reported there two months earlier, had been present during the massive enemy air raid on the Guadalcanal-Tulagi area on 7 April that launched Yamamoto's Operation I-GO. The *APc-38* arrived at Guadalcanal on the last day in June, bringing the total number of wooden-hulled cargo ships then present to sixteen. After reaching Noumea, she had made the final leg of her voyage from the United States with the fleet tug *Sioux* (AT-75) towing the gasoline barge *YOG-41*, the yard patrol craft *YP-418* (ex-fishing trawler *Crest*), and the yard minesweeper *YMS-237*.[9]

The below table lists these ships as well as other APcs that arrived at Guadalcanal through 6 September 1943, which collectively totaled twenty-eight vessels. Another twenty-two of these type ships—APcs 1 through 22—were initially based at Milne Bay, New Guinea, after arriving in Australia, and the remaining ten APcs serving in the Pacific supported bases at Noumea; Efate Island; Espiritu Santo, New Hebrides, Funa Futi, Ellice Islands; and, Honolulu, Hawaii. The assignments

Chapter 4

of some vessels changed over the course of the war as operational requirements dictated.

Commander Amphibious Force, Third Fleet (CTF 32):
Rear Adm. Richmond K. Turner, USN
Commander, Landing Craft Flotillas (CTG 32.3):
Rear Adm. George H. Fort, USN
Coastal Transport Flotilla Five: Lt. Dennis Mann, USNR

Ship	Commanding Officer	Date Arrived at Guadalcanal
APc-23	Lt. Dennis Mann, USNR	29 Mar 1943
APc-24	Lt. Bernard F. Seligman, USNR	29 Mar 1943
APc-25	Lt. John D. Cartano, USNR	29 Mar 1943
APc-26	Lt. (jg) James B. Dunigan, USNR	29 Mar 1943
APc-27	Lt. Paul C. Smith, USNR	27 May 1943
APc-28	Lt. (jg) Austin D. Shean, USNR	27 May 1943
APc-29	Lt. (jg) Eugene H. George, USNR	27 May 1943
APc-30	Lt. John R. Shepard, USNR	27 May 1943
APc-31	Lt. R. H. Loomis	27 May 1943
APc-32	Lt. Thomas M. Beers	28 May 1943
APc-33	Lt. James E. Locke	29 Mar 1943
APc-34	Lt. (jg) H. B. Palmer	29 Mar 1943
APc-35	Lt. Robert F. Ruben, USNR	28 May 1943
APc-36	Lt. (jg) Kermit L. Otto, USNR	28 May 1943
APc-37	Lt. Arthur W. Bergstrom, USNR	28 May 1943
APc-38	Thomas Lee Ray	30 Jun 1943
APc-39	Franklin L. Knox, Jr.	6 Sep 1943
APc-40	Lt. (jg) A. H. Heitzler, USNR	4 Sep 1943
APc-41	J. E. Fuld Jr.	6 Sep 1943
APc-42	Lt. (jg) C. E. Voyles, USNR	3 Sep 1943
APc-43	Lt. H. R. Swanson, Jr., USNR	4 Sep 1943
APc-44	Joseph M. Price, USNR	3 Sep 1943
APc-45	Lt. R. D. Williams, USNR	6 Sep 1943
APc-46	Lt. (jg) R. M. Ross, USNR	3 Sep 1943
APc-47	Lt. W. E. Durin, USNR	3 Sep 1943
APc-48	Dwight D. Currie, USNR	4 Sep 1943
APc-49	Lt. (jg) Ross A. Cunningham, USNR	6 Sep 1943
APc-50	Lt. (jg) R. L. Linder	4 Sep 1943

TASK UNIT FORMED

Task Unit 32.3.1, comprised of the APcs *28, 29, 35, 36*, formed at Koli Point on the north coast of Guadalcanal on 4 June, with direction by Fort to embark troops at Aola Bay on the northeast coast of Guadalcanal the following day. Lt. Comdr. Baily embarked in the *APc-29* was the task unit commander. The operational order specified that the *APc-29* was also to embark Lieutenant Harper, and the company headquarters of the Solomon Island Patrol, as well as one Fijian Patrol. The *APc-35* and *36* were to each embark one Fijian Patrol, and the *APc-28* two Solomon Island Patrols. Actually, a Navy radio countermeasures unit, an Army radio field unit, and two Fijian patrols under Sargent Love, New Zealand Army, reported aboard the *APc-35*, and the *APc-36* embarked a Fijian patrol and radio unit. The composition of units that the other vessels likely carried is unknown. Having boarded all necessary personnel, the group of ships departed Aola Bay in early evening on 6 June, bound for waters in the vicinity of Lark Shoal, San Cristobal.[10]

Photo 4-1

USS *APc-29* at anchor off Guadalcanal, circa 1944. (Courtesy of Tom De Mott Jr., NavSource: www.navsource.org/archives/09/23/092302901.jpg)

The *APc-35* left the formation at 0130 to proceed to Selwyn Bay, Ugi Island. Following her arrival, she anchored at 0605 and disembarked the Fijian patrols by means of rubber landing boats, followed by the Army and Navy radio units. She remained at anchor the next two days as the teams searched the island. The morning of 9 June, the vessel embarked one Fijian patrol and radio countermeasures unit and proceeded to Bio Island, disembarked the personnel and returned to Selwyn Bay to embark the remaining troops. The *APc-35* made a second trip to Bio Island, retrieved the teams ashore and proceeded to Kira Kira, San Cristobal Island to rendezvous with the remainder of the task unit. After anchoring, she disembarked the Fijian patrols at 1800.[11]

While the *APc-35* was engaged at Ugi and Bio Islands, the other ships split up to search the other islands; the task unit commander in *APc-29* at Kira Kira, the *APc-28* at the Olu Malau (Three Sisters) Islands, and the *APc-36* at Suumoli Harbor, Ulawa. These islands, located to the southeast of Guadalcanal (today, a part of the Makira-Ulawa Province), were populated mostly by Melanesian natives. San Cristobal (now known as Makira), the largest in the group, had the distinction of having more inland swamps, due to the many rivers joining the ocean in roughly parallel lines every two to five kilometers, and saltwater crocodiles than any other island in the Solomons.[12]

In early evening on 11 June, the *APc-35* embarked the Fijian patrols and then remained at anchor until 0100 before departing Kira Kira for Star Harbor, Cristobal Island. Following arrival there five and one half hours later, she put two sections of the Fijian patrol ashore before moving to the north shore of Star Harbor to land the remainder of the patrol and two radio units, and then anchored in the bay. The *APc-28* departed the Three Sisters Islands for Tulagi Harbor that night arriving at its destination two hours past midnight on 12 June.[13]

The remaining three small coastal transports were then all at San Cristobal. The *APc-36* was anchored off Fanarite Point after having disembarked her Fijian patrol and radio unit, while the *APc-29* and *APc-35* were both on the north coast of the island at Kira Kira and Star Harbor, respectively. On 13 June, Lieutenant Ruben assumed responsibility for the task unit, after the task unit commander, Lieutenant Commander Baily, received an injury to his back. On the 16th, the *APc-36* relocated from Fanarite Point to Kira Kira, after which patrols from the *APc-35* conducted a search of the Fanarite Point area. Between 18 and 21 June, the *APc-36* put her patrol and radio unit ashore at Hawa Bay and Bia Village before arriving at Maru Bay, San Cristobal. The *APc-28* meanwhile searched the Mauru Sound, Guadalcanal area. The four ships rejoined at Maru Bay on 21 June before departing in the early evening for Koli Point, Guadalcanal; arriving the following day.[14]

NOTHING FOUND, BUT SUSPISIONS AROUSED

> *Possibly of some note is the fact that up to the day this vessel arrived at Star Harbor, enemy traffic was fairly active, but, from that time on was almost completely silenced.*
>
> Lt. Robert F. Ruben, commander Task Unit 32.3[15]

Ruben submitted a report on 22 June which conveyed that efforts by the radio countermeasures units and Fijian patrols put ashore on the islands had failed to reveal the presence of enemy spies and coast watchers, or any other enemy activity. The islands were thoroughly covered and possible local sources of information were fully exploited. The bearings obtained by directional finding equipment were few, and of little value as the low quality of reception indicated that the sources of this traffic were at a distance well outside of the suspected area, and a majority of the bearings pointed to known Japanese-held territory.[16]

Following this factual overview, Ruben offered a cautionary warning about the possible connection between a local man and the failure of the operation. Ruben made the acquaintance of a German planter at Star Harbor who had been in the area for thirty-two years, and who was reputedly a deserter from the German navy. This individual, Mr. Kuper, resided on Santa Ana Island, and maintained a small place on Anchor Island in Star Harbor as a trading post. Ruben described him thus:

> He is anti-British and has open contempt for the local authorities. This man, however, is said to be above suspicion. It is the opinion of this command that this is questionable. However remote, the possibility of a connection between the acquaintance of Mr. Kuper and the sudden diminishing of enemy radio traffic should not be overlooked. On the other hand, he claims to be very pro-American and apparently could not do to[o] much for the *APc 29* at Santa Ana.[17]

PRECEDING ACTION IN THE RUSSELL ISLANDS

Between 11 May and 7 June 1943, the *APc-25* and *APc-34* operated from Renard Sound, a deep water sheltered anchorage on the northeast side of Banika Island in the Russell Islands group, to perform a variety of tasks for commander, Naval Base Russells. The duty consisted mostly of hauling army supplies to various outposts in the islands, including Paddy Bay on the northeast coast of Pavuvu Island. The Russell Islands, which lay northwest of Guadalcanal, consisted of Banika and Pavuvu, separated by Sunlight Channel, as well as several surrounding small islets, shoals and reefs. The two coastal transports and some motor torpedo boats ordered on 30 May to the islands in preparation for the invasion of New Georgia, which including John F. Kennedy's *PT-109*, were the only naval vessels then operating in the Russells. Pavuvu had appeared to Army staff officers flying over the island in search of a rest camp to be a tropical paradise due to the gentle surf, white beaches, and palm tree-lined coastal areas devoid of brush they observed below. In reality, the uninhabited island was the home to muddy tidal swamps in many of the inlets that indented its coast, as well as armies of coconut (land) crabs that subsisted on the thick mat of rotten coconuts covering the island, beneath which there was more repugnant smelling thick goo. Pavuvu had served as a coconut plantation until 1941 when, as the Imperial Japanese Navy swept through the Solomons, it was abandoned. Troops sent to Pavuvu for rest did not relish the experience; a Marine wryly observed the only benefit time spent on the island offered was, due to the universally-hated conditions, as a means for inexperienced replacements to bond with hardened combat veterans before they went into battle together.[18]

Map 4-2

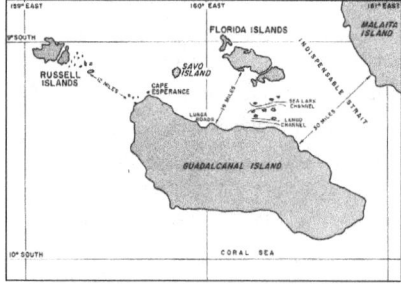

Although U.S. Marines and soldiers sent to Pavuvu—the largest of the Russell Islands—for "rest" from combat hated the miserable conditions, the islands offered the Allies a site to stage troops and materials for the planned invasion of New Georgia in the central Solomons.
Source: http://www.ibiblio.org/hyperwar/USN/ACTC/img/actc-38.jpg

There were a few variations in duties assigned the two coastal transports. The *APc-25* was sent on 26 May and 7 June to Macquitti Bay on Pavuvu's northwest coast to take soundings of the harbor and search for a possible embarkation point for troops. In the mid-afternoon of the latter date, she picked up Maj. Roger B. Fraser, USMC, pilot of a P40 shot down in an air battle that morning off Pavuvu's south coast in the vicinity of Cape Baloka. Fraser, commanding officer of Marine Fighting Squadron 112 based at Guadalcanal, had received orders at 1020 to scramble all available aircraft to intercept an enemy force 150 miles away and coming down the Slot. Fourteen planes took off from No. 1 Fighter Strip on Guadalcanal, took station at 20,000 feet above the Russell Islands, with Fraser leading the first of three flights. One aircraft was forced to return to the strip and another to Carney Field on Guadalcanal near Koli Point before they reached the Russells. Fraser's flight made contact with twelve to fourteen Japanese Zeros that came in for an attack from behind and above the eight planes. The after action report vividly described the engagement, as well as the bravery, skill and good fortune of the pilots involved:

> Major Fraser went after the first Zero which he shot down. Lieutenant Synar went after the second which was pursing the Major; he shot it down. Lieutenant Johnson, in pursing the third was attacked from behind and over one half of his rudder, his hydraulic system and a tire were shot away. He continued in spite of the damage and destroyed the third Zero before proceeding home where he was able to land his plane in spite of the extensive damage. Lieutenant Percy, while chasing the Zero after Lieutenant Johnson, became separated and was attacked by at least six Zeros. He fought until his controls were shot away then he jumped at a very low altitude. Because of the low altitude his parachute streamed behind him but did not open and it is a miracle he is still alive. He hit the water sustaining a broken pelvis, two sprained ankles and numerous bruises. He was able to swim to a coral reef 5 miles east of the Russell's [air] strip where he remained all afternoon and night finally reaching the adjacent island where he was found by natives and returned to the Russells that afternoon. Captain Donahue attacked the remaining Zeros and destroyed two. Lieutenant Harter's plane was hit and he made a landing on the Russell strip.

After the first engagement the remaining Zeros reformed south of the Russells. Major Fraser and Lieutenant Synar, who were now flying alone, proceeded to a spot midway between the Russells and Buraku [Island] where they were attacked by twelve Zeros from above. Major Fraser shot down one Zero and had his oil line hit by another. He was forced down when his engine froze and made a water landing off Pavuvu Island of the Russell Group. He was followed down by the Zero which exhausted it ammunition just before the Major landed. Fraser had some trouble getting out of his plane when underwater but finally managed to get free and was picked up and returned to the Russell Strip four hours later.[19]

As the air battle continued, Lieutenant Logan got into the second fight when he spotted a Zero on the tail of a P40. He attacked the plane and drove it away but, while thus engaged, was hit from behind and his own controls were shot away, requiring him to bail out at 18,000 feet. The report provided a chilling account of the ensuing action:

> In this helpless altitude, while descending in the parachute, the enemy exhibited the most base cruelty, by making repeated firing runs on Lieutenant Logan. On the third run Logan was trying to spill his chute and the enemy, evidently miscalculating, the increased speed of descent, hit Lieutenant Logan with his propeller and cut half of the right foot away. The enemy still persisted in these attacks until Logan's plight was observed by flight leader Herrich (RNZAF) who drove the enemy away in spite of the fact that his supply of ammunition was exhausted. Lieutenant Logan showed great presence of mind in applying a tourniquet, injecting morphine and taking sulfathiazole tablets. Upon reaching the surface of the water midway between Buraku and the Russells, he inflated his boat, dusted his wound with sulfanilimide powder and displayed sea markers to aid his rescue. He was picked up very shortly afterwards by the J2F-5 [a Grumman single-engine amphibious biplane] piloted by Lt. Col. Clifford of MAG [Marine Air Group]-21. It was found necessary to amputate the right foot on his arrival at the hospital.[20]

In the final tally, twenty-three of forty Zeros engaged by the Marine Squadron were destroyed at the cost of five planes lost and all pilots rescued with the exception of one Army P40 pilot. The VMF-112 lost three planes in stopping the brunt of the attack, and raised the squadron total to 86 enemy planes destroyed. Fraser, who was plucked from the sea by the *APc-25*, became a Marine Corps ace during the war—credited with six kills—and also received the Distinguished Flying Cross.[21]

5

New Georgia Campaign

> *[Munda] is a most magnificent defensive area from the sea. There is a dense jungle behind. In front is the Munda Bar. . . . The water is chock full of reefs. . . . Some people think Munda's not going to be tough. I think it's a very tough nut to crack. I know we can do it.*
>
> Observations by Rear Adm. Richmond K. Turner
> at a pre-invasion conference[1]

By early 1943, some Allied leaders, and most notably General MacArthur, wanted to focus on capturing the powerful enemy base at Rabaul, but Japanese strength there and a lack of landing craft meant that such an operation was not practical in that year. Instead, on the initiative of the Joint Chiefs of Staff, Operation CARTWHEEL was developed, which proposed to envelop and cut off Rabaul without capturing it, by simultaneous offensives in New Guinea and northwards through the Solomon Islands. The New Georgia Campaign, a series of battles that took place in the New Georgia group of islands, in the central Solomon Islands from 20 June-25 August 1943, was part of CARTWHEEL, the Allied grand strategy in the South Pacific.[2]

Commander Third Fleet, Admiral Halsey, provided the initial planning guidance for the occupation of New Georgia on 17 May 1943. Forces of the South Pacific Area were to seize and occupy positions in the southern part of the New Georgia Island Group preparatory to a full-scale offensive against Munda Point on New Georgia, and Vila on Kolombangara Island, also a part of the island group. From there assigned forces would move to the northwest to attack Buin airfield on the south end of Bougainville Island, and to Faisi, a small island off Bougainville southeast of Buin, which hosted the headquarters of the Japanese 8th Fleet and a seaplane base. Bougainville—about 130 miles long and 30 miles wide—was the largest island of the Solomon Islands, and mountainous, dominated by the Emperor and Crown Prince ranges. The specific tasks for the assigned forces were to seize, hold, and develop:

- A staging point for small craft in the Wickham Anchorage Area in the southeastern part of Vangunu Island and 50 miles from the Munda airstrip.
- Viru Harbor on New Georgia Island 30 miles southeast of the Munda airstrip.
- A fighter airstrip at Segi, New Georgia, 40 miles from the Munda airstrip.
- Rendova Island, whose northern harbor was just 10 short miles south of Munda, as a supply base, advanced PT Base, and an adequate support base to accommodate amphibians prior to their embarkation of troops for an assault on Munda and/or Vila.

More detailed planning for the operation was predicated upon the arrival in the South Pacific of an adequate number of LSTs (tank landing ships), LCI(L)s (large infantry landing craft) and LCTs (tank landing craft), some being built by commercial shipyards themselves newly constructed. Ultimately, Halsey's desire for an April or May D-Day was not realized due to constant slippage of the arrival dates of the necessary landing craft.[3]

PREPARATORY OCCUPATION OF THE RUSSELL ISLANDS

Immediately following the evacuation of all Japanese forces from Guadalcanal in February 1942, Admiral Halsey had set in motion plans for occupying the Russell Islands, so that they might be used as a staging point for the planned advance into New Georgia. About 9,000 infantrymen and Marines from New Caledonia landed unopposed at three different points in the Russells at about dawn on 21 February. Accompanying the landing forces was a major portion of the Navy's 33rd Construction Battalion, and the "Seabees" immediately began construction of a radar station, PT boat base, and an airstrip. A steady stream of men, supplies, and equipment arrived nightly. By the end of February there were in the Russells units of the 43rd Army Infantry Division, the 3rd Marine Raider Battalion, the 10th Marine Defense Battalion, the 33rd Construction Battalion, and Naval Base personnel. By early June the Seabees had completed building two airstrips and the fuel tanks and other supporting facilities necessary for an invasion of New Georgia.[4]

Map 5-1

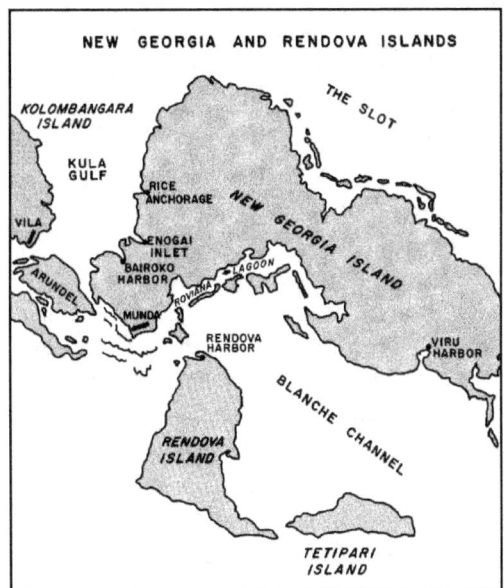

The Allies invaded the New Georgia Islands to capture Japanese airfields at Munda and Vila, and other enemy positions in the islands, as a part of Operation CARTWHEEL, a strategy designed to isolate and bypass Rabaul without capturing it.
Source: http://www.ibiblio.org/hyperwar/USN/ACTC/maps/actc-p486.jpg

SMALL COASTAL TRANSPORTS MOVE MEN AND MATERIALS FORWARD

Among the forces allocated to Rear Adm. George H. Fort for the forthcoming operation to take New Georgia, code-named "TOENAILS," were fifteen small coastal transports, which included the four ships engaged temporarily in hunting for enemy spies and coast watchers. The fifteen ships were formed into two divisions: APc Division 25—comprised of APcs *23* through *29*—under Lt. Dennis Mann (who was also the flotilla commander as well as the commanding officer of the *APc-23*), and APc Division 26—APcs *32* through *39*—under Lt. Arthur W. Bergstrom, the commanding officer of the *APc-37*.[5]

As planning and preparations for the operation continued, APcs made repeated runs from Guadalcanal to the Russells to deliver men and stocks of combat material to staging areas before the invasion commenced on 30 June. The task units of which the APcs were a part included one or more tank landing craft transporting troops and equipment. In early evening on 11 June, the *APc-23* moored alongside the attack transport *President Jackson* (APA-18), anchored off Koli Point on Guadalcanal's north coast, to embark personnel and gear of Carrier Aircraft Service Unit No. 8 for movement to the Russell Islands. The *APc-24* outboard the *23* took aboard 150 enlisted men of the unit. A third cargo ship, the *APc-26*, took 120 men and four officers, and *APc-27* another 125 officers and men. After the loading was completed, the APcs departed in company with the *YP-421* (ex-fishing trawler *Surf*), which had been designated the command ship, and the tank landing craft LCTs *67* and *180*. Upon arrival at Renard Sound the following morning, a pontoon barge came alongside to take off the CASU 8 personnel and gear, following which the vessels in the convoy departed in late morning to return to Guadalcanal. Over the next thirteen months, the carrier aircraft service unit operated from the Russell Islands; Munda, New Georgia; Green Island, New Guinea; and the Treasury Islands, while maintaining various land-based aircraft. These included the F4F, SBD, TBF, F6F, Australian P40s, F4U Corsairs, P38s rigged as night fighters, P39 Bell Airacobras, B25s rigged with 75mm breach loaded cannons, and a few F8 aircraft. The unit returned to the United States in late July 1944, after providing support for aircraft striking the Japanese base at Truk.[6]

Shortly after departing the Russells and while still in the channel the ships were warned via radio of an expected enemy air raid. The *APc-23* set general quarters at 1040 and witnessed dogfights off her port bow and four or more planes shot down. The *APc-24* meanwhile steered various courses as a protective measure against attack, while keeping under the shelter of shore anti-aircraft batteries, and the *APc-27* lay to off the islet Laun during the air battle. Afterwards the *APc-23* received orders to proceed independently ahead of the other ships back to Koli Point. After increasing speed to 10 ½ knots, her best speed, she set off and following her arrival in the early evening at Guadalcanal, boarded a reconnaissance party of twenty-seven officers and men at Koli Point for transport to Wernham Cove, Russell Islands.[7]

PROTECTION FROM DETECTION BY ENEMY PLANES

The APcs in the Guadalcanal-Tulagi area went to general quarters on several occasions in June due to sightings or reports of enemy planes. The *APc-26* was at anchor off Lunga Point on 16 June when, in mid-afternoon, a group of Japanese aircraft arriving from the southwest attacked two ships. The bombers were Vals sporting very dark paint except for white tails. As aircraft dove on the bow, bridge, and stern of the freighter USS *Celeno* (AK-76) releasing their bombs from a height of 250 to 500 feet, other planes strafed the ship from stem to stern. One bomb hit the ship's starboard side, forward of the 5-inch gun platform and inboard of the No. 7 20mm gun tub. The detonation knocked both guns out of action, penetrated 7/16" thick plating and twisted and tore the entire after deckhouse and deck platform. A direct hit aft blasted a large hole in the ship and broke a frame near the stern tube seal, resulting in flooding. The freighter's stern was also set on fire by bomb blasts, and she suffered additional damage from strafing.[8]

Three planes attacked the tank landing ship *LST-340*. A direct hit created a massive fire among deck-loaded trucks due to—in addition to flammable loads of cans of oil and gasoline, wooden crates, trunks, bedding, and barracks bags—full tanks of gasoline. Six other aircraft joined in the attack, and daylight soon streamed in through more than one hundred holes created by fragments from near bomb misses and strafing. The fire main piping was damaged and with no water to fight flames, the commanding officer ordered troop passengers to abandon ship. The port engine was knocked out of commission, and after it became too hot for the watch team in the main engine room to remain, they were ordered to put the starboard throttle at flank speed ahead, and leave the space. All hands, other than gun crews and repair personnel, were then ordered to abandon because of the danger of explosions from magazines, the gasoline cans in trucks, and rapidly spreading flames. The commanding officer beached the LST at Tenaru on Guadalcanal, and *LST-398* came alongside and put out the fires.[9]

No enemy planes came within range of the *APc-26*'s 20mm guns, which was fortunate for her as based on the damage the bombers had done to the steel-hulled 328-foot LST and even larger 441-foot AK, even a near miss would have likely reduced the wooden vessel to a mess of floating debris, and killed or severely injured a majority of her crew. Enemy planes returned in the evening the following day, at 2030, and the coastal transport fired twelve rounds of 20mm at those closest overhead. Across the Slot, a lone aircraft flew low over the Tulagi Harbor, coming in from the southwest. Despite anti-aircraft fire from shore batteries and from vessels present—including the *APc-23*'s No. 1, 2, and 3 20mm guns—it apparently escaped. If possible, small vessels—including PT boats—sought to shield themselves from the view of enemy aircraft. The previous day, the *APc-23* had been moored starboard side to the *LST-180* at a water hole at Govona Inlet, Florida Island, when warning came in the early afternoon of an impending air raid. She had cast off immediately, proceeded to a "hideout" in the inlet, anchoring in eleven fathoms of water, and remained there until after Condition Red changed to Green at 1515. The *APc-24*, at Tulagi, had quickly made its way to a hideout in a small cove off Purvis Bay, Florida Island, and moored to the bank to gain shelter from nearby foliage.[10]

Commander, Task Force 31 had directed preparation of hideouts for small craft, as well as the indoctrination of all units and individuals in the necessity for dispersal and use of overhead cover and camouflage. Such action was common among the APcs and amphibious landing craft, particularly in forward areas. Four large infantry landing craft—LCI(L)s *327, 328, 329, 336*—hid from Japanese dive-bombers in a small cove at Poko Plantation on Rendova Island several times during August.[11]

SMALL COASTAL TRANSPORT DOWNS TWO, MAYBE THREE, AIRCRAFT

Of course, the hideouts were only of use if you could get inside one before the arrival of enemy aircraft overhead. At a little past daybreak on 16 July, *APc-34* got under way from alongside the *APc-24* at anchor in Tulagi Harbor, and made Sturgis Dock. There she took aboard mail, freight, and seventeen army-navy personnel for transportation to Guadalcanal and departed Tulagi at 0800. Arriving off Lunga Point a little over two hours later at 1015, the *APc-34* anchored in twenty fathoms of water, discharged the mail, freight, and passengers, and began to load cargo, mail and twenty-two army or navy men for transport to Tulagi. At completion, she set a return course, steering course 025 true at 9 ½ knots. At 1345, a Condition Red warning came over the radio, upon which her commanding officer, Lt. (jg) H. B.

Palmer, ordered General Quarters set, ship's speed increased to flank, and commencement of zigzag evasive steering.[12]

At about 1420, her lookouts detected a group of ten enemy planes approaching low and fast the *APc-34*'s starboard quarter (at a height of 1,200 to 1,500 feet above the water) from the direction of where the *Celeno* and another cargo ship, the *Deimos* (AK-78), were located off the north coast of Guadalcanal. All four of her guns opened as the aircraft came within range. The initial target angle was 45 (degrees above the horizon), but increased to 70 as the planes closed, and the range to the targets decreased from 1,000 yards to 300 yards. Two aircraft passed down her port side and one other close aboard to starboard, strafing but not bombing the APc, which seemed to indicate the enemy had expended their ordnance on the *Celeno* or another ship. Two planes would not make it home to their airfields. Using tracer rounds to improve their aim, the gun crews aboard the small coastal transport scored hits on two of the planes, and they fell into the sea off the port bow and port quarter of the wooden ship. The third plane also took fire but was not seen to crash. The *APc-34* suffered no casualties, and all aboard received a battle star. After Condition Red changed to Green, it was back to business as usual. The coastal transport passed through the Tulagi Harbor anti-submarine net at 1540, made Sturgis Dock, and began unloading her freight, mail, and passengers. At completion, she moored portside to *APc-24* at anchor in the harbor, ending another day in the Solomons.[13]

PALM THATCHES GREATLY VALUED

Navy leadership respected the sanctuary that hideouts afforded ships small enough to traverse shallow waters. Thus, while other APcs transported personnel, boxes of ammunition, drums of gasoline, rations, and medical supplies to forward areas, the *APc-31* journeyed to Malaita Island—sixty nautical miles to the southeast across Indispensable Strait from Guadalcanal—to obtain a supply of palm fronds. At the completion of loading, she left Mallu Harbor on the north coast of the island in the early morning darkness on 1 July, bound for Kukum Beach, Guadalcanal, with 7,500 palm fronds. These materials in large quantities were unavailable locally because of considerable damage done palm trees during the Guadalcanal Campaign, when fronds were shot or bombed away as a result of land combat and air raids.[14]

Three days later, the *APc-31* sallied forth to obtain addition fronds, this time bound for Auki Harbor on the northwest coast of Malaita under escort by the New Zealand minesweeper HMNZS *Gale* (TO4). The *Gale* and two sister ships, the *Breeze* and *Matai*, comprised the 9th Auxiliary Minesweeping group which operating from Tulagi carried out night-time patrol and escort duties under the operational control of commander Third Fleet. Embarked aboard the wooden cargo ship were a group of six American navy and army officers for transport to the island, and in tow astern a "terra ramp." This device allowed cargo, including thatches, to be loaded faster and more efficiently. Following a day and a half of backbreaking work, spent cutting and loading 8,300 palm thatches, the *APc-31* left in the early afternoon of 6 July for Lunga Point, Guadalcanal, escorted by the *Gale*.[15]

INVASION TASK FORCE FORMED

Rear Adm. Richmond K. Turner's Task Force 31 was formed for the invasion of New Georgia on 17 June with 12 LSTs, 12 LCI(L)s, 28 LCTs, 10 APcs, three APDs (high-speed transports), two DMs (destroyer-minesweepers), and two ATs (fleet tugs). The number of ships and landing craft assigned to it increased daily thereafter, while the supporting force (Task Force 32), shrinking by a compensatory amount, continued to carryout administrative and support tasks. Halsey's general concept was that movements of the amphibians on 30 June into the New Georgia Group were the necessary prelude to capturing in succession the Munda and Vila airfields and other enemy positions in the islands. The final planning included making the major assault on Munda airfield from its eastern flank while simultaneously landing a holding assault against its seaward front and closing off its support lines to the north by a small landing on the Kula Gulf. The gulf bordered the northwest coast of New Georgia. The plan also specified building an airstrip at Segi Point, after taking this area on New Georgia's southeast coast, to provide close air support for the assault on the Vila airfield, and making Rendova Island to the south of New Georgia into a combination staging point and artillery support position for the Munda assault. Experience had shown that tank landing craft—characterized by frequent breakdowns, small crews and slow speed—required ports or protected anchorages at about sixty-mile intervals where they could receive repairs and daytime crew rest as they transited at night towards the landing beaches. This led to a search for havens in the middle Solomons, and the selection of Viru Harbor, New Georgia, and Wickham Anchorage at the eastern approaches to Vangunu Island, as areas to be seized as well.[16]

Rear Admiral Turner divided the amphibious assault force of Task Force 31 into two major groupings for 30 June, based on whether their tasking was to be in the eastern or western part of the New Georgia Group, and termed them the Eastern Force and the Western Force. Turner, the commander of Task Force 31, retained immediate command of Task Group 31.1, all of the large transports and cargo ships, a portion of the destroyer-type transports and minesweepers, most of the tank landing ships and the necessary protecting destroyers. Rear Admiral Fort commanded Task Group 31.3, an organization of destroyer-transports and minesweepers, infantry and tank landing craft and small coastal transports. Task Group 31.1 (the Western Force) was assigned the Rendova Island task, while Task Group 31.3 (the Eastern Force) was allocated the assault chores at Viru Harbor, New Georgia, Segi Point, New Georgia, and at Wickham Anchorage. These three places all could serve as service locations for LSTs or PT boats moving forward from the Russell Islands to Rendova or Munda.[17]

The assault force carried in the Western Force ships was to go ashore in four echelons, the troops aboard the transports and cargo ships as part of the first echelon, with the remaining echelons carried by the LSTs and LCI(L)s. The occupation units carried in the Eastern Force were also to land in four echelons. The vessels carrying the first echelons at Viru Harbor and Wickham Anchorage included destroyer-transports, with coastal transports, LCI(L)s, and LCTs making up the succeeding echelons as well as the first echelon at Segi Point. Most landing craft were a part of more than one echelon. Commander Eastern Force had logistic responsibility for "embarking troops and supplies from the Russells destined for the support of TOENAILS" after the initial movement, and for all ship lift to Viru Harbor, Segi Point, and Wickham Anchorage.[18]

EARLY ASSAULT LAUNCHED TO SAFEGUARD ALLIED COAST WATCHER

On 20 June, ten days before the planned invasion, Turner learned by radio from New Zealander Donald Kennedy, a longtime coast watcher with a private army of about 200 Melanesian locals armed with captured Japanese weapons, that three barge loads of Japanese troops had landed at Segi Point on New Georgia and that he needed help to avoid capture. Kennedy's guerilla activities had so angered Lt. Gen. Minoru Sasaki—commander of the Southern Detachment who would lead the Japanese forces during the Battle of New Georgia from June to August 1943—that he had sent a company of infantry to hunt him down. In order to provide assistance and ensure that the enemy would not have an opportunity to dig in, Companies O and P of the 4th Marine Raiders landed there from the destroyer-transports *Dent* (APD-9) and *Waters* (APD-8) the next morning to ensure possession of this particularly valuable real estate. Segi Point was desired as the site for an airstrip to support close fighter aircraft air support during the landing operation against Munda or Vila. No Japanese resistance developed, and airfield construction began there on 30 June.[19]

OCCUPATION OF NEW GEORGIA

> *All boats away, all troops away. You are the first to land, you are the first to land—expect opposition.*
>
> Orders given aboard Rear Adm. Richmond K. Turner's flagship, the attack transport USS *McCawley* (APA-4), prior to the first wave of boats departing her side and those of three *President*-class APAs in company to land the 43rd Army Infantry Division and 4th Marine Raider Battalion on Rendova beaches at New Georgia Island on 30 June 1943.[20]

The occupation of New Georgia was coordinated with operations by MacArthur's Southwest Pacific forces against Woodlark and Kiriwina Islands in Milne Bay and Salamaua and Lae on New Guinea. The second landing in the New Georgia area took place at Rendova Harbor on the north side of Rendova Island, a boot-shaped islet 20 miles long and 8 miles wide separated from New Georgia Island by only a few miles of water. The landing force went ashore on 30 June in the face of machine gun fire from the beach, and a little after 0700, the batteries on Munda Point opened fire. The first salvo straddled the *Gwin* (DD-433), one of the four destroyers patrolling off shore that comprised the screening unit, and a moment later a round struck her, killing three men, wounding seven, and knocking out her aft engine room. Another round just missed the *Buchanan* (DD-484), and two other batteries on Baanga Island and one or two at Lokuloku Reef joined in. Despite the damage she had sustained, the *Gwin* laid down a heavy smoke screen to protect the unloading transports, while the *Buchanan* and *Farenholt* (DD-491) sought to silence the enemy guns. They put seven batteries out of action, but an exchange of fire between shore batteries and screening destroyers continued intermittently throughout the day.[21]

By 0730, all troops except ship working details had been landed; within two hours from the time of initial debarkation newly emplaced shore batteries on Kokurana Island were shelling enemy installations at Munda. Throughout the landing operation a combat air patrol, comprised of aircraft from Marine Fighting Squadrons VMF 121, 122, 213, and 221 from Guadalcanal and the Russells, was maintained. (The famous fighter, Ace Major Gregory "Pappy" Boyington had commanded VMF 122 until a week earlier when relieved, on 22 June, by Maj. Herman Hansen, Jr. His famed Black Sheep Squadron, VMF 214, was officially activated on 7 September 1943.) Twice during the forenoon, these aircraft drove off enemy planes that threatened ships and some were downed in combat with Japanese Zeros over Rendova. The Zeros were of a dark green or black color and sported a red rising sun inside a dark circle. Around noon, the *APc-23* plucked aviator Capt. W. A. Baron, USMCR, from waters off Vangunu Island and the *APc-24* similarly retrieved a second pilot, 1st Lt. Robert Dailey, Jr., USMCR, of VMF-121. Both of the coastal transports earned a battle star for their actions that day.[22]

That afternoon the combat air patrol over Rendova received warning of bogies ("enemy aircraft") high and low, twenty miles out, approaching from the northwest. The group proved to be 24 to 28 Betty (Mitsubishi type 96) torpedo planes, escorted by Zeros flying high cover at 12,000 to 15,000 feet coming in over the northwest corner of New Georgia near Munda Point. "There they go" was heard in cockpits coming over radio circuits, and Rendova aircraft control urged the pilots, "Go get them Boys, protect your shipping." The tally claimed by VMF-221 was 13 Bettys and 3 Zeros shot down, and with an additional ½ Betty and ½ Zero shared with other fighters, or ships below. The ships of Rear Admiral Turner's task group were then in a cruising formation, en route back to Guadalcanal via the Blanche Channel. Enemy bombers circled the formation, using land background to mask their movement, before making very low approaches at speeds of nearly 250 knots. Approximately one minute before the leading planes reached the screening ships, the formation executed "Emergency Turn 9" from a base course of 139 degrees. All vessels opened fire, and immediately scored hits. The bombers, despite losses, attacked with great determination, releasing torpedoes from only 500 yards away. The transport *McCawley*, Turner's flagship, was hit by a torpedo—after escaping a bracket of three—resulting in the admiral and his staff shifting to the *Farenholt*. By 1558 the attack was over; the action lasted only eight minutes in which only two enemy aircraft survived the efforts of protecting fighters and anti-aircraft fire of the ships. More suffering for the *McCawley*, however, was yet to come. About an hour later, she was attacked by a group of 12–15 Vals that broke through the overcast about 1,000 feet overhead. Although the ship was "dead in the water" and thus a sitting duck, the salvage crew aboard her manned guns and drove the planes off. The crew was subsequently ordered to abandon following a decision that the *McCawley* could not be saved. She was sunk later that night by three torpedoes fired by PT boats that believed she was a Japanese transport.[23]

LANDING AT WICKHAM ANCHORAGE, VANGUNU ISLAND

Concurrent with the amphibious assault at Rendova Island to the south of New Georgia Island, the first landing at Oloana Bay in Wickham Anchorage—on Vangunu Island, eastward off the southeast coast of New Georgia—was made at 0630 on 30 June. The selection of Oloana Bay as the site to come ashore took Japanese defenders by surprise, and by late morning all landing operations had been completed unopposed. The previous evening, Rear Admiral Fort embarked in the destroyer-minesweeper *Trever* (DMS-16), and the LCI(L)s *24, 233, 332, 333, 334, 335,* and *336* had left Wernham Cove in the Russells to proceed northwest towards Vangunu. They were joined by the transports *Schley* (APD-14) and *McKean* (APD-5) at sea. The *Trever* was a former *Clemson*-class destroyer commissioned in 1922, and the two APDs even older ex-*Wickes*-class destroyers, commissioned in 1918 and 1919, respectively. Aboard the *Schley* and *McKean* were companies N and Q of the 4th Marine Raiders, as well as elements of other Marine Corps units.[24]

The *APc-35* and the LCTs *63, 133,* and *482,* comprising the second section of the above task unit, also stood out of Wernham Cove the evening of 29 June for Oloana Bay. They reached their destination in the early afternoon the following day. An hour later, Japanese planes passed over Oloana Bay at 1430. The *APc-35* and *LCT-63* opened fire but were unable to score any hits; the small coastal transport did however earn a battle star. Other APcs and LCTs had also moved forward from Guadalcanal in late June to Banika Island in the Russells. The vessels were staged for the forthcoming operations at either Renard Sound, a deep water sheltered anchorage on the northeast side of Banika, or Wernham Cove on the southwest coast. A small peninsula enclosed and completely sheltered the cove, except for an opening from Sunlight Channel which separated Banika and adjacent Pavuvu Island.[25]

As required, groups of small coastal transports and tank landing craft moved forward to Oloana Bay. Task Unit 31.3.12—the *APc-24* with LCTs *134, 330,* and *369*—stood into the bay in the mid-afternoon of the 29th, Task Unit 31.3.32—*APc-36* with LCTs *60, 127,* and *144*—on the morning of 1 July, and TU 31.3.33—*APc-37* with LCTs *132, 145, 325, 367* and *481*—the following morning.[26]

LANDING AT VIRU HARBOR, NEW GEORGIA

The planned landing at Viru Harbor on New Georgia Island was delayed by one day until 1 July because of the late arrival of the advance assault unit—Companies O and P of the 4th Marine Raiders—which had landed at Segi on 21 June and been dispatched overland to Viru. The Marines had been delayed at Choi River near Nono, New Georgia on 28 June by enemy action. The first echelon of the Viru occupation unit, the destroyer-minesweeper *Hopkins* (DMS-13) with a landing craft in tow and the transports *Kilty* (APD-15) and *Crosby* (APD-17) arrived two miles south of Viru Harbor at 0610 on 30 June. At 0703 shore batteries opened and straddled the *Crosby*. The ships returned fire and, since the location of the advance unit was not known, they opened the range and established a patrol approximately 4,000 yards from the harbor entrance. The directive governing the operation specified that the landing force embarked in the transports—Company B, 103rd Army Infantry Division, reinforced by one-half of Company D—was not to land until the guns guarding the entrance to the harbor had been immobilized by the advance assault unit attacking from the direction of Segi.[27]

In view of the unknown position of the Raiders, and the inadvisability of attempting a frontal assault at Viru Harbor without a simultaneous land attack, Comdr. Stanley Leith, who was in charge of both Mine Squadron Two and of the task unit, decided to land the embarked troops at Choi River. There would also have been little sea room to avoid enemy fire during an approach to Viru Harbor, as the entrance was through a narrow passage with sheer cliffs about one hundred feet high on each side. The embarked troops were landed in early afternoon at the mouth of the Choi River. The morning of the following day, 2 July, the advance unit captured Viru Harbor unaided at 0900. The *APc-24* accompanied by the LCTs *134*, *330*, and *369* arrived from Oloana Bay on adjacent Vangunu Island a little over an hour later. These amphibious craft were the first to land, and functioned as a source of water and supplies for the Marine Raiders.[28]

The APcs *27*, *36*, and *38* received battle stars for their actions on 1 July during the New Georgia Rendova-Vangunu occupation. The *APc-36* was en route that day from Wernham Cove to Oloana Bay with four tank landing craft, the *APc-27* was bound for Segi Point, New Georgia, with LCTs *58*, *62*, *129*, and *323* loaded with occupation troops and equipment, and the *APc-38* was moored at the government dock at Tulagi unloading cargo.[29]

Two other APcs would also earn battle stars for the New Georgia occupation, the *APc-26* and *APc-35* on 5 July and 21 July, respectively. Few details exist about the qualifying actions of the former vessel. Despite no pre-warning of an impending attack, the gun crews of the *APc-35* shot down a Japanese aircraft. Ten minutes after the wooden ship had left anchorage at Rendova Harbor to join LCTs *60*, *64*, *65*, *66*, and *375* for transit to Oloana Bay, dive-bombers attacked the harbor. The *APc-35* claimed destruction of one of the enemy planes, but was ineligible for a star. Navy vessels could only receive a single battle star for any particular operation, and the fighting small coastal transport had previously qualified for one on 30 June.[30]

IN HARM'S WAY

On 28 July, the *APc-25* and *APc-38* received orders to load diesel oil, rations and supplies at Lunga Point for delivery to the 1st and 4th Marine Raiders at Enogai. The Raiders, supported by two Army infantry battalions, had attacked and destroyed a Japanese garrison guarding the small port of Enogai—which lay on New Georgia Island's northwest coast, on the Dragons Peninsula, between Enogai Inlet and Bairoko Harbor—on 10-11 July 1943. The Japanese used Bairoko Harbor and it facilities to resupply and reinforce its troops guarding Munda airfield to the south. Per orders of a Marine major, one hundred water cans and friction tape were also put aboard at Lunga Point. The two vessels took their departure at 2020 for Segi Point, New Georgia, to pick up native guides, who were to pilot them to Enogai via Mongo channel along the northeastern coastline of New Georgia. After embarking two pilots aboard the *APc-25*, and one aboard the *APc-38*, the vessels left Segi Point in the mid-afternoon of 29 July.[31]

Photo 5-1

USS *APc-38* under way in San Francisco Bay on 15 February 1943; she is fitted with four 20mm anti-aircraft guns that became standard for her class. (U.S. Naval History and Heritage Command photo # NH 96395, Navsource: www.navsource.org/archives/09/23/092303801.jpg)

The passage through the channel to the Mongo entrance in the Kula Gulf was winding and over considerable shoal water full of reefs. The commanding officer of the *APc-25*, who commanded the two-ship task unit noted about the perilous journey:

> Several times the fathometer registered only 1 fathom below us and on two occasions it registered no water. It was apparent to the eye there was only a minimum of water at several points. The guides were indispensable, but were uncertain how much water we required even after we told them our draft. Twice my guide remarked with surprise, "No touch'em bottom yet?" No bottom was touched, but the passage would be extremely difficult without guides.[32]

The vessels cleared the entrance at dusk and entered Kula Gulf just as a heavy squall set in, which only a few minutes earlier would have made it impossible to see reefs or continue the passage. Three PT boats met them abeam Grassy Lagoon and as rain continued to fall the APcs proceeded almost entirely by dead reckoning. The PT boat escort that was to guide them temporarily disappeared, and the darkness and rain prevented the ships from picking up Rice Anchorage. Continuing on, dead reckoning indicated they must be approaching Enogai, but the person who was supposed to flash a light to identify the entrance failed to do so; they were told later that the man who was to signal them—via a brief red flashing light each minute after 2320—could not be found at the scheduled time. One of the PT boats had by then rejoined, and the two APcs following it went past Enogai to Bairoko, the Japanese stronghold. Fortunately, their presence was not detected due to the foul weather, and the little cargo ships retraced their course and picked up the red signal at twenty minutes past midnight.[33]

After receiving direction from someone ashore in a Higgins boat about where to anchor, the unloading of cargo commenced. The support from shore was excellent, there were plenty of boats, and all hands—including officers—turned to and unloaded with all dispatch. The *APc-25* had been loaded with several cargo nets, holding about 2,000 pounds each. The boatswain's mates initially employed a double whip to lift the heavy nets out of the hold, until it was found that unloading by hand, except for the heavier boxes, was faster than through the use of the slow winch. The *APc-38* finished unloading her cargo first and received permission at 0230 to depart. The *APc-25* followed at 0400, caught the other vessel at the entrance to Mongo Channel at 0940, and they arrived together at Segi Point around noon on 30 July. Each of the ships had embarked twenty-one ambulatory cases at Enogai, as well as one additional stretcher case aboard the *APc-38*, which they discharged along with medical supplies at Lunga Point the next morning.[34]

The intrepid ships had been very lucky. In his after action report, the commanding officer of the *APc-25*, and task unit commander, Lt. John D. Cartano, observed that departure from Enogai should not be attempted a minute later than 0400. He elaborated that on a dark clear night, even one moonless, Japanese outposts or observers at Wilson Harbor could hardly fail to detect a vessel passing by less than three miles off shore. This would certainly be true if the Japanese garrison had radar of any effectiveness and, if not, there would be sufficient light closer to daybreak to profile ships passing by Wilson Harbor or Lever Harbor, unless visibility was reduced by rain or low lying clouds. He further recommended:

> Laying over at Grassi Lagoon both in going to and coming from Enogai might well make an easier schedule if full darkness of night is to be obtained. If air coverage during the operation off New Georgia is possible, protection of night is, of course, less important.[35]

In addition to having avoided detection by Japanese forces ashore—as a result of good fortune coupled with bad weather—the ships had also dodged aircraft and a surface craft while en route to and returning from their mission at Enogai. Cartano mentioned these incidents, and emphasized the importance of air coverage:

> While proceeding to Mongo Entrance, following a report of enemy planes from the *APc 23*, we sighted what appeared to be 12 enemy planes. On our return to Mongo Entrance, two natives in a canoe informed us a boat with 5 Japs had just a few minutes before passed through. With the likelihood of detection of ship movements from Wilson Harbor and the strong possibility of detection by outposts and planes, the trip would be rather difficult without air coverage.[36]

Measures to make any such future transits by small vessels less perilous were, however, not required. After Allied forces captured Munda airfield, the Japanese abandoned Bairoko on 24 August 1943.[37]

LIVE SAVING ACTIONS BY SMALL COASTAL TRANSPORT

Two weeks after returning to Guadalcanal, the *APc-25* rescued crewmen of the attack transport *John Penn* (APA-23), which had come under attack off Lunga Point on 13 August by enemy torpedo planes. The APA shot down one aircraft, which burst into flames and crashed near her mainmast, at about the same time a torpedo from another plane hit the ship. Eight minutes later, the *John Penn* began settling by the stern and sank at 2150. The small coastal transport was about 700 to 800 yards shoreward of the attack transport at the time of the attack. She had orders to convey medical supplies and mail to American forces at Enogai, to evacuate casualties, and to escort LCTs *325* and *327* to the same place, and had been "marking time," circling Lunga Point waiting for the tank landing craft to form up. The small wooden ship was thus the first vessel to arrive alongside the *John Penn*. The stern of the attack transport was aflame and oil spilling out was burning on the water's surface near this area of the ship.[38]

The *APc-25* hove to just short of the burning oil near the stern of the ship, where a large number of her crew were swimming, floating, or struggling in the water. Many of the men were injured and having difficulty staying afloat. Without waiting for life rafts to be launched, Lt. (jg) E. L. Burdick, S1/c William Hull, RM3/c Thomas Burke, and F1/c Willard Daniel Persson, and perhaps others dove over the side to rescue whoever they could. Each was able to take in tow at least one of the injured men. All suitable gear was put over the side of the *APc-25*, including a rubber life raft, two ten-man life rafts, and a wherry crewed by ship force personnel. Cargo nets rigged fore and aft enabled survivors, able to do so, to swim to the side of the ship and climb up. Stretchers were lowered for those too severely injured to climb aboard and those who could not otherwise be raised.[39]

While first aid was being administered aboard, life rafts and boats searched for additional injured men. Some survivors were picked up in a semi-conscious condition, talking incoherently and badly injured and bleeding. Many were shock victims resulting from the explosion; many had leg injuries; some had concussions, deep gashes on the head and face; and a few were burn victims. Higgins boats and other amphibious craft dispatched from shore assisted greatly. The *APc-25* joined the two waiting LCTs and left Lunga Point at 2249.[40]

For his prompt action in taking his wooden ship in near the burning attack transport, and thereby saving many men that would have perished, Cartano received the Navy and Marine Corps Medal. The citation reads:

Lieutenant John D. Cartano, United States Naval Reserve

For heroism displayed in the rescue of approximately thirty-five survivors from a burning transport which had been subjected to an enemy aerial attack in the Solomon Islands area on August 13, 1943. Lieutenant Cartano, as the Commanding Officer of a small craft, went promptly to the rescue of survivors from the stricken ship which at the time was exploding and burning violently. His efficient conduct of rescue operations resulted in saving the lives of many wounded men who would undoubtedly have been lost but for his prompt and fearless action. His conduct was in keeping with the highest traditions of the United States Naval Service.

6

Voyage to Australia and Initial Operations

> *Surface firing just witnessed was of a very low order. If we ever hope to stand a chance against the enemy definite improvement must be had. Commanding officers will take steps to have pertinent and applicable parts of Chapter 43, Blue Jackets Manual, 1940, explained to gun crews, also elementary principals of exterior ballistics. Sight setting pointing and communication drills will be regularly held.*
>
> *This kind of shooting spells no good for the enemy which is exactly what we want . . . get behind your guns, stick to your guns, use them skillfully and intelligently; they stand between you and Davey Jones' Locker.*
>
> Signals sent by Capt. Grayson B. Carter, USN, following gunnery practice conducted by a group of twelve tank landing ships, the *APc-4*, and submarine chaser *SC-742*, soon after the flotilla's departure from Balboa, Panama, and later during the transit to the Southwest Pacific after gunnery proficiency had improved dramatically.[1]

Twenty-two small coastal transports comprising APc Flotilla 7 were based in Australia, under Rear Adm. Daniel E. Barbey, USN, commander Amphibious Force, Seventh Fleet. The ships arrived at Sydney and Brisbane between 15 May and 16 August 1943, with the journey of the first group likely representative of the others. The APcs *1, 2, 3, 5, 13, 15, 17,* and *19*, built in Maine and Rhode Island yards and having proceeded down the eastern seaboard of the United States and across the Caribbean, arrived in the Canal Zone on 27 February 1943. A little over two weeks later, they departed Balboa, Panama, on 15 March with the oiler *Sepulga* (AO-80), assigned as task unit commander and logistics escort. The other vessels comprising the group were the infantry landing craft *LCI(L)-329*, minesweepers *YMS-72, YMS-237,* and *YMS-238,* and the sub-chaser *SC-703*.[2]

Launching of *APc-17* at Camden Shipbuilding and Marineway, Camden, Maine, on 8 August 1942. (Courtesy of Tom De Mott Jr., Navsource: www.navsource.org/archives/09/23/092301701.jpg)

The group, led by the *Sepula* with the *APc-13* in tow, stood into Fanui Bay, Bora Bora, on 5 April. Of frugal design and outfit, the wooden ships had but a single propulsion engine, and breakdown or malfunction resulted in their being dead in the water and requiring a tow. A sailor who served aboard an infantry landing craft succinctly noted in a personal diary he kept his view on the potential disaster associated with possessing no redundancy:

> At 7:30 APc#32 pulled up alongside us. An APc is a small coastal transport. Unlike the LCI(L) which runs a total of 8 diesel engines, an APc runs only 1. I would hate to be in an APc when one of THEIR engines quit![3]

Bora Bora in the Society Islands lay midway along the Panama to Sydney route. From there, ships destined for Australia sailed through or close to a number of the South Pacific island groups. First were the Cook Islands, then the Samoa, Tonga, and Fiji groups, and finally, a thousand miles or so from the Australian coast, the New Hebrides group and New Caledonia, forming the eastern rim of the Coral Sea. Arriving at Tearanui Harbor, Bora Bora, four of the eight APcs anchored. The remaining small coastal transports moored alongside them to form four two-ship nests, a standard convention.⁴

Following a welcome reprise, the ships formed Task Unit 36.6.13 five days later bound for Tutuila in the Samoan Islands. The steel-hulled minesweeper *Advent* (AM-83) replaced the *Sepula* in the group and the *APc-13* was made up for tow alongside the *LCI(L)-329*. In the late morning of 16 April, the vessels passed through the anti-submarine nets of Pago Pago Harbor, Tutuila, and as space allowed moored alongside the refueling pier to top off. The group stood out four days later, bound for Suva, Fijian Islands. Arriving a little past noon on 25 April, the ships moored to King's Wharf. Following three days in port, the group got under way at dawn, formed a column to pass out through the anti-submarine nets of Suva Harbor and rang up 10.5-knot transit speed.⁵

The last stop for *APc-1, 2, 3, 5, 13, 15, 17,* and *19* on their long journey to Australia was at Noumea, New Caledonia; a French colony and the site of the Navy's principal fleet base in the South Pacific that marked the end of the island-protected shipping lane to Australia. From New Caledonia westward was but the open Coral Sea. The officers and crewmen of the small coastal transports enjoyed their layover at Noumea, while awaiting assignment to a task unit for the final push to Australia. The eight APcs reached Sydney on 15 May and reported for duty. The *APc-4*, which crossed the Pacific with LST Flotilla Five, arrived there ten days later. During her transit with the first large fleet of tank landing ships to arrive in the South Pacific, there had been time for traditional Navy rites. Shortly before crossing the equator, the below message had appeared in the Navy Press Broadcast News aboard the *LST-340*, which all hands read daily:

> From: Neptunus Rex—Ruler of the Raging Main. Ye officers and crew of the USS *LST 340* soon will be within the limits of our Royal Domain. Be it known by all ye sailors, mariners, landlubbers and others—horrible but just punishment awaits ye lowly, loathsome, scummy pollywogs. My faithful and trusty shellbacks among ye have kept us informed of sins committed in disregard to our royal decrees. The great day shall come—the time grows short—make amends lest ye be weighted in the balance and found wanting.

The remaining small coastal transports dispatched from the United States touched Australia at Brisbane; a group of five—APcs *6, 7, 11,*

14, and *18*—arrived there on 12 July, another seven—APcs *8*, *9*, *10*, *12*, *20*, *21*, and *22*—on 10 August, and finally the *APc-20* on 16 August.[6]

The flotilla was organized into two subordinate groups of ships. Group 19 comprised ships constructed in yards in Rhode Island—which included famed yacht builder, Herreshoff Manufacturing—and Group 20 those in Maine yards. Although the Navy provided builders common specifications, there were likely some differences in boat construction techniques and availability of materials in different regions. A summary of the ships of the flotilla follows, as well as the names of commanding officers:

Commander Seventh Fleet: Vice Adm. Arthur S. Carpender, USN
Commander Amphibious Force, Seventh Fleet (CTF 76):
Rear Adm. Daniel E. Barbey, USN
APc Flotilla Seven

Group 19 Ship	Commanding Officer	Group 20 Ship	Commanding Officer
Herreshoff Mfg., Bristol, Rhode Island:		**Henry G. Marr, Damariscotta, Maine:**	
APc-1	Lt. Frank E. Shine, Jr., USNR	APc-13	Lt. (jg) O. Knapp, USNR
APc-2	Lt. (jg) Porter L. Fortune, Jr., USNR	APc-14	Lt. (jg) B. H. Kowlkes, USNR
APc-3	Lt. (jg) P. C. Lindley, Jr., USNR	**Camden Shipbuilding, Camden, Maine:**	
APc-4	Lt. (jg) Edwin R. Edwards, Jr., USNR	APc-15	Lt. (jg) Kemper Goffigon, USNR
APc-5	Lt. (jg) Claude E. Fike, Jr., USNR	APc-16	Lt. W. W. Harris, Jr., USNR
APc-6	Lt. C. R. Rosebro, Jr., USNR	APc-17	Lt. C. O. Smith, USNR
APc-7	Lt. W. T. Conlan, USNR	APc-18	Lt. R. O. Love, USNR
APc-8	Lt. L. E. Hansen, USNR	**Hodgdon Brothers, East Boothbay, Maine:**	
APc-9	Lt. W. V. French, USNR	APc-19	Lt. C. B. Link, Jr., USNR
APc-10	Lt. (jg) R. T. Kelley, USNR	APc-20	Lt. (jg) S. P. Johnston, Jr., USNR
Warren Boat, Warren, Rhode Island:		APc-21	Lt. (jg) W. J. Bates, USNR
APc-11	Lt. (jg) S. Touchet, USNR	APc-22	Lt. (jg) V. G. Martin, Jr., USNR
APc-12	Lt. (jg) W. O. Gay, Jr., USNR[7]		

Map 6-1

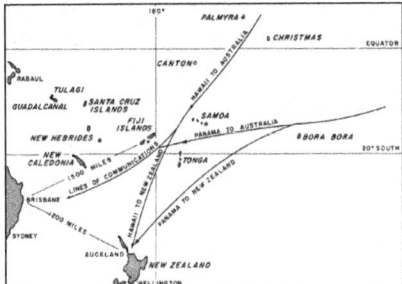

New Caledonia Island: This French colony lay at the end of the island-protected shipping lane from the Americas to Australia, and was the site of the U.S. Navy's principal fleet base in the South Pacific.
Source: http://www.ibiblio.org/hyperwar/USN/ACTC/img/actc-21.jpg

OPERATION CHRONICLE

> *The operation accomplished the movement overseas of a total of more than 16,000 men, their equipment and supplies, over distances of approximately 180 miles beyond our advance base at Milne Bay, in waters subject to Japanese air, surface, and submarine attack, without the loss of a single man, ship, or craft.*
>
> Rear Adm. Daniel E. Barbey in this report to commander-in-chief United States Fleet on Operation CHRONICLE, the occupation of Woodlark and Kiriwina Islands off the northeastern coast of New Guinea, during the period 30 June to 15 August, 1943[8]

In the winter of 1942–1943 Lt. Gen. Robert L. Eichelberger, USA, had led an Allied force which, following the Battle of Buna–Gona, captured the main Japanese beachheads in New Guinea, at Gona (9 December 1942), Buna (2 January 1943), and Sanananda (18 January 1943). Following this defeat, the Japanese began to strengthen their garrisons at Lae and Salamaua—on the Huon Gulf further up the eastern New Guinea coast—which became MacArthur's next objectives as well as Finschhafen, located fifty miles to the east of Lae on the Huon Peninsula. Allied control of Finschhafen was considered necessary for the capture of the western cape of the Vitiaz Strait for the construction of airfields and naval facilities to support the planned

Chapter 6

New Britain campaign as part of Operation CARTWHEEL. From February to June 1943, Japanese and Allied efforts to gain an advantage over the other in eastern New Guinea lapsed into a stalemate as the opponents reinforced and replaced earlier losses. The Imperial Navy could not make good its heavy losses in planes and pilots so the Japanese Army Air Force was gradually taking control of operations in New Guinea. For the Allies, carrier-based aircraft in the Pacific remained firmly under U.S. Navy control, as did the greater part of the Pacific Fleet. MacArthur was thus limited to cruisers, destroyers, and submarines, and he lacked transports, cargo vessels, and landing craft. Neither side had the resources in early 1943 to force a decisive victory over the other, and the campaign seemed likely to continue as a war of attrition. This impasse was, however, soon to change.[9]

Shortly after the arrival of the first group of APcs at Sydney, some were dispatched to Milne Bay, New Guinea, along with the other units of Rear Adm. Daniel Barbey's Amphibious Force Seventh Fleet (Task Force 76). Barbey and the forward echelon of his staff arrived by air at Milne Bay on 22 June and he broke his flag (embarked) in the repair ship *Rigel* (AR-11). The APcs *1, 5, 15,* and *19* had reached Milne Bay a day earlier via stops at the amphibious training center at Port Stephen, Brisbane, and Townsville. Port Stephen, a large natural harbor ninety-nine miles northeast of Sydney, was named by Royal Navy Captain James Cook when he passed by on 11 May 1770, honoring Sir Philip Stephens, the Secretary to the Admiralty. Stephens was a personal friend of Cook and had recommended him for command of the voyage. Brisbane, 316 miles further up the Australia coast, was the location of the Southwest Pacific headquarters for Gen. MacArthur and the Seventh Fleet commanded by Vice Adm. Arthur S. Carpender. From Brisbane, the *APc-1, 5, 15,* and *19*—in company with the *LST-456* and *458* and escorted by the destroyer-transports *Gilmer* (APD-11) and *Sands* (APD-13)—stopped at Townsville, 600 miles further up the coast, before leaving for Milne Bay across the Coral Sea. Located near the center section of the Great Barrier Reef, Townsville was host to American and Australian troops and air crew, and was a major staging point for battles in the Southwest Pacific. Leaving Townsville on 18 June, the ships arrived at Milne Bay three days later on 21 June.[10]

The *APc-3* was assigned from 1 June to 30 November 1943 to Commander Naval Base, Port Stephens, New South Wales, for duty associated with training Allied troops in amphibious and raiding

Map 6-2

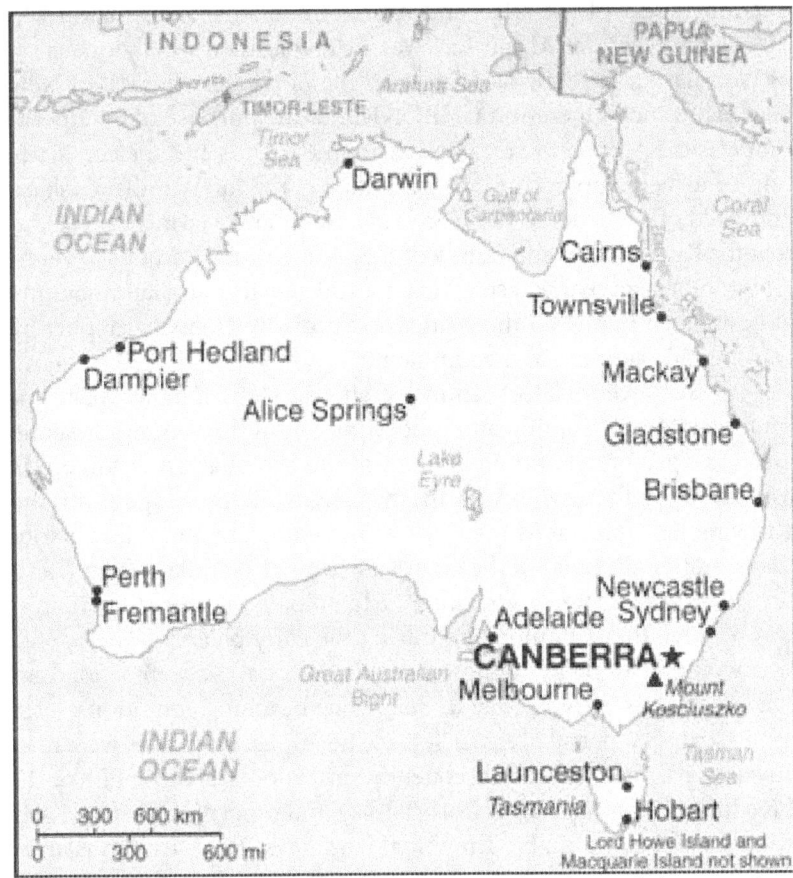

Shortly after the first group of APcs reached Australia, they and the succeeding small coastal transports arriving from America were dispatched to Milne Bay on the southeast tip of Papua, New Guinea.
Source: http://www.lib.utexas.edu/maps/cia13/australia_sm_2013.gif

landing operations. The U.S. Army First Cavalry Division, which would later make landings on the Admiralty Islands and on Luzon in the Philippine Islands, received instruction at the amphibious training center as did a part of the Sixth Australian Rifleman Division, fresh from the North African Campaign, and a portion of the First Marine Division. The Marines' training included particular attention given to small raiding parties that were to land behind enemy lines from rubber boats.[11]

Chapter 6
INVASION OF WOODLARK AND KIRIWINA ISLANDS

The movement of the APcs and large numbers of forces forward to the advance base at Milne Bay was in preparation for the invasion of Woodlark and Kiriwina Islands off the northeastern coast of New Guinea, termed Operation CHRONICLE. The purpose of the operation was the occupation and defense of the islands and the construction of airfields on each. The occupation force for Woodlark Island consisted of elements of the U.S. Army, Navy, and Marine Corps, and that for Kiriwina Island entirely of U.S. Army units. Barbey's Seventh Amphibious Force was responsible for transporting and landing units at designated points on the islands and providing logistic support by transporting supplies and equipment.[12]

All the Seventh Fleet landing craft and ships for the operation underwent basic training and indoctrination in the Sydney-Brisbane area. The personnel and equipment of the Woodlark task force was assembled at Townsville well in advance, while the staging for the Kiriwina task force at Milne Bay was not completed until just before the operation. Because of the lack of air cover at Woodlark Island, and the risk from enemy air attack on LSTs unloading during daylight, it was decided that all unloading during the early phases of the operation would be done at night. Reconnaissance parties were landed on the two islands early in May to determine beaching conditions, sites for airstrips, dispersal areas, defensive positions, etc. There were also advance parties landed subsequently on Woodlark the night of 22 June for preliminary beach work, and a similar party landed on Kiriwina the following night. The initial landing in force at both islands was made on 30 June; at 0630 at Kiriwina and in the early evening at 2100 at Woodlark. By 15 July, two weeks after construction had begun; an airstrip on Woodlark was usable. Eight days later, U.S. Army Air Corps Squadron 67, comprised initially of sixteen P39 Airacobra fighters, commenced operations from Woodlark.[13]

COASTAL TRANSPORTS SUPPORT THE KIRIWINA LANDING

The APcs at Milne Bay were not involved with supporting the troops and equipment landed by tank landing ships, infantry landing craft, and destroyer-transports at Woodlark Island through 2 July; or in subsequent supply echelons through 4 August. They were, however, directly involved with the operations at Kiriwina. The LCT first echelon for Kiriwina sailed from Milne Bay an hour past midnight on 29

June, bound for Boro Boro at Goodenough Island, to spend the night before proceeding to Kiriwina the following morning. Comprised the first section of the echelon were *APc-1* and *15* with twelve LCTs—*61, 83, 85, 173, 177, 178, 179, 183, 368, 371, 372,* and *373*—escorted by the Australian corvette HMAS *Benalla* (J323). The second section was the *APc-5* escorting seven mechanized landing craft (LCM), one of which it had to tow a portion of the way. The first echelon of infantry landing ships carrying assault forces departed Milne Bay nearly eleven hours later, escorted by four *Mahan*-class destroyers, *Mahan* (DD-364), *Drayton* (DD-366), *Flusser* (DD-368), and *Perkins* (DD-377). But, proceeding directly to Kiriwina, the group arrived first off the island, at 0500 on 30 June, and was joined an hour later by the APcs and LCTs for the landing. Between 1 and 11 July, other LCT echelons continued to deliver equipment and supplies to Kiriwina, making the run from Milne Bay to Kiriwina via Boro Boro and return to Milne Bay. The *APc-19* escorted the second and tenth echelons, *APc-1* the seventh, and *APc-5* the eleventh.[14]

The seizure of undefended Woodlark and Kiriwina Islands in the southern Solomon Sea served as dress rehearsals for other forthcoming amphibious operations for headquarters planners, and commanders of combat and service support units. Considerable hydrographic and navigational difficulties were encountered in the approaches to Kiriwina during the assault landing, but these challenges resulted in the development of better beach points, by improved selection of beaches for landing craft, indoctrination of beach and shore parties, and overall training. As a part of this effort, Barbey established a school for amphibious scouts in the vicinity of Cairns, a city located in the far north of Queensland—748 nautical miles up the Australian coast from Brisbane—on 7 July 1943. Gen. Walter Krueger, commander Sixth Army and Alamo Force, the task force created by MacArthur for Operation CARTWHEEL—which included the 6th Army—decided that he also needed to have a reconnaissance capability, based on the difficulties encountered by Alamo Force in its first operation at Woodlark and Kiriwina Islands. In November, he formed the "Alamo Scouts" as a special unit for reconnaissance and raiding. An Alamo Scout Training Center for volunteers was established on Fergusson Island, New Guinea under Col. Frederick W. Bradshaw. The top graduates of the training course were assigned to the Alamo Scouts, and the other graduates were returned to their units where they could be used for similar work. Over the course of their two year existence, the Scouts evolved from a simple reconnaissance unit to a sophisticated intelligence collection group which supplied and coordinated large-scale guerrilla operations on Leyte and Luzon in the Philippines. In addition to its other achievements, the unit liberated 197 Allied prisoners in New Guinea, and provided forward reconnaissance and tactical support of the Sixth Ranger Battalion in the liberation of 511 Allied prisoners from the Cabanatuan Prisoner of War Camp on Luzon, in February 1945.[15]

PREPARATION FOR THE LAE-SALAMAUA CAMPAIGN

At 0600 on 16 July, three LCTs—*83*, *173*, and *183*—escorted by the *APc-1* departed Milne Bay for Oro Bay and Nassau Bay. The craft had been urgently requested by the commanding general, New Guinea Force, Australian Edmund F. Herring, to assist in supplying the U.S. 41st Army Infantry Division engaged in offensive operations against the enemy in the Nassau Bay area. To assist readers in better understanding the sequence of events described in this and the following chapters, a summary of significant Japanese-held areas on the eastern New Guinea coast, or relatively close inland, and the associated dates that Allied amphibious forces and/or ground troops moving northward landed on beaches or captured enemy bases follows. The distance to each area from Milne Bay helps to show the geographical relationships between different areas:

From Milne Bay to	Nautical Miles	Significance of Geographic Area
Oro Bay	160	U.S. Base used as staging area for the battles of Buna-Gona, and Sananada (16 Nov 1942–22 Jan 1943) and for further operations
Popondetta:	178	17 Nov 1942: Captured by Australian 16th Brigade
Buna	180	2 Jan 1943: Beachhead captured by Allied forces
Sananada (near Buna)	18	Jan 1943: Beachhead captured by Allied forces
Gona (near Buna)		9 Dec 1942: Beachhead captured by Allied forces
Cape Ward Hunt	225	12 Apr 1943: Australian Air Force radar site established
Morobe	245	20 Apr 1943: U.S. PT boat base established at this site

From Milne Bay to	Nautical Miles	Significance of Geographic Area
Nassau Bay (near Salamaua)		30 Jun 1943: American landing in support of Salamaua
Salamaua	295	11 Sep 1943: Japanese base at Salamaua captured
Lae	314	4 Sep 1943: Australian 9th Division landing on Red Beach followed by the capture of Lae on 16 Sep 1943
Hopoi (near Lae)		4 Sep 1943: Site of 9th Division landing on Yellow Beach
Hanisch Harbor	340	27 Sep 1943: Allied troops occupy en route to Finschhafen
Finschhafen	366	22 Sep 1943: Allied landing on Scarlet Beach followed by capture of Finschhafen for further operations[16]

A little over two weeks earlier a task force of infantry from the 41st Division had on 29 June, embarked from a staging area above Morobe in twenty-nine LCVPs—Landing Craft Vehicle, Personnel, but more commonly known as Higgins boats—and two captured enemy barges, and escorted by three PT boats had set out for a landing behind Japanese lines at Nassau Bay only a few miles below Salamaua. (Designed by Andrew Higgins of Louisiana, each shallow-draft, LCVP barge-like boat, typically constructed from plywood, could ferry a platoon-sized unit of 36 men to shore at 9 knots.) In murky darkness, ever increasing rain and wind, and heavy seas, the amphibious craft arrived off the beach and, despite surf running about twelve feet, landed. The boats were tossed about, and equipment, weapons, and ammunition were lost in the landing but every soldier was put safely ashore. Most of the LCVPs were unable to retract and twenty-one of them were left swamped on the beach.[17]

The landing had been undertaken so that the Allies could secure a beachhead to establish a supply point for the forthcoming Salamaua-Lae campaign. The *APc-1*, commanded by Lt. Frank E. Shine, Jr., arrived with tank landing craft at Oro Bay in the late morning of 17 July. His orders were to base in the Oro Bay-Buna area to tend LCTs and to arrange with local Army authorities for aerial coverage and coordination of operations. Two days later, the LCTs *173* and *183* left Oro Bay in the mid-afternoon to deliver their loads to Cape Ward Hunt and Morobe further up the New Guinea coast.[18]

Small coastal transports and tank landing craft continued to sail up the coast to support combat operations. The *APc-15* left Milne Bay on 6 August in company with LCTs *61*, *174*, and *178* to deliver supplies to Buna and, after discharging cargo, to load equipment there for deliver to Nassau Bay. Three days later, the *APc-5* stood out of Milne Bay around noon on 9 August en route the Oro Bay-Buna-Morobe area with a group of officers and men aboard, and on 10 August the *APc-4* and LCTs *87*, *184*, and *387* with 375 tons of ammunition left there for Nassau Bay. With these and other ships transporting men and materials to forward areas, Rear Admiral Barbey decided that the facilities in the Buna area were insufficient to receive all necessary equipment, and that vessels should proceed to Morobe to discharge their cargo.[19]

Thereafter, APcs began operating from Morobe, a small coastal village on Morobe Bay, about midway between Buna and Salamaua. U.S. Army forces had liberated Morobe from the Japanese on 3 April, and it became a staging point for American and Australian troops. The *APc-4* arrived with *LCT-184* and *387* at Oro Bay from Morobe at noon on 15 August, and left again with the *LCT-184* for Buna. That evening the *APc-5* and *APc-15* stood out of Milne Bay for Morobe, with aboard the former ship Commander Farrar to assume control of shipping at the port. The wooden ships also worked other ports. At 0500 on 22 August, the *APc-1* departed Oro Bay for Tufi, the site of an advanced Navy motor torpedo boat base on the southeastern peninsula of Cape Nelson, and returned in the early evening two days later.[20]

Much of the activity along the New Guinea coast in July and August was associated with preparations for Operation POSTERN, an amphibious landing of the Australian 9th Division on the Huon Peninsula that would take place between 4 and 6 September 1943. The operation was to be a three-pronged offensive with the 9th Division landing east of the Japanese base at Lae, a paratrooper force landing to the northwest of the base, and an infantry force pushing up from the south. All three forces were to converge on the objective and annihilate any opposition. In the late afternoon of 31 August, the first and second sections the fifth echelon, comprised of twelve LCTs, *APc-4* and *21*, and submarine chasers *SC-637* and *648*, sortied from Milne Bay for Buna. During the amphibious operation at Lae, and subsequent ones at Finschhafen and Arawe in late autumn and early winter, APcs of Flotilla Seven would earn their pay. Ten coastal transports—APcs *2*, *4*, *6*, *9*, *15*, *16*, *18*, *20*, *21*, and *22*—collectively garnered sixteen battle stars; the *APc-21* was lost, and the *APc-2* and *APc-15* damaged due to enemy action.[21]

AMPHIBIOUS SCOUTS RELOCATE TO FERGUSSON ISLAND

On 26 August 1943, amphibious scouts boarded the infantry landing craft *LCI(L)-224* and *226* at Milne Bay, for movement under escort of the sub-chaser *SC-637* to Fergusson Island located off the southeast end of New Guinea. There, they would occupy an abandoned PT base at Kalo Kalo for use as a training camp to prepare for reconnaissance missions. Admiral Barbey had on 7 July ordered the establishment of a school for amphibious scouts in the vicinity of Cairns and as a cover designation directed that the group be titled "Special Service Unit No. 1."[22]

Volunteers from the 7th Amphibious Area—Americans and Australians from the Navy, Marine Corps, and Army—were sought with many and varied skills including knowledge of the geography, native customs, and language of the theater; reconnaissance experience; small-craft handling; hydrographic knowledge; and the ability to evaluate beach suitability for amphibious craft. By 18 July, the majority of the group was at Cairns and began physical conditioning and training in martial arts, panoramic sketching to identify precise locations, and rubber-raft work. Instruction also included jungle survival training, Pidgin English and recognition of underwater coral formations and dangerous sea life.[23]

The scouts first recon-mission would be at Finschhafen in early September, and the unit would later conduct pre-landing reconnaissance for nine amphibious landings on New Guinea's east coast and the Bismarck Islands into July 1944.[24]

7

Capture of Lae and Finschhafen

> *Those planes don't look friendly to me.*
> A radio transmission heard by the destroyer *Conyngham* (DD-371)
> from the *Lamson* (DD-367) to the *Mugford* (DD-389) and *Drayton*
> (DD-366), on 4 September, regarding a flight of Japanese planes
> from Rabaul, approaching off New Guinea during the Lae invasion[1]

On 4 September 1943, as part of Operation POSTERN, Barbey's 7th Amphibious Force landed the 9th Australian Division on two assault beaches eastward of Lae; Red Beach to the east of the mouth of the Buso River and Yellow Beach near Hopoi. In a coordinated action the U.S. Army's 503rd Parachute Infantry Regiment made an unopposed airborne landing the following day at the town of Nadzab, located fifty miles to the west of Lae in the Markham Valley. Accompanying it were two gun crews of the Australian's Army 2/4th Field Regiment who, after brief instruction in the use of parachutes, jumped along with cut-down 25-pounder artillery pieces. The airborne force was to secure the Nadzab Airfield, so that the Australian 7th Division could be flown in to cut off any possible Japanese retreat into the Markham Valley.[2]

LANDINGS OPPOSED LARGELY BY JAPANESE AIR STRIKES

The first green-clad Australian soldiers to storm ashore were landed by "Higgins boats" of the U.S. Army's 2nd Engineer Special Brigade. William F. Heavey, the commanding general of the brigade, and other officers had boarded an APc the previous evening at Morobe and left at 1930 with a convoy of forty Ramped, Personnel Landing Craft, LCP(R)s—which, although referred to as Higgins boats after their designer, Andrew Higgins of Louisiana, were built by Chris Craft—to make their way across the Huon Gulf. MacArthur had requested amphibian engineers for his theater of operations early on because of the Navy's initial reluctance to risk its ships in the dangerous and confined waters off the New Guinea coast. After the brigade arrived in Australia, its first task had been to assemble the 36-foot landing craft, which to greatly speed delivery were shipped in sections for assembly in Australia. For sand beach landings, the initial assault troops were generally transported in high speed transports (APDs) and went ashore in the LCP(R)s that these ships carried. As the first faint streak of dawn crept over the eastern horizon, the ships and craft of the invasion force began moving toward the landing beaches, behind which a 10,000 foot mountain range towered up into the clouds. Nearer the shore, warships began shelling the beach to drive the enemy off it. The Japanese shore batteries opened fire, but were soon silenced as the destroyers bombarded the beaches with increasing fury.[3]

The naval gunfire stopped as suddenly as it had started, and Amphibian scouts of the 2nd ESB, dressed in Aussie uniforms, were quickly ashore to reconnoiter the beach, ascertain enemy positions, and guide in the landing craft. They signaled back that any remaining opposition was negligible; most of the Japanese had been killed in the bombardment or had fled to the safety of the hills behind the beach. Infantrymen of the 9th Division were already boarding landing craft waiting alongside Navy transports. As each landing craft moved away from an APD and headed toward the line of departure, another took its place alongside. Wave after wave of landing craft formed, and each shot forward on signal from their leader. Nearing the shore, coxswains yelled, "Hold on! Prepare to land," after which boats struck sand with a thud, ramps dropped, and forty Australians from each craft jumped across the surf and were into the jungle in less than a minute. The initial landing of nearly six hundred troops was made on the beaches almost simultaneously, a few minutes after the planned time of 0630. The landing force had wanted an approach during the darkness with a landing at dawn. However, the shore was low-lying swampy jungle with no distinguishing contours, and the landing beaches themselves had no prominent features by which they could be located in darkness with radar. In daylight, clumps of coconut palms and a river bed were the main aids to identification.[4]

The ramped, personnel landing craft were followed by waves of infantry landing craft LCI(L)s delivering additional soldiers to the beachhead. Tank landing craft (LCTs) and tank landing ships (LSTs) came next to land anti-aircraft batteries, vehicles, ammunition, and still more infantrymen. During the troop movement ashore, ground opposition was limited to incidents of sniper fire. However, in a surprise attack at 0705, three Vals accompanied by six Zeros came in at a low altitude and dropped about thirty bombs among landing craft. Two of them—LCI(L)s *339* and *341*—were badly damaged and suffered high personnel casualties. The *Conyngham*, one of the screening destroyers, believed that the planes had come in from the westward or from over the mountains to the north. The latter route would have prevented their being detected on the ship's SC-2 radar screen, which was saturated with land echoes.[5]

A second, more deadly attack followed in the mid-afternoon of D-Day. The USAAF 5th Air Force was providing a protective air umbrella over the movement of echelons of vessels en route to and from the beach. However, at 1350 a portion of a group of about seventy Japanese planes evaded the fighters, proceeded toward Morobe and attacked retiring forces. Four dive-bombers targeted the *Conyngham*, scoring a near miss that pierced the ship with many shrapnel holes and wounded one man, and five planes made runs on the destroyers *Drayton*, *Lamson*, and *Mugford*, resulting in some superficial topside damage to the *Lamson*. Two enemy planes were shot down by destroyers. Another group of eighteen dive-bombers and torpedo planes attached the sixth echelon en route from Buna to Red Beach. A torpedo passed about twenty feet astern of the *LST-473* and a second one passed under her bow without exploding, before she sustained serious damage from two bomb hits and two near misses. The LST-*471* evaded one torpedo, but was struck by the second one. The two torpedo bombers that had singled her out came in at masthead height and dropped their torpedoes. The first one missed the ship, passing harmlessly by its bow. The second one hit the LST in the stern, portside, detonated, and almost completely demolished the ship aft of frame 41, killing one American officer and six sailors, and forty-five Australian soldiers. The two disabled ships were taken in tow by LSTs *452* and *458* for Morobe. Three hours later, enemy aircraft bombed landing areas on the beaches at 1700, setting fire to an ammunition dump, and further damaged two landing craft abandoned earlier after bomb strikes had knocked them out of action.⁶

ATTACK ON LCT CONVOY

In the days to come, enemy aircraft approached convoys nearly every night, but in the darkness appeared to not know with certainty the positions of individual ships. Accordingly, vessels had been instructed to hold fire, unless planes adopted attack positions, to preclude disclosing their locations to the enemy. During an attack in the evening of 8 September, six LCTs escorted by the minesweepers *YMS-49* and *YMS-51* and coastal transport *APc-4* were en route to Red Beach. Aboard *YMS-49*, the first hint of danger came at 1925, when one or more of the four destroyers serving as an outer screen on the starboard beam of the echelon opened fire. General quarters was set aboard the minesweeper and, as bombs fell in the area of the DDs, she and other ships opened fire in the direction of the destroyers' gunfire. Thereafter, a few bombs fell on the LCT formation, a third group of bombs dropped a distance from it, and a fourth farther away almost over the horizon. The planes remained at a good altitude overhead, out of range of the vessels below and, having risked little, retired at 2005 having scored no hits.⁷

AIR RAID ON MOROBE

On 12 September, a flight of about thirty planes from Rabaul arrived over Morobe Harbor, a deep-water, nearly landlocked bay, protected to seaward by several islands and surrounded from shore to foothills by mangrove. It was regularly bombed by the enemy, but offered in addition to a spacious anchorage and port facilities, good hideouts nearby for PT boats, trawlers, and barges. Present in the harbor that day was a large concentration of amphibious and escort craft. At 1055, a group of LCTs and two sub-chasers were in the process of proceeding out of the harbor as Vals were sighted at a high altitude to the northwest. The movement by this group of ships prevented any significant maneuvering by individual vessels to avoid attack. In the case of the *SC-703*, she had another sub-chaser abaft her port beam, an LCT on her starboard quarter, and LCTs on either bow. As planes began their dive-bombing runs, the first attacks were on vessels well back in the bay, followed by ones against targets further out toward the entrance.

A bomb hit the *LST-455*, disabling the tank landing ship and causing many personnel casualties. Another struck a loaded LCT and put it out of commission. The *LST-455* had been serving as the control and repair ship for the northern movements of landing craft. (The *LST-453*, located at Buna to provide services to craft moving between staging and assault areas, subsequently assumed those duties as well.)[8]

Morobe was famous among the men of the Navy's 7th Amphibious Force and Army's 2nd Engineer Special Brigade using the harbor for an unusual tragedy. The 2nd ESB had established a small base at Morobe in late June and soon thereafter found that it was not only the Japanese that presented danger to them, as one member later recounted:

> One day a couple of doughboys were sunning on the beach. Suddenly a streak like a submarine came in from the sea. It was a crocodile. Before the men could get away, the crocodile grabbed one by the leg and dragged him off to sea, never to be seen again. Before our move to New Guinea we had been warned of the ferocious crocodiles and sharks we would encounter. Outside of this one incident we did not actually have any encounters with "crocs" or sharks. The men rarely saw any and found that when they moved in a new area, the animals invariably moved away and left the area to man. The bugs and mosquitoes, on the other hand, multiplied wherever we moved.[9]

The Army raised six Engineer Amphibious Brigades in 1942 before the Navy protested the blatant infringement on one of its traditional roles. After some negotiation, the Navy agreed to expand its own beach and shore activities and thus provide greater capacity, and let the Army keep the brigades already in existence. The Army agreed not to create any more of the brigades, and renamed its Engineer Amphibious Brigades, "Engineer Special Brigades," due presumably to the sensitivity of the word Amphibious to the Navy. Each brigade had three "Boat and Shore regiments" comprised of two battalions; one of landing craft and the other of troops trained and equipped to unload men and equipment from the landing craft to the beach. Not possessing the amphibious lift of the Navy, the Army only conducted shore-to-shore operations, in which boats loaded with soldiers left a friendly area, moved along the coast to an unfriendly area and landed. The 2nd Brigade was only placed under the operational control of Admiral Barbey for a short period during the Lae and Finschhafen campaigns. However, it continued to enjoy close relations with the 7th Amphibious Force in shore party work and in the joint operation of amphibious craft. In January 1945, Barbey, while commander of the San Fabian Attack Force for the Lingayen Gulf landings on Luzon, Philippine Islands, praised the Army organization thus:

> It is believed that the Engineer Special Brigade as organized in the Southwest Pacific Area is the most efficient Shore Party organization now functioning in amphibious warfare and that the permanent organizations of these regiments have contributed in a large measure to the successes of amphibious operation in the theater.[10]

Buna, located further up the coast and controlled by the Australians, had few facilities. Vessels arrived via a one-way entrance among reefs to berth at a single *Liberty*-ship dock, and access from landward was by muddy roads through a mangrove swamp. However, it offered a port closer to the operations under way and those forthcoming. The *LST-464* was positioned at Buna to serve as a first aid ship and collection point for naval casualties. Although stretchers could best be accommodated on the tank decks of LSTs, in an emergency an APc could carry eighteen stretcher cases and the infantry landing craft six apiece.[11]

LAE CAPTURED

Following the dive-bomber attack on 12 September, the operation settled into a supply problem as Lae and Salamaua were virtually in the hands of the Allies. In a classic pincer movement, the 7th and 9th Divisions entered Lae on 16 September and captured the Japanese bastion. There had been relatively little initial resistance by shore based forces at Lae but enemy air attacks in strength commenced about noon on D-Day, followed by night attacks by groups of enemy planes. Ships leaving the landing areas, and resupply echelons, were under persistent and determined air attacks until airfields were eventually developed after the capture of Finschhafen and aircraft were brought forward to neutralize nearby Japanese air bases. Operation POSTERN concluded swiftly allowing the landings at Finschhafen to take place much earlier than originally envisioned. The *APc-4*, *APc-6*, and *APc-21* received battle stars for the Lae operation.[12]

FINSCHHAFEN OPERATION

> *Andrew Higgins is the man who won the war for us. . . . If Higgins had not designed and built those LCVPs [Personnel and Vehicle Landing Craft], we never could have landed over an open beach. The whole strategy of the war would have been different.*
>
> President Dwight D. Eisenhower, 1964 interview

The capture and occupation of Finschhafen, which lay approximately sixty-four miles beyond Lae up the New Guinea coast, was undertaken to develop the area as a concentration point and staging area for future operations against New Britain and the Bismarcks, and for its use as an advance base for aircraft and light surface ships. Located on the blunt eastern extremity of the Huon Peninsula, Finschhafen offered three ports, none suitable for amphibious landings due to their restricted areas. Ships arriving at Finsch Harbor entered from the north as a narrow, hook-shaped peninsula enclosed the port on the other three sides. Passage into the long, narrow inlet to Langemak Bay, southward of Finsch Harbor, was from the east. Dreger Harbor, located still farther south, was protected from the open sea by islands. The 20th Australian Infantry Brigade, reinforced, was selected to land on Scarlet Beach at the mouth of the Song River in a small bay approximately seven miles to the north of Finschhafen. A detachment of the 2nd Engineer Special Brigade comprised the Shore Party, along with a Royal Australian Navy beachmaster and small detachment.[13]

In preparation for the operation, landing craft and their escorts were first staged at Buna. After bulk supplies were loaded in six tank landing ships, they proceed just before midnight on 20 September for "G Beach" east of Lae, escorted by the four destroyers of the covering group and the fleet tug *Sonoma* (AT-12). There they loaded vehicles, equipment, and personnel of the assault force and—in company with sixteen LCI(L)s, flagship *Conyngham*, and the four DDs of the naval bombardment group that had followed them to Lae—proceeded in darkness to Finschhafen for a pre-dawn landing. A party of ten amphibious scouts, that included four natives, had earlier been put ashore near the beach the night of 11 September by PT boats, and withdrawn on 14 September. They were unable to obtain the desired hydrographic information because of native and Japanese activity on the beach. No beach defenses were observed but machine gun nests were thought spotted at the north end of the beach.[14]

LANDING ON SCARLET BEACH

In early morning darkness, at 0433, on 22 September, four destroyers—*Drayton*, *Flusser*, *Lamson*, and *Mugford*—commenced naval bombardment, each covering an allotted sector along or on the flank of Scarlet Beach. Twenty minutes later, assault troops landed in sixteen wooden-hulled LCVs (vehicle landing craft) carried there by four high-speed transports—the *Brooks* (APD-10), *Gilmer* (APD-11), *Humphreys* (APD-12), and *Sands* (APD-13)—of Transport Division Sixteen. The ships were old World War I flush-deck destroyers that had been modified to transport U.S. Marine raiders (in this case Australian troops) and to get them ashore, to carry "Higgins boats" suspended in davits. The landing craft available for this operation were LCVs, unadorned, ramp-less, unarmed early Higgins boats.[15]

The LCVs were the precursors to the LCP(R), a variant of the famous Higgins LCVPs, which would revolutionize military strategy. The boat's designer, Andrew Higgins—a fiery Irishman who drank whiskey like a fish and who had opined that the Navy "doesn't know one damn thing about small boats"—had attempted during the prewar years to convince the sea service of the need for small wooden boats. Once the war broke out, he was sure that the Navy would require thousands of small craft, and he also believed that steel would be in short supply. Accordingly, Higgins bought the entire 1939 crop of mahogany from the Philippines and stored it on his own. In 1941, he finally received a Navy contract to develop what would be the LCVP. The resultant 36-foot long Higgins boat could hold a platoon of thirty-six fully equipped men or twelve men and a jeep, and its use allowed soldiers to storm open, less fortified beaches, instead of attacking well-defended ports. Waves of the boats could withstand punishing sea conditions, and still safely and rapidly deliver huge numbers of troops to the shoreline due to the numerous innovations that Higgins had incorporated in the design of the landing craft. These included the use of durable veneer marine mahogany plywood—enabling the boats to absorb the stresses of pitching and rolling—and a solid pine log in the bow to allow collisions with objects without sustaining hull damage. A single 225-horsepower Gray diesel marine engine propelled the boat at speeds up to 12 knots, and a steel bow ramp protected passengers from gunfire and facilitated discharge of troops. In addition to being fitted with a rudder for normal movement, there was a second one forward of the propeller for backing, allowing the craft to quickly retract off hostile beaches and head for open water. The boats also had two .30-caliber machine guns, providing embarked troops a more robust means of self-defense than the personal weapons they carried.[16]

Thereafter waves of LCI(L)s began hitting the beach. The first group of seven landing craft took enemy fire from the right flank during the approach but return fire from the LCI(L)s silenced the beach guns. Two Betty type twin-engine enemy bombers approached at 0520 and were driven off by gunfire from DDs, SCs, and LSTs, but other planes continued to shadow the formation from the horizon. Another twenty-five Higgins landing craft, LCM(3)s and LCVPs, landed at 0610 with troops and equipment. The much larger tank landing ships (LSTs) began beaching and unloading forty minutes later.[17]

The landing area was protected during the assault by a PT boat screen at the northern entrance to the Vitiaz Strait, by an anti-aircraft group of five destroyers nearby, and by an anti-submarine screen of one destroyer and two sub-chasers. The submarine chasers were a part of Task Unit 76.7 (titled the Sub-Chaser Group) comprised of the *APc-16* and SCs *648, 698, 699, 703, 734, 736,* and *742*. The small coastal transport served, as was usual practice, as a navigation ship and escort. The sub-chasers escorted their respective echelons to the beach and then joined an anti-submarine circular screen one mile to seaward of the destroyer anti-aircraft screen until it was time to accompany an echelon back to Buna. At 0645 the Allied aircraft assigned to form a high and low fighter umbrella arrived on station over the landing area. At 0920 the tug *Sonoma* sighted a group of Vals approaching over the hilltops, hoisted the signal "Strange aircraft sighted bearing 285° T[rue]", and opened fire with her starboard battery. Destroyers drove off the planes with their 5-inch batteries, and the enemy retired to the northward pursued closely by P38 fighters. A few bombs were dropped but no damage was sustained.[18]

LARGE JAPANESE AIR RAID REBUKED

A large group of Betty type torpedo-bombers and Zero fighters from the naval 11th Air Fleet at Rabaul fiercely attacked the amphibious force in the early afternoon. At 1242, a destroyer escort detected the enemy and signaled "Unidentified aircraft sighted." One minute later the officer in tactical command ordered "scatter," and individual ships began maneuvering on various courses at full boiler power. Japanese torpedo bombers began making attacks on the formation—from a northeasterly direction at an altitude of approximately fifty feet—at 1245. Destroyers and tank landing ships opened fire with anti-aircraft batteries at a range of about 2,500 yards, and all ships opened with smaller weapons when planes came within range. Entries in the *Sonoma*'s deck log described the ensuing action:

> Enemy planes passing through formation, at approximately 30 feet altitude. All guns on all ships firing heavily. Two torpedo planes seen to drop torpedoes 1500 yards astern of formation. One plane seen to drop torpedo while in the middle of the formation on starboard beam. All ships using evasive tactics. DD escorts circling convoy at close range and at high speed. Torpedo on starboard beam seen to broach several times and then disappeared. No run observed. Torpedo wake from torpedoes dropped astern last seen 400 yards on starboard quarter.
>
> Enemy plane shot down on port quarter. Two enemy planes shot down on starboard bow after passing through formation. One enemy plane shot down astern. P38s engaged torpedo bombers on port beam and port quarter. Zero fighters seen being engaged by P38s overhead.

At 1249, four minutes after it had begun, the torpedo attack ceased, and all guns stopped firing. The convoy suffered no damage, during an attack in which eight torpedo bombers and six Zero fighters were reported shot down by ships and air coverage.[19]

FINSCHHAFEN TAKEN

After coming ashore, the 20th Infantry Brigade Group of the 9th Australian Division had begun advancing toward enemy-held Finschhafen, as the division's 22nd Infantry Battalion moved east along the coast from Lae to threaten Langemak Bay, located just south of Finschhafen. The 20th Infantry captured Heldsbach, the airfield, and part of the shore of the harbor before meeting stiff resistance at the Bumi River, where three hundred Japanese sailors and one company of soldiers defended the south bank. Two companies of the 2/15th Battalion then moved inland to outflank the enemy, and the next morning the Aussies crossed the river in the face of stalwart resistance. The brigade commander asked Maj. Gen. George Frederick Wootten, commanding the division, for an additional battalion to hold Scarlet Beach so that he could concentrate his brigade against Finschhafen. Wootten agreed to this request. The 2/43rd Battalion landed at Scarlet Beach on the night of 29 September to relieve the 2/17th, which then immediately moved out for Finschhafen. Following air and artillery bombardment, the three Australian battalions—2/13th, 2/15th, and 2/17th—attacked on 1 October, fought all day, and overwhelmed the defenders. The next morning the Aussie brigade occupied the village and harbor of Finschhafen, and made contact south of Langemak Bay with patrols of the 22nd Battalion that had advanced overland from Lae. The final enemy stronghold, Sattelberg mission, located atop a hill about five miles inland from Finschhafen, fell to the Australian 26th Brigade on 25 November.[20]

The Japanese, after eighteen months of occupation, had been cleared from Huon Gulf, allowing MacArthur to continue his drive towards the Philippines. The small coastal transport *APc-16* received a battle star for her actions on D-Day at Finschhafen.[21]

MOTOR TORPEDO BOAT BASE DREGER

The *APc-20* received orders to proceed on 22 November to Motor Torpedo Boat Advance Base Six at Kana Kopa, a tiny circular bay 250 yards across at the southeastern end of Milne Bay, and upon arrival to report for duty to Commander Torpedo Boat Squadrons, Seventh Fleet, Comdr. Morton C. Mumma, Jr., USN. After Mumma observed that the existing PT boat base at Cairns, Australia was "so far in the rear as to be practically useless," Navy Seabees, one company of the 55th Battalion, had arrived in Milne Bay on 23 May 1943. Despite excessive tropical rains and adverse soil conditions they had the base in operation in time for its boats to strike the Japanese at Salamaua and Nassau Bay on 29 and 30 June. On the whole, it was a good base, as sites in New Guinea go, although everyone ashore wallowed in apparently bottomless mud for months until concrete slabs were poured, and a truck was actually lost in the mud of Kana Kopa.[22]

Dreger Harbor, where the *APc-20* served as an advance base tender for PT boats, and which would eventually supplant Kana Kopa as the main supply and repair base in New Guinea, was established as an advance base on 25 November. Motor torpedo boats of Squadrons

12 and 21 began patrols from Dreger Harbor five days later. The new base added sixty-five miles to the distance the boats could patrol northward along the New Guinea and New Britain coasts from the previous advance base at Morobe, which was later abandoned as an operating base in December.[23]

The length of patrols was further extended after landings at Arawe, on the southwestern coast of New Britain, on 15 December, and at Saidor, on the New Guinea coast, on 2 January 1944. Fuel barges were placed at these points, so that PT boats could leave Dreger Harbor in the morning or early afternoon, top off their tanks at Arawe or Saidor, and then begin their patrols. The coastal transport was kept busy much of the time towing fuel barges back and forth from Dreger Harbor to the advance fueling points. When not thus engaged the *APc-20*, like the Australian HMAS *Potrero*, was used for carrying supplies between bases. The latter ship was a 70-foot, wooden-hulled, diesel-driven coaster that Mumma had acquired somewhere for use as a cargo craft.[24]

The *APc-20*, commanded by Lt. (jg) S. P. Johnston, Jr., would receive two battle stars for Eastern New Guinea operations. The first award was for 7th Fleet supporting operations from 15 October to 4 December 1943, and the second star for the period 5 December 1943 to 30 January 1944 of the Finschhafen occupation. In addition to APcs *16*, and *20*, the *APc-18* also supported the Finschhafen occupation, and would earn a battle star for the period 25 December 1943 to 17 February 1944. Small wooden ships of APc Flotilla Seven went in harm's way at Lae and Finschhafen, and escaped unscathed while serving as navigation ships and escorts for LCT echelons. This good fortune would change in late December at Arawe, New Britain.

Photo 8-1

Enemy Strike from Rabaul depicting the USS *APc-15* engaged off Arawe, New Britain, in a desperate battle with 20–25 Japanese dive-bombers and fighters attacking the small 103-foot wooden ship. (Painting by Richard DeRosset)

> Richard DeRosset's depiction of the *APc-15* during its battle with a flight of Japanese dive-bombers and fighters takes me back to that day seven decades ago and reminds me of the heroic efforts of my officers and crew. He captures the minute details of the ship engaged in a life-and-death fight for its survival against overwhelming odds. His magnificent painting is a masterful work of power, passion, and detail.
>
> Kemper Goffigon III
Former Commanding Officer USS *APc-15*

8

Coastal Transports Sunk and Damaged at Arawe, New Britain

> *Volume of fire power is all important.*
> Comment by the commanding officer of the sub-chaser *SC-743*, one of the small ships—which included the *APc-2, APc-4, APc-9, APc-15, APc-21,* and *APc-22*—that escorted tank landing craft to the New Britain beach during the assault on Arawe.[1]

On 22 November 1943, General MacArthur issued a directive for the seizure on 15 December of Arawe, a very small harbor—just an indentation really—on the south coast of New Britain; the largest island in the Bismarck Archipelago which lay across the Dampier and Vitiaz Straits from New Guinea. The objective was to obtain a suitable location from which PT boats could protect the southeastern flank of Allied forces during seizure of the Gloucester Peninsula, sixty miles to the north-northwest. It was anticipated that the control of Arawe would isolate western New Britain from Japanese supplies and reinforcements arriving via the island's south coast and help protect future Allied use of the Vitiaz and Dampier Straits. The term "Z-Day" was used to denote 15 December, the planned date for the amphibious landing on Arawe, to avoid confusion with the main landing on 26 December by the 1st Marines at nearby Cape Gloucester, which was designated D-Day following the normal convention. For the Arawe operation, it was considered necessary for the final approach to the beach to take place in daylight owing to the prevalence of reefs; otherwise the landing was set as early that day as possible.[2]

The landing force, the 112th U.S. Cavalry Regiment, was withdrawn from garrison duty at Woodlark Island and assembled at Goodenough Island two weeks before the operation. Admiral Barbey's 7th Amphibious Force was responsible for the overwater movement. The landing force embarked in ships at Goodenough Island, and joined the attack force convoy assembled at Buna. Following a deceptive move by the group towards Finschhafen, the vessels proceeded for Arawe after dark. The LCT echelons—groups of tank landing craft—loaded equipment and supplies at Cape Cretin near Finschhafen and proceeded under escort directly to Arawe.[3]

The plan called for two surprise landings in darkness, preceding the main landing, with about 150 soldiers in rubber boats carried in APD transport ships allocated to each. One party was to seize Blue Beach 5,000 yard east of Arawe and block the entrance to and exit from the narrow intervening peninsula. The other party was to land at the northern tip of Pilelo Island in order to capture a suspected Japanese wireless telegraph station. The landing on Blue Beach was repulsed by Japanese defenders with approximately fifty percent casualties. It was believed that the strong defenses were due to detection of a small party of amphibious scouts that had landed a few days earlier to reconnoiter the beach, and spent a couple of hours ashore before returning to Milne Bay. (Earlier in the month, Special Service Unit No.1 had completed relocation to Milne Bay, when on 8 December the *APc-12* and *LCT-72* arrived there from Fergusson Island with the remainder of the 10 officers and 29 men that made up the scouts, and associated equipment.)[4]

The main landing was to take place on Orange Beach, situated on the western shore of Arawe Peninsula after initial bombardment by destroyers positioned off Cape Merkus, Orange beach, and its flanks. For initial movement ashore over shallow coral reefs, Alligator LVTs (tracked landing vehicles) and DUKWs (six-wheel-drive amphibious trucks referred to as "Ducks") generally had to be used. The amphibious vehicles were launched in moonlight at 0500 about five miles off the beach, but due to confusion and the slow speed of the Alligators, the timing broke down, naval bombardment was delayed, and so was the landing. Fortunately the troops went ashore against light opposition, and by mid-afternoon had secured the eastern half of the peninsula, their objective for Z-Day.[5]

FIRST LCT ECHELON LANDS AT ARAWE

The first group of tank landing craft—LCTs *172*, *174*, *176*, *374*, and *381*—with the *APc-4*, sub-chaser *SC-699* and minesweeper *YMS-70* as escorts, was designated Echelon Three. It was to land at Arawe immediately following the tank landing ships of Echelon Two. Accompanying it to Arawe were fourteen Army mechanized landing craft (LCMs). The weather was bad during the crossing from Cape Cretin, and the group of vessels encountered strong currents that slowed its advance but, by proceeding at maximum speed, reached New Britain on time. On arrival the echelon received notice that H-hour had been delayed, so extra time was consumed by entrance through Pilelo Passage instead of via Arawe Passage as planned. The change in approach route proved fortuitous to large numbers of army personnel in rubber boats and in the water, survivors of the unsuccessful attack on Blue Beach, encountered and picked up by the echelon. Word was then communicated from the command element on the beach that they were ready to receive the LCMs, and that the LCTs were to land immediately thereafter.[6]

The echelon, less the submarine chaser and minesweeper, entered Arawe Harbor but the ensuing operations were slowed by intense cross traffic on the beach—unloading of seven LSTs and the LCMs and some LCTs concurrently. At 0855, the harbor was attacked by approximately fifteen dive-bombers and seven fighters. The only casualty was one member of the beach party embarked in a tank landing craft, who was slightly wounded, and three enemy planes were shot down. It was now apparent that concentrating a number of landing craft in a confined harbor at one time was a bad idea. All LCTs not immediately required for unloading were withdrawn and kept dispersed in the area east of Pilelo Island, and sent in on call. There was no further contact with the enemy.[7]

Chapter 8
SMALL COASTAL TRANSPORT *APC-21* SUNK

> Allied air support was light and not very effective from what could be seen. The only Allied planes were [USAAF] P-47's [Thunderbolts], and each time, they were not able to engage the enemy till after surface vessels had already been attacked.
>
> Comments made by the commanding officer of the submarine chaser SC-743, describing attacks made by Japanese fighters and bombers on vessels at Arawe in which the *APc-21* was sunk by a direct bomb hit[8]

The first re-supply echelon, designated Echelon Four, was comprised of the LCTs *88, 382, 384, 386, 387,* and *388*, with the *APc-21, SC-743,* and *YMS-50* as escorts. The task unit commander was Lt. (jg) W. J. Bates, the captain of the small coastal transport. The sea was calm and the sky clear with light winds from the southeast during the transit on 16 December. Aboard the *SC-743* general quarters was ordered at 1518 to prepare for the final approach to Arawe, and she then led the group of LCTs single file through Arawe passage into the harbor. A dozen Vals and "Zekes" (the Allied name for Zero fighters) came in low over Pilelo Island at 1643 and began strafing and bombing ships in the harbor. Army Air Force P47 Thunderbolts appeared overhead about four minutes later and engaged enemy planes on various bearings. The silhouettes of the P47s and enemy fighters, which crewmen aboard the sub-chaser believed were either Zekes or "Oscars" (Nakajima Ki-43 Army type 1 fighters) were very similar. This made it difficult to distinguish between friendly and enemy aircraft, especially when positioned against the sun and markings could not be seen. The *APc-21*, surprised by eight Vals, opened with 20mm, .50-caliber and .30-caliber machine gun fire, damaging three of the planes making bombing and strafing runs. One bomb fell near her, but inflicted no damage. From then on the echelon would be under almost continuous air attack while at Arawe.[9]

Deciding it was neither necessary, nor wise, for the escort vessels to remain inside the harbor the *SC-743, YMS-50* and *APc-21* stood out and took up patrols off Arawe and adjacent Pilelo Island waiting for the LCTs to unload. Two LCTs were immediately emptied by soldiers, but then the work stopped—it then being Army policy to not unload during darkness—and the echelon was dispersed for the night. At 2030, the sub-chaser hove to off Arawe to search with WEA-1 sound gear and surface radar for Japanese ships or submarines. She did not detect any, but for the next several hours remained at the same location, with her engines stopped to keep from producing a phosphorescent wake which might despite the darkness reveal her position to enemy planes. At 2035, the *SC-743* secured from general quarters and set Condition II; the port watch section on duty, with all guns cocked, loaded and manned, while the starboard watch (the other half of the crew) lay down at their battle stations to try to get some rest.[10]

Fifty-three minutes past midnight, Japanese aircraft began bombing Pilelo Island by the light of the three-quarter moon. Planes came in from a westerly direction with level bombing and dive-bombing at intervals of about five minutes. One plane flew directly across the moon, which appeared to be a "Rufe" (a Nakajima A6M2-N Navy Type 2 interceptor/fighter-bomber). It dove and dropped a bomb that produced white light with a pyrotechnic effect due to its wide burst. The explosion of bombs released by planes in level flight at higher altitudes resulted in heavier concussions and an orange glow in the burst. Per operating orders, vessels were not to fire on aircraft in the dark unless they were attacked, to preclude revealing their position. The *SC-743* had occasion to use her guns, and learned that those firing the weapons, especially the gunner on the 40mm, were blinded by the flashes and firing was not as accurate. She secured from general quarters at 0330, and set the starboard watch with weapons readied and manned; and the port watch in turn lay down at battle stations.[11]

The remaining LCTs to be unloaded were to be off the beach by 0730, so the echelon could be clear of Arawe before an expected morning attack by aircraft from Rabaul. At 0800, when some remaining craft had not exited the harbor, the commanding officer of the *APc-21* took his ship into the constricted area to find out the situation. He did not have a walkie-talkie radio, the only means by which to communicate with the beach. At 0810, a large group of 40-50 Vals and Zeros attacked the harbor by dive bombing and strafing. All the fighters had used the surrounding hills and islands for cover during their approach, while the Vals attacked in a steep dive directly out of the morning sun from the east over Pilelo Island.[12]

The *APc-21* received three direct bomb hits which broke the ship in two and she sank in three or four minutes. Other escorts and craft maneuvered radically to dodge bombs, as enemy planes in turn employed evasive banks and changes in altitude to confuse anti-aircraft fire. All of the ships except the *SC-743* and *LCT-388* were extensively damaged. High overhead, P47s were engaging Zeros in dogfights.[13]

Following the attack, the sub-chaser proceeded to where the *APc-21* had slipped beneath the ocean surface to search for survivors, and found that LCMs and an LCT had already picked them up. The small coastal transport suffered one man killed and eight wounded, and LCTs two killed and eight wounded. The echelon left at 0830 on 17 December for Dreger Harbor with the landing craft only half unloaded. Four days later the *APc-12* delivered fourteen survivors of the *APc-21* to Milne Bay.[14]

APC-2 DAMAGED

> *Not once, even with seventy-five (75) enemy planes in the air and with the ship rocking from bomb bursts, did the complete cooperation and mutual confidence disappear from the men.*
>
> Lt. (jg) Porter L. Fortune, Jr., commanding officer of the *APc-2*, remarking on the performance of his crew while under attack[15]

Enemy aircraft made a determined effort to destroy Echelon Eight—LCTs *85*, *171*, *172*, *176*, *374* and *381*, with the *APc-2* and submarine chasers *738* and *743* as escorts—with three heavy attacks on 21 December. Despite bad weather, the echelon had arrived at Arawe from Dreger on time that morning at about 0830. At five minutes shy of noon, lookouts aboard the small coastal transport sighted with binoculars in the clouds above about fifty planes approaching from the east. A group of approximately thirty Vals dove down from about 8,000 feet on the ships below, while the remaining planes, Zeros, engaged Allied fighters. The attack lasted for several minutes during which time every ship present was attacked. At least ten of the planes dove on the *APc-2*, dropping eight bombs that landed within forty feet of the ship. A near miss on the portside close to the fantail caused the ship to temporarily heel over far to starboard and covered the stern and the 20mm gun mount with a deluge of water. The ordnance was apparently 132-lb bombs with delayed action fuses as they burst some distance under the water. The APc was hit with sprays of shrapnel, but no one was injured, nor was there any apparent significant damage to the ship.[16]

In his after action report, the commanding officer cited the "leadership and coolness of action" of the executive officer and gunnery officer, Thomas G. Fitzgerald, during this and two subsequent attacks, in which he "kept every gun firing at its maximum seemingly at exactly the right times at the right planes." Fitzgerald also dispatched one aircraft himself:

> When a gunner on a starboard .50 caliber gun was temporarily jarred to the deck by a near bomb miss, a lone plane was coming in low from the opposite side to which the mass of planes were approaching. Lt. (jg) Fitzgerald took the .50 caliber and personally shot down the plane.

This Val came within 400 feet of the ship, dropping bombs and attempting to strafe, before being filled with bullets and crashing a few seconds later.[17]

A second attack five hours later was even more ferocious than the first. As an enemy flight approached from the east at approximately 8,000 feet, Lt. (jg) Porter L. Fortune, Jr., ordered the *APc-2* brought right to minimize the ship's cross-section by presenting only her stern to the aircraft. He then directed speed increased to flank, and the commencement of zigzag steering. Anti-aircraft fire opened when planes were about 5,500 feet away, and continued until the last one was approximately 3,000 feet distant. During the attack of some two minutes in duration, planes in groups of five dove on the small coastal transport, with the center aircraft descending lower to strafe, while the others released bombs from about 1,550 feet in altitude. Each time, the ship's gunners held the bombers at bay and drove the strafing plane away. Some eighteen planes attacked the *APc-2*, and two were likely shot down by her, as overhead an estimated twenty-five Zeros were heavily engaged by P38s and P47s.[18]

The ship suffered no personnel casualties, although the gun crew of the after 20mm was shaken up. However, excessive vibration made it apparent that the propulsion engine had been jarred loose by bomb blasts and that the shaft was out of alignment. When the ship turned to starboard, it slowed down twenty-five RPMs, whereas it sped up during changes to port, and the rudder was sluggish. Additionally, while the engineers had previously pumped about 750 gallons of water from the bilges each day due to hull seepage, the amount had increased five-fold, likely due to the stern tube seal having been knocked out of position.[19]

In a third attack at 1750, twelve Bettys with fighter cover appeared out of the sun as they were being heavily engaged by P38s and P47s. They dropped bombs from a mid-level altitude in the water to the north and east of Pilelo Island. None fell within 500 yards of the *APc-2*, and fire was not opened because Allied fighters drove the bombers off.[20]

Despite three attacks and damage to the *APc-2* and *LCT-171*, the echelon left Arawe at 1900—completely unloaded and on time—for Dreger Harbor. The group was intercepted at 2340 by the minesweeper *YMS-70* and sub-chaser *SC-703*, sent from Hanisch Harbor. The two ships graciously offered to assist the *APc-2* if necessary (she declined and continued to proceed unaided) and then escorted all the vessels to Hanisch.[21]

APC-15 DAMAGED WITH CREWMEN KILLED AND INJURED

> It had been decided previously that APcs were too vulnerable for [direct] combat duty, and would no longer be employed as escorts in spite of their many other advantages. However, shortage of escorts required that an APc be sent with this [the 9th] echelon [to Arawe]. It was considered that this would probably be a reasonably safe trip, as the initial attack on Cape Gloucester was scheduled for the same time and it was hoped that the enemy would be fully occupied with more important events.
>
> Comdr. B. C. Allen, Jr., commander LCT(5) Flotilla 7 and Task Unit 76.5[22]

In the early evening of Christmas Day of 1943, Echelon Nine, a resupply convoy of four tank landing craft—LCTs *259, 260, 298,* and *400*—departed Tare Beach, Cape Cretin for Arawe, New Britain, escorted by the *APc-15* and sub-chaser *SC-743*. Following the loss of the *APc-21* (Echelon 4) to Japanese bombers a week earlier, and subsequent damage to *APc-2* (Echelon 8), Navy brass had determined that using the small wooden coastal transports to escort amphibious craft to assault beaches was not advisable. However, there had not been a larger, better armed vessel available. During the night transit, periodic light flashes associated with fighting were observed to the north, but were sufficiently distant as to arouse no anxiety. Just after dawn, Lt. (jg) Kemper Goffigon, III, the commanding officer of the *APc-15*, ordered general quarters set aboard his ship in preparation for the approach to the island. Upon arrival two LCTs proceeded to the designated beach to discharge their cargo, while the sub-chaser, coastal transport, and the remaining LCTs patrolled off shore. The wind was light and variable, the sea calm, and the sky clear overhead with cumuli around the horizon. At 0845, a large flight of Japanese aircraft—approximately twenty bombers and sixteen fighters from Rabaul—was sighted to the east-southeast, using the sun to mask their approach. Goffigon ordered flank speed and evasive maneuvering. The bulk of the planes concentrated their main attack on the *APc-15*, while the others targeted an LCT, the motor torpedo boats *PT-110* and *138*, departing Arawe with Army passengers, and targets in the harbor.[23]

A group of 20 to 25 aircraft assaulted the *APc-15* from off her port bow, bombers in the center and Zero fighters on the flanks of the flight. Two of the bombers were Bettys—twin-engine Mitsubishi G4M land-based attack aircraft—and the others Vals—smaller Aichi D3A dive-bombers. Goffigon described the approach of the aircraft, during which the Bettys dropped bombs from a high altitude, while the Vals and Zeros dove steeply down to attack, with both the fighters and dive-bombers strafing the wooden ship as they closed her:

> All aircraft came in one attack; Betty's dropping bombs at approximately 1,200 feet, the rest pulling out of the dive at heights ranging [downward] between 1,000 and 100 feet. Two or three Vals pulling out at the latter height. The aircraft made an exceptionally steep dive, approximately 60 degrees with no glide approach, starting about 12,000 feet.[24]

As the massed planes came within range, the *APc-15*'s guns—four 20mms, four .50-caliber machine guns, and two .30-caliber guns—opened. Recognizing that in dangerous New Guinea and New Britain waters, additional guns increased one's chances of survival, crewmen had been on the lookout for weapons in every port the ship visited, and had commandeered six machine guns to augment the standard outfit of four 20mm anti-aircraft guns. To best fight his ship, Goffigon had assigned everyone except four members of the crew and himself to the gun positions. Each 20mm normally had a crew of four; a gunner, range setter, loader, and a fourth individual to raise and lower the mount trunnion. A gunner and a loader were assigned to each of the .50-cals, and a gunner only to each of the .30-caliber machine guns. The larger machine guns were mounted on the raised deck aft of the deckhouse, two on the portside and two on the starboard, and one .30-cal. on each bridge wing. The executive officer, Lieutenant (junior grade) Dowd, was the gunner on the starboard .30, and Lieutenant (junior grade) Weiner, the third officer assigned to the ship, the port gun. A single engineer was assigned to the engine room tending machinery, and the captain, a quartermaster third, radioman second, and signalman second were on the bridge for ship control and communications.[25]

Within a span of two to three minutes, the flight of bombers had released 20 to 30 bombs, ten of which fell within 100 yards of the *APc-15*. The detonations of three dropped close aboard off the starboard quarter of the ship, lifted her stern and heeled the vessel to port. The stern then settled, and the ship righted itself, but the propulsion engine went from ahead-flank speed to idle due to the concussion. Water spray from bomb blasts enveloped the vessel, obscuring the vision of gunners, whom nevertheless shot down one Betty and one Val.[26]

Despite heroic efforts aboard the diminutive ship—which an Australian had, upon first viewing the APc, likened to a "little Dutch wooden shoe"—she took a terrible beating from the Japanese air armada. In addition to structural damage and machinery derangement, the ship also suffered two crewmen killed and sixteen injured. Only one officer and a dozen enlisted escaped injury, and they were dazed from bomb blasts. One gunner and one loader were killed outright, and five of the remaining nine gunners were severely wounded, being in exposed positions and the obvious targets of enemy pilots trying to silence anti-aircraft fire. Motor Machinist's Mate Second Siek, the gunner on the No. 4 20mm gun, was killed instantly by shrapnel, and his gun crew was blown over the side. Storekeeper Second Anderson, the loader for the No. 1 .50-caliber machine gun, was killed by strafing. Another gunner had his right hand practically blown off, a third suffered stomach wounds due to strafing, a fourth had his right hand laid open, and a fifth gunner had his right leg badly mangled. The executive officer, who was the sixth gunner killed or wounded, had injuries common to practically everyone that was topside, bleeding from the body, arms, and face. On the bridge, the signalman lost an eye and the commanding officer was hit in the arm by shrapnel. A bomb blast propelled the Flotilla 7 surgeon and priest out of the deckhouse onto the deck, and water deluge from another near miss washed them over the side.[27]

Following the attack by the Japanese planes, which lasted for only two to three minutes before P47 Thunderbolts drove off the attackers to the northwest, the commanding officer gave the order to abandon ship. He has received word from the chief boatswain's mate that the vessel was sinking, several men had been blown or washed into the sea, and those still aboard that had not been killed or injured were dazed from bomb concussions. The ship could not maneuver, as the engine was not responding to bell changes, and the *APc-15* and crew were in no shape for an ensuing attack. So, one by one, the remaining men jumped into the water. The captain believed he was the last to leave the ship, but Motor Machinist's Mate Second Cilly had elected to remain in the engine room. The survivors were plucked from the water by the sub-chaser and LCTs and taken to the Army Field Hospital on the beach for medical treatment. After being treated aboard the *SC-743*, Goffigon ascertained that the drifting ship was not sinking. At his request, Lieutenant (junior grade) Weiner, ten able crewmen, and three members of the flotilla staff returned with him to the ship after about a thirty minute absence and boarded. The fire party went below, put out burning mattresses, and checked the engine room, where they found Cilly. Through his efforts, the ship could now make way although the helm was sluggish, and the captain took the damaged vessel into shallow water very close off Arawe and anchored. While the wounded continued to receive medical treatment, shipmates able to do so, made repairs, and rigged for tow. In addition to the damage wrought to the ship's engine room and bridge by bomb blasts and staffing, exterior derangement included:

- Entire starboard side above waterline smashed, split and punctured by shrapnel
- Most of the fasteners and deck fittings and deck stations on the starboard side had started to work, and some had come loose
- Fo'c'sle hatch distorted
- Bridge and radio shack shrapnel filled
- Bridge door blown off
- Both peloruses shot up and their stands on the hand rail around the bridge catwalk badly distorted

Chapter 8

- Guard rail piping and wind breaker around bridge and flying bridge smashed, and flag bag smashed
- Radio aerial shot down
- One wherry boat destroyed, another one badly damaged, and starboard 15-man life raft blown to bits
- Starboard .50-caliber machine gun blown over the side

There was a general weakening of the ship's structure due to the terrific concussions; the engine had a pronounced vibration, due to a loosing of the main engine to the engine bed and starboard-side weakness; and the helm was sluggish.[28]

As the remaining LCTs unloaded their cargo on the beach, Army doctors started tending to the wounded and operating as necessary. The flotilla doctor was badly shaken up after being swept overboard into the sea, but assisted greatly. After all the wounded had been treated and were placed aboard a LCT, the *APc-15* weighed anchor. Being unable to back her engine, she required an Army LCM to pull her clear into deeper water. During the return transit to Dreger Harbor the commanding officer was assisted by a skeleton crew and staff officers. Entering harbor, the sub-chaser *SC-743* made up alongside the wooden ship as she proceeded to anchorage. The LCTs in company made the beach and discharged the wounded men to the 54th Evacuation Hospital, and medics removed the deceased crewmen from the *APc-15*. The *SC-743* then towed the small coastal transport alongside the *LST-453*—a tank landing ship converted to serve as a tender and repair ship, which was positioned at Negin Island—where emergency repairs to the *APc-15* to correct battle damage began immediately.[29]

It is a wonder that the *APc-15* survived an attack by such a large group of aircraft bent on her destruction and continued her war service. The commanding officer received the Navy Cross for his leadership and heroism during the battle and ensuing efforts to save the ship, as described in an excerpt from the award citation:

> He courageously disregarded his own painful injuries and, showing forceful leadership and outstanding skill, immediately undertook strong protective measures to control damage and care for the wounded personnel. With the engineering plant and rudder badly damaged, he reassembled his remaining men and labored tirelessly for five hours in the combat zone to effect repairs which enabled his ship to return to a place of safety under her own power. The

conduct of Lieutenant, Junior Grade, Goffigon throughout this action reflects great credit upon himself, and was in keeping with the highest traditions of the United States Naval Service.

Photo 8-2

Official photograph of Lt. (jg) Kemper Goffigon III, the commanding officer of USS *APc-15*. (Courtesy of Kemper Goffigon III)

Signalman Second Warren C. Borneman received the Silver Star for continuing to carry out his communications duties, despite his own brutal wounds including the loss of an eye, resulting in the rescue by small craft of wounded shipmates who might have otherwise drowned, as detailed in his medal citation:

> Though severely wounded in one eye, he continued to perform his duties in a cool and efficient manner. After receiving his wounds he sent signals to nearby ships regarding the rescue of personnel struggling in the water. Thereafter he assisted in further measures for the safety of surviving personnel. Only after all possible measures had been taken did he give consideration to his own severe wounds.

Following limited repairs able to be performed by *LST-453* personnel the *APc-22* towed the *APc-15* to Buna for access to the repair ship *Amycus* (ARL-2) and temporary hull repairs. A survey of the wooden ship identified additional defects, summarized in a damage report:

> The primary hull damage was sustained by the starboard deck house side above the rub rail. This structure was badly torn, fasteners were loosened and steel over [covering] head gussets torn or loosened. . . . The plugs over the side planking fasteners were started throughout the starboard side of ship. The starboard bridge keel had started to leave the hull forward and causing leaks. . . . It is probable that the ship [engine and shafting] has suffered misalignment since the vessel can make only one third of its maximum turns. Shims under the engine have been knocked loose adding to misalignment difficulties.[30]

The *APc-2* towed the *APc-15* from Buna to Milne Bay, where she underwent additional repair to make her seaworthy for tow across the Coral Sea to an escort base on Trinity Bay at Cairns, Australia. Following her arrival at a recently completed maintenance facility at U.S. Navy Base, Gown, she entered the floating dry dock *ARD-7* for considerable hull repair and refitting, requiring the ship to remain in Australia for several months.[31]

SUMMARIZATION

A few more re-supply echelons arrived at Arawe; none, following the devastation to the *APc-15*, escorted by a small coastal transport. During the period 15 to 31 December 1943, the LCTs and escort ships of

Task Group 76.5 were credited with shooting down twenty-two Japanese aircraft, with six more probable. As a result of enemy action, the *APc-21* was sunk, *APc-2* and *APc-15* damaged, and LCTs *82, 382, 384, 386, 387,* and *396* damaged as well. A total of six Navymen were killed and thirty-nine were wounded, most aboard the *APc-15* and *APc-21*. Both of these ships received a battle star for the Arawe operation as did the APcs *2, 4, 9,* and *22* as well.

The Arawe landings were begun eleven days before the initial landing by the 1st Marines at Cape Gloucester. Because the operation did not add up to a great deal, strategically or tactically, and the scale of fighting was overshadowed by that which took place on the island's opposite shore, many observers tended to discount its importance. However as a diversionary action, the invasion implicated one Japanese battalion which otherwise could have fought at Cape Gloucester. Thus, the Arawe landings indirectly contributed to the destruction of enemy air power in New Britain. If the Japanese ground defense of Arawe was not particularly robust, the violence of their reaction by air exceeded all expectations. Attacks on the beachhead began within hours of the first landings and persisted for a week; far heavier opposition than the enemy had offered previously at Bougainville or the operations in northern New Guinea.[32]

9

Support for PT Boats and the Treasury Islands Landings

> *Steering various courses entering Blanche Harbor, Treasury Island. Mortar Fire from enemy on beach; also machine gun fire. Laying to inside harbor at designated beach. . . . Frequent bursts of shell fire heard...Enemy planes attacked; fighters and dive bombers. . . . Enemy planes dropped bombs and flares at beach in Blanche Harbor.*
>
> Excerpts from the combined deck log/war diary of the *APc-37*, describing the Treasury Islands landings on 27 October 1943.[1]

While Rear Admiral Barbey's Seventh Amphibious force was battling its way up the coast of New Guinea with the goal of breaking the Bismarcks Barrier, Rear Adm. Theodore S. Wilkinson was pushing up through the Central Solomon Islands headed for the same destination. Wilkinson had relieved Rear Adm. Richmond K. Turner as the commander, Third Amphibious Force on 15 July 1943, allowing Turner to move on and assume the duty of commander Amphibious Force Pacific Fleet in the Central Pacific.

EXPANDING ROLE OF MOTOR TORPEDO BOATS

From the meager force and limited facilities—four PT boats and one grass shack—with which Motor Torpedo Boat Squadron Three had initiated operations at Guadalcanal on 12 October 1942, the MTB organization in the Solomons had continued to expand and evolve. By early 1944, there were twelve Motor Torpedo Boat Squadrons— No. *2, 3, 5, 6, 9, 10, 11, 19, 20, 23, 27,* and *28*—and numerous bases ranging in size from small forward temporary operating bases to large overhaul and repair facilities. During this period some PT boats also evolved from true motor torpedo boats into hybrid "motor torpedo boat-motor gunboats" with the addition of a 37mm gun in the bow. To compensate for the increased weight that would otherwise degrade the boat's speed, two of their four torpedo tubes were removed. The addition of one USAAF automatic 37mm gun was standard, but there were variants. Three PT boats were stripped of their torpedo tubes and other armament, except for a pair of twin .50-caliber gun mounts, and two 40mm cannon were installed, fore and aft, as well as additional machine guns. The main occupation of PTs had evolved into finding and destroying Japanese alongshore barge traffic, which, by virtue of the American command of adjacent waters, had become the enemy's only surface supply line. The PT hybrids proved to be excellent gunboats against the armed barges employed by the Japanese Army. They, and other PT boats, would also receive improvements and upgrades to communications and reconnaissance capabilities. The PTs were equipped with radio gear for communications with their base or tender and with each other. A VHF (very high frequency) capability was added to provide greater communications security between the boats and aircraft, and PTs were also fitted with radar sets to give them eyes to see in the dark.[2]

The Japanese were using shallow draft motor-driven barges in the Solomons, Bismarcks, and New Guinea to transport and supply troops in areas that could not be served by cargo ships, due to the sinking of enemy merchant vessels by the Allies. The barges could easily be run into shallow coves and creeks, where a little camouflage, together with the natural cover, made them extremely hard to detect from the air during the day. With suitable overhead screening, even open beaches could be used. In areas patrolled by Allied air forces, most barge movement took place at night. It seemed likely that as the destruction of Japanese shipping continued, the 6,000 barges that were believed to be in service in spring 1943 would continue to be augmented, and more widely employed for supply, reinforcement and evacuation.[3]

Although a number of barges were used by the Japanese, including Chinese junks, the most common was the *Daihatsu*-class, meaning "large motorized boat." The 49-foot barge was similar to the U.S. Navy's Higgins boat with a bow ramp that was lowered to disembark troops or cargo after it was run up on a beach. Each barge could carry one tank, or seventy men, or 10 tons of cargo. Despite its welded steel hull, the Daihatsu was less boxy than a LCVP, giving it better sea keeping and, powered by an economical diesel engine, the barges had a range of 100 nautical miles at 7.5 knots, and a top speed of about 9 knots. The standard armament was two light machine guns or two to three 25mm/60 anti-aircraft guns, but the barges were commonly field-modified to carry weapons as large as 37mm. Improvised armor was also often added to protect the crew quarters.[4]

DUTY IN THE CENTRAL SOLOMONS

The main bases for PT boat operations in the central Solomons were Lever Harbor on the north coast of New Georgia Island, and just to the south of New Georgia, Rendova Harbor on the north side of Rendova Island. The motor torpedo boats were well adapted for duties in the area, which offered relatively smooth water and many temporary operating positions close to targets. Their primary task was intercepting barges supplying enemy forces in the Kolombangara-Vella Lavella area, but the versatile boats also performed other duties. These included transporting servicemen between bases, rescuing pilots of downed aircraft, evacuating casualties, and conducting coastal reconnaissance.[5]

Operating chiefly at night when in enemy waters, the motor torpedo boats were subject to a myriad of navigational hazards—as the waters around Vella Lavella and Kolombangara were studded with coral reefs—in addition to fire from enemy shore batteries, and from float planes, the natural enemy of the boats. Although they usually hunted at night, PT boats occasionally conducted day operations. On 14 September, three boats from Rendova Harbor searched coves from Doveli Cove to Takisukuru on the northern and western coast of Vella Lavella. Two other PTs covered the northeastern coast of the island from Marisi Bay to Lambu Lambu. Proceeding inside uncharted reefs, the boats pushed into bays occupied by enemy forces and shot up houses, wharves, and observation stations, and set fire to and destroyed five camouflaged barges.[6]

Many night encounters with barges were inconclusive, as damaged craft were often able to slide past reefs or into coves, where it was possible to elude their pursuers. During the month of September 1943, motor torpedo boats did, however, destroy at least twelve enemy barges, and damage eight or ten others. Near month's end, Lt.

Comdr. Leroy T. Taylor arrived at Lambu Lambu Cove on the northeast coast of Vella Lavella on 25 September, with Motor Torpedo Boat Squadron 11, and the *APc-25*, and established a new PT base. The small coastal transport was to serve as "station ship," fueling, provisioning, and providing fresh water for the seven boats using the cove as an operating base, and to function as the base communications center. This concept was not a new one. Three months earlier, Motor Torpedo Boat Squadron 9 arrived at Rendova on 30 June and set up its base on Lumbari Island, on the north side of the harbor. Squadrons 5 and 10 arrived there in July, and Squadron 11 in August. It soon became evident that while the PT boats could cover the western portion of the New Georgia Islands group from Rendova, they could not effectively patrol the eastern area. To solve the time/distance problem, Lever Harbor on the northeast coast of New Georgia was selected as a new operating point. Lt. Craig C. Smith arrived there on 24 July with four boats of Squadron 6 and *APc-28* to serve as a tender, since there was no plans to establish a shore base.[7]

Taylor later wrote a brief history of his unit entitled "Too Many Months in the Solomon Islands or Sex Takes a Holiday." The following excerpts help to convey what the duty was like, particularly the deadly struggle between Japanese and American forces engaged in frequent running battles in the darkness:

> We arrived at Rendova just as the New Georgia Campaign was in full swing. We got into the harbor at 9 o'clock at night without being shot up by our own guns there. At first the Japs used to dive bomb the boats in the harbor in daytime, coming in low just over the hills on Rendova Island where the radar couldn't pick them up.
>
> Hunting barges around Kolombangara and the Vella Gulf wasn't what one would call fun. They traveled in convoys and carried plenty of machine guns. One of the other squadrons operating in Kula Gulf had the worst time. There, they had to contend not only with armed barges but with big guns and little guns on the beach. And down near Diamond Narrows [a special passage between New Georgia and Arundel islands where the channel was no more than 50 meters wide] it wasn't so far from shore to shore. There were Japs on both sides.
>
> The float planes used to chase our boats at night, bombing and strafing. It was bad. Every time you opened fire on a barge you had a float plane on your neck in 2 minutes. It was a war of nerves.

Night fighters seemed to be a solution and a plan was arranged to get a float plane. One of the section leaders volunteered to be the bait. He would go out and raise a racket by steaming at high speeds and firing his guns. Our night fighter would stay overhead waiting. The float plane would jump in to knock off a torpedo boat and the night fighter would shoot him down in the process. This first night everything went according to plan. The float plane came in and the night fighter was there. Then the first word from the night fighter came over the radio. "I'm being attacked by a float plane!" The word went back from the boat, "Bring him down to 2 feet and I'll get on his tail."[8]

Taylor also described the navigation hazards associated with hunting Japanese barges in uncharted shoal waters, the previously discussed operation along the Vella Lavella coastlines to find and destroy enemy sanctuaries, and experimentation in using Army weapons on PT boats:

The charts of these islands are not what you'd call up to date. Probably because nobody was ever interested in them but a few traders. There are such reassuring notes as "Reefs reported 6 to 8 miles offshore," "Shoal sighted by H.M.S. *Dart*, 1792," "White water seen here by Capt. Bligh but position doubtful." These things don't help you much when you have to hunt three or four hundred yards off the coast at night. One goes slowly and somewhat nervously. Then some damn fool drops his tin hat [battle helmet] or jumps down on deck and you go straight up in the air. You're sure you've hit a reef which is the surest way of finding it. This is the way we were so successful in locating most of the reefs around Vella and Choiseul. Once we made a daylight barge hunt around Vella and had such good luck that we asked to try the same thing at Choiseul. The answer was "No," because of the navigational hazards. The same night we were ordered to patrol the Choiseul coast arriving on station at midnight.

While at Vella we experimented with regular trench mortars mounted on our boats. Getting in to 500 yards of the beach and throwing mortar shells into enemy outposts was fun. The first night we heaved a few over onto the back side of Moli Island. After the first good explosion we heard a loud, exasperated voice scream "Jesus Christ! What next? [presumably by a Japanese who spoke English]." We knew there were Japs in there.[9]

Chapter 9
STATION SHIP DUTIES

The *APc-31* arrived at Lambu Lambu the morning of 1 October from Guadalcanal, via a stop at Rendova, to relieve the *APc-25* as station ship. After unloading her cargo, stores and drums of gasoline, she remained moored to the beach in Lambu Lambu Cove at Vella Lavella Island for the next eight days, operating her radio to provide communications for the base and supplying PT boats with fresh water. Relieved of this duty by the *APc-33* on 9 October, she proceeded to Guadalcanal for a ship maintenance availability with the *Argonne* (AG-31) and repair of ship's equipage. The *Argonne* was a former submarine tender and had been Admiral Halsey's flagship before he moved his 3rd Fleet Headquarters ashore at Noumea, New Caledonia. The *Argonne* was at Purvis Bay, adjacent to Tulagi Island to conduct repairs to the destroyer *Selfridge* (DD-357), which had been damaged in an engagement with Japanese destroyers off Vella Lavelle on the night of 6 October 1943.[10]

On 17 October, the *APc-31* received orders and proceeded the short distance to the PT boat base at Mocambo Island, Florida Islands, Guadalcanal. After loading one hundred fifty cases of 37mm ammunition

Map 9-1

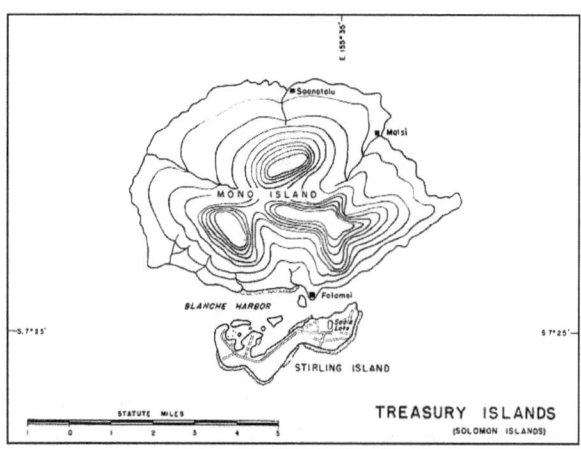

Motor torpedo boats were based at Stirling in the Treasury Islands to blockade the waters around southern Bougainville Island, as well as those of the Shortland Islands and the Choiseul Bay area to the immediate south and east-southeast.
Source: http://www.ibiblio.org/hyperwar/USN/Building_Bases/maps/bases2-p269.jpg

and twenty-five cases of 40mm ammunition for the PT boat base at Rendova Harbor, she took aboard one-half ton of torpedo supplies for the base at Lambu Lambu. The following morning, she loaded an additional 100 drums of aviation gasoline and dry stores for Lambu Lambu and seven Marines for transport. The *APc-31* arrived at Lambu Lambu via a stop at Rendova, discharged the Marines, unloaded cargo at the gasoline dock, and then moored to the bank and took up the now routine duty. She operated her radio for the base, and supplied boats with fresh water until relieved on 27 October by the *APc-34*. Returning to Guadalcanal, the *APc-31* loaded 170 drums of aviation gasoline and dry stores. She departed Kulcum Beach in early morning darkness on the last day of the month, escorted by a destroyer, to join a convoy of six infantry landing craft, two tank landing craft, and four destroyers bound for Blanche Harbor. This deep water strait separated Stirling and Mono, which together comprised the Treasury Islands, located to the northwest of Guadalcanal in the western Solomon Islands.[11]

OCCUPATION OF THE TREASURY ISLANDS

American and New Zealand troops had only days earlier occupied the Treasury Islands after the 8th Brigade Group, 3rd New Zealand Division landed on Mono and Stirling Islands on 27 October 1943. To obtain last minute, current information about the enemy, a reconnaissance party of two New Zealand non-commissioned officers and some natives had been landed by PT boat the night of 21-22 October. The group learned from local natives that:

- the enemy had recently landed reinforcements;
- medium-caliber guns were emplaced on both sides of Falami Point;
- machine guns were emplaced on Mono Island along the approaches;
- there was an observation post at Laifa Point with direct wire communications to a radio station near the Saveke River; and,
- Stirling Island was unoccupied.

The scouts were evacuated by the same means the following night, and brought with them some Mono Island natives to act as guides for the landing. An advance party consisting of once again, New Zealand non-commissioned officers and some natives, was landed by PT boats the night of 25-26 October to cut the communication lines between the observation post and the radio station just prior to the scheduled landing.[12]

The main landings comprised five transport groups commanded by Admiral Fort. Eight high-speed transports—*McKean* (APD-5), *Stringham* (APD-6), *Talbot* (APD-7), *Waters* (APD-8), *Dent* (APD-9), *Kilty* (APD-15), *Ward* (APD-16), and *Crosby* (APD-17)—and an equal number of infantry landing craft—LCI(L)s *24, 62, 67, 69, 222, 330, 334*, and *336*—made up the first two groups. They were followed by two tank landing ships, *LST-339* and *LST-485*, of the Third Transport Group, and LCTs *321, 325*, and *330* of the Fourth Group, escorted by the *APc-37*. The final transport group, the *APc-33*, six LCM(3) landing craft, and one crash boat, entered the harbor last. The *APc-33* moored to bushes at a prescribed spot awaiting her turn to discharge cargo. In early afternoon, she went alongside a tank lighter on the beach to unload. Enemy fighters and dive-bombers attacked shipping in the harbor at 1530; none came within range of her guns. The small coastal transport cleared the side of the lighter at 1750 and made fast to a nearby nest of ships. That evening, as enemy planes dropped bombs and flares on the beach, she took up station-ship duties at Treasury until relieved by the *APc-31* on 1 November.[13]

Enemy resistance was relatively light on D-Day, 27 October, and Blanche Bay, the main objective, was taken by nightfall. The landing was opposed by machine gun, sniper, and mortar fire on the beached LSTs, but the enemy guns were silenced and unloading continued. While screening the tank landing ships, the destroyer *Cony* (DD-508) was hit by two bombs during the afternoon air raid. The blasts knocked her after engine room and after guns out of commission, killed eight men, and wounded ten seriously. The Japanese lost fourteen planes in exchange for the damage to the *Cony*. That night a group of ships—destroyers *Philip* (DD-498) and *Saufley* (DD-465), the *APc-37*, and LSTs *339* and *485*—were in transit back to Guadalcanal, when an enemy "snooper" arrived overhead. After making a pass to drop floatlights for illumination, it released two bombs that fell near the *399*, but inflicted only superficial damage to the ship.[14]

The following day, a temporary PT boat base was quickly set up on Stirling Island upon the arrival of Lt. Comdr. Robert B. Kelley and his Motor Torpedo Boat Squadron Nine. Patrols to guard the approaches of the Treasury Islands against counter-attack commenced that evening. With the establishment of this base, PT boats were now in a strategic position to blockade the areas around southern Bougainville Island, and the Shortland Islands and Choiseul Bay area to the immediate south and east-southeast. Remnants of the enemy that had escaped from the New Georgia Islands to Choiseul Island were travelling north on foot to the Choiseul Bay area where nightly barges shuttled them across the Bougainville Straits to Fauro Island, the Shortlands, and southern Bougainville.[15]

Four small coastal transports earned battle stars for the Treasury operation; the *APc-33* and *APc-37* for the landing on 27 October and the *APc-31* for station ship duty on 1 November 1943. The star received by the *APc-30* for the occupation and defense of Cape Torokina on 15 December involved survey ship duties.[16]

SURVEY OPERATIONS

Pursuant to orders from Admiral Fort, the *APc-30* embarked a surveying party consisting of two officers and four men and equipment from the survey ship *Oceanographer* (AGS-3) and departed Guadalcanal in mid-December 1943 for Advance Base, Torokina, Bougainville Island. Arriving there on the 15th, she commenced a survey of Express Augusta Bay the following day. The work entailed first setting up control beacons on the beach to assist in fixing the positions of reefs, and then taking soundings with leaded lines as far as eight and one half miles off shore, to obtain the data necessary to produce accurate charts. The *APc-30* departed there on 13 January to return to Blanche Harbor and arrived the following day to carry out her new orders to fix the geographical location of the Treasury Islands. She was relieved of this duty on the 20th and, after transferring personnel and gear to the *APc-34*, left Express Augusta Bay for some much needed repair work. The weary little wooden ship entered dry dock at Renard Sound, Russell Islands to have worm-eaten planking replaced, and her propeller shaft realigned, and its shaft stern bearing and spring bearing replaced. During this work, her engine was found to have settled on its bed, which had caused the shaft misalignment and worn bearings.[17]

Other small coastal transports were also soon engaged in survey work. The *APc-48* was at Vatilau, Ramos, and Maliata Islands in February 1944. In mid-February, the *APc-23* returned to the *Oceanographer* the survey party that had charted the approaches to Cape Torokina and left with a different group of surveyors for Vatilau Island—about four miles in length and of horse-shoe shape—to chart Munda Harbor and the lagoon east to Onaiavisi Entrance.[18]

GROUNDING AND LOSS OF SMALL COASTAL TRANSPORT

The availability of accurate charts was incredibly important to safe navigation as attested to by the loss that previous autumn of the *APc-35*. After departing Renard Harbor for Renard Sound, Russell Islands on 22 September, she had run aground in the early evening on a reef at Latitude 8° 47.8′ South, 157° 46.2′ West Longitude. The *LCT-69*, whom she had been escorting, tried to pull the coastal transport off the reef without success. In the process a towing cable parted and badly injured the skipper of the tank landing craft. After being worked against the reef during the night, the forward hold of the APc began taking water the following morning, upon which her crew began removing gear from it. Two LCMs arrived from Segi Point at 0830. One took the gear and departed while the other stood by. The fleet tug *Pawnee* (AT-74) arrived in the mid-afternoon and anchored about 500 yards from the wreck.[19]

At 1508 the tug's captain and salvage officer left the ship to inspect the *APc-35*, aground bow on, with approximately thirty degrees list to starboard, and by now all lower spaces flooded. After putting three three-inch pumps aboard the stricken wooden ship, the tug passed a tow wire to the *APc-35* at 0715 on 24 September and began pumping operations. Following nearly eleven hours of dewatering, she made preparations to pull the APc free and at 1806 began heaving in on her winch. At 1838, the tug discontinued pulling with the only results apparent slight slewing of the stern to starboard. The *Pawnee* took off all personnel later that night as the list had increased to 50 degrees and the vessel was in danger of capsizing. The following day, the tug anchored off the reef to the northward of South Island, and commenced removing portable equipment from the stranded vessel. Divers then patched two holes in the flooded engine room beneath the ship's waterline, and made repairs to her inoperative sound gear. On 27 September, the intrepid tug—anchored off South Island with seventy-five fathoms of chain veered and having placed beach gear to the port side of the *APc-35* to assist in righting, so that pumping might resume—began hauling on the beach gear. With the *Pawnee*'s anchor dragging due to the strain and all pumps working, the list decreased only from fifty degrees to thirty degrees starboard. Salvage efforts continued the following day, until—with the small wooden ship pounding heavily on the reef and all efforts to refloat her unsuccessful—Admiral Fort's staff directed the tug to abandon the operation and to land the crew and salvaged equipment at the Russell Islands.[20]

Photo 10-1

Salvation from the Sea depicting USS *PT-59*, under the command of Lt. John F. Kennedy, taking U.S. Marines pinned down by Japanese forces at the mouth of the Warrior River off Choiseul Island. Cover boat *PT-236* is in the background. (Painting by Richard DeRosset)

10

JFK Rescues Marine Paratroopers on Choiseul Island

> When all seemed lost, you can well appreciate my relief to see the landing craft returning, escorted by PT boats, one commanded by you. As I recall, we both had our hands full and there was little time for amenities. Please accept again my heartfelt thanks.
>
> Letter to President John F. Kennedy from retired Marine Corps Colonel, Warner T. Bigger[1]

In addition to providing support for the Treasury Islands landings and engaging in barge hunting, PT boats also evacuated U.S, Marines pinned down by enemy forces on Choiseul Island, which lay across the New Georgia Sound from their base on Vella Lavella, during this period. On 2 November 1943, the base at Lambu Lambu Cove received a radio call from Lt. Col. Victor H. Krulak, commander 2nd Marine Parachute Battalion, 1st Marine Parachute Regiment, for PT boat assistance to take off a group of Marines. The battalion had landed on the southeast coast of the island a week earlier from the high-speed transports *Kilty*, *Ward*, *Crosby*, and *McKean*, to carry out Operation BLISSFUL. This "Choiseul diversion" was a feint designed to make top Japanese brass believe that it was the objective of an impending amphibious assault, vice at Torokina, on Bougainville Island to the northwest, where the 3rd Marine Division would land on 1 November. The intent was to conceal the true objective of landing at Torokina for as long as possible and to also draw enemy troops to Choiseul that might otherwise fight on the Bougainville beachhead. To prevent the enemy from discovering the Marines were considerably less in number than an invasion force, the 650-man battalion had gone ashore the night of 27–28 October on unguarded beaches near Voza, an abandoned village which lay between concentrations of Japanese forces at Sangigai and Choiseul Bay. Intelligence indicated there were some 4,000 to 5,000 enemy on the island, dispersed in small camps along the coast.²

Map 10-1

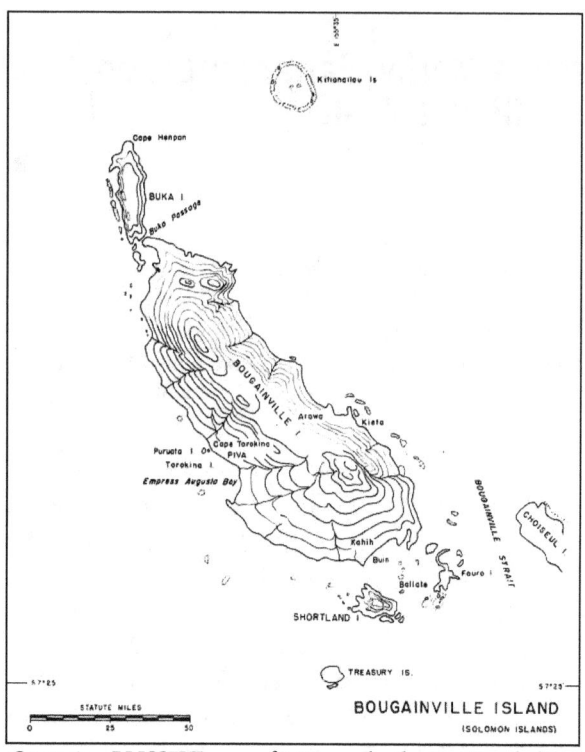

Operation BLISSFUL was a feint to make the Japanese believe that Choiseul Island was the objective of an impending amphibious assault vice at Torokina on Bougainville Island to the immediate northwest
Source: http://www.ibiblio.org/hyperwar/USN/Building_Bases/maps/bases2-p271.jpg

In succeeding days, the Marines carried out raids to destroy installations, barges, and supplies. These activities, along with skirmishes with enemy in the jungle, created the intended impression of a larger force at work. On the afternoon of 2 November, a group of Marines led by the battalion executive officer, Maj. Warner T. Bigger, shelled Guppy Island—which, located in the middle of Choiseul Bay, was the site of an enemy barge replenishing-center and fuel base for the area—with 142 rounds of 60mm mortar fire. At completion, the group made its way southward to the west bank of the mouth of the Warrior River, which lay to the east of the entrance to the bay. The Japanese located the raiding party, and enemy forces attacked the Marines from both upstream and from across the river. Outnumbered and outgunned, pinned down, and cut off from the remainder of the battalion, Bigger desperately required extraction from the hostile beach.[3]

When the radio call came in at Lambu Lambu, there were only two PT boats available, the *PT-59*, commanded by Lt. John F. Kennedy, and the *PT-236* of Ens. William F. Crawford. Kennedy was refueling and had only one-third of a tank of fuel in the *PT-59*, enough to make it to the Warrior River, about 65 miles distant, but not enough to get back. Due to the urgency of the situation, a decision was made that the *PT-59* and *236* would leave immediately, and when Kennedy's boat ran out of fuel, the other boat would tow it.[4]

The account of John F. Kennedy's command of *PT-109* and her loss in the early morning darkness of 2 August 1943 when, while on patrol in Blackett Strait off the Kolombangara coast in the Solomon Islands, she was sliced in two by the Japanese destroyer *Amagiri*, is well known. So too are his efforts to get crew members safely to a small island and to secure their rescue, for which he earned the Navy and Marine Corps Medal and was also awarded a Purple Heart. Less familiar is Kennedy's subsequent tenure as the skipper of the *PT-59*. He accepted command of the motor torpedo boat, which was to be converted to a gunboat to serve as a more formidable weapon against armed enemy barges, at Tulagi on 1 September. Following its modification to PTGB-1 (Gunboat No. 1), he joined Motor Torpedo Squadron 19 at Vella Lavella. (Since the Navy did not ultimately officially adopt this designation, it was a colloquial term. However, a Squadron 19 war diary entry does refer to "Gunboat 1" commanded by Lt. J. Kennedy, USNR.) Changes made to the boat involved removal of her torpedo tubes to facilitate the installation of Bofors 40mm cannons fore and aft. She was also fitted with six .50-caliber machine guns (four twin mounts and two single barrel guns) to augment the two twin-mounts she already had. This gave her an impressive fourteen mounted .50-caliber machine guns, and for more punch the two Bofors guns on the bow and stern. The installation of more and heavier armament resulted in an associated increase in manning. Typically there were one to three officers and twelve enlisted men of various ratings aboard a PT boat; the crew size of the three Solomons PTs converted to gunboats swelled to eighteen. Since there were only twelve bunks for the crew, the men had to "hot rack," meaning a man relieved on watch would occupy a bunk vacated by someone taking over the duty.[5]

Kennedy was cognizant of the greater combat capabilities his *PT-59* offered. An officer assigned to the same squadron later recalled that during briefing sessions, before the boats went out on patrol, he would frequently ask [the squadron commander]: "Skipper, why don't you let me go in first with my boat? This is going to be a strafing operation [presumably referring to barge hunting missions at night] and I can fire many more rounds than an ordinary PT boat."[6]

Back on Choiseul, Bigger's patrol, consisting of Marines mainly from Company G plus several from Headquarters Company, was involved in a firefight with the Japanese at the mouth of the Warrior River—resulting in the wounding of corporals Schnell and May—when boats were sighted approaching the river mouth from seaward. As the Higgins boats began taking fire from the east bank, Marines on the west bank attracted the attention of personnel in the two craft. With all guns firing at the east bank, which combined with that of land forces caused the enemy to temporarily cease fire, the LCP(R)s made the west bank. As the Marines waded out to board the two boats, the enemy began to lob mortar rounds at them. Luckily, good fortune intervened. A storm was gathering—with a heavy sea rising and winds from the southwest creating rough surf—and a heavy rain began to fall, screening the Marines from view.[7]

The first landing craft, having taken more than thirty Marines, reversed its engines and began backing to prepare for departure. Now sitting much deeper, the boat scraped against the shallow coral reef beneath its keel, bending the rudder and making steering difficult. Maj. Warner Bigger and the remaining thirty plus men boarded the other wooden-hulled boat. As the LCP(R) retracted, it too worked against the coral, opening a seam, and the boat began to fill with water. The engine compartment flooded—and the engine stopped and could not be restarted—and the boat began to drift dangerously towards the hostile shore before finally grounding. The PTs appeared at dust to find one LCP(R) hard aground and the other damaged.

Although the sliver of a crescent moon and a few stars visible through patches in the overcast provided little illumination, the boats were clearly distinguishable as landing craft versus Japanese barges. One Marine though, upon hearing gunners aboard the *PT-59* rack their machine guns, worried that they might be shot by their own guys.[8]

The two PT boats had earlier reached the Choiseul coast and began looking for a landing craft to help guide them to Bigger's force. At around 1800, it appeared and Kennedy found that much to his delight Lt. (jg) Richard E. Keresey, Jr., a PT boat skipper who had accompanied the 2nd Marines to investigate possible sites for a PT boat base on the island, was aboard. Keresey transferred to the *PT-59*, and Kennedy set out, headed full-out for the river mouth with the boat's fuel gauge reading almost empty and little daylight remaining. With Keresey guiding, Kennedy arrived on the scene, "coming in on mufflers." This expression refers to PT boats, when wanting to run silent, feeding engine exhaust out under the water at low speeds. Positioning his boat between the shore and the immobile craft to shield the Marines, Kennedy drew fire from the shore. Despite the rain squall, enemy mortar rounds and machine-gun fire had continued to seek the immobile Marines. As the *PT-236* lay starboard side to the beach and drove the Japanese back up into the jungle with 20mm and .50-caliber machine-gun fire, the crew of the *PT-59* began pulling Marines up on deck. Kennedy took aboard all of the Marines from the grounded boat as well as its Navy crew, and also the Marines from the other LCP(R). The damaged, but operable Higgins boat had stood off, well clear of enemy fire until the arrival of the PT boats. Once all the Marines were aboard—crammed onto the fantail and packed into the crew's quarters below, leaving scarcely any room for sailors to move about—the reefed Higgins boat was scuttled. Approximately twenty-five Marines were subsequently transferred to the *PT-236*.[9]

Following their departure the two PTs boats transited, with the remaining Higgins boat struggling to keep up, around the southwest coast of Choiseul to Voza without incident. Upon arrival there at 2130, Kennedy transferred the Marines to waiting craft that took them to shore. Their work done, the PT boats set a course south back across the New Georgia Sound to Vella Lavella. Halfway there, the *PT-59* ran out of fuel and was taken under tow by the *PT-236* until the arrival around dawn of the two boats at Lambu Lambu Cove. A few hours earlier, Corporal Edward J. Schnell had died quietly in

Kennedy's bunk at 0100. Due to his critical injuries, he had been kept aboard, vice transferred ashore at Voza, in the hopes of getting him much better medical treatment at the field hospital on Vella Lavella.[10]

On Choiseul Island, the entire battalion was withdrawn by three infantry landing craft at 0130 on 4 November, leaving behind only minefields and booby traps set by Marines to delay an anticipated enemy attack. During embarkation, the sounds of exploding mines signaled a timely departure. The 2nd Marines returned later that morning to their encampment on Vella Lavella.[11]

As it turned out, Kennedy would have only a little over two weeks still in command. On the night of 5 November, he led three PT boats to the Moli Point/Choiseul Bay area, where they attacked Japanese barges. During the next week and a half, the *PT-59* prowled off Choiseul Bay looking for barges, and Kennedy's final action, on the night of 16 November, was an uneventful patrol. On 18 November, a doctor directed Kennedy, who was physically and mental exhausted and had lost twenty-five pounds, to go to the hospital at Tulagi. He gave up his command of *PT-59* that same day to Ens. John N. Mitchell (who would later be United States District Attorney under President Richard M. Nixon) and left the Solomons on 21 December 1943. Back in the States, Kennedy appeared to have lost the edge that drove him on *PT-59*. He jumped back into the nightlife scene and assorted romantic dalliances. Assigned in March to Submarine Chaser Training Center, Miami, Florida, Kennedy joked about the easy duty, "Once you get your feet upon the desk in the morning, the heavy work of the day is done." He was discharged from active Navy duty due to a physical disability in March 1945.[12]

The relatively unknown Marine Corps diversion on Choiseul Island and the action of the PT boats in taking off a small portion of the 2nd Parachute Battalion were overshadowed by other events occurring at the same time. These included the landing by the 3rd Marine Division on 1 November at Cape Torokina on Empress Bay, Bougainville, and the ensuing Battle of Empress Augusta Bay on 1-2 November, in which U.S. Navy Task Force 39—comprised of the twelve combatant ships of Cruiser Division 12 and Destroyer Divisions 45 and 46—achieved a clear victory over an adhoc Japanese naval force of two heavy cruisers, two light cruisers, and eight destroyers from Rabaul.

11

Assault and Capture of Tarawa

> *The capture of Tarawa knocked down the front door to the Japanese defenses in the Central Pacific.*
>
> Observation by Adm. Chester Nimitz regarding the acquisition of the Gilbert Islands, which came at a high cost in terms of lives lost.

In addition to the twenty-eight coastal transports of APc Flotilla 5 in the South Pacific and the twenty-two vessels of APc Flotilla 7 in the Southwest Pacific, ten other APcs served in the Eastern, Central, or South Pacific. Four of these ships, constructed at the Anderson & Cristofani yard in San Francisco, California, were assigned duty with Service Squadron 2 in Hawaii transporting personnel and cargo between bases in the islands. Two—the *APc-108* and *109*—subsequently joined a small number of other ships at Funa Futi, Ellice Islands to form Mobile Service Squadron 4, newly created to support the invasion and capture of Tarawa Atoll in the Gilbert Islands. Code named GALVANIC, the operation would begin on 20 November 1943. The remaining six APcs made their way from builders' yards on America's east and west coasts to Noumea, New Caledonia, for duty with Service Squadron, South Pacific Force. During the war, these ships often worked directly for the commanders of bases in the South Pacific—and in one case an Army command—while remaining under the operational control of a Service Squadron. Summary information about the coastal transports follows, including the dates the ships were commissioned, and later arrived in the Hawaiian Islands, or at Noumea or Funa Futi.

Map 11-1

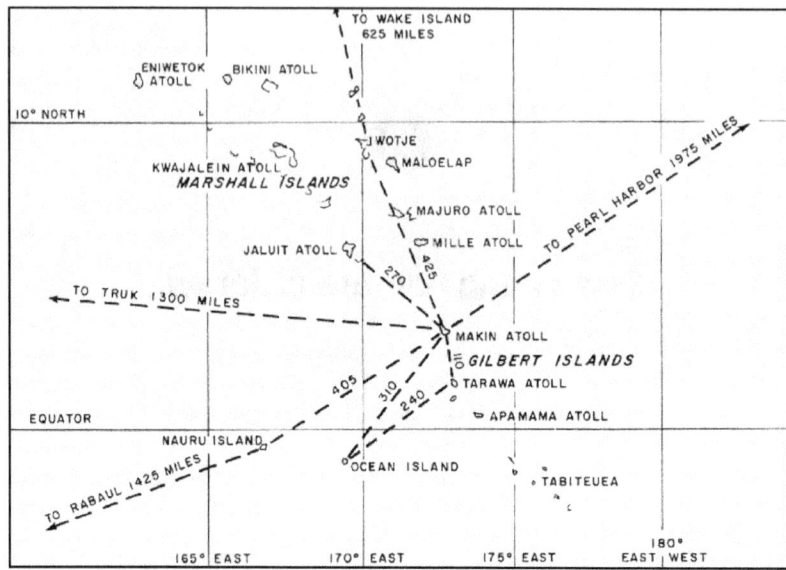

Two small coastal transports supported the occupation of Tarawa in the Gilbert Islands. One, the *APc-108*, rescued the crew of the Army freight ship *F-14* from Tabiteuea Island. After suffering an engineering casualty, the ship had drifted for thirty days before being deposited off the island.
Source: http://www.ibiblio.org/hyperwar/USN/ACTC/maps/actc-16-p612.jpg

Ship	Commanding Officer	Ship Commissioning	Date Reported
Service Squadron, South Pacific Force: Noumea, New Caledonia			
Built at Herreshoff Manufacturing, Bristol, Rhode Island			
APc-95	Lt. (jg) Roswell B. Milligan, USNR	15 Jul 1943	26 Oct 1943
APc-96	Lt. (jg) Richard A. Green, USNR	28 Jul 1943	10 Nov 1943
Built at Noank Shipbuilding, Noank, Connecticut			
APc-98	Lt. (jg) Gordon D. Winsor, USNR	18 Dec 1943	14 Jun 1944
Built at Fulton Shipyard, Antioch, California			
APc-101	Lt. (jg) J. J. Snel, USNR	2 Apr 1943	14 Aug 1943
APc-101	Lt. (jg) William F. Grandy, USNR	17 Apr 1943	14 Aug 1943
APc-103	Lt. R. J. Wissinger, USNR	1 May 1943	14 Aug 1943
Service Squadron Two, Pacific Fleet: Honolulu, Hawaii			
Built at Anderson & Cristofani, San Francisco, California			
APc-108	Lt. (jg) Keith L. Davey, USNR	1 May 1943	17 Jul 1943
APc-109	Lt. (jg) J. S. Horton, USNR	5 Jun 1943	17 Jul 1943
APc-110	Lt. (jg) R. M. Raffelson, USNR	3 Jul 1943	27 Sep 1943
APc-111	Lt. (jg) W. J. Jolly, USNR	31 Jul 1943	27 Sep 1943
Service Squadron Four, Pacific Fleet: Funa Futi, Ellice Islands			
APc-108	Lt. (jg) Keith L. Davey, USNR	1 May 1943	19 Nov 1943
APc-109	Lt. (jg) J. S. Horton, USNR	5 Jun 1943	19 Nov 1943

THE GILBERT ISLANDS

The Gilbert Islands, which included Tarawa, Apamama, and Makin, was a group of coral atolls that lay in a roughly north-south line across the equator. The Japanese had invaded the British-held islands on the same day as the attack on Pearl Harbor and occupied them by 10 December 1941. The location of the islands immediately south and east of other important Japanese bases in the Carolinas and Marshalls added to their strategic importance to the enemy. For the Allies, the Gilberts offered sites for air fields necessary for progress along the road through the Central Pacific toward Japan. The planned assault and capture of Tarawa and Makin in November 1943 was a part of the overall American strategy of conducting an offensive through Micronesia—the Gilbert, Marshall, and Carolina Islands—at the same time as MacArthur's New Guinea-Mindanao approach to Japan. In order to set up forward air bases capable of supporting operations across the Central Pacific to the Philippines and on to Japan, the U.S. needed to take the heavily defended Marianas Islands. However, use of land-based aircraft to weaken enemy defenses and provide some measure of protection for the invasion forces necessitated capturing the Marshall Islands, northeast of Guadalcanal. An enemy garrison and air base on Betio, one of the islands of Tarawa Atoll in the Gilberts, guarded against invasion forces arriving from Hawaii. Thus, the starting point for the planned invasion of the Marianas lay far to the east, at Tarawa.[1]

SERVICE SQUADRON FOUR

During the preparatory period for GALVANIC, Adm. Chester Nimitz approved use of floating mobile bases to provide logistic support, and on 1 November 1943, Service Squadron Four was commissioned. Based at Funafuti, and under the command of Capt. H. M. Scull, the squadron consisted of the destroyer tender *Cascade* (AD-16) and twenty-three other ships and craft—including the *APc-108* and *109*—ranging from the repair ships *Phaon* (ARB-3) and *Vestal* (AR-4) through tugs and patrol craft to fuel-oil barges and 500-ton lighters.[2]

CAPTURE OF TARAWA AND MAKIN

Two regiments from the 27th Infantry Division landed at Butaritari Island Makin Atoll, on 20 November and, following light Army losses—64 killed and 150 wounded—signaled "Makin taken," three

Map 11-2

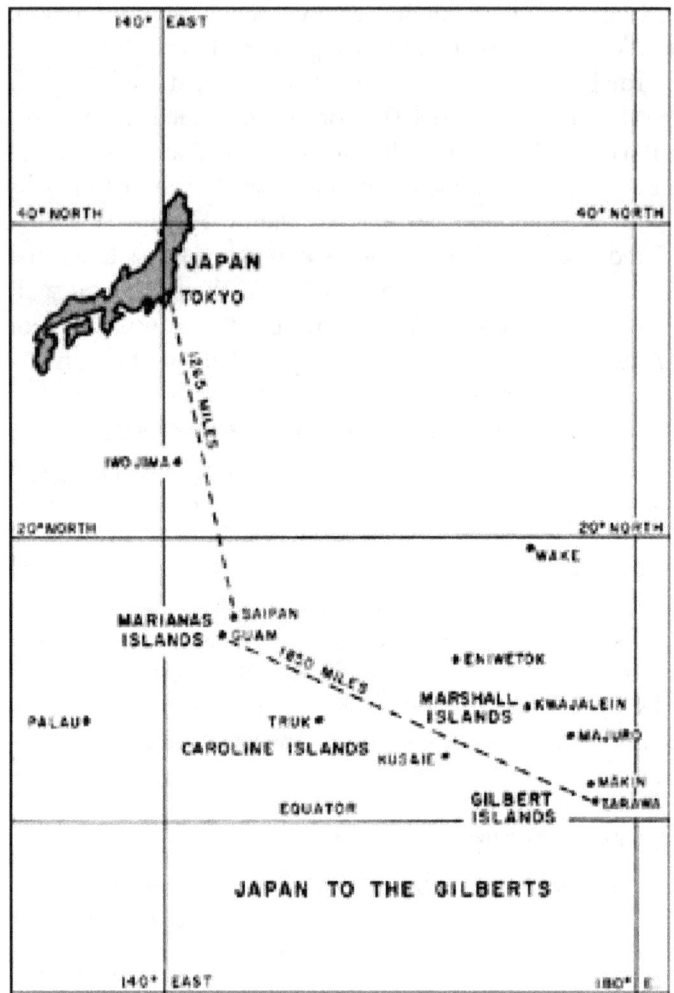

Principal route of the Central Pacific forces towards Japan.
Source: http://www.ibiblio.org/hyperwar/USN/ACTC/maps/actc-p735.jpg

days later. The assault on Tarawa that same day was bitterly contested. Heavily fortified, and garrisoned by several thousand Japanese troops on Betio, the principal island of the atoll, Tarawa had been attacked repeatedly from the air for weeks preceding the assault, and the previous day by naval shore bombardment. Although these efforts silenced the heavy guns and killed approximately half the Japanese troops, the enemy was able to concentrate his remaining forces beside the only

Assault and Capture of Tarawa {133}

beach where a landing was possible and inflicted heavy casualties. The 2nd Marine Division suffered heavy casualties—871 killed, an additional 124 men who would succumb to their wounds, and 2,306 wounded or missing in action. The fighting lasted nearly four days, at the end of which time the island was considered secure, although subjected to air raids and isolated sniper action.[3]

Map 11-3

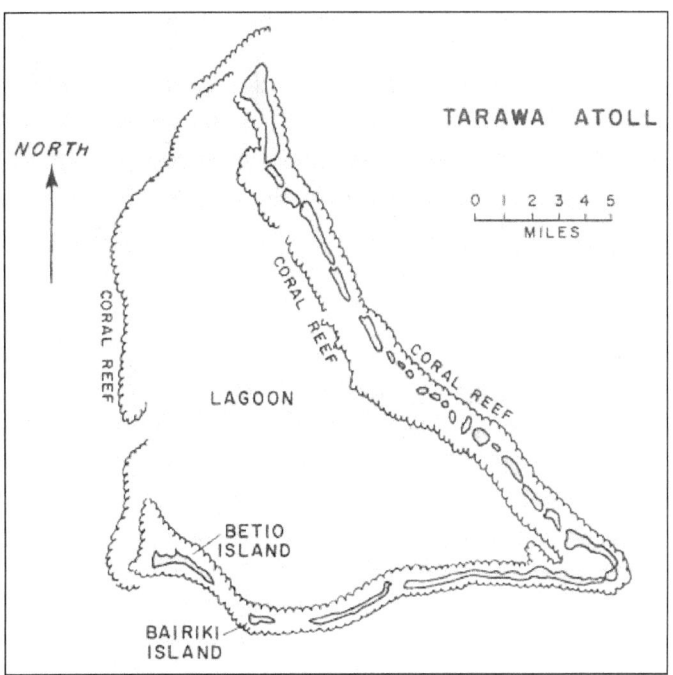

The 2nd Marine Division encountered heavy opposition after coming ashore on the lagoon side of Betio Island at Tarawa Atoll.
Source: http://www.ibiblio.org/hyperwar/USN/ACTC/maps/actc-p683.jpg

SMALL COASTAL TRANSPORTS MOVE FORWARD

The morning of 8 December, the *APc-108* and *109* got under way from Funa Futi, to proceed to Tarawa, Gilbert Islands, and to, upon arrival, report to the island commander for temporary duty. Loaded aboard the *APc-108* were forty-six tons of 90mm projectiles. The ships made landfall on Tarawa, a triangular-shaped atoll, in the late afternoon of the 11th and after taking aboard a pilot, stood into the lagoon and anchored off Betio Island. The lagoon, about seventeen miles long and tapering from eight miles to less than a mile in width, was open to the west, though partially barred by a section of the submerged reef. Betio, at the southwest corner of the Tarawa atoll, measured roughly two-and-one-quarter miles in length by less than half a mile in width. The following day, the ships proceeded in the late forenoon through the lagoon to a new anchorage off Eita Village at Ella Island, part of the Tarawa Atoll. The coastal transports began unloading ammunition into LCVP and LCM craft on 13 December, slowed because the landing craft could only beach to land their cargos at high tide.[4]

While unloading in darkness an hour and a half past midnight, the coastal transports experienced their first air raid when two enemy bombers flew over at about 20,000 feet and bombed the island airstrip located about seven miles from the anchorage. These bombs all appeared to land in the water. All ammunition was transferred by around first light, and the ships returned to the Betio anchorage that afternoon.[5]

Three days later, the *APc-109* received orders to report to commander Mine Squadron 1, embarked aboard the 454-foot minelayer *Terror* (CM-5), the only minelayer specifically built for the fleet during World War II, and to proceed at his direction to Makin Island, Gilbert Islands, and assist in a survey of lagoon entrances. That same day, 17 December, the small coastal transport embarked a survey party and the squadron commodore, cast off from the *Terror* at 1714, and proceeded out of the harbor. She arrived at Makin Lagoon in the early evening the next day, and the following morning the survey party commenced its work, transported by a LCVP. The *APc-109* proceeded to Nabuni Island a day later on 20 December, embarked the survey party and returned all personnel to the *Terror* the following day.[6]

Enemy aircraft returned to Tarawa on 23 December, while the *APc-109* lay anchored in the lagoon. The alert sounded in the early evening at 1918, and two aircraft high up, dropped bombs on the airstrip on Betio Island. Several hours later, in early morning darkness at 0315, the alert sounded again. A single plane passed over the island and dropped several bombs and was followed thirty minutes later by several aircraft that, from a great height, released bombs; one appeared to score a direct hit on a grounded plane. This convention continued every few days; on 27 December, a single plane bombed the island from a great height, with the bombs landing in water off the end of Betio Island.[7]

RECRUITMENT OF NATIVE LABORERS

While the *APc-109* was assisting with the survey, the *108* received orders from the Assistant Port Director to proceed to Tabiteuea, Tarawa, which lay two hundred miles to the south, to embark native laborers for passage back to Betio. They were to assist three Seabee battalions, the 74th, 95th, and 98th, that had arrived at the atoll to construct fighter and bomber runways and to build bases on Betio and Buoto Islands. At Betio the greatest obstacle was the condition of the island. The former Japanese base had been wrecked as a result of the air strikes and fighting, and chaos, ruins, a litter of corpses and decaying food dumps extended over the entire 285 acres. Flies and mosquitoes, with ideal breeding conditions, existed in countless swarms; all water sources were brackish and polluted; and only salt water was available for washing purposes. It appeared that literally every square foot of the island had to be cleared and graded in order for the Seabees to begin with installations and improvements.[8]

The coastal transport left her anchorage at 0714 on 19 December for Tabiteuea, with a British Colonial officer who was also a member of the Fiji military force embarked as recruiting officer. The *APc-108* arrived at Peacock anchorage the following morning and began boarding sixty natives. She returned to Betio anchorage around noon on 21 December, and disembarked the passengers into two LCM landing craft. Another trip to Tabiteuea followed a couple of days later, this time with a native recruiting officer aboard. The ship arrived at Peacock anchorage on Christmas Day and the recruiting officer went ashore and began enrolling laborers. The last party of a total group of 125 men came aboard on 27 December by means of outrigger canoes. Following her return to Tarawa the following day, the ship anchored opposite Eita Village and began to disembark passengers via an outrigger canoe and completed the operation with an LCM.[9]

Both the *APc-108* and *109* traveled to islands in the Gilbert Islands Group in January to find more laborers for work in the Pacific areas. During a representative trip, the *109* anchored in a confined anchorage off a native canoe channel on the western side of Beru Island, embarked 103 natives, and discharged them and a British officer off Abaokoro Village at Tarawa two days later. The recruitment continued during short jaunts to Arorae, Nukunau, Onotoa, Tabiteuea, and Tamana islands to collect still more native laborers.[10]

The ships also brought thousands of bales of Pandanus thatch back to Tarawa. The thatch, leaves from an evergreen tree (Pandanus tectorius, a type of screwpine) stitched together in sheets, were used to roof and also cover the walls of island huts. During a representative trip, the *APc-108* loaded 279 bales of thatch while at anchor off Tabontebra Village at Abaing using native outriggers and eight natives aboard to help load. Upon return to Tarawa, the thatch was unloaded at Cora Island. (Presumably the thatch was obtained to provide natives recruited to work on Tarawa and elsewhere materials to build dwellings in which to live.) Through month's end in January 1944, other trips to Abaing yielded still more bales; recruitment and transport of natives continued; and Japanese aircraft occasionally bombed Betio Island, always releasing the ordnance from a very high altitude. The *APc-108* and *APc-109* each earned a battle star for the Gilbert Islands operation.[11]

12

Army/Navy Support for Allied Coast Watchers

> *The coast watchers saved Guadalcanal and Guadalcanal saved the Pacific.*
>
> Observation by Adm. William Halsey, regarding the contributions of coast watchers in the Solomon Islands, including those on islands in the Santa Cruz Group to the southeast of Guadalcanal.

The other eight APcs assigned to Service Squadrons did not garner any special laurels or battle stars in the war. On the other hand, the *APc-95* did have the distinction of relieving a renowned sailing vessel of its cargo ship duties in the New Hebrides. The war service of the two-masted scow was the basis for a Hollywood comedy war film released in 1960, titled *The Wackiest Ship in the Army*, starring Jack Lemmon, Ricky Nelson, and Chips Rafferty. The storyline involved a secret mission to deliver an Australian coast watcher to a location only a shallow-draft vessel could reach, and its encounter with Japanese surfaces forces and role in helping to win the Battle of the Bismarck Sea. In actuality, the scow supported coast watchers, rescued many downed American aircraft crews, and is thought to have helped track down two Japanese submarines, in addition to its more mundane cargo ship duties.[1]

Information about the Unclassified Miscellaneous Vessel *Echo* (IX-99), a designation used by the U.S. Navy for ships that did not fit into one of the standard categories, is sketchy as the *Echo* did not keep a war diary. Entries from that of the seaplane tender *Mackinac* (AVP-13) do cite two instances in which the sailing vessel was involved with coast watchers. On 7 March 1943, the *Makinac* arrived at Peou Bay, Vanikoro Island, in the Santa Cruz Group, to relieve the *Thornton*

(AVD-11) as patrol plane tender. The *Echo* stood into the bay a couple of hours later, with embarked aboard her coast watchers and supplies destined for the Swallow Islands, a part of a larger cluster of islands—lying between Latitude 9° and 11° South and Longitude 165° and 169° East—generally referred to by the name of Santa Cruz. The Santa Cruz Islands included the big islands of Santa Cruz, Utupua, and Vanikoro; the Swallow or Reef island group; and the Duff group. The Swallow Islands were all quite small, the largest being not more than four miles in length, and several of the smaller ones containing only a few acres. In 1766 an English vessel, the HMS *Swallow* commanded by Capt. Philip Carteret visited the islands, which he named after his ship. Resembling reefs, they were also called the Reef Islands. Patrol planes from the *Mackinac* delivered the coast watchers to their destinations the following day, along with Captain Echols, U.S. Army, and two radio technicians to set up "teleradio" sets for them. Following the return of the soldiers to the *Echo*, she departed the bay on 11 March. The scow revisited Peou Bay two months later in May.[2]

Vanikoro was home to the only female coast watcher in the Solomon Islands. The 51-year-old Australian, Ruby Boye, was living on the island with her husband Skov, the manager of the Vanikoro Kauri Timber Company, when the Japanese occupied Tulagi and Guadalcanal in May 1942. A ship was sent from Australia to evacuate the island's European residents, but Ruby and Skov elected to stay on the island as coast watchers, monitoring the movements of enemy ships and aircraft. Boye's coded reports via wireless radio quickly proved invaluable to Allied forces and enraged the Japanese, who several times sent planes to bomb the island. Japanese vessels were prevented from reaching the coast watchers by a near impenetrable reef around the island with entrances known only to inhabitants.[3]

Map 12-1

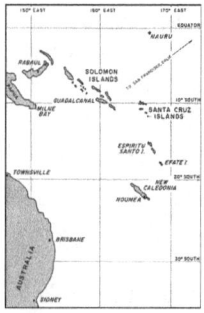

Vanikoro, one of the Santa Cruz Islands, was home to the only female coast watcher in the Solomons. Source: http://www.ibiblio.org/hyperwar/USN/ACTC/img/actc-19.jpg

Being civilians, coast watchers risked execution as spies if captured by the enemy. To provide a measure of protection, the Royal Australian Navy began in March 1942 to grant naval rank and to provide these individuals the requisite uniform. The hope was that if seized, they would be viewed as members of Australia's armed forces and be treated accordingly. On 27 July 1943, Boye was appointed a third officer, Women's Royal Australian Naval Service, an honorary rank that carried with it no pay, setting her apart from her male contemporaries. The Japanese knew of her presence and who she was, having sent her in 1942, a threatening radio message in English: "Calling Mrs. Boye, Japanese commander say you get out!" She was unfazed, and continued to act as a relay station between coast to watchers further north and to the program's naval intelligence office at Vila, New Hebrides. Halsey made a special flight to Vanikoro to meet Boye, and when she fell ill late in 1943 he sent a Navy aircraft to evacuate her for treatment. Boye returned to Vanikoro in 1944 and, in recognition of her contributions, she received the British Empire medal; bestowed for military service worthy of recognition by the Crown. Her WRANS appointment concluded on 30 September 1946.[4]

Map 12-2

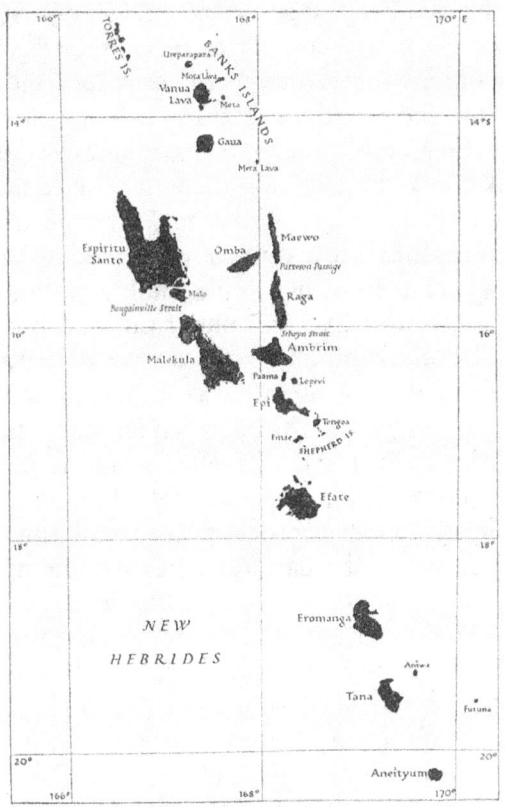

Fig. 165. The New Hebrides
Based on G.S.G.S. map no. 4298 (on a conical projection).

Following modification for duty as a refrigeration ship, the small coastal transport *APc-95* provisioned army and navy bases and outposts in the New Hebrides. Source: http://www.loc.gov/item/82692644

The *APc-95* was at Noumea, New Caledonia, when ordered on 18 December 1943 to Ships Repair to undergo conversion for duty as a refrigeration ship. The modifications included the installation of a 10-ton refrigeration box, requiring the removal of all berthing for passengers in her forward hold. At completion, she departed Noumea on 11 January 1944 for Efate Island, New Hebrides, for assignment to Service Command, U.S. Army at Vila Harbor as the relief for the only ship of the United States Navy to be named for the nymph Echo.[5]

The large two-masted flat-bottomed schooner was built in 1905 by William Brown & Sons, at Te Kopuru near Dargaville in New Zealand, of kauri throughout. The generally straight-grained wood had exceptional strength-to-weight ratio and was rot resistant, making it ideal for yacht hull construction. She was originally topsail rigged; twin diesel engines were installed in 1920. The U.S. Navy had acquired the 104-foot vessel from the New Zealand government under reverse Lend-Lease and, following her conversion by the repair ship *Rigel* (AR-11), placed her in commission on 4 November 1942 at Auckland. Operating from Vila Harbor, she served for over a year in the New Hebrides and adjoining island groups. Relieved of these duties by the *APc-95*, the *Echo* proceeded to Wellington, was decommissioned on 15 March 1944, and was returned to the New Zealand Government.[6]

The exceptionally well-built scow, which was fitted with centerboards in lieu of a keel to allow her to ply shallow waters, and lowered to prevent leeward drift when under sail, still had many years of service ahead. Originally built for the Kaipara timber trade, she also hauled coal, plied between Wellington and Karamea, and carried meat from Wairoa to Napier. In 1920, she was bought by Charles Ekford and thereafter would make thousands of crossings across Cook Strait between Blenheim and Wellington, carrying any and every sort of cargo, including Ford cars and tractors on top of the cargo hatches. Following her Army stint the *Echo* resumed working out of Blenheim and was the last vessel commercially under sail in New Zealand waters. In June 1972, the *Echo* was placed "on the hard" (on blocks ashore) at Picton, a town in the Marlborough region of New Zealand close to the head of Queen Charlotte Sound, and fitted out as clubrooms for the Marlborough Cruising Club. Since then she has served as a small scow museum and café, and is currently a well-appointed café and bar which also displays the history of trading scows in New Zealand.[7]

For the first couple months of her service the *APc-95* hauled mail and passengers, fresh beef, Army rations, and general cargo between Undine Bay and Havannah and Vila Harbors on Efate Island. She then started making "milk runs" to other islands in the New Hebrides as well, including Epi, Espiritu Santo, Makekulu, and Ouaco.[8]

13

Through the Bismarcks

> *It was the jungle and the rain, too, that made New Britain so different from Guadalcanal. I knew that it was going to be different the moment that I ran down the ramp of our L.C.I. [Infantry Landing Craft] and across a narrow black beach,scrambling up a small steep bank to burst from sunlight into the gloom of the jungle. For, in that moment, the rains began to fall; and in that moment we began to hunt the foe.*
>
> Robert Leckie, a member of the 1st Marine Division during the Assault on Cape Gloucester, in *Helmet for My Pillow*, his personal narrative of World War II

CAPTURE OF CAPE GLOUCESTER

After a hot and stuffy Christmas spent at sea in landing craft of the Seventh Amphibious Force, the 1st Marine Division landed near Cape Gloucester, New Britain, in the early morning of 26 December 1943. Before the landings, Alamo Scouts accompanied by Marine officers and a former coast watcher who knew the country had conducted three separate reconnaissances of Cape Gloucester. Based on the intelligence obtained, two small beaches—designated Yellow 1 and 2—on the east coast of the broad peninsula that ended at Cape Gloucester were selected for the main landing, providing access to a 3,900-foot airstrip about five miles away at the northern tip of the cape. A diversionary landing also took place at Tauali (Green Beach) on the Dampier Strait side of the island, six-and-one-half-miles southwest of the cape. This operation came just eleven days after the landing at Arawe on Cape Merkus to the south-southeast, which, although later criticized regarding its overall value, tied up one Japanese battalion that could have fought at Cape Gloucester.

From seaward Cape Gloucester unpleasantly resembled Guadalcanal Island, where the 1st Marines had last fought. In actuality, the "leathernecks" found New Britain—a 250 mile long crescent-shaped island that lay northeast of New Guinea across the Vitiaz and Dampier Straits—to be even worse than "the Canal." This was due to a waist-deep swamp that extended from the beaches inland up into tropical rainforest and persistent heavy rain that never stopped falling on the heavily wooded island. About 7,500 enemy troops bivouacked in the vicinity of the airstrip, and at Borgen Bay on New Britain's north coast comprised the enemy defense forces. The bay was an important staging area for barge traffic making runs between Rabaul and Japanese positions across the straits on New Guinea. After two weeks of dirty fighting and general wretchedness, the Marines were able to secure a beachhead and a perimeter by 16 January 1944 at the cost of 248 killed and 772 wounded.[1]

Prior to the landing on 26 December, the destroyers *Flusser* (DD-368) and *Mahan* (DD-364) had first been sent in the early morning darkness into Borgen Bay as entry was considered risky because of barriers in its uncharted waters. As the destroyers proceeded cautiously, using their radar to navigate and sound gear to locate shoals, minesweepers *YMS-49* and *52* followed, marking the hazards with buoys improvised from gunpowder cans. In trail was the amphibious force carrying assault troops.[2]

SMALL COASTAL TRANSPORTS SENT TO BORGEN BAY

It appears the initial effort to define and mark a safe channel through shoal water into Borgen Bay was not ideal. The *APc-12* left Cape Sudest for Cape Gloucester in darkness at 2243 on 3 February 1944 to proceed independently for the Borgen Bay area. Her orders were to remove the buoys at designated locations A and B and reposition them at points C, D, and E. For this action, the coastal transport received a battle star. On 10 February, while returning from Cape Gloucester with an echelon of tank landing ships—LSTs *66, 204, 206,* and *463*—under escort by three destroyers, an enemy plane dropped one bomb off the port bow of the *APc-12*; releasing the ordnance on its third run after first making two passes over the ships. The plane was thought to be a reconnaissance aircraft capable of carrying only a single bomb. Three days later, it made a similar attack, dropping one bomb a hundred feet off the port quarter of the cargo ship *Etamin* (AK-93), bound for Cape Sudest from Cape Cretin under escort by the *APc-12* and sub-chasers *PC-1131* and *SC-736*. There was no resultant damage from either of the attacks.[3]

Two months later, the *APc-13* entered Borgen Bay on 19 April 1944 and moored alongside the light cruiser *Nashville* (CL-43) aboard which MacArthur and his staff was embarked. The ship's commanding officer requested that the coastal transport take the general ashore, but these orders were subsequently changed and the *APc-13* instead proceeded to the entrance of the bay to assist the departing *Nashville* to clear the reef at night. The small coastal transport left the bay four days later with twelve Japanese prisoners under Marine guard aboard. Later that same day, 22 April, the *APc-13* arrived at Langemak Harbor, New Guinea and made up alongside the miscellaneous auxiliary *Goldstar* (AG-12). After discharging her prisoners to the former cargo ship, she shaped a course east-southeast for Milne Bay.[4]

ADMIRALTY ISLAND LANDINGS

> Within a week after the initial landing the First Cavalry Division had buried a Jap[anese] for each cavalryman landed on D-Day, with estimated total garrison of between 4000 and 5000 troops.
>
> Commander Attack Group reporting on the Admiralty Islands operation, which was launched with a "reconnaissance in force" at Los Negros Island after an ineffective air reconnaissance had revealed no evidence of human activity. This misconception was discounted two days before the assault when Army scouts, who had gone ashore after being dropped off by a Catalina seaplane, reported that the area was "lousy with Japs."[5]

The capture and utilization of the powerful Japanese base at Rabaul, located on the northeast coast of New Britain, had been the main objective of Operation WATCHTOWER (which had opened with the landings at Guadalcanal in August 1942). However, after Allied movement up the New Guinea coast and finally into New Britain, the enemy stronghold still had close to 100,000 defenders. The garrison also had enough munitions, weapons, provisions, and supplies to withstand a long siege while inflicting large numbers of casualties on Allied invasion forces. Thus, the decision was made to bypass Rabaul and to instead, leap into the Admiralty Islands, which were ideally situated to develop facilities necessary to assist in isolating Rabaul and to support the approach to the Philippines. Manus, the largest island in the group—spanning approximately 49 miles from east to west and 16 miles from north to south—offered ample space for military installations as well as Seeadler Harbor on its northeast coast, which could accommodate a task force. Los Negros Island, which located adjacent to Manus formed the eastern half of the harbor, had sufficient flat land to construct an airfield that would enable the Allies to deny the Japanese access to the Bismarck Archipelogo and to dominate a 1,000-mile square of neighboring ocean whose corners were Bougainville, Truk, the Palaus, and Biak.⁶

Map 13-1

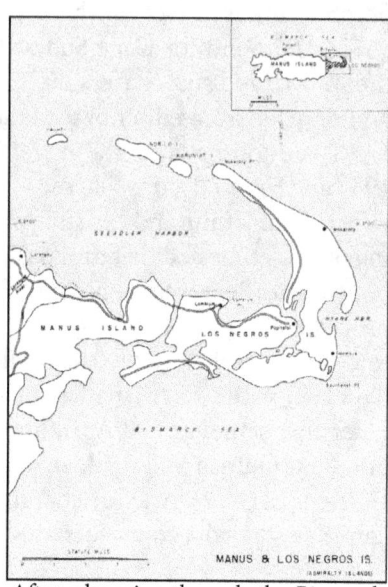

After advancing through the Bismarck Archipelago, the Allies bypassed the Japanese stronghold at Rabaul and leapt into the Admiralty Islands; ideally located to assist in isolating Rabaul and to support the approach to the Philippines. Source: www.ibiblio.org/hyperwar/USN/Building_Bases/maps/bases2-p297.jpg

In the late afternoon of 27 February 1944, an attack group comprised of three ADPs and nine DDs sailed from Cape Sudest, New Guinea for the Admiralty Islands, preceded by the light cruisers *Nashville* (CL-43) and *Phoenix* (CL-46) and four destroyers. The group of ships arrived off Hyane Harbor, on the eastern shore of Los Negros Island, shortly after 0700 on 29 February. A landing inside the harbor would facilitate the seizure of Momote airstrip which touched its south shore. Entry into the harbor, however, required negotiating a narrow, treacherous 50-yard wide entrance, and its shore except near the airstrip was a mass of tangled mangrove. Planners had chosen the small, nearly landlocked Hyane, instead of the much larger and more accommodating Seeadler Harbor—some 15 miles long by 4 wide—or good beaches on the southeast coast of Los Negros, because the site was not an obvious choice and thus would likely not be as heavily defended.⁷

Embarked in the ships of the attack group were one squadron of the 1st Army Cavalry Division and detachments totaling 1026 troops; 170 each in the *Humphreys* (APD-12), *Brooks* (APD-10), and *Sands* (APD-13) and the remainder in the nine DDs averaging 57 per destroyer. Following standard pre-landing aerial bombing and naval shore bombardment to soften up the enemy, the APDs proceeded to the Transport Area approximately 5,000 yards from the harbor entrance. From this position the entire assault force landed in twelve LCP(R)s; three waves of four boats each. Commander Attack Group, Rear Adm. William M. Fechteler, USN described the ensuing action:

> Enemy machine gun fire was opened on the landing boats, which maneuvered radically as they stood in. Machine gun fire and heavier shore batteries opened on the destroyers, and on the *PHOENIX* group to the south. One battery, . . . on the southeastern tip of LOS NEGROS, later proved to be a 4.7" naval gun. . . . Close support was rendered by the destroyers, which moved in to within less than a mile of the shore as the landings progressed. Sporadic but inaccurate fire broke out from the beach each moment the bombardment slackened.

A scheduled strike by Army Air Force B25 bombers and surface bombardment enabled the landing craft to round the southern point of the harbor and make the shore. No opposition was encountered on the beach, and by 0950 the assault force had captured the airstrip and began to establish a perimeter around it.⁸

The foul weather greatly assisted the unmounted waterborne troopers. At 0945, heavy rain began to fall making supporting ship gunnery more difficult, but also providing sufficient cover for the landing to continue. If the visibility decreasing to 1,000 yards had not prevented Japanese gunfire from being effective, it is unlikely it could have been completely silenced by the destroyers outside the harbor. The landing force thus encountered little enemy opposition during daylight on D-Day, but was heavily attacked that night and on the succeeding one. The commander of the landing force later stated that support of the destroyers, which had remained on the scene and provided gunfire support, was his salvation.⁹

The following morning, 2 March, the first resupply echelon—six tank landing ships aboard which were a total of 3,550 Army and Navy men, support elements of the 1st Cavalry Division, and one naval construction battalion—arrived. The LSTs encountered mortar fire after entry into the harbor, but soon silenced it with 3-inch and automatic weapons fire, and sustained no casualties or damages. Two destroyer-minesweepers—the *Long* (DMS-12) and the *Hamilton* (DMS-18)—tried to enter Seeadler Harbor to sweep magnetic mines planted by Royal Australian Air Force Catalina seaplanes in May 1943. Enemy guns emplaced on islands flanking the entrance drove the ships off. On 4 March, cruisers of Task Force 74 shelled these positions with undetermined results. Two days later the destroyer *Nicholson* (DD-442) approached the entrance and, after delivering considerable shore bombardment, drew return enemy fire; sustaining a hit in the handling room of her No. 2 5-inch gun that killed three men and wounded two. The intrepid DD thereafter destroyed the two guns that had fired on her. On 8 March 1944, the minesweepers entered the harbor without opposition and lifting eleven "ship killers" swept a channel to the eastern end off Salami Plantation. The following month, smaller 136-foot wooden-hulled minesweepers—the *YMS-8, 10, 46, 47, 48,* and *51*—worked the remaining areas of the harbor denied the deeper draft DMSs.[10]

SMALL COASTAL TRANSPORT ARRIVES IN THE ADMIRALTIES

The *APc-7* departed Cape Sudest at midnight on 10 March 1944 to rendezvous at the four-mile buoy with a crash boat and a picket boat, and escort them to Cape Cretin. She and her charges joined Echelon H-3A—LSTs *452, 454, 456, 457, 459,* and *465*—escorted by five American destroyers, *Flusser* (DD-368), *Gillespie* (DD-609), *Hobby* (DD-610), *Kalk* (DD-611), and *Reid* (DD-369), and the Royal Australian destroyer HMAS *Warramunga* (I44), off Cape Cretin the following evening for passage to the Admiralty Islands. The night of 12 March, LSTs *456* and *457* left the formation at 2242 to proceed onward to Seeadler Harbor under escort by *Kalk* and *Hobby*. At a little after 0600 the following morning, the main body—the remaining four tank landing ships and the *APc-7*—entered Hayne Harbor while the destroyers, designated the fire support group for Army troops on Los Negros, patrolled to the east of the harbor entrance. After unloading, the six LSTs departed that evening with six destroyers for Cape Sudest.[11]

The *APc-7* remained behind, having been ordered to duty in the Admiralties to serve as headquarter ship for Capt. Karl J. Christoph,

USN, Landing Craft Control Officer, Admiralties. Her movement orders directed arrival at Seeadler Harbor, Manus Island, but hostilities delayed these plans. Captain Christoph shifted his flag at Hayne Harbor in the late afternoon of 13 March from the destroyer *Drayton* (DD-366) to the destroyer *Reid*, and later in the month to destroyers *Roe* (DD-418) and *Welles* (DD-628) before finally taking up residence aboard the wooden vessel in April. Resistance on Los Negros—from a strong enemy force that had withdrew into rugged terrain covered with dense jungle on the western part of the island—did not end until 24 March when the 5th Cavalry and 12th Cavalry prevailed in battle against the Japanese. On Manus Island, the enemy was largely obliterated the following day on 25 March, at a place called "Old Rossun" south of Lugos Mission. The *APc-7* received a battle star for the period 11-18 March 1944.[12]

After taking the Admiralty Islands—thereby finally breaking the Bismarck Barrier and contributing to sealing off Rabaul—MacArthur's next objective was to leapfrog the Japanese garrison at Wewak, New Guinea, into Hollandia, and to establish a new headquarters there.[13]

Map 13-2

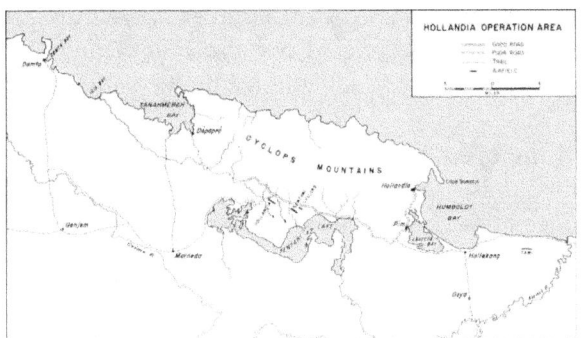

Following the Allies' capture of Hollandia on the northeast coast of New Guinea, MacArthur's general headquarters relocated there from Brisbane, Australia. The naval, air, and troop supply base would support the landings on Leyte, and, thereafter, virtually everybody and everything en route to the Philippines campaign would pass through Hollandia.
Source: http://www.ibiblio.org/hyperwar/USA/USA-P-Approach/maps/USA-P-Approach-2.jpg

Chapter 13
INVASION AND OCCUPATION OF AITAPE AND HOLLANDIA, NEW GUINEA

> *Convoy in gross disorder but finally underway in same direction by follow the leader tactics. No signal facilities being available with small harbor craft.*
>
> Commander, Escort Division 37 noting in a war diary entry on the difficulty in forming Echelon R-5—comprised of small Navy and Army vessels—for movement from Finch Harbor to Aitape and Hollandia, New Guinea, in support of the assault and occupation of these areas in April 1944.[14]

On 22 April 1944, the Allies launched the largest amphibious operation yet carried out in the Southwest Pacific involving over 200 ships. It was intended to initiate the final stages of the isolation of Rabaul and involved concurrent landings at three locations on the northwest coast of New Guinea. The western landing took place at Tanahmerah Bay—about thirty miles to the northwest of Hollandia, the site of an enemy army and air force base—the central landing was thirty miles to the east in Humboldt Bay; and the eastern landing about ninety miles further eastward at Aitape. Hollandia, the name by which the entire area would become known to American forces, was a tiny settlement nestled at the head of Challenger Cove, an arm of Humboldt Bay and formerly the easternmost Dutch outpost in the Netherlands East Indies.[15]

The objective of the operation was to seize and occupy the Tanahmerah Bay-Humboldt Bay-Aitape areas, and to establish at Aitape minor air and naval facilities, and in the Humboldt Bay-Tanahmerah Bay areas a major airbase, minor naval facilities, and an intermediate supply base for the purpose of supporting further operations to the westward. Rear Admiral Barbey commanded the overall attack force and the attack group at Tamahmerah Bay, Rear Admiral Fechteler the attack group at Humboldt Bay, and Capt. Albert G. Nobel, USN, that at Aitape. All the landings were a complete surprise which—following the intense pre-assault air and naval bombardment that broke the back of any resistance—eliminated Japanese opposition, resulting in practically no casualties during the landings. The enemy at Humboldt Bay retired into the hills and a party at Aitape left their defenses prior to the assault. Both Aitape airfields were captured by 22 April, and fighter operations commenced two days later. The airfields at Hollandia were taken thereafter, on 26 April, and one strip was ready for use at month's end.[16]

On 26 April, Echelon R-5 formed off Finch Harbor, New Guinea, for escort by four destroyer escorts and three patrol frigates—*Eichenberger* (DE-202), *El Paso* (PF-41), *James E. Craig* (DE-201), *Neuendorf* (DE-200), *Ogden* (PF-39), *Van Buren* (PF-42), and *Whitehurst* (DE-634)—up the New Guinea coast to Aitape and Hollandia. The *APc-2*, fleet tug *Sonoma* (AT-12), and the tank landing ship *LST-201* took positions as column leaders, and the remaining vessels of the echelon, seven Army "F Ships": *F-55, F-73, F-78, F-93, F-126, F-127,* and *F-128*; four Army harbor tugs: *WT-1, 33, 36,* and *63,* and the *TP-246* fell in behind in the formation. All of the ships, except for the escort vessels, and the *Sonoma* and *LST-201*, had small boat ways and dock sections in tow astern. The *APc-2* was towing a ninety-pontoon PT boat dry dock, per orders of Comdr. Morton C. Mumma Jr., USN, the commander PT Boats Seventh Fleet (Task Group 70.1).[17]

This may have been the first operation in which a Navy "Pacific island hopper," the *APc-2*, operated with newly constructed Army island hoppers, in this case the group of seven 99-foot steel-hulled freight ships. If the craft of the Catboat Flotilla which MacArthur employed along the New Guinea coast were the initial island hoppers, and the Navy's APcs and YPs the second generation of small cargo vessels, the large numbers of Army freight and freight-supply ships now arriving in the Pacific were the final phase. A lot of wear accrues to vessels during Pacific crossings, and some of these ships were dispatched to the theater before all construction-related problems could be identified and corrected.[18]

Such was the case of the 99-foot U.S. Army freight ship *F-14*, newly built by Sturgeon Bay Shipbuilding in Sturgeon Bay, Wisconsin. While in passage to the Southwest Pacific, she departed Honolulu on 31 March 1944 in company with another freight ship, the *F-117*, and an Army small tug, *ST-381*, bound for Funa Futi. The *F-14* became separated from the other two ships that night, but transited independently as routed until 7 April when, about 420 miles north of Canton Atoll, her main reduction gears were stripped. Canton—whose shape when viewed from above resembled that of a pork chop—was located roughly halfway between Hawaii and Fiji. Completely disabled by machinery derangement, the freight ship and her sixteen officers and men drifted for thirty days, during which no land, vessels or aircraft were sighted, and all efforts to send a radio message of her plight were of no avail. The wind and sea deposited the freight ship off Tabiteuea Island in the Gilberts on 7 May and she anchored in the Taponteaba area.[19]

Except for a five-man watch maintained aboard ship, the captain, Mr. Owen, and crew lived ashore in native villages until in early June, when the M.V. *John Williams*, a London Missionary Society supply ship, sighted the anchored freighter during one of her periodic calls to the island. On 5 June, a "Dumbo" rescue plane from Apamama Atoll, located to the north-northwest in the Gilberts, about eighty miles south of Tarawa, arrived and took the Chief Engineer to Tarawa to arrange for towing services. The *APc-108* was sent to Tabiteuea and arrived on scene two days later. Sighting the freight ship anchored in a small bight on the windward side of a reef off the island, she positioned herself ahead and towed the *F-14* clear. During this rescue operation, an officer swam to shore through the reef to locate the captain and the remaining members of the crew, all merchant mariners. They were brought off the island using the *F-14*'s lifeboat which was ashore. The *APc-108* arrived with the ship in tow at Betio Anchorage, Tarawa on 9 June.[20]

The seven freighters of Echelon R-5—which departed Finch Harbor on 26 April 1944 for transit up the New Guinea coast—were also operated by Merchant Marine crews. One of the other vessels was the *TP-246*, assigned to the Army's Small Ships Section for use as a tug. Formerly the *Sea Tern*, she was one of the many civilian or commercially-owned trawlers, tow boats, purse seiners, or sailing schooners of under 100 feet in length taken by the Army early in the war and classified as "small freight and passenger vessels." Commander, Escort Division 37, expressed (in the preceding quoted material below the chapter title) his frustration regarding the lack of a signaling ability aboard the ships. However, it is unlikely that masters of Army ships would be familiar with formation maneuvers performed regularly by Navy surface combatants.[21]

During the transit the convoy was slowed by breakdowns and parting of towing gear in heavy seas. The group stood into Humboldt Bay a little before noon on 3 May, and the *APc-2* delivered the bulky dry dock to the motor torpedo boat tender *Oyster Bay* (AGP-6). The 311-foot steel ship was a converted small seaplane tender that would tend PT boat squadrons in the forward area through the war's end. That evening, the coastal transport went to general quarters in response to a Condition Red alert, and again at a little past midnight. The sky over Hollandia was still an area of action, and air raids were frequent. Mopping up operations against remnants of enemy land forces continued until 6 June, when the operation, which had cost 152 servicemen killed and missing and 1,057 wounded, was officially declared closed.[22]

On 5 May 1944, the *APc-2* stood out of the bay at 1845 as part of a convoy bound for Dreger Bay. Shortly before midnight the convoy went to general quarters and at 0015, crewmen aboard the coastal transport observed what might have been a segment of a burning aircraft fall into the sea on the starboard quarter of the formation. The group reached its destination around noon on 7 May. Two days later, a large, approximately three-ton refrigerator was placed on the fantail of the *APc-2* per orders of Commander Mumma to enable the ship to provision motor torpedo boat squadrons in extreme forward areas. She left the next day for Saidor, a coastal town 110 miles further up the New Guinea northeast coast, with cargo and foodstuffs. Mumma had previously acquired operational control of the *APc-20*, which mostly towed fuel barges back and forth between Dreger Harbor and advance PT fueling points. When she was not thus employed, she hauled supplies between bases, as did Army freight ships. As the supply lines to PT boat bases lengthened due to the movement of the Allies forward, and the number of motor torpedo boats increased, it became necessary to acquire more cargo ships to carry spare parts and equipment between bases. At the time of the Aitape and Hollandia landings, commander Motor Torpedo Boat Squadron 21, Comdr. Selman S. Bowling, had obtained from the Sixth U.S. Army the permanent assignment of four 99-foot diminutive steel-hulled freighters, each with a cargo capacity of about 100 tons. For the rest of the war these ships plied back and forth between bases; making at best eight knots.[23]

Motor torpedo boats began operating from Nom Plantation, the site of their base on Saidor, following the arrival there on 4 March 1944 of Squadron 24, and their numbers grew when Motor Torpedo Boat Squadron 10 reported on 28 April. The Allies had acquired Saidor on 2 January, when the 32nd Army Infantry Division landed on the north coast of New Guinea and against little opposition seized its harbor and airstrip. These facilities were ideally situated to enable Allied forces to cover the Dampier and Vitiaz Straits, and Saidor would also serve as a stepping stone towards Madang, which lay further north, the ultimate objective of MacArthur's Huon Peninsula campaign. This goal was met on 24 April, when the Australian 8th Infantry Brigade pursuing remnants of the Japanese 20th Division entered Madang unopposed. Saidor remained in use through the end of June 1944, longer than any other advance PT base in eastern New Guinea due to the heavy enemy barge traffic in the area. However, good hunting aside, a strongly defended coastline offered dangers other than those ordinarily posed by barges and floatplanes; PTs drew shore fire at least sixty-four times in March, April, and May.[24]

Hollandia was quickly developed into an important naval, air, and troop-supply base, and MacArthur's general headquarters and those of the Allied Land, Naval, and Air Forces relocated from Brisbane to Hollandia on 8 September 1944. The base would supply the landings on Leyte, and virtually everybody and everything en route to the Philippines campaign would pass through Hollandia. In addition to the *APc-2*, *APc-4*, and *APc-9*—which were each awarded a battle star for the Aitape-Humboldt Bay-Tanahmerah Bay operation—many other Pacific Island hoppers would base or stop at Hollandia while carrying out their duties. Among this group of unsung diminutive cargo vessels were Navy small coastal transports and some yard patrol craft (YP), and larger numbers of Army freight-supply ships, as well as some freight ships (F), large tugs (LT) and a few harbor tugs and small freight and passenger vessels (TP).[25]

14

Capture and Occupation of Guam

My aim is to get the troops ashore standing up.
Comment by Rear Adm. Richard L. Conolly, commander Southern Attack Force (Task Force 53) during the invasion of Guam, who had earned the nickname "Close-in Conolly" for his insistence on having his naval gunfire support ships firing from stations very close to the beaches.[1]

As MacArthur pushed up the northeast coast of New Guinea—after having finally pierced the Bismarcks Barrier—towards the Philippines, Nimitz's Central Pacific forces drove westward along a separate, and soon to become the principal, route toward Japan. After taking Tarawa and Makin in the Gilberts, Navy amphibious forces captured Kwajalein and Eniwetok in the Marshalls and moved into the Marianas to launch Operation FORAGER. The purpose of the operation planned against the Mariana Islands was to neutralize Japanese bases in the Central Pacific, to support the Allied drive to retake the Philippines, and to gain island airfields for a strategic bombing campaign against Japan. A portion of the operation was an assault against Peleliu—an island in the westernmost cluster (today the Palau archipelago) of the Caroline Islands—which would be fought between September and November 1944.

The Marianas offensive began with the 2nd and 4th Marine Divisions, and the 27th Army Division landing on Saipan. While these assault forces and the enemy ashore fought the Battle of Saipan between 15 June and 9 July 1944, the Japanese Navy's Combined Fleet sortied to engage the U.S. Navy fleet supporting the landings. In the ensuing 19-21 June Battle of the Philippine Sea, the American battle force defeated the Japanese in what would be the greatest carrier battle of the war. Following the loss of two carriers, the *Shokaku* and *Taiho*, 346 planes, and an associated large numbers of pilots, Japanese naval air was unable for the duration of the war to engage Allied forces with parity. This reality resulted in Japanese leadership turning to the use of suicide planes.[2]

Following heavy fighting, U.S. forces took Saipan on 9 July and then executed landings on Guam and Tinian in the Marianas. The Allied plan for the invasion of the Marianas called for heavy preliminary bombardment, first by carrier aircraft and planes based in the Marshall Islands to the east, then, once local air superiority was gained, close bombardment by battleships. This convention was used at Guam. On 5 July, a series of air strikes began and three days later naval bombardment. The bombing and naval gunfire steadily increased as additional supporting units arrived in the area. Battleships *Idaho* (BB-24), *New Mexico* (BB-40), and *Pennsylvania* (BB-38) arrived off Guam on 12 July; the *Colorado* (BB-45) on 14 July; and the *California* (BB-44), and the *Tennessee* (BB-43) on 19 July. Also present were the cruiser *Indianapolis* (CA-35), aboard which Adm. Raymond A. Spruance, commanding the Fifth Fleet, was embarked, as well as the light cruisers *Birmingham* (CL-62), *Cleveland* (CL-55), *Honolulu* (CL-48), *Montpelier* (CL-57), and *St. Louis* (CL-49).[3]

From 17 to 20 July 1944, Underwater Demolition Teams Three, Four, and Six worked on clearing obstacles and improving beach approaches. Obstructions found on the Agat landing beaches consisted mainly of palm log cribs filled with coral, connected by 3/8-inch to 1/2-inch wire cable. Off the Asan beaches, obstructions were largely wire cages—four feet square and three to four feet high—filled with cemented coral and spaced five feet apart. Barbed wire on beaches was sparse, poorly installed and considered to offer no obstruction to LVTs (tracked landing vehicles), but was removed where practical. By midnight on 20 July, the frogmen had cleared all obstructions from the reefs in front of the assault beaches at Agat and Asan. Agat, the southern landing area stretching from Bangi Island to Apaca Point, had been strategically chosen to help secure Orote Peninsula to the north. The peninsula hosted an airfield and bounded Apra Harbor, a deep-water port on the western side of the island. The primary landing site, however, was at Asan, which lay northeast of the harbor on Guam's western shore.[4]

Capture and Occupation of Guam {157}

Map 14-1

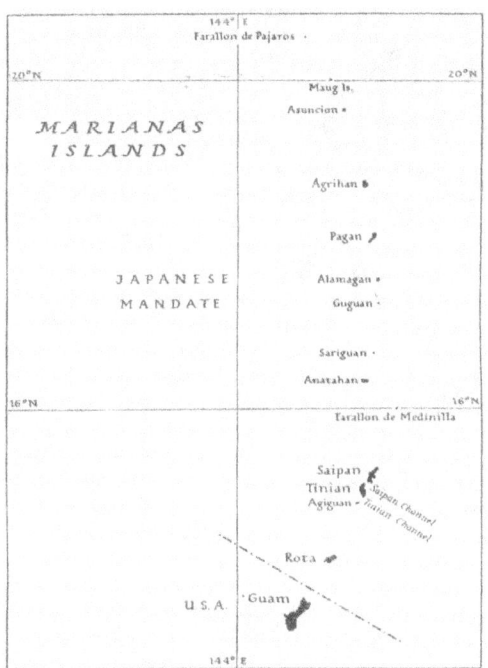

Guam had fallen to Japanese forces at war's commencement, on 10 December 1941, because America's defense of the Philippines was negligible without ownership of nearby Saipan and Tinian, which Japan had acquired in 1921 along with the remainder of the Marianas, except for Guam.
Source: http://www.lib.utexas.edu/maps/historical/pacific_islands_1943_1945/marianas_islands.jpg

On the morning of 21 July, W-day (the designation of D-day on Guam) the 4th and 22nd Regiments of the 1st Provisional Marine Brigade stormed ashore at Agat. The 305th Regimental Combat Team, a part of the 77th Army Infantry Division, landed in mid-afternoon that same day. The fighting at Agat was severe, particularly during the first night as the Japanese 38th Regiment launched a major counterattack. At Asan, the Marine assault forces crossed the reef offshore and landed, opposed by the Japanese 320th Independent Infantry Battalion and naval troops manning the coastal defense guns. The plan was to fight between Adelup and Asan Points, referred to as "the devil's horns." From east to west, two battalions of the 3rd Marine Regiment landed on Beach Red 1, one battalion of the 3rd Marines on Beach Red 2, three battalions of the 21st Marines came ashore on Green Beach, in the middle, and three battalions of the 9th Marines on Blue Beach adjacent to Asan Point. Against heavy Japanese defenses, it took until 10 August to eliminate all organized resistance on Guam, and 1,866 servicemen were either killed in action or died of wounds during twenty-one days of combat. Japanese casualties were estimated to be over 10,900.[5]

Present among the fleet off Guam on W-Day were the *APc-46* and the seaplane tender *Williamson* (AVP-15), a converted flush-deck

Map 14-2

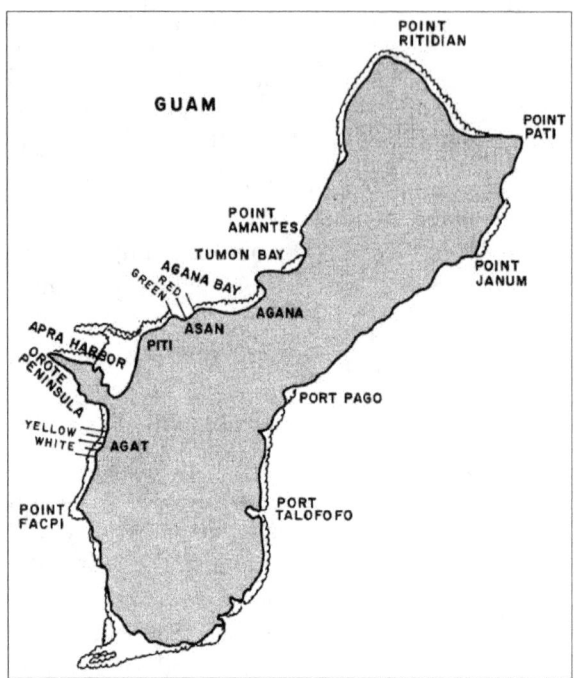

During the Allied invasion and occupation of Guam in 1944, the *APc-46* served as a seaplane tender, rearming and refueling aircraft, off Yellow Beach during the assault phase and later in Apra Harbor.
Source: http://www.ibiblio.org/hyperwar/USN/ACTC/maps/actc-p926.jpg

Clemson-class destroyer. The latter steel-hulled ship had recently been fitted with a rig for the under way fueling of floatplanes from battleships and cruisers. Observation of the fall of gun rounds was critical to surface gunnery in World War II, particularly during the early years before radar was perfected, and battleships often had to fire on targets far beyond visual range. To assist them in directing gunfire, BBs carried up to four Vought OS2U Kingfisher floatplanes aboard. Cruisers, which had shorter range guns, used Curtis-Wright SOC Seagull floatplanes primarily to locate enemy surface ships and submarines, but the small biplanes could also "spot" the fall of rounds. The Seagulls had folding outer wings to enable their storage in aircraft hangers aboard the cruisers. Since battleships lacked hangers, Kingfishers had rigid non-folding wings. Accommodations were, however, not an issue. The aircraft were simply parked on launch rails when not used.[6]

The *Williamson* was kept busy in the days leading up to the landing on Guam refueling floatplanes in order that the parent battleships and cruisers could continue shore bombardment unencumbered by the necessity to retrieve and refuel the aircraft. Following her arrival at Guam on 21 July 1944, the *APc-46* joined the *Williamson* to form Task Unit 53.2.2, the "seaplane re-servicing unit." Before dusk that first day, the small coastal transport rejoined the ships of LST Flotilla Sixteen, Group 46, Tractor Group Four—with whom she had transited to Guam—for night retirement well clear of the island. The designation "Tractor Group" referred to the LVTs (Landing Vehicle, Tracked) carried aboard the tank landing ships. Called amphibious tractors, the LVTs, which were originally intended solely as cargo carriers for ship-to-shore operations, had evolved into assault troop and fire support vehicles. Per her orders, the *APc-46* arrived off Agat Beach each morning following night retirement and remained well clear of the shore while the *Williamson* re-serviced seaplanes.[7]

On 25 July, this convention changed. The commander of the seaplane unit boarded the *APc-46*, and directed the small ship to proceed to Agat Beach, where she anchored off Yellow Beach 2 in eight fathoms of water. She was joined later that day by the *Williamson*, which had been engaged in planting seaplane moorings off the beach. Six mooring buoys were laid near the *APc-46* to create with her serving as headquarters ship, an improvised seaplane base. The *Williamson* anchored nearby to act as the terminal vessel. Taking up her new duties, the small coastal transport re-serviced eight planes the following day. That night, Japanese 37mm shore batteries began shelling the beach a little before midnight, forcing the vessels to clear the area. The *APc-46* lay off the Transport Area that night, returning to the anchorage the following morning and resuming her duties. A few days later the *APc-46* and *Williamson* received orders on 31 July to shift the improvised seaplane base to the southeast area of Apra Harbor, which had fallen two days earlier following the capture of Orote Peninsula by the First Provisional Marine Brigade.[8]

The *Williamson* spent the bulk of her time over next several days—until departure on 16 August for Eniwetok Atoll—patrolling off Orote Peninsula, leaving the *APc-46* to her duties as seaplane base. The wooden ship had been equipped with communications equipment to

Photo 14-1

USS *APc-46* at anchor off Guadalcanal, circa 1944. (Courtesy of Tom De Mott Jr., Navsource: www.navsource.org/archives/09/23/092304601.jpg)

contact planes on 6,500 or 6,970 KHz for landing directions or special instruction and, upon their arrival, facilities to service seaplanes. To deliver fuel, ammunition, and personnel, she had one Bowser boat with 1,500 gallons fuel capacity, one aircraft rearming boat, and one aircraft personnel boat. The *APc-46* continued her aviation service at Guam into October 1944, during which she earned a battle star for the period 21 July to 5 August.[9]

The remaining phase of Operation FORAGER, the assault and occupation of Palau—located to the southwest of Guam and north of New Guinea—commenced in mid-September. In order to secure the flank, and also gain airfields for American forces preparing to invade the Philippines, U.S. Marine and Army forces landed on Peleliu and Angaur in the Palau Islands on 15 and 17 September, respectively. The fighting was protracted on both islands, particularly on bloody Peleliu, where after heavy and intense combat the island was finally secured on 27 November 1944. At Peleliu, the 1st Marine Division and the 81st Army Infantry Division collectively suffered 1,794 killed and 8,010 wounded or missing—the highest casualty rate for U.S. military personnel of any battle in the Pacific War.[10]

15

Support for Motor Torpedo Boat Squadrons

> *A relatively small fleet of such vessels, manned by crews thoroughly familiar with every foot of the coast line and surrounding waters, and carrying, in the torpedo, a definite threat against large ships, will have distinct effect in compelling any hostile force to approach cautiously and by small detachments.*
>
> > Statement made before the war by Gen. Douglas MacArthur, who was an advocate of PT boats, in *American Caesar: Douglas MacArthur 1880—1964*. However, experience demonstrated that PTs were more effective against barges than warships, and a majority of the boats were accordingly retrofitted with machine guns and larger 20mm, 37mm, or 40mm cannons.

With the ending of the New Guinea campaign and the beginning of operations in the Philippines, plans were made to establish both an advance base and a large operating, repair, and supply base for PTs in the Leyte Gulf area and to move all available squadrons and floating equipment there as rapidly as possible. Construction was begun on PT Advance Base 5 at Tinaogan Point in San Juanico Strait, the narrow strip of water separating Leyte from Samar, but never completed due to poor conditions. The site was characterized by muddy hillsides and flat areas alike that were detrimental to morale for the squadrons based there. Things improved when a Seabee battalion vacated the camp they had built for themselves on a knoll just below the site of the PT base and the advance base was moved there. Bobon Point, on the Philippine Sea in northern Samar, was chosen as the site for the other much larger operating, repair, and supply base.[1]

The first equipment for PT Base 17 did not arrive at Bobon Point until 26 January 1945, and the preceding period from 21 October on through January was characterized by heavy rain, typhoons and frequent air raids that interfered greatly with the servicing of PT boats by tenders. The advance base was a sea of mud, and two typhoons, heavy enemy air oppositions, the Battle of Surigao Strait, and operations against enemy surface ships in the Camotes Sea had built up a backlog of repair work. All repairs and servicing were done by tenders anchored in San Juanico Strait or in San Pedro Bay, Leyte, and by floating equipment—work shop barges, crane barges, radar barges, fuel barges, and dry docks—anchored near the advance base.[2]

It was also necessary during this period, in addition to maintaining current operations, to stage PT boats and supporting equipment through Leyte for the Mindoro, Ormoc, Lingayen Gulf, and Subic Bay operations. Moreover, fewer motor torpedo boats were available; one tender and three squadrons of PTs had been transferred temporarily to the operational control of commander LCI(L) Flotilla 24 for a special operation from Mindoro. The availability of PT Base 17 would have helped immeasurably, but the facility was of little value to motor torpedo boat squadrons until March 1945. The floating equipment and the four F ships and two FS ships assigned to the task group were the saving features during this period.[3]

To supply advance bases, commander Motor Torpedo Boats 7th Fleet (Task Group 70.1) operated what amounted to a private shipping line, using four F ships acquired earlier from the Army and two larger freighters, *FS-167* and *FS-170*, recently assigned to the task group by the commander Service Force, Seventh Fleet. At the time of the Aitape and Hollandia landings in April 1944—as the number of PT boats increased and supply lines lengthened—it became imperative to acquire more cargo vessels to carry spare parts and other special PT equipment between bases. Comdr. Selman S. Bowling, USN (who had relieved Comdr. Morton C. Mumma, Jr. as commander Motor Torpedo Boats 7th Fleet) had obtained from the Sixth Army four F-ships, little freighters with a capacity of about 100 tons each. These diminutive vessels plied back and forth between PT bases, making a maximum speed of 8 knots. The larger, 180-foot *FS-167* and *FS-170* earned battle stars for the periods 13 September—15 November and 28 September—15 November 1944, respectively, for "duty in connection with motor torpedo boats operations" in western New Guinea. The *FS-167* received a second battle star for the period 23-29 November for her participation in landings on Leyte.[4]

Photo 15-1

Assigned to the 2nd Engineer Special Brigade, the USA *FS-175* was the same type 180-foot steel-hulled Army freight-supply ship as the *FS-167* and *FS-170*. (Courtesy of the 2nd Engineer Special Brigade.org website: www.2esb.org/04_History/Book/Chapter_24.htm)

Another freight-supply ship, the *FS-255*, earned a battle star for western New Guinea operations at Morotai from 1 December 1944 to 9 January 1945. MacArthur had in July 1944 selected the Japanese held island of Morotai—located in the Netherlands East Indies about midway between the Philippines and the western tip of New Guinea—as the location for air fields and naval facilities needed to support the planned liberation of Mindanao. United States and Australian forces landed on Morotai on 15 September 1944, and secured their objective in two weeks, but the Japanese, mindful of the strategic importance of the island, sent reinforcements to the island, and intermittent fighting continued until the end of the war. The fighting would have been worse, had not the U.S. Navy quickly established a PT boat base at Morotai on 16 September when the tenders *Mobjack* (AGP-7) and *Oyster Bay* (AGP-6) arrived with Motor Torpedo Boat Squadrons 9, 10, 18, and 33, and their forty-one boats. The PT boats' primary mission was to prevent the Japanese from moving troops from nearby Halmahera to Morotai by blockading the 12-mile-wide strait between the two islands. The seizure of Morotai ultimately proved to be even more advantageous than MacArthur had envisioned. Allied forces invaded Leyte Island in the central Philippines in late October. The air bases at Morotai were the closest Allied airstrips to Leyte and from there, fighters and bombers flew strikes against targets in the southern Philippines and Netherland East Indies in support of the landings at Leyte.[5]

Map 15-1

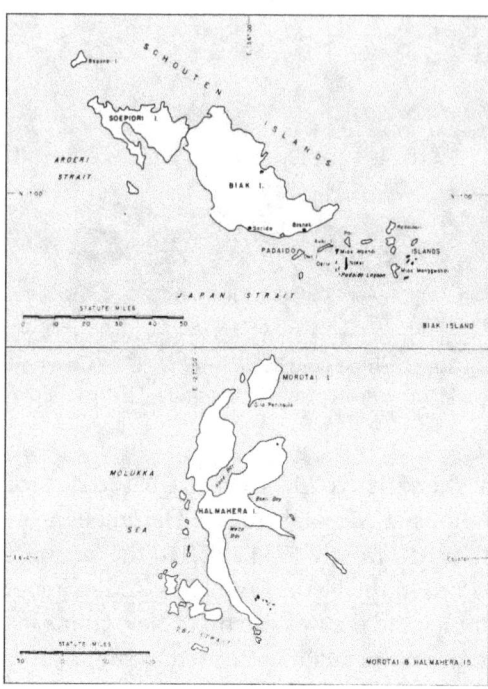

Allied forces captured air fields and naval facilities on Morotai Island to support the Philippine Islands Campaign, but the Japanese sent reinforcements and fighting continued until war's end.
Source: www.ibiblio.org/hyperwar/USN/Building_Bases/maps/bases2-p309.jpg

CONTRIBUTIONS OF PT BOATS IN THE SOUTHWEST PACIFIC

When combat patrols from the last operating base in New Guinea—PT Boat Base 21 on Mios Woendi, a small triangular island approximately one mile long and about 3,000 feet across in Western (Dutch) New Guinea,—were secured on 16 November 1944, it had been less than twenty-three months since the *PT-121* and *122* had made their first patrol from Porlock Harbor in Papua. Task Group 70.1 had expanded from one small tender and six boats to eight tenders and fourteen squadrons of motor torpedo boats, supported in forward and far forward areas by Navy small coastal transports and Army freight and freight-supply ships. During this period, PT boats engaged in almost nightly action along 1,500 miles of the coastline of New Guinea, and along the coasts of New Britain and the Admiralties. Their efforts had wrought a terrible toll on the Japanese. Littered along the coastlines was the wreckage of hundreds of barges, whose loss denied cargos of supplies, food, and munitions to thousands of the enemy ashore. In the case of barges employed as transports, there were fewer Japanese soldiers to fight Allied ground forces on the beach and in the jungle.[6]

16

Leyte and Mindoro Landings

> *Should we lose in the Philippines operations, even though the fleet should be left, the shipping lane to the south would be completely cut off so that the fleet, if it should come back to Japanese waters, could not obtain its fuel supply. If it should remain in southern waters, it could not receive supplies of ammunition and arms. There would be no sense in saving the fleet at the expense of the loss of the Philippines.*
>
> Adm. Soemu Toyoda, Imperial Japanese Navy, discussing Vice Adm. Takeo Kurita's mission to destroy completely the transports in Leyte Bay following the American invasion of the Philippines, and why there were no restrictions as to the damage that his force might take.[1]

The Sixth Army went ashore at Leyte Island on 20 October, 1944, two months and two years after the first landings were conducted in the Guadalcanal area of the Solomon Islands. During the intervening period, Halsey's South Pacific Forces had occupied or neutralized the remainder of the Solomon Islands, and MacArthur's Southwest Pacific Forces had forged a route through the New Guinea/New Britain area. Nimitz's Central Pacific Forces had taken the Gilberts, the Marshalls, the Marianas, and the Southern Palau Islands. The Japanese counter-attacked in the Battle of the Philippine Sea, fought between the First Mobile Fleet and American Fifth Fleet from 19 to 21 June 1944. In what one American aviator termed "The Great Marianas Turkey Shoot," the U.S. Navy destroyed three enemy aircraft carriers—the *Hijo*, *Shokaku*, and *Taiho*—some 480 planes, and nearly as many aviators. The devastating loss left the Japanese with virtually no carrier-based aircraft or experienced pilots for the forthcoming Battle of Leyte Gulf.[2]

Chapter 16

The naval force, comprised of units of the American 3rd and 7th Fleets, assembled for the invasion of Leyte was not quite as large as the one that had taken part in June 1944 in the invasion of Normandy, but it had more striking power. Embarked aboard the assault vessels were the Sixth Army's Tenth and Fourteenth Corps. The weather at the entrance to Leyte Gulf at daybreak on 20 October was cloudy with altostratus and partial swelling cumulus, a visibility to seaward of twelve miles, and light winds from the southeast. Planners had been concerned that a typhoon might pass through the area and cause retirement or diversion of the forces en route from New Guinea. However, the conditions on "A-Day" were perfect as described by commander, Third Amphibious Force:

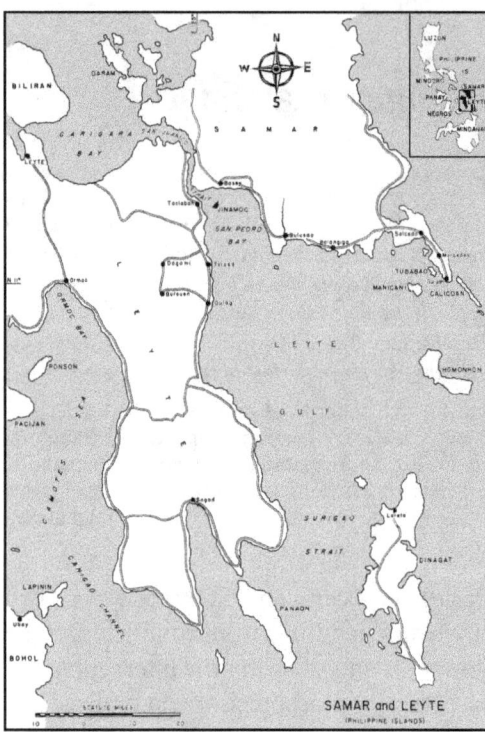

Map 16-1

Landings on Leyte Island launched the Allies Philippine Islands Campaign. During the ensuing Battle of Leyte Gulf, Japanese aircraft carried out organized kamikaze attacks for the first time.
Source: http://www.ibiblio.org/hyperwar/USN/Building_Bases/maps/bases2-p379.jpg

The assault proceeded on schedule following the preliminary bombardment by ships' gunfire and aircraft, a slight onshore tendency of the almost imperceptible wind conveniently drifting the smoke and dust of the bombardment off the beaches and into the interior. The airborne beach observer had made his required report earlier, but the report was unnecessary in this case due to the almost complete absence of surf.[3]

The landings at Tacloban, located in northeast Leyte on an inlet of the Leyte Gulf, and at Dulag, twenty-five miles to the southward, were made against little opposition. Naval historian Samuel Eliot Morison noted about the operation: "The Leyte landings were easy, compared with most amphibious operations in World War II—perfect weather, no surf, no mines or underwater obstacles, slight enemy resistance, mostly mortar fire." With this beginning, the liberation of the Philippines was off to a good start.[4]

Among the armada of ships that arrived off Leyte on 20 October was a group of five vessels—the Navy escort patrol craft *PCE(R)-848*, *PCE(R)-849*, and *PCE(R)-850*, the S.S. *Apache*, and the *FP-47*—designated as the "commander Army Headquarters Unit." A few months earlier, MacArthur had directed his chief signal officer, Maj. Gen. Spencer B. Akin, to establish a fleet command post to facilitate communications during complex land, sea, and air attacks. The unit was at Leyte to provide ship-to-shore and ship-to-ship communications for MacArthur's general headquarters and the Sixth Army Headquarters throughout the Leyte operation. The *FP-47* (later reclassified *FS-47*) served as the communications ship and the *Apache* as broadcast ship, while the PCE(R)s berthed the Army officers and men. The light cruiser *Nashville*—MacArthur's flagship—arrived at 1050 that morning with the Supreme Commander Southwest Pacific Area embarked. That afternoon, a motor whaleboat left the side of the *PCE(R)-848* with Akin and party to accompany MacArthur to Red Beach. Moments after he waded ashore and thus fulfilled his pledge to return to the Philippines, the general spoke with great emotion as he delivered a rousing speech to the Filipino people—transmitted in a radio address from the beachhead—enjoining them to drive the Japanese invaders from the islands:

> TO THE PEOPLE OF THE PHILIPPINES:
>
> I have returned. By the grace of Almighty God our forces stand again on Philippine soil—soil consecrated in the blood of our two peoples. We have come, dedicated and committed, to the task of destroying every vestige of enemy control over your daily lives, and of restoring, upon a foundation of indestructible, strength, the liberties of your people.

At my side is your President, Sergio Osmena, worthy successor of that great patriot, Manuel Quezon, with members of his cabinet. The seat of your government is now therefore firmly re-established on Philippine soil.

The hour of your redemption is here. Your patriots have demonstrated an unswerving and resolute devotion to the principles of freedom that challenges the best that is written on the pages of human history. I now call upon your supreme effort that the enemy may know from the temper of an aroused and outraged people within that he has a force there to contend with no less violent than is the force committed from without.

Rally to me. Let the indomitable spirit of Bataan and Corregidor lead on. As the lines of battle roll forward to bring you within the zone of operations, rise and strike. Strike at every favorable opportunity. For your homes and hearths, strike! For future generations of your sons and daughters, strike! In the name of your sacred dead, strike! Let no heart be faint. Let every arm be steeled. The guidance of divine God points the way. Follow in His Name to the Holy Grail of righteous victory!

Aboard the Army freight and passenger vessel *FP-47*, which was serving as a press ship, were war correspondents. They, and the ship's officers and crew, would witness in the ensuing days several attacks by conventional and kamikaze aircraft on other ships. The 114-foot wooden ship would also later serve in the Lingayen Gulf and at Manila during the Philippine Islands Campaign.[5]

The capture of Leyte was part of a strategy to isolate Japan from the countries it had occupied in Southeast Asia, and in particular, to deprive its forces and industries of vital oil supplies. Leyte Gulf was about forty miles wide east and west and about fifty miles long, and the southern part of the gulf was, in effect, a part of the Surigao Strait which formed a wide waterway between the Pacific and the Sulu Sea. Allied control of the Leyte Gulf area and San Bernardino Strait only 100 miles to the north would deny the Japanese all water routes between the Pacific and the South China Sea except via the northern end of Luzon Island, the economic and political center of the Philippines, being home to the country's capital city, Manila, on the southern end of Mindoro island.[6]

The lull following the lightly opposed Leyte landings was short-lived. After receiving word on 17 October of the presence of the

Map 16-2

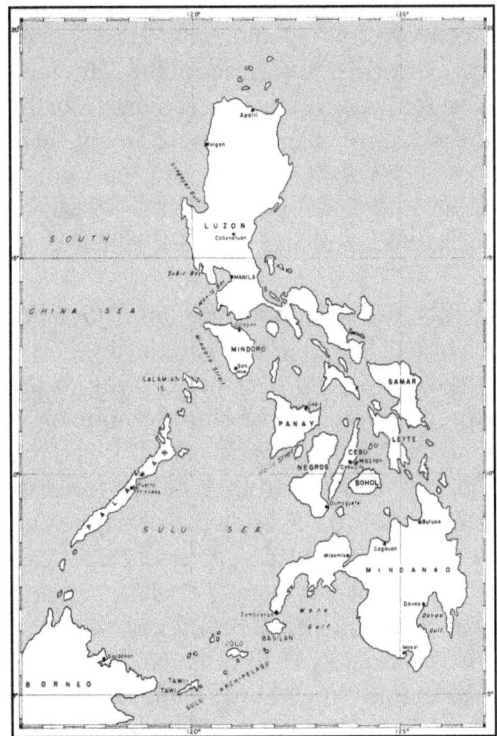

Philippine Islands.
Source: www.ibiblio.org/hyperwar/USN/Building
_Bases/maps/bases2-p376.jpg

advance American minesweeping and hydrographic group in the entrances to the Leyte Gulf, Adm. Soemu Toyoda, the commander-in-chief of the Combined Fleet issued the alert for SHO-1. This plan for a naval battle with the American fleet off Leyte was a part of the larger Operation SHO-GO, a defense plan against American advances toward Japan. Thus, as amphibious ships were unloading on assault beaches and the Sixth Army was extending the beachhead, Japanese naval forces were en route to Leyte Gulf to give battle.[7]

ECHELON L-5 TO LEYTE

In the mid-afternoon of 8 October 1944, many of the commanding officers or masters of the tugs that would comprise Echelon L-5 (of Task Force 77) to Leyte met at U.S. Army Services of Supply Headquarters at Hollandia to discuss the operation. Also in attendance was the commanding officer of the patrol frigate *Coronado* (PF-38), the single escort ship assigned to the convoy of Army and Navy tugs. One or more of the masters may have expressed concern about the Navy having assigned but a single escort for protection of the convoy. If so, the answer may have conveyed reassurance, such as, "Not to worry, there are plenty of Allied aircraft and combatant ships in the Leyte Gulf to deal with the threat." Of course, no one then knew that the Japanese would soon adapt the use of kamikaze planes to attack Allied shipping.[8]

The echelon departed Humboldt Bay at about 0800 on 10 October and formed a cruising disposition of five columns. The convoy—once joined by the Army large tugs *LT-131* and *225* that evening to the north of Tanahmerah, and three days later in the late afternoon of 13 October by the Army tug *LT-1* and Navy tugs *Hidatsa* (AT-102), *Lark* (ATO-168), and *Vireo* (ATO-144) arriving from Woendi—consisted of twenty-four vessels. In addition to the Navy patrol frigate and three tugs, there were twenty Army craft: the freight vessel *F-15*; three coastal tankers *Y-6*, *14*, and *20*; four harbor tugs *TP-1*, *124*, *128*, and *381*; and twelve large tugs *LT-1*, *129*, *131*, *134*, *225*, *229*, *231*, *455*, *633*, *634*, *635*, and *637*. The tugs had collectively 58 tows which slowed and rendered the ships less maneuverable. The fleet tug *Hidatsa* was particularly burdened. She had in tow astern of her: the gasoline barge *BK-07*, the crane barge No. 3, and a PT dry dock for Motor Torpedo Boat Squadron 12; a part of the equipment being forwarded to Leyte to establish a PT operating base.[9]

Photo 16-1

The USA *F-15*, one of the Army's 99-foot freighters, at anchor. (Courtesy of the 2nd Engineer Special Brigade.org website: www.2esb.org/04_History/Book/Chapter_24.htm)

Disposition of Ships in the Five-Column Formation

		Coronado		
Vireo (3 tows)				*Lark* (3 tows)
	Y-6	Y-14	Y-20	
LT-131 (3 tows)	*LT-231* (3 tows)	*LT-129* (3 tows)	*LT-455* (3 tows)	*LT-229* (5 tows)
LT-225 (3 tows)	*LT-633* (3 tows)	*LT-634* (4 tows)	*LT-635* (3 tows)	*LT-637* (4 tows)
LT-1 (3 tows)	*LT-134* (3 tows)	*TP-381* (3 tows)	*F-15* (3 tows)	*TP-128* (3 tows)
TP-1		*Hidatsa* (3 tows)		*TP-124*

The initial convoy speed was 4–5 knots. That night the group encountered frequent heavy rain squalls, accompanied by fresh to strong southeast breezes. The low visibility and increasing seas caused the convoy to become ragged and scattered, and at daylight the formation speed was reduced to allow stragglers to rejoin. The echelon commander embarked aboard the *Coronado* admonished numerous units to stay on station, to keep closed up, and to pay better attention to signals, and noted in a war diary entry the diversity of personnel operating the vessels:

> Some of the tugs are manned by Coast Guard officers and crews, some by Army Transport Service and two (2) by Army Engineers [personnel of an Army Engineer Special Brigade(s)]. The latter two (2) developed to be the poorest station keepers.

Station keeping was much improved the following day.[10]

On 14 October the *LT-225*'s boilers became salted and she had to "blow them," loosing considerable water in the process. She then dropped her tow, came alongside the *Coronado* and received 3,000 gallons of feed water. The following day the diesel-powered wooden harbor tug *TP-124* took the *LT-633* in tow so that her engineers could secure the boilers to make condenser repairs, which were completed the next morning. The next couple of days were uneventful until 19 October, when the harbor tugs TPs *103* and *124* had to take the *LT-225* and her barges in tow while she again attempted boiler repairs. In mid-afternoon on the 21st, the commanding officer of the *Coronado* sent a USCGR officer to provide assistance in making repairs. He returned on board the next day and reported that the boilers were in terrible condition and that one had been temporarily repaired and could probably be steamed at about 80 percent capacity. The tug remained under tow as she would otherwise have been unable to keep up.[11]

At daylight on 24 October, the northeast end of Siargao Island and the east coast of Dinagat Island became visible on the port bow of the convoy, and in late morning the convoy stopped to shorten tows and to reform into three columns for passage into the Leyte Gulf that evening. Shortly before dark a large convoy of ships, primarily LSTs and LSIs, passed close aboard to port heading southeast. As the group of tugs proceeded through the gulf, scattered anti-aircraft fire was observed to the west and north, and from 0425 to 0510 flashes of light beyond the horizon to the southwest. The commanding officer of the *Hidatsa* described the scene:

> The lights appeared to be from gunfire in the vicinity of Hibuson Island. The light flashes appeared to indicate opposing forces and were taken to be either a bombardment of shore batteries who were returning the fire or a close range engagement between opposing surface forces.[12]

What they were observing as darkness gave way to the first gray of dawn over Dinagat Island was the climax of the Battle of Surigao Strait. The remaining units of Vice Adm. Shoji Nishimura's component of the Japanese Southern Force—originally the battleships *Fuso* and *Yamashiro*, heavy cruiser *Mogami*, and four destroyers—were headed for the Surigao Strait to pass into the Leyte Gulf when they encountered an American battle line blocking the entrance. Earlier attacks by PT boats and destroyers of DesRon 24 against the Japanese force as it crossed the Mindoro Sea had already taken a heavy toll. Ship-launched torpedoes scored hits on both the battleships as well as the destroyers *Asagumo*, *Michishio*, and *Yamagumo*. The *Yamagumo* blew up and sank, the *Fuso* and *Michishio* began to sink, and the *Asagumo*—her bow knocked off—was put out of action and later finished off by gunfire from cruisers and destroyers. Nishimura's force, reduced to the battleship *Yamashiro*, cruiser *Mogami*, and destroyer *Shigure*, now had the misfortune of running into Rear Adm. Jesse Oldendorf's cruisers and battleships. As a barrage of American naval gunfire pummeled the Japanese ships, the *Shigure* retired—the only one of the three enemy combatants that would survive the day.[13]

The climax came with the American battle line scoring repeated hits on the *Yamashiro* after she had been struck by two torpedoes fired by destroyers of DesRon 56. Despite damage from gunfire, the battleship increased speed to 15 knots and set a southward course in an effort to escape, when the torpedoes, which had not detonated on contact, exploded in her. Eight minutes later, as her list increased to forty-five degrees, she went down taking the admiral and almost all of the ship's officers and men with her to the bottom. The *Mogami*, also badly damaged by the battle, was destroyed later that morning by torpedo bombers. By this engagement, Oldendorf prevented the Japanese from bringing their battle fleet through Surigao Strait, and attacking the beachheads on Leyte Island.[14]

At 0600 on 25 October the convoy entered San Pedro Bay, proceeded to the Northern Transport Area, and anchored in the forenoon off the mouth of the Palo River. (This marked the *Lark*'s return to the Philippines, having escaped Manila as the minesweeper AM 21 at midnight on 10 December 1941 in company with the gunboats *Asheville* (PG-21) and *Tulsa* (PG-22), and the minesweeper *Whippoorwill* (AM-35) bound for Makassar Strait. The waterway between the islands of Borneo and Sulawesi in Indonesia join the Celebes Sea to the north with the Java Sea to the south. Following arrival in the strait, the ships received orders to proceed to Surabaya, Java, in the Netherlands East Indies and to join the rest of the U.S. Asiatic Fleet able to escape the Philippines.) Throughout the remainder of 25 October and in ensuing days Japanese planes made numerous raids in the vicinity of and against shipping in the Northern Transport Area. To help shield the ships from view of attackers, smoke generating craft patrolled the anchorage area. The anchored ships as a group put up heavy anti-aircraft fire during raids but, due to the smoke, some vessels were unable to sight the planes and thus did not engage in gunfire. A considerable amount of shrapnel fell on the fleet tug *Hidatsa* during one attack, as well as a 20mm projectile from one of the firing ships, which exploded after hitting her deck slightly wounding a machine gunner.[15]

Information about the actions of the small Army ships is scant. The coastal tanker *Y-6* and large tugs *LT-134, 229, 231,* and *637* earned battle stars. Two other Army large tugs, not a part of this particular convoy, would also receive battle stars for Leyte landings; the *LT-454* for the period 2-9 November while a unit of the next echelon of tugs and tows dispatched to Leyte, and the *LT-20* for a more lengthy interval, 10 October to 10 November 1944.

ECHELON L-7 TO LEYTE

Echelon L-7 departed Humboldt Bay, Hollandia at 1000 on 20 October for Leyte. Comprising the convoy were one Navy tanker, the Australian merchant vessel S.S. *James Cook*, one OS type vessel, one

Army freight-supply ship, and ten tugs with various tows. The tug *LT-454* was one of the tugs, as were likely five other large tugs—*LT-108*, *113*, *116*, *348* and *529*—the harbor tug *TP-109*, and the small tug *ST-18*. The types but not the identities of the vessels which made up the convoy were recorded by the patrol frigate *Ogden* (PF-39), the escort for the convoy, in a war diary entry. However, the *LT-454* and the other tugs all left Hollandia on 20 October. The *ST-18*, belonging to the Army 2nd Engineer Special Brigade, was operated by a civilian skipper and seven soldiers comprising the crew. The steel-hulled tug, spanning a mere 75 feet, was the smallest vessel in the convoy, could make 9 knots unburdened, and had a towing ability of 300 tons at 6 knots. The 12-day transit to Leyte was uneventful except for the night of 28 October, when the convoy passed through the outskirts of a typhoon area encountering strong winds and rather rough seas. The foul conditions lasted through late afternoon the following day when the weather began to moderate as the storm receded to the northwestward.[16]

The convoy entered the Leyte Gulf at 0925 on 2 November and proceeded across it to an area off Dulag where the convoy ships anchored at 2000 for the night while the *Ogden* patrolled at slow speed nearby. Frequent enemy air raids occurred thereafter in the vicinity of the airstrip at Dulag. Shortly after midnight an enemy plane dropped a bomb which hit the water about fifty yards from the patrol frigate and exploded. Water and bomb fragments fell on her deck but no damaged resulted. Several more bombs hit the water in the vicinity of the anchored convoy; all were misses with no damage incurred. Frequent air raids on Dulag shore installations continued throughout the hours of darkness. The convoy got under way after daylight on 3 November and proceeded to the White Beach area in San Pedro Bay where the ships dispersed. Enemy air raids on shore installations began shortly after dark and continued throughout the night, and following days brought more of the same. Smoke-generating small craft endeavored to screen the ships at anchor in San Pedro Bay, but the bright moonlight rendered concealment difficult. Several raids occurred after dawn on 5 November, and all the ships in the harbor fired on enemy aircraft until friendly planes took off from the airstrip and drove them away.[17]

On 9 November, a convoy comprised of nine merchant vessels, two tank landing ships, and eight miscellaneous small craft—presumably some of them tugs—left San Pedro Bay for Hollandia, New Guinea. Screened by the destroyers *Claxton* (DD-971) and *Reid* (DD-369) and patrol frigates *Belfast* (PF-35), *Glendale* (PF-36), and *Hutchison* (PF-45), the convoy (Task Unit 78.2.30) entered Humboldt Bay on 16 November and was dissolved.[18]

KAMIKAZE ATTACKS AT LEYTE GULF

The Battle of Leyte Gulf is generally considered to be the largest naval battle of World War II. It was fought in waters near the Philippine islands of Leyte and Samar from 23 to 26 October 1944, between U.S. and Australian forces and the Japanese Navy. It was also the first battle in which Japanese aircraft carried out organized kamikaze attacks. The Japanese still had plenty of planes, as their aircraft factories were not yet subject to American bombing raids, and were replacing the heavy losses suffered by the air groups of the Imperial Navy in the Battle of the Philippine Sea. The loss of experienced aviators was not so easy to overcome, since pilot training lagged behind aircraft production. The main reason the Japanese turned to the use of kamikaze aircraft was the growing inability of their pilots to break through Allied fighter plane protection, and Navy ship anti-aircraft gunfire—whose effectiveness had been increased greatly by the implementation of proximity-armed fuses—to hit vessels with conventional bombs and torpedoes. The new tactic was to crash into a ship and to sink or damage it by the spread of gasoline and the detonation of bombs. Of course the pilot had to be expended, but thousands of fatalistic young Japanese men volunteered for a duty that was certain to result in their death. The first organized kamikaze attack was made on 25 October 1944 against escort carriers *Santee* (CVE-29) and *Suwannee* (CVE-27) during the Battle off Sumar, a part of the Battle of Leyte Gulf. The efforts to defeat the Allies through the use of suicide planes (essentially pilot-guided explosive missiles) as well as conventional aircraft continued as kamikaze attacked fleet units and shipping in Leyte Gulf waters and convoys plying between the islands of Leyte and Mindoro.[19]

The Battle of Leyte Gulf secured the beachheads that the Sixth Army had established on Leyte from attack from the sea. However, hard fighting would be required before the island was completely in Allied hands. The ground combat on Leyte was fought in parallel with an air and sea campaign in which the Japanese reinforced and resupplied their troops on Leyte while Allied forces attempted to interdict them and establish air-sea superiority in preparation for amphibious landings at Ormoc Bay, located on the opposite, southwest side of the island. The Allies had the same need to resupply ground troops on Leyte, and subsequently on Mindoro, Luzon, and other Philippine islands. Meeting this requirement was a joint Army and Navy responsibility. Thus, among the large numbers of merchant and amphibious ships comprising the resupply convoys were Army and Navy island hoppers.[20]

ECHELON L-13 TO LEYTE

The first Navy "island hopper" to earn a battle star for Leyte was the small coastal transport *APc-18*, commanded by Lt. W. S. Fox. In the early evening of 12 November, Echelon L-13 to Leyte (Task Group 76-5) formed off the entrance to Humboldt Bay, New Guinea. Leading the convoy were four columns of tank landing ships, with the *APc-18* positioned in the rear of column one. Five hundred yards behind the group of twenty-two LSTs was the Navy cargo ship *Triangulum* (AK-102), serving as fleet guide for ten merchant ships formed in three columns astern of her. Comprising the escort screen were the destroyer escorts *Lovelace* (DE-198) and *Whitehurst* (DE-634), the patrol frigates *Coronado* (PF-38) and *Eugene* (PF-40), and the subchasers *SC-703* and *SC-743*.[21]

En route to Leyte, two tank landing ships joined on 13 October and another seventeen LSTs—as well as the provision stores ship *Pastores* (AF-16)—the following day; swelling the ranks of these type amphibious ships to forty-two. The convoy arrived off Cartmon Hill, Leyte Gulf, on 19 November, hove to and disbanded as groups of vessels began to proceed to their assigned beaches. Five days later, during a surprise attack by Japanese aircraft on shipping in San Pedro Bay, the *APc-18* shot down an enemy plane, one of a group of three bombers and two fighters. The attackers were first sighted visually at only five miles distant, leaving little time to react, but all four of the *APc-18*'s 20mm anti-aircraft guns and one .30-caliber machine gun opened on the group as it closed to 1,600 yards off the vessel's port beam. The guns continued to blaze away until the flight had opened to 2,200 yards off her port quarter—which departed less one plane brought down by 20mm gunfire. The wooden ship was neither bombed nor strafed, apparently because the passing flight of aircraft had been after other targets. The next day, 25 November, kamikazes pressed home attacks on the fleet off Leyte, damaging four carriers; the *Essex* (CV-9), *Intrepid* (CV-11), *Hancock* (CV-19), and *Cabot* (CVL-28).[22]

ECHELON L-14 TO LEYTE

The next echelon to Leyte, L-14,—eighty-three merchant vessels, amphibious ships and craft, the freighter *FS-167*, and escort vessels— formed at noon on 19 November 1944. The mission of the echelon was to transport, protect, and land various Army and Navy reinforcements on the east coast of Leyte. The ships carrying personnel or cargo had loaded at Finschafen, Hollandia; Biak-Owi, New Guinea; or Morotai, Dutch East Indies, before joining at the rendezvous point. The four high-speed transports—*Liddle* (APD-60), *Kephart* (APD-61), *Cofer* (APD-62), and *Lloyd* (APD-63)—of Transport Division 103, and destroyer escorts *Craig* (DE-201) and *Manning* (DE-199), and frigates *El Paso* (PF-41) and *Van Buren* (PF-41) were assigned as screening ships. The APDs were former *Buckley*-class destroyers converted to carry invasion troops. Although the addition of a topside berthing compartment for embarked troops, and davits for the Higgins boats to land them, had resulted in the loss of some fighting capability, the gun mounts the ships retained made them viable escort vessels. Aside from their distinct silhouettes, ADPs were easy to distinguish from other destroyers due to the dark green mottled camouflage paint they sported, resulting in the moniker "Green dragons." [23]

En route to Leyte, the convoy passed various echelons returning from the assault beaches. In the early morning darkness on 22 November, it met Battleship Division Two steering an opposite course, ten miles to port. The following day, two or more torpedo planes attacked the convoy in the evening. One was destroyed by gunfire from LSTs and screening ships. As it disintegrated five miles distant and to the left of sunset glow, it was clearly discernible in the night sky to men aboard the ships. A few hours later, the convoy entered Leyte Gulf at ten minutes past midnight on 24 November. Seven hours later, all LSTs proceeded at 0700 toward beaching areas and the remaining ships of the convoy and screening vessels to San Pedro Bay. The *FS-167* carried PT spares to support motor torpedo boat squadrons. That evening, as the ships returning in convoy were forming up, they were attacked by enemy aircraft. One plane, believed to be a Japanese twin-engine bomber, was hit by 40mm fire and fell in flames.[24]

Chapter 16
KAMIKAZE ATTACKS INCREASE

One of the Army freight-supply ships recently arrived in the Southwest Pacific was the *FS-366*. Built by Sturgeon Bay Shipbuilding, in Sturgeon Bay, Wisconsin, the 176-foot ship was manned by a Coast Guard crew under the command of Lt. (jg) Charles E. Mashburn. She left Hollandia on 7 November 1944 with 292 tons of ammunition for delivery to the Philippines. As the *FS-366* and the other ships comprising the convoy of which she was a part entered the Leyte Gulf by day on 18 November, intense anti-aircraft fire was visible ahead. Mashburn described his ship's arrival at San Pedro Harbor, and witnessing attacks by enemy aircraft—including kamikaze—against shipping:

> We nonchalantly steamed to anchor. Saw our first two [Japanese] planes, one shot down by ack-ack [anti-aircraft fire] dive out of clouds. Raids continuously day night. Saw P-38 shoot down single seater plane with bomb. Was watching with glasses. To date Nov. 24 have seen many planes, many shot down. . . . Nights are panorama of tracers, big guns and search lights. . . . Planes shot down in flames. Often recite [the] 23rd Psalm.[25]

On 24 November, thirty Japanese planes of an eighty-plane raid broke through the combat air patrol of Allied fighters overhead to bomb and strafe the airstrips ashore and shipping in the harbor. A 20mm shell hit the gun deck of the *FS-366*, spraying shrapnel among her .50-caliber machine-gun crews, wounding the gunnery officer and five men. Although the injuries received were not life threatening, four men required hospitalization. Mashburn expressed regret his men were hurt, and wryly observed that the event would, however, induce sailors to be in full battle dress when at general quarters:

> Very painful. One almost lost leg. I'll have no more trouble keeping my crew in helmets, jackets, and clothes from now on. Nor will they remain exposed unnecessarily. I'm sorry for my boys. Fragments had to be picked from legs. Some since will go home and keepers of toes and feet will stay in [injured men who did not lose all or significant portions of their extremities would continue their service]....The shell today burst 3 feet or less from my head. I was protected by the deck.[26]

As the enemy attacks continued, seemingly without end, day after day, the officers and crew members of the freight-supply ship spent long hours at their battle stations:

- 25 Nov: Several alerts today. Clear moonlight night. Ack-ack should be very accurate. Smoke screen being laid tonight to cover shipping. We're being left out again. . . . Four raids have been over. 2 [Japanese] bombers shot down. No bombs dropped for some reason. 3 planes straffed ships. 1 plane set afire passed over our stern with fire from over 50 ships directed at it. Momentarily I expected us to be riddled by friendly fire. We still have a cargo of TNT! Must call ships tomorrow and warn them to watch their fire.

- 26 Nov: Have been at G.Q. [general quarters or "battle stations"] over 15 hrs this day. Men worn out. Several attacks. Five Japs shot down at noon today over docks. 1 parachuted. No damage. . . . Expect several more attacks. Smoke screen effective. No bombs dropped in the area tonight.

- 27 Nov: Several raids today. G.Q. till late in night. Bombers high above ack-ack.

- 28 Nov: 54 [Japanese] planes headed this way, detoured over Ormac [a port city on the southwest coast of Leyte] thank goodness they did. Planes might have been interrupted [by Allied fighters]. . . heavy rain and overcast helped us. No bombs dropped so far tonight.[27]

In his 29 November journal entry, Mashburn summarized the combat action of the past few days, and he poignantly described brief pauses when the war seemed far away. The entry closed with an observation that the men who survived the war should do something worthwhile with their lives to honor the sacrifice made by those who lost theirs on foreign soil:

> Five [Japanese] planes were shot down within sight noon the other day. One [Japanese] parachuted. A few days before a P-38 shot one down close by, the bullets hit the water astern. I had my glasses trained on them. A[n] FS [freight-supply ship] got the first plane of our ships the other day. They now have its wing aboard. Saw a[n] enemy plane come out of clouds the other day. Watched him with glasses as he dove, dropped his bomb and escaped. A beautiful piece of work. That night I believe a plane was shot down in flames as he crossed our stern. Today we found several dents in our hull where shells had hit. One 20mm hit 2 feet or 4 feet from my head and exploded.

The moon is full—The bay is a mirror shimmering through the smoke screen with ship after ship, barge after barge silhouetted in silver light. The night is clear and cool. Were the war a million miles away the universe could seem no calmer—not a breeze ripples the water. There has not been an enemy plane over head in over 36 hours. A large flight of planes approached Ormoc last night while a rain squall hid this bay....This night of a bombers moon (full) may bring disaster.... I've been in [the] service [for] 2 ½ years [at] most. Has it been 2 ½ years taken from me—has it been my whole life? The men who are spared by God's grace must endeavor to make their lives worthwhile to humanity to recompense for the lives of gallant, just, and brave who have given their blood on foreign soil that our principals might prevail against aggression, violence and hate. God grant us the strength![28]

ANOTHER LARGE CONVOY ATTACKED

> *It is my opinion this convoy should have been given air cover from at least 200 miles off Leyte Gulf to destination, because of the size of the convoy, (36 ships and 5 escorts), and because half of the ships in this convoy were carrying troops. Five escorts are not adequate protection for a convoy of this size, where air and submarine attack are imminent.*
>
> Comdr. H. J. Doebler, USCG, commander Task Unit 76.4.7, in his report on a series of Japanese air attacks that occurred on 5 December 1944 against the convoy for which he was responsible, while en route from Hollandia to the Leyte Gulf

The *FS-170*, manned by a Coast Guard crew under Lt. (jg) G. T. Mahoney, Jr., left Biak, Dutch New Guinea, on 30 November 1944. She and the *F-120* joined a convoy (Task Unit 76.4.7) en route to San Pedro Bay, Leyte, comprised of the attack transport *Gilliam* (APA-57), cargo ship *Boots* (AK-99), station tanker *Porcupine* (IX-126)—five tank landing ships—LSTs *460, 735, 741, 911,* and *1018*—the infantry landing craft *LCI(L)-984*, five Army freight-supply ships—*FS-145, FS-158, FS-163, FS-171,* and *FS-310*—and the Army tug *LT-454*, as well as eighteen large merchant vessels—most *Liberty* ships—and five patrol frigates.[29]

The convoy was formed in six columns of six ships each. The ships in columns two, three, and four, and the remaining column

Photo 16-2

The former USA *LT-455* —a sister ship of the *LT-454*—during post–World War II service as the auxiliary fleet tug USNS *A-ATA-20*. (Courtesy of Jim Swank, NavSource: www.navsource.org/archives/09/38/093824003.jpg)

leaders were all carrying troops. Three tankers and one ammunition ship were stationed in outboard columns, and in the after part of the formation, to minimize damage to other vessels if attacked and blown up or set aflame. The remainder of the vessels, including the freight and freight-supply ships carried miscellaneous cargoes. Five patrol frigates—the *Belfast* (PF-35), *Coronado* (PF-38), *Glendale* (PF-36), *Ogden* (PF-39), and *San Pedro* (PF-37)—were assigned to screen the convoy.[30]

The first few days of the 1,300 mile-voyage from Hollandia was peaceful. This changed on 5 December, when the convoy sustained a series of attacks from Japanese dive-bombers and torpedo planes which began in the morning and continued until early evening. All attacks were concentrated on columns two and three, which were composed entirely of troop ships. The first challenge, however, resulted from the track specified for the convoy being apparently the same as the route of the U.S. Army Air Transport Service. Numerous bogies were picked up by radar and most were later visually identified as C47 Skytrains. The first enemy aircraft that attacked the convoy apparently used the C47s as cover, as it was undetected by radar. A Zeke came in fast on the starboard quarter of the convoy at 0840, bombed and missed the S.S. *Marcus Daly*, and retired over the port quarter of the convoy.[31]

The *Daly* was a 442-foot *Liberty* ship, one of many such rapidly constructed in American shipyards during the war as mainstays of the dry cargo fleets. Developed from "a proven British design, readily adaptable to mass production methods," the 7,176-ton ships were propelled by a reciprocating steam engine to speeds up to eleven knots. Although *Liberty* ships had received some criticism for this limitation and had been termed plodding, the large size of their hatches and deep tween deck spaces with much freedom from hull obstructions made them suitable for a variety of roles. The Army employed *Liberty* ships for myriad missions other than hauling cargo, including service as emergency troop ships, as afloat field hospitals, and as aircraft repair ships.[32]

Over the course of that day, 5 December, several different type enemy planes, including the below fighters, bombers and attack aircraft, made attacks on the convoy:

- Jill   Nakajima B6N Tenzan Navy Carrier Torpedo Bomber
- Kate   Nakajima B5N Navy Type 97 Carrier Attack Bomber
- Oscar Nakajima Ki-43 Hayabusa Army Type 1 Fighter
- Zeke   Mitsubishi A6M Navy Type Zero Carrier Fighter[33]

The next attack came at a little past noon, when a Kate launched a torpedo at the *Liberty*-ship S.S. *Antone Saugrain* from off her port beam. It struck the freighter's stern, exploded, and carried away the rudder. The dive-bomber then crossed over the middle of the convoy and the bow of the *FS-170* at an altitude of approximately 200 feet and escaped by zigzagging violently while under heavy convoy fire. Ten minutes later, two aircraft—Kates or Jills—came in fast and low. The first plane dropped one torpedo. It struck the *Saugrain*'s hull at the number two hold and exploded, fatally wounding the vessel aboard which were 413 crew and Army troops. The patrol frigates *Coronado* and *San Pedro* and the Army tug *LT-454* came to the freighter's assistance and saved all hands. The Coast Guard crew of the 143-foot long diesel-electric tug recovered a total of 277 survivors for which ten members earned the Bronze Star Medal:

Name	Rank or Rate
Alan W. Davis	Coxswain, USCG
David Garner	Radioman, First Class, USCGR
Paul E. Hagen	Boatswain's Mate, Second Class, USCGR
Abraham Krohn	Seaman, Second Class, USCG

Name	Rank or Rate
George A. Lowery	Chief Boatswain's Mate, USCG
Edward E. Macklin	Fireman, First Class, USCGR
Robert W. Owen	Seaman, First Class, USCG
Louis Rua	Fireman, First Class, USCGR
Ned E. Smart	Seaman, First Class, USCGR
Wilbert Williams	Seaman, Second Class, USCGR

The award citation for Seaman Second Class Wilbert Williams, which is representative of those of the other men, reads "For heroic achievement at sea on 5 December 1944. When the U.S. Army large tug on which he was serving put about to render assistance to the crew of a freighter torpedoed by enemy aerial action he as a member of the life boat detail was instrumental in the rescue efforts. The number of survivors of the abandoned ship brought safely to the tug totaled 277." The *LT-454* did not garner a battle star as a member of this convoy, but she had one for the Leyte landings (2–9 November 1944), and would earn another star for the Lingayen Gulf landing (14–18 January 1945).[34]

The second plane turned away from gunfire of the *Ogden*, *Coronado*, and convoy ships. As the formation continued in transit towards Leyte, the *Antoine Saugrain* was left astern but not forgotten. The fleet tug *Quapaw* (ATF-110) arrived that night to find the *Saugraine* proceeding for Leyte under tow by the *LT-454*. All efforts to save her, however, would be for naught. The freighter was sent to the bottom two days later by a torpedo bomber off Leyte, taking with her a very valuable cargo of radar equipment.[35]

The weather conditions that entire day were ideal for enemy aircraft. The sky was three-tenths to seven-tenths covered with cumulus, whose average cloud base was four thousand feet, and there were occasional rain squalls in the area. In mid-afternoon, a Zeke came in at 1452 on the starboard side of the convoy, went into a steep dive and dropped a bomb, which was a near miss on the S.S. *John Evans*. The *FS-170*, ideally situated on the starboard beam of the *Liberty* ship, was the first convoy vessel to open fire and followed the plane through its run, scoring .50-caliber machine-gun hits. After taking fire from other ships including the *Ogden* and *Glendale*, the bomber retired on a course of 270° relative, smoking noticeably as it disappeared from view in a rain cloud. All the remaining attacks that day were against the *Marcus Daly*, which earlier that morning had escaped damage from a bomb drop during the first air raid on the convoy.[36]

A little over a half hour later, a Zeke or Oscar came in from the starboard side of the convoy and dive-bombed the *Marcus Daly*. The ordnance missed, and the aircraft then joined a Zeke or Oscar on the port side of the convoy and both planes came in on suicide dives. The first one hit the bow of the *Marcus Daly* and exploded, setting her foc'sle on fire. Three crewmen—one Navy Armed Guard and two Merchant Marine—were killed and seven wounded, and 200 embarked troops were either killed, wounded, or missing in action. The commanding officer of the *FS-170* described the attack:

> Two dive bombers approached from 165° relative under fire from this ship and others present. Forty millimeter hits were scored by this ship causing the plane to cease zigzagging, drop one wing and plunge into the bow of a liberty ship on our port bow, seemingly out of control.[37]

Clifton H. Linville, the master of the *F-120*, attested to the singular role of the freight-supply ship in bringing down the aircraft that damaged the *Marcus Daly*:

> On 5 December, 1944, I witnessed a 40 M.M. projectile strike a Japanese Dive Bomber aft of the wings on the fuselage. Immediately after this, the plane burst into flames and crashed into the bow of a liberty ship. At the time the plane burst into flames, only the *F.S. 170* and *F-120* were firing at said plane, and, inasmuchas the *F-120* has only .50 cal., there is no doubt in my opinion that the *F.S. 170* was responsible for the destruction of 1 Jap[anese] plane.

Despite this written certification by a credible eye witness, the *FS-170* was not awarded a battle star. Large convoys were spread out over several miles, and thus task force commanders had to, in the absence of witnessing events themselves, sort out from among two or more ships claiming destruction of an enemy plane which one should get credit. Often in the case of uncertainty, an escort received the laurel; the logic for such a decision being that surface combatants, possessing more potent, longer range weapons, were more likely to bring down an aircraft.[38]

The second plane came in on the S.S. *Mactan* but, badly damaged by gunfire, overshot the ship by about 100 feet and exploded when it hit the sea. A member of the Catboat Flotilla, the *Mactan* had escaped the Philippines dressed in hospital colors during the siege of Bataan in 1942. Built in 1896, the dilapidated coastal steamer transported a load of casualties to Australia unmolested by the Japanese who were notified of its sailing via Swiss diplomats. Maj. William Fairfield, U.S. Army Air Force, who made the voyage, described how the ship had come to be pressed into that duty:

> It seems that General MacArthur had ordered Colonel Romalo, an officer on his staff, to secure a boat and there being only two in the harbor, one a lumber schooner which was unfit, and this "Mactan," General MacArthur said, "Use the Mactan." The Colonel said, "You can't put them on that because it's suicide, the ship has been condemned!" General MacArthur said, "It's suicide to leave them here; put them on!" and gave orders to the Red Cross to make it ready. In two days, they had renovated the ship as much as possible, had completely painted it with the use of Filipino labor, also had put the necessary Red Cross insignia on it and had hung the Red Cross Flag from one of the main halyards. So, with a glow in the sky and thunderous concussions, as the oil storage and supply dumps were being blown up behind us, we saw Manila die.[39]

The voyage aboard the *Mactan* took a miserable twenty-seven days, during which the wounded suffered from ants infesting the ship, an engine breakdown, a violent storm, and barely missed being caught in a Japanese air raid on Darwin. The vessel, which had been employed for inter-island service and had passenger accommodations for only approximately fifteen, had some 248 wounded aboard as well as Filipino medical attendants, doctors, nurses, and crew. Following its arrival in Australia, the S.S. *Mactan* was ruled unseaworthy but continued to serve, presumably following repairs.[40]

At 1647, a torpedo bomber—identified as a Kate or Jill—came in low down the port side of the convoy, apparently intending to attack the *Marcus Daly*, but was forced to turn away by gunfire from that side of the formation. The same thing occurred forty minutes later. Heavy fire by the *Glendale*, *Ogden*, and other ships caused the pilot of an attacking torpedo bomber to drop his fish well short of the *Marcus Daly*, at whom the attack was again directed. The master of the freighter had earlier voluntarily left the convoy without confusion after being crashed by the kamikaze, heading downwind until the blaze was under control before returning to station. The personnel casualties had been heavy due to the blast from the exploding plane;

twenty-two killed, fifty missing, and thirty wounded. The *FS-145* had picked up twenty-three survivors of which three expired and eighteen of the remaining twenty required medical attention.[41]

After being besieged for nearly an entire day, the convoy finally reached its destination on 6 December. The ships hove to five miles south of San Pedro Bay at 0652, awaiting orders regarding their disposition and the removal of passengers and survivors. The personnel losses suffered as a result of numerous Japanese air attacks would have been much greater but for the combined actions of the ships' gun crews as succinctly noted by the task group commander:

> The volume of fire from the escorts and ships in convoy was responsible for the convoy not suffering more severe damage by badly crippling one suicide dive bomber thus causing a miss, causing two dive bombers to pull out early undershooting target, one torpedo plane to drop fish about three miles from intended victim, and one torpedo plane to turn away before dropping torpedo.[42]

SLOW TOW TO MINDORO

> *The business of forming up this motley assembly of 4-knot tows was extremely difficult, radio facilities in doubt and a semblance of balance in station assignments difficult to obtain considering various lengths of tows, armament, speeds available, etc. Some members of the convoy could man a VHF circuit, others a HF circuit, others none. Even the U.S.S. WHIPPOORWILL could only listen on a[n] HF wardroom radio and nothing else. Some could read international signals, some understood mersigs [Merchant Signals used in WWII ship convoys], and some could read U.S. Navy flag hoists of speed and course signals only. After attempting a few radio checks with no success, I decided that course and speed flag hoists, and plain language flashing light BT's would have to be the maneuvering methods. No unit understood the IXBT method for executive signals, including the U.S.S. WHIPPOORWILL. He had to be taught because I designated him guide and Convoy Commodore.*
>
> Comdr. J. B. McLean, USN, commander Destroyer Division 48[43]

Although the Battle of Leyte would not be officially over until 26 December 1944, preparatory steps for the next phase of the Philippine Islands Campaign, a landing in the Lingayen Gulf on Luzon, scheduled for 9 January 1945, were under way. As a prelude to this major amphibious invasion, an assault force—comprised principally of a regimental combat team of the 24th U.S. Army Infantry Division, and the 503rd Parachute Regiment—landed on Mindoro Island on 15 December, and except for mopping up secured it within two days. The small island was greatly desired due to its geographical position to the south of Luzon across the 7 ½-mile-wide Verde Island Passage. Establishment of airfields there would enable Southwest Pacific Air Forces to operate against enemy air forces on Luzon and to cover the Lingayen landings.[44]

The first task unit (78.3.12) supporting the planned landing at Mindoro on 15 December to leave the Leyte Gulf, and the last to arrive at Mindoro, was an aggregation of tugs and barges termed the Slow Tow Convoy. The Army operated hundreds of tugs—designated large, small, and harbor—during the war. Although their exact numbers are unknown, there were still 256 harbor tugs in the Pacific four months after V-J Day, let alone other types. Just as Navy Yard Craft (which planners had not envisioned would operate very far from a Navy base or yard due to their small size) crossed ocean expanses, so too did TP vessels. The Army had initially used this designation for private or commercially owned vessels it acquired for use as "small freight and passenger vessels." Later, following the Army's procurement of forty-three new, bright and shiny 96-foot diesel-powered, wooden, harbor tugs, the TP classification applied to them as well. Two of these type ships—the *TP-113* and *TP-129*—were members of the slow tow convoy to Mindoro and earned a battle star for the period 12-18 December 1944.[45]

The convoy was formed in three columns with *Whippoorwill* as the formation guide and leader of the center column, and the Australian rescue tug HMAS *Reserve* (W149) and *TP-129* as left and right column leaders. The *Reserve* had been acquired by the Australian Commonwealth Marine Salvage Board on 10 December 1942. Commissioned into the RAN on 17 August 1943, she served off eastern Australia and in the Southwest Pacific during the war and would receive the battle honour "'New Guinea 1943-44." Such honors for participation in a battle or campaign were displayed on a solid wooden board (traditionally teak) mounted on the ship's superstructure, carved with the ship's badge and scrolls naming the ship and the associated honors. The board was either left completely unpainted, or with the lettering painted gold.[46]

The other ships took their positions astern of the column leaders, with the 168-foot Army coastal tanker *Y-14* the last vessel in column one. She was one of 112 such tankers, constructed by eight small American shipbuilders for the U.S. Army. All of the ships were of steel and were of either 162 or 182 feet in length. The Y-tankers were designed to transport fuel oil, including gasoline, for distribution from larger tankers, and, like the TP tugs in this convoy, were intended primarily for harbor duty. The tankers could carry a light deck load of freight or a small number of troops, but were not considered true oceangoing ships or intended to make long voyages. The Y-tankers, tank barges really, had practically no freeboard amidships (distance from the water to the main deck), and as the master of one vessel noted, "during very rough weather, it was almost necessary to rig up a breeches buoy in order to travel safely from the after to the forward part of the vessel." A Breeches buoy was a rope-based rescue device used to remove mariners from a sinking ship or to transfer them from one location to another in situations of danger. By September 1943, sixteen Y-tankers had already arrived in the Southwest Pacific and more were en route to the theater. In a representative voyage to Australia, the *Y-5* left New Orleans on 18 August 1943 and traveled unescorted until her arrival at Brisbane on 9 November. The ship's master reported that during the voyage the decks of the coastal tanker were constantly awash and on one occasion the *Y-5* was mistaken for a submarine due to her low profile.[47]

Photo 16-3

The 182-foot former Army coastal tanker USA *Y-87*—one of 112 such small ships—under way during her service as the Navy fuel oil barge *YO-242*. (Courtesy of Stanley Svec, NavSource: www.navsource.org/archives/14/141224201.jpg)

During formation of the convoy, the task unit commander found that the largely Army contingent had only the vaguest sort of verbal orders. He was startled by this realization, and recorded the substance of the replies to his inquiry to the convoy, "What are your orders?"

U.S.S. *WHIPPOORWILL*	Turn tow over to PT Unit
H.M.A.S. *RESERVE*	Deliver to PT Base
T.P. 113	We have no instruction, Sixth Army is to give us instructions
L.T. 1	As far as we know the Army will take them
T.P. 129	Don't know
S.T. 381	Only orders are verbal to drop barge and return
L.C.T. 675 and *389*	Report to SOP [Senior Officer Present] on arrival
Y 14	Awaiting orders

Of the vessels in convoy, the 187-foot *Whippoorwill* was the largest. Commissioned on 1 April 1919 as a *Lapwing*-class minesweeper (AM-35), she had been reclassified an old fleet tug (ATO-169). The two tank landing craft, LCTs *389* and *675*, were also naval vessels and the remaining *LT-1* and *ST-381* were Army large and small tugs, respectively.[48]

The smallest vessel in the convoy, the 72-foot *ST-381*, was a unit of the 2nd Engineer Special Brigade and was operated by four civilians and seven soldiers. Her master, first mate, chief engineer, and first assistant engineer were ably assisted by GIs serving as the second mate, second assistant engineer, cook, signalman, or as a seaman. The master, R. E. Carpenter, described in a report to the brigade commander duty at Tacloban on Leyte and his efforts to acquire additional machine guns for his tug before departing for Mindoro:

> Using Cancabato Bay, 500 feet off the Tacloban Air Strip as our permanent mooring, we have found it to be a rather hot corner at times. You know of the numerous attempts to knock that strip out since our arrival here. With all fairness to the other men who are in the same game and trying their best to bring them down, I can say honestly that we gave one "Bogie" [enemy aircraft] all that a single fifty [caliber machine gun] could pump into him for a half a minute.
>
> Hunting being good and being informed we had a mission coming up, we applied strongly to the Brigade Ordnance Maintenance to give us more guns, and they complied. Before leaving on our mission [the slow tow to Mindoro] we had five single fifties, two forward, two aft and one midship. Our ESB gunners were fit and ready for any Jap[anese] planes.

The added self-defense capability was important as the *ST-381* had limited maneuverability imposed by a fuel barge full of distillate she had in tow astern of her.[49]

Photo 16-4

The *ST-381*—one of the many Army large, small, and harbor tugs to serve in the Southwest Pacific during World War II—was the only small tug to earn a battle star. (Courtesy of 2nd Engineer Special Brigade.org: www.2esb.org/04_History/Book/Chapter_24.htm)

Of the vessels in the Mindoro-bound convoy only the *Whippoorwill* was truly a seagoing ship. The LCTs were intended to be shipped aboard larger vessels until off a landing beach and the others were harbor craft. However, the troops ashore and the Motor Torpedo Boat Base at Mindoro needed the tows astern of the tug boats and landing craft. The *Whippoorwill* was delivering to the PT base a pontoon crane barge and a pontoon drydock and the other tugs barges with loads of cargo. Screening the nine vessels were the destroyers *Bush* (DD-529), *Halford* (DD-480), and *Radford* (DD-446), and the smaller destroyer escorts *Holt* (DE-706) and *Jobb* (DE-707). Since this was a 4-5 knot convoy, ships of the screen continually circled the group during daylight at a speed of 12-15 knots, increasing to 20-24 knots upon an air alert. This disposition allowed freedom of movement by the ships and kept a maximum number of guns bearing outboard at all times.[50]

The convoy departed Dulag in the northern Leyte Gulf the morning of 12 December and proceeded south towards Surigao Straits. The master of the *ST-381* reported, "We were swung into Cabalian Bay, in the lower Surigao Straits [for a period of time] on account of some trouble which was not revealed to the ships of the convoy." At 2100, the convoy made the narrows and entered Mindanao Sea. There was light anti-aircraft fire from the tip of Mindanao—the second largest and southernmost island in the Philippines—but the vessels were under strict orders not to fire at night unless directly attacked.[51]

The task unit was attacked on the 13th, 14th, 15th, and 16th by Japanese aircraft that broke though the defense of the CAP (combat air patrol) overhead. Nine planes were shot down by the CAP and three aircraft were downed and two damaged by gunfire from the convoy or escorts. In each instance, enemy planes took advantage of the sun to help shield them from view during the approach phase of their attacks. Well aware of their increased vulnerability to attack when the sun was low on the horizon, ships went to general quarters for dawn alert and sunset alert each day. The enemy aircraft, however, appeared somewhat confused by the continuously changing screen of escort ships, and often modified their approaches and targets at the last moment. The first such attack occurred in the mid-afternoon of 13 December when a fighter appeared suddenly over the formation without any previous warning and was driven off by fire from the convoy and escort. A twin-engine bomber—a Betty or Sally—then approached from the southeast. The plane released two bombs near a ship in convoy and then, hit by fire from escort ships, its port engine began smoking and it crashed into the sea several miles astern.[52]

Five or six planes attacked the convoy from different directions the following morning. Several were shot down by CAP, but two dive-bombers escaped and came in from astern of the convoy at 0812 pursued by Navy fighter aircraft. The master of the *ST-381* described the attack:

> Two Japs were coming into the convoy's stern from a northeasterly direction. . . . We were grateful as we spotted them to see a Navy Corsair on the tail of the lower one astern. He had winged him but the Nip tried to keep himself up after his dive to reach and crash one of our escort destroyers. He failed to reach his mark by 200 yards.

Gunfire from screening destroyers found the lower plane and it went out of control in a downward spiral and likely crashed. The other plane, a Betty, dove on the *Halford*. It took fire from ships of the escort and convoy, and disappearing northward was smoking slightly from the port engine.[53]

Chapter 16

At 1105 on 15 December, a medium bomber approached from ahead of the convoy and dove on the *Bush*, dropping a bomb at very low altitude close aboard her starboard quarter. The escort and convoy opened fire on the Sally-type (Mitsubishi Ki-21 Army type 97) heavy bomber and it began to smoke and fell into the sea about two miles astern of the formation and 200 yards off the *Bush*'s port quarter. The master of the *ST-381* described the role his machine guns played in the action:

> A twin engine Jap bomber dove at the convoy from the northeast, leveled off and picked on the second column, the next to our right, just the way we wanted him, for we had three fifties to greet him and they emptied what they had into him. The after gun hit him for 15 seconds, knocking one of his bombs off. The bomb missed the after barge in column 2.
>
> One of the escort destroyers was making the rear swing of his patrol and was very glad the Nip was not under control and crashed 300 feet off his starboard bow. The Commanding Officer and the crew of the DE acknowledged this by saying 'We were doing a splendid job,' also by gesturing as grasping their hands in a warm hand shake.[54]

That afternoon the *ST-381*'s towing cable parted which proved fortuitous for her, relative to events the following day. The cable was repaired and the tug was under way in thirty minutes but now at the rear of column one, the tanker *Y-14* having taking up her old position. Saturday, the 16th, started as a quiet and peaceful day with good seas as the southern end of Mindoro came into sight. This tranquility did not last long. At 0824 an aircraft crashed near the port side of the coastal tanker *Y-14*. The master of the *ST-381* described the attack:

> A bomber came in from the northwest on our side of the convoy and leveled off low, leaving the destroyers in a hard position for their heavy guns to be effective. After he crossed the bow of the outside destroyer our two forward and midship guns kept pumping him. He attempted a left bank, but was out of control, trying to crash the *Y-14* tanker, who was now in our former position of the convoy. He could only give her a glancing blow off the port quarter while in a vertical bank and dive. He crashed immediately after rounding the tanker's stern. At least 5 or 6 of the tanker's crew jumped overboard and were picked up by the two LCTs of our convoy. I believe some of her crew were lost, as the Escort Commander

asked all ships if they had picked up any men. The tanker proceeded under her own power.[55]

Two of the tanker's crew members perished and the ship was slowed by the damage it had sustained to a maximum speed of five knots. The aircraft had appeared at a range of 6,000 yards headed apparently in a suicide run at the destroyer escort *Holt*—which was then beam on to the enemy and the closest ship to it in the formation—closing rapidly at a speed of about 300 knots. Recognizing danger, the destroyer changed course radically to the right, and the aircraft, finding the *Holt*'s new target angle unfavorable, chose instead to crash the tanker. The loss of life and damage it suffered would have been greater but for the actions of the gunners aboard the *Holt*. Hit by 40mm and 20mm gun rounds, the plane, with cockpit on fire and smoking, lost altitude gradually and fell into the water short of the *Y-14*, exploding on impact.[56]

The convoy arrived off Ilin Island, Mindoro at about dusk on 16 December, upon which the *Whippoorwill* and *Reserve* proceeded to the Mangarin Bay PT boat base, and the remainder of the vessels stood towards White Beach. In addition to the enemy attacks, there had been five breakdowns and one broken tow en route to Mindoro. Each time the convoy had slowed to bare steerageway until the cripple rejoined. At 0608 the next morning, the last tug having cleared its tow in darkness to Army craft alongside, the task unit commander formed the returning convoy, once again by the "herding method" and departed. The damaged *Y-14* was left at the beachhead as were also the two LCTs as scheduled.[57]

The return trip was uneventful, except for having to ride in the trough of the sea during two days of rough weather. The passage was made at 8 to 8 ½ knots, occasionally slowing due to the *ST-381*'s overheating engines. On Sunday, 17 December, the flags were half-masted in the convoy for a burial at sea from the *LST-605*. The convoy arrived at San Pedro Bay, Leyte Gulf, two days later in the early afternoon and dissolved. During the slow tow to Mindoro and return, Commander McLean had developed an admiration for the resolute tugs, noting in his report:

> It was a pleasure to watch the tugs effort to stay closed up and to keep station on course changes. They handled themselves excellently and made every effort to cooperate. Their signalman (probably one each) were on the job day and night and they went in boldly

and anchored on an unknown shore at night with little to go on. In fact, their performance amazed everyone on the flagship [the destroyer *Bush*] bridge. The last day, homeward bound, the smallest tug, *ST 381* fell out. His engines were overheating and he was burning salt water. He signaled for the convoy to go ahead, that he could come in alone. However, by slowing the convoy to 7 knots he was able to keep up. He deserved a "Well Done" and got it.[58]

The *ST-381*'s civilian Army Transportation Service members would later be replaced by an all 2nd Engineer Special Brigade crew with Staff Sgt. Benjamin H. Sooy, Jr. in command and nine soldiers comprising the crew. As a result of downing a Betty bomber, the men had painted a small Japanese flag on the vessel's stack and it was soon followed by two more. The *ST-381* and the much bigger, relatively speaking, 113-foot large tug *LT-1* each received a battle star for the period 12-18 December 1944. The *ST-381* would be the only Army small tug to garner such an award during the war, and the *LT-1* one of seven large tugs; the others being the *LT-20, 134, 229, 231, 454,* and *637*.[59]

RESUPPLY CONVOY TO MINDORO ISLAND

> Five of the seven ships sunk or rendered inoperative by enemy attack were put out of action by suicide divers—human bombers. Only one suicide bomber out of six attacking on 28 and 30 December failed to hit his target—the first one shot down the morning of 28 December by LCI(L) 1076. The suiciders were, therefore, 83% effective. Dive bombers and torpedo bombers were relatively ineffective—out of uncounted numbers of bombs and torpedoes released at vessels of convoy only one sank a ship. This new weapon employed by the enemy—the suicide diver, or human torpedo, constitutes a serious threat to Naval forces and shipping.
>
> Observation by Comdr. A. Vernon Jannotta, USNR, commander Task Group 77.11 and LCI(L) Flotilla 24, in an action report describing the loss of ships in convoy from Leyte to Mindoro, Philippine Islands

At month's end, a large convoy of ninety-two ships (designated U plus 15, L-13) sailed on 27 December from Leyte for Mindoro via the Sulu Sea. Leading it were twenty-five tank landing ships formed in five columns. Next were the merchant freighters and other supply or support ships; three *Liberty* ships, six Army "F ships," the Navy tanker

Porcupine (IX-126), the Navy seaplane tenders *Half Moon* (AVP-26) and *San Pablo* (AVP-30), and the Navy motor torpedo boat tender *Orestes* (AGP-10) also positioned in five columns. Bringing up the rear were the twenty-three infantry landing craft of LCI(L) Flotilla 24, carrying the ordnance, supplies and equipment of embarked Beach Jumper Units as well as spare ammunition, smoke pots, dry stores, aviation gasoline, base equipment and 176 personnel to support PT boats. Also aboard the landing craft were 965 troops of the 21st Inf. Reg., 24th Army Division, and the 130 officers and men of Beach Jumper Units No. 6 and No. 7. The convoy also included some Army crash boats, small vessels designed to dash out from land to rescue downed aviators.[60]

Disposed ahead and on either side of this mass of ships were nine destroyers—*Bush* (DD-529), *Edwards* (DD-619), *Gavsevoort* (DD-608), *Hamilton* (DMS-18), *Philip* (DD-498), *Pringle* (DD-477), *Sterett* (DD-407), *Stevens* (DD-479), and *Wilson* (DD-408)—serving as an outer screen. Inside them on the flanks of the convoy were the twenty-nine PT boats of Motor Torpedo Squadrons 8, 24, and 25, formed in six units of four or five boats. The convoy speed was eight knots with the screen patrolling at up to ten knots.[61]

The weather was generally fair, calm seas, and light northeasterly winds, none in excess of five knots, and maximum visibility. The latter factor aided enemy aircraft to locate shipping as did a full moon during the entire transit. The Japanese mounted thirty-one attacks against the convoy between Leyte and Mindoro, and an additional ten during the first forty hours following the arrival of the ships at Mindoro, using kamikaze and dive-bombers during daylight hours and dive-bombers, torpedo bombers, and minelayers during darkness. The series of concentrated and nearly continuous air attacks began on the second day as the convoy passed through the Surigao Straits, the Mindanao Sea, the Sulu Sea and the Mindoro Straits.[62]

The first hint of danger came with airborne "snoopers" reconnoitering the convoy in the early morning darkness of 28 December between 0332 and 0420. There soon followed reports and sightings of several bogies in the area. At 1014, an attack developed suddenly when six Vals screamed in from the starboard quarter of the convoy. Three of these aircraft proved to be suicide divers. The *LCI(L)-1076* shot down one of the planes attempting to crash the group of infantry landing craft and it fell in flames into the sea. With all the ships in the convoy firing, a second Val crashed the *Liberty*-ship S.S. *John Burke*, which loaded with ammunition, exploded and completely disintegrated. A search by the *LCI(L)-624* found no survivors of the ship's 40-man merchant marine crew and 28-man Armed Guard. The cataclysmic blast also damaged the tanker *Porcupine* and opened seams in the motor torpedo boat *PT-332*, though 500 yards away. Fragments from the *John Burke* hit the freighter S.S. *Francisco Morozan*, wounding three of her merchant complement. At 1022, a third plane crashed the *Liberty*-ship S.S. *William Sharon* in the bridge area, setting the vessel on fire and causing it to go dead in the water. The destroyer *Wilson* went alongside her and extinguished the blaze which had engulfed the freighter. After embarking the survivors, the DD rejoined the convoy. About this time, fighter cover from the 5th Army Air Force arrived—eighteen P38s, eight P47s, and four Corsairs—and thereafter daytime CAP and night fighter protection was provided for the balance of the transit.[63]

That night the salvage ship *Grapple* (ARS-7) accompanied by the destroyers *Converse* (DD-509) and *Stanley* (DD-478) was sent from Leyte to recover the *William Sharon* adrift in the Mindanao Sea. They located the disabled ship early the following afternoon nearly twenty-five miles to the west-southwest from her reported position. After a smoldering fire on the bridge was put out, the *Grapple* took her under tow for San Pedro Bay.[64]

Gunfire from the freight-supply ship *FS-309* had found and set on fire the aircraft that crashed the ammunition-laden *John Burke*. The resulting shock wave from the explosion lifted crewmen aboard the Army ship off their feet, and tore the flying bridge to pieces, pulverizing all shatterproof windows that were not down. Remnants of the *John Burke* were seen falling from the sky and as shrapnel littered the deck of the *FS-309*, larger debris including booms, life rafts, and hatches dropped into the sea not twenty feet ahead of her. Out of the smoky area where the *Liberty* ship had previously been came three huge mountainous waves, and sailors topside sighted two men in the oil-covered, debris-filled water frantically waving and shouting. As the *FS-309* maneuvered closer, Hospital Apprentice, Second Class Francis L. Owens, USCGR, "voluntarily jumped overboard endangering his own life to bring the dazed and bruised men to safety." It turned out the two sailors were not *John Burke* survivors. They had been blown overboard from a Navy ship in the column to the left of the *FS-309*. For this act of heroism, Owens received the Bronze Star Medal.⁶⁵

Commencing in the late afternoon and lasting until nearly midnight, Japanese Vals and Bettys in small groups of two to six planes made a series of attacks against the convoy. During this action, ships of the convoy shot down six enemy aircraft in flames, but took damage as well. Several LCI(L)s and PTs suffered personnel casualties from strafing, shrapnel, and crashing planes, and craft narrowly missed by bombs received slight underwater damage. The *LCI(L)-624* was grazed by an aircraft-dropped torpedo, which although passing under her from bow to stern did not explode. The tank landing ship *LST-750* was not so fortunate. She was rocked by a torpedo which struck her engine room and detonated at 1917. With the convoy still under attack, four large infantry landing craft—LCI(L)s *1000, 1001, 1005*, and *1006*—went to her aid, and by midnight had retrieved from the damaged ship and life rafts 183 Navy and Army personnel of the total 212 embarked. When all survivors had been removed, the LST—rendered completely inoperative by the damage—was sunk by gunfire from the *Edwards*.⁶⁶

The following day, 29 December, brought more of the same. Bogies were in the area between 0403 and 0510 but launched no attacks. This lull did not last long and beginning at 0717, Vals and Bettys attacked the convoy, which was now northeast of the Cagayan Islands, almost continuously for an hour and a half. Vessels of the convoy shot down three planes in flames and damaged two others which, as they left the area smoking, jettisoned their bombs well clear of the convoy. One of the planes was plummeting down in a suicide dive on a tank landing ship, when gunfire from the *PT-352* found it and it crashed into the sea alongside its intended target. The *FS-349*'s port twin .50-caliber machine gun then took a single-engine aircraft approaching the convoy under fire. The pilot's apparent objective was to crash the tanker *Porcupine*, a converted *Liberty* ship loaded with volatile aviation gas, positioned 700 yards on the freight-supply ship's starboard beam. Tracer hit the cockpit, and the kamikaze impacted the water off the *FS-349*'s starboard bow without inflicting damage to the convoy.⁶⁷

During this series of attacks, bombs fell near several ships but they caused no damage, and for the remainder of that morning and afternoon, there were no additional enemy attacks. Bogies were seen in the convoy area, but friendly air intercepted effectively and no serious threats to the ships developed. Enemy aircraft attacks resumed at dust and for the next several hours all ships were engaged at battle stations fighting off dive and torpedo bombers. Gunfire from the *FS-349* downed one of an undetermined number of planes that launched a raid at 2130. During the night action, which lasted until 0125 on 30 December, planes repeatedly strafed and bombed the convoy, but no serious damage was incurred and ships accounted for six planes shot down. Enemy aircraft were not the only threat to the convoy and escorts. At 2225, dark objects were sighted in the water and reported as probable floating mines. An LST struck a mine but suffered no serious damage, and all other ships passed through the field safely.[68]

ATTACKS CONTINUE AT MINDORO

Groups of enemy aircraft followed the same practice on 30 December as in the preceding two days; bogies in the area around the convoy in the early morning darkness followed by attacks. As part of an attack at 0655, a plane bombed the destroyer *Philip*—which by maneuvering with full rudder caused the ordnance to fall into the sea 200 yards off her starboard beam—and the aircraft was shot down by fire from her and PT boats. Another plane was "splashed" at about the same time. Immediately thereafter, a single enemy aircraft was reported at 0702 approaching from the south, but was chased away by a "Black Widow," a Northrop P61 night fighter. Three minutes later a "Helen"—Nakajima Ki-49 Donryu Army Type 100 heavy bomber—circled the convoy and came in on a long glide, approaching the flotilla of infantry landing craft from ahead and to port. The *LCI(L)-624*, ideally positioned at the head of the port column, found her with a burst of 40mm fire and the aircraft crashed in flames about 500 yards off the port quarter of the formation. This was the last attack on the convoy in transit and it occurred as the ponderous group of ships was standing into San Jose Bay on the southwestern tip of Mindoro.[69]

Throughout the late morning while the LSTs and freighters were disembarking troops, survivors and wounded, no Japanese aircraft were sighted or reported in the area. By 1500 the LCI(L)s had completed unloading their troops and were anchoring singularly in Mangarin Bay in the vicinity of the tender *Orestes*; the PT boats being moored nearby. A short time later, four single-engine Japanese planes were observed circling overhead in the bay area at an altitude of about 14,000 feet. There were a part of a flight of twelve aircraft which P38 interceptors had engaged, but these planes broke through. Three of them started their suicide dives successively—one at the *Gansevoort*, patrolling outside the bay; one at the tanker *Porcupine*, laying outside off Bulong Point; and one at the *Orestes*. In spite of intense anti-aircraft fire, each plane roaring downward was able to crash its target. The commander of the LCI(L)s described the destruction wrought by the kamikazes:

> The destroyer *Ganevoort* was hit amidships; her engines and guns rendered inoperative, she was later beached and abandoned. The tanker *Porcupine*, containing the greatly needed aviation gasoline resupply for the Mindoro area was totally destroyed by fire. At 1548 the *Orestes* was hit by the third suicider, which was in flames from the fire of PT's and LCI(L)'s in immediate vicinity, but which bounced off the water to the ORESTES' starboard side at frame 29; its bombs deflecting upwards and exploding inside. The ship burst into flames immediately. Many of the officers and men of the ORESTES were blown into the water by the explosion; orders to abandon ship were apparently given soon thereafter; and the waters surrounding the ship were quickly covered with swimming men.

A few small boats and several PTs in the vicinity started to pick up *Orestes* survivors and were joined by other PTs and LCI(L)s. By 1610 all survivors had been recovered. Firefighting efforts by one LCI(L) alongside both the port and starboard sides of the *Orestes* took longer, slowed by the blaze and exploding ammunition, but by 1945 all fire had been extinguished.[70]

Off Bulong Point a suicide plane had first made a low-level strafing and bombing attack on a group of LSTs unloading at White Beach blowing the stern off one of them, and then turned towards the *Porcupine*, into which it crash dived. The tanker immediately burst into flames and a number of her crew were blown or jumped into the water. (At the same time another aircraft, employing the same tactic, had in a low-level attack straddled two destroyers with bombs before crashing into the *Gansevoort*.) Proceeding to assist the *Porcupine*, the *FS-367* took several men aboard via their climbing a boarding net. Crewman James D. Ellis sighting a man struggling in the water and calling for help, dove into the water and supported him until both were picked up by a craft. At 1615 it was obvious that the fire aboard the tanker had spread beyond control and there was no help available. The *FS-367* stayed alongside the *Porcupine* until all the survivors were off. The

Gansevoort then received orders to fire a torpedo into the tanker in an attempt to sink her and extinguish the fire before it reached the aviation gasoline stowed forward. In spite of a torpedo hit, the burning ship remained afloat and fire ignited escaping gasoline cascading into the sea. The spreading flames endangered the damaged *Gansevoort*, and her captain requested that the *FS-367* come alongside and take off her crew. By the time the freight-supply ship reached her, the DD was in immediate danger of being engulfed. The *FS-367* thus warped alongside the destroyer and began towing her to a safe anchorage. During this evolution an air alert sounded and an enemy plane was shot down immediately overhead, however the *FS-367* got the *Gansevoort* to safety several hundred yards off White Beach.[71]

Between 1800 and 2300 enemy planes were seen and heard in the Mangarin Bay area but the ships of the disbanded convoy were not attacked. The salvage of supplies and cargo aboard the *Orestes* commenced the following day amidst periodic duals between Japanese aircraft and fire from short batteries, LCI(L)s and PT boats. At dusk these vessels were dispersed in small groups to concealment by shoreline in the Manarin Bay and Ilin Island area for the night.[72]

Total convoy losses were three ships sunk or destroyed—*John Burke*, *LST-750*, and *Porcupine*—with an additional three ships—*William Sharon*, *Orestes*, and *Gansevoort*—rendered completely inoperative—requiring salvage, towing, and extensive yard repair—and various DDs, PTs, LSTs, and LCI(L)s damaged. The primary targets of the Japanese aircraft had been the large merchant ships heavily laden with materials for the resupply of the Allied force on Mindoro. Service in the U.S. Merchant Marine was particularly dangerous in World War II, and 1 in 26 mariners aboard merchant ships would die in the line of duty, a percentage higher than that of all the military services. In recognition of the danger posed to mariners, MacArthur had previously directed that merchant seamen of ships anchored in the Mindoro area occupy foxholes during the night for their own protection. Commenting on this decision and on the role the Merchant Marine played in the invasion of Mindoro and in preceding Pacific operations and campaigns, he stated:

> I have ordered them off their ships and into foxholes when their ships became untenable targets of attack. At our side they have suffered in bloodshed and in death. The high caliber of efficiency and the courage they displayed mark their conduct throughout the en-

tire campaign in the Southwest Pacific area. I hold no branch in higher esteem than the Merchant Marine services.

Most of the mariners chose to remain aboard the vessels as long as the ships were afloat in spite of this order under the guise of "volunteer skeleton crews."[73]

17

Lingayen Gulf Landings

> *The enemy's large scale employment of suicide planes give rise to highly concentrated and desperate anti-aircraft fire....About forty-three planes reached their targets[Allied ships], many after flying through the heaviest concentration of gun fire. A plane diving at speed in excess of four hundred fifty knots becomes in effect a low velocity projectile; its momentum is so great that is may not be deflected by volume of hits alone. The loss of a tail or the total disintegration of a wing generally, but not always, causes the plane to swerve from its general course. Killing the pilot may or may not deflect the plane.*
>
> Vice Adm. Thomas C. Kinkaid, commander, Luzon Attack Force, highlighting the grave danger that kamikaze aircraft presented to Allied shipping during Lingayen Gulf Landings in January 1945[1]

Assault forces of the Sixth Army under Lieutenant General Krueger, commenced landing on beachheads in the Lingayen-Dagupan-San Fabian-Rabon area of Luzon Island in the Lingayen Gulf at 0930 on 9 January 1945. The objectives of the amphibious operation—which, code named MIKE-ONE, was the largest operation of General MacArthur's Operation MUSKETEER, a four-phased plan to liberate the Philippine Islands—were the prompt seizure of central Luzon, the reoccupation of the Manila–central plains area, the establishment of bases for the support of operations to the north of the Philippines, and the complete occupation of Luzon Island. The weather conditions that day—deemed "S-Day"—were favorable; sea and surf conditions were slight, there was no precipitation, and visibility was limited only by bombardment smoke the morning land breeze carried offshore. As the Lingayen Attack Force (Task Force 79) landed, the enemy offered little opposition to either landing craft moving shoreward or to soldiers running across the beaches, the only resistance coming on the northeastern flank. This reflected new tactics adopted by the Japanese to withdraw from established beach defenses and to instead fight inland in the jungle. The landing of the San Fabian Attack Force, a few miles to the east, was unopposed. Over the next two days, ship-to-shore movement of follow-on assault troops and equipment continued smoothly and on 11 January, Krueger assumed command of Sixth Army forces ashore. That afternoon MacArthur and his staff left the light cruiser *Boise* (CL-47), for his headquarters at Dagupan near the Lingayen Gulf.[2]

The above brief description of the launching of the American invasion of Luzon Island provides no inkling of the destruction that Japanese kamikaze aircraft vested upon Allied ships during the movement of Army troops, equipment and supplies to the objective area. Moreover, the air attacks continued during and after the landings as well. Much has been written about the loss of life aboard scores of Navy ships, with associated damage to dozens of those ships and the loss of four; the escort carrier *Ommaney Bay* (CVE-79), and the destroyer-minesweepers *Hovey* (DMS-11), *Long* (DMS-12), and *Palmer* (DMS-5). The focus of this chapter is the "island hoppers" that received battle stars for the Lingayen Gulf operation. These ships were the small coastal transports *APc-12* and *APc-16*, the freight-supply ships *FS-156, 171, 174, 254, 364,* and *366*, the large tugs *LT-229, 231,* and *454*, and the coastal tankers *Y-6* and *21*. All of the freight-supply ships and the large tug *LT-454* were manned by Coast Guard crews. The identities of the commanding officers of the other ships are unknown, as is whether Coast Guardsmen, Merchant Mariners, Army Transport Service, or Army Engineer Special Brigade personnel comprised the crews of these ships. Summary information about the thirteen vessels follow, including the time periods of the 4-18 January Lingayen Gulf operation for which each ship received a battle star, and the names of commanding officers if known:

Ship	Length/Type Construction	Award Dates	Commanding Officer
Flagship of LCT Flotilla 23, Group 79			
USS *APc-12*	103-ft.; wood	4-18 Jan 1945	Lt. W. O. Gay, Jr., USNR
Echelon G-2 (Reinforcement Group Luzon Attack Force) Leyte to Lingayen			
USA *FS-174*	180-ft.; steel	11-18 Jan 1945	Lt. E. R. Sneeringer
USA *FS-364*	176-ft.; steel	11-18 Jan 1945	Coast Guard crew

Ship	Length/Type Construction	Award Dates	Commanding Officer
Echelon G-3 (Task Group 78.9) Leyte to Lingayen			
USA *FS-171*	180-ft.; steel	4-18 Jan 1945	Lt. (jg) Lemuel K. Hartsook, USCGR
USA *FS-366*	176-ft.; steel	4-18 Jan 1945	Lt. (jg) Charles E. Mashburn, USCGR
USA *FS-254*	176-ft.; steel	9-18 Jan 1945	Lt. Robert A. Copeland, Jr., USCGR
Echelon G-4 (Task Group 78.3) Leyte to Lingayen			
USA *LT-229*	149-ft.; steel	7-14 Jan 1945	
USA *Y-6*	182-ft.; steel	12-18 Jan 1945	
USA *Y-21*	162-ft.; steel	12-18 Jan 1945	
Echelon G-5 of Task Force 78 (Luzon Attack Force) Leyte to Lingayen			
USS *APc-16*	103-ft.; wood	4-18 Jan 1945	Lt. W. W. Harris, Jr., USNR
Support for Lingayen Gulf Operation			
USA *LT-231*	149-ft.; steel	14-18 Jan 1945	
USA *LT-454*	143-ft.; steel	14-18 Jan 1945	Coxswain Alan W. Davis, USCG
USA *FS-156*	180-ft; steel	15-18 Jan 1945	Lt. (jg) William H. Burgess, USCG

LUZON ATTACK FORCE

Of course, the aforementioned ships were only a very small part of the huge attack force assembled for the Lingayen Gulf landings. Vice Adm. Thomas C. Kinkaid commanded the Luzon Attack Force (Task Force 77) comprised of Task Force 78 (San Fabian Attack Force) under Vice Adm. Daniel E. Barbey and Task Force 79 (Lingayen Attack Force) under Vice Adm. Theodore S. Wilkinson, Jr. The below listed task groups supported these task forces:

Task Force 77 Task Groups Supporting Both Task Force 78 and Task Force 79	Task Group Commander
TG 77.1 Fleet Flagship Group	Capt. A. M. Granum
TG 77.2 Bombardment and Fire Support Group	Vice Adm. Jesse B. Oldendorf
TG 77.3 Close Covering Group	Rear Adm. Russell S. Berkey
TG 77.4 Escort Carrier Group	Rear Adm. C. T. Durgin
TG 77.5 Hunter-Killer Group	Capt. J. C. Cronin
TG 77.6 Minesweeping and Hydrographic Group	Comdr. W. R. Loud
TG 77.7 Screening Group	Capt. John B. McLean
TG 77.8 Salvage and Rescue Group	Comdr. B. S. Huie
TG 77.9 Reinforcement Group	Rear Adm. Richard L. Conolly
TG 77.10 Service Group	Rear Adm. R. O. Glover

In the final days leading up to the invasion of Luzon, there were 138 ships in the Lingayen area engaged in minesweeping and bombarding the coastline, and on the morning of 9 January 1945, 344 additional ships arrived to take part in the amphibious landings at

Lingayen and nearby San Fabian. The Army and Navy island hoppers arrived in the operations area as units of resupply groups after the initial assault. Five of the small ships earned battle stars prior to the landings, reflecting their involvement in combating Japanese attacks made against task groups of which they were a part while en route to Lingayen Gulf. The first convoy to transport Army personnel and supplies to the beachhead for resupply of assault forces was Task Group 78.9, designated Echelon G-3 of Task Force 78.[3]

ECHELON G-3, LEYTE TO LINGAYEN GULF

Echelon G-3 was a large task group, composed upon its arrival in Lingayen Gulf of 122 vessels, including the Army freight-supply ships *FS-171*, *FS-254*, and *FS-366*. Escorting them and the other vessels in convoy—fifty-three tanking landing ships, twenty-five merchant vessels, three tankers, three infantry landing craft, and a motor torpedo boat tender with twenty-three PT boats—were five destroyers and six destroyer escorts. The merchant ships had sailed on 3 January from Hollandia, located on Humboldt Bay on the northern coast of New Guinea. The following day, a group of LSTs from Biak, a small island just northwest of New Guinea, joined them, and this ever growing task group was augmented by other LSTs and miscellaneous vessels at Leyte on 9 January. The last units to hitch on were the *Wachopreague* (AGP-8) and her charges—PT boats from Motor Torpedo Boat Squadrons 28 and 36—at Mindoro for the final four days of the transit to Lingayen Gulf.[4]

Among the ships that joined at Leyte was the *FS-366*, loaded with perforated steel strip matting required for rapid construction of temporary runways and aircraft landing strips. Her commanding officer, Lt. (jg) Charles E. Mashburn, described difficulties ships in convoy faced, including the challenges of maintaining station in low visibility and avoiding collision, heavy seas, and a lack of adequate communications:

> Terrible weather, good in that it gave us perfect protection from [Japanese] planes as we steamed to Luzon's west coast. Terrible days of bad visibility. Large convoy, no communications. We kept station by grace. Had we broken down or become lost the Japs would have found us. We had no stragglers points [where a ship that fell out due to a casualty or battle damage might attain assistance]. We rolled in [the] trough hour after hour. Cargo shifted and we were in danger

of capsizing. Pumped water out to maintain equilibrium, . . . I spent remainder of days [in transit] sleepless and nervous for fear each roll would be our last.[5]

The weather cleared during the latter part of the transit, making detection by the enemy easier. The first hint of danger came the morning of 12 January when, at 0700 a single aircraft reconnoitered the convoy. A few hours later at 1250, as the convoy approached the southwest coast of Mindoro, a kamikaze that had made an undetected approach crashed into the starboard side of the *Liberty*-ship S.S. *Otis Skinner*, stationed alongside the *FS-366*. The ship was holed amidships above the waterline and great clouds of smoke poured forth, but her crew brought the fire under control, and there were no killed or wounded. A second enemy plane retired without attacking. At 1437 an "Oscar" (Nakajima Ki-43 Hayabusa Army Type 1 fighter) was sighted. It was likely a scout, for a group of aircraft attacked the convoy at 1830—centered on the rear of the formation, which contained the *Liberty* ships, tank landing ships, and various types of small craft. The pilots of five of the six aircraft tried to crash ships; four failed, due to a lack of skill and/or fire from escort and convoy guns seeking their air space. Nevertheless, this handful of zealous Japanese aviators caused many casualties aboard two of the ships and damage to four:

- One plane crashed the deck of the *Liberty*-ship S.S. *Kyle V. Johnson*, causing a large fire and many casualties
- One crashed close aboard the tank landing ship *LST-778*, causing numerous casualties and minor damage
- One crashed close aboard the *Liberty*-ship S.S. *David Dudley Field*, causing minor engine room damage
- One crashed close aboard the *Liberty*-ship S.S. *Edward N. Westcott*, causing superficial damage on the main deck and one man seriously wounded
- One was believed to have crashed near the rear of the convoy without damage to any ship
- The remaining plane retired without attacking[6]

The convoy entered Lingayen Gulf the following morning, at 0800 on 13 January. The gulf, which lay about one hundred miles north of Manila, was of rectangle shape, approximately twenty-miles wide and thirty-miles deep, with the long axis orientated nearly north-south.

The massive formation proceeded onward for two hours until, as the ships neared their destination, the LSTs detached to proceed to designated beaches. The *Liberty* ships anchored at 1130 while awaiting specific instructions from commander Task Force 78. After the destroyers shepherded the merchantmen to their designated beaches, the task group dissolved.[7]

Map 17-1

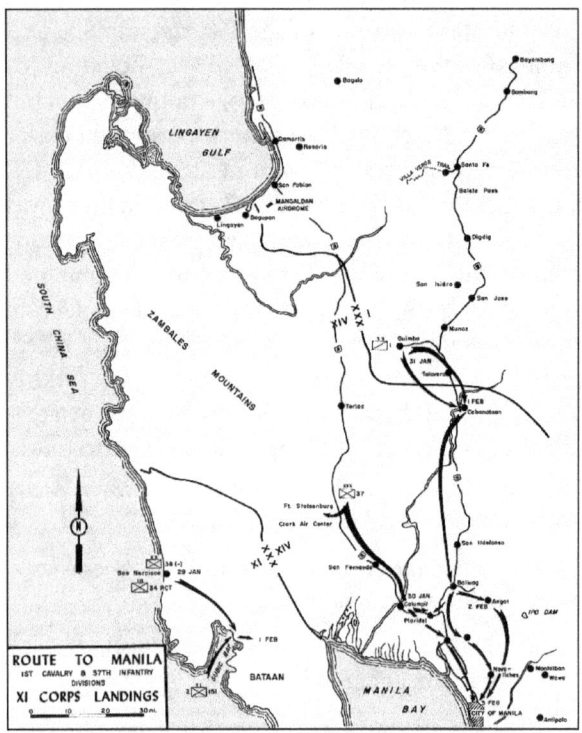

Although assault forces of the Sixth Army met little opposition on landing beaches in Lingayen Gulf, many ships suffered kamikaze attacks while en route there, and during and after the initial assault of Luzon Island.
Source: http://www.ibiblio.org/hyperwar/USMC/IV/maps/USMC-IV-20.jpg

The *FS-366* arrived at the beachhead to find a heavy swell, no docks, and the constant threat of attack by the enemy. After discharging her cargo, the freighter remained anchored in Lingayen Gulf in an emergency standby status for other tasking, on guard—and especially at night—for Japanese suicide swimmers with bombs on their backs and "Q boats." The latter term referred to suicide motorboats that were a part of the wider Japanese Special Attack Units program. Toward the end of 1943, in response to unfavorable progress in the war, the Japanese command had entertained suggestions offered by junior officers for various suicide craft. These suggestions were initially rejected but later deemed necessary, particularly after the loss of a majority of the empire's experienced pilots. The Navy accepted the idea of kamikaze ("divine wind") planes, kaiten ("turning of the heavens") mini-submarines, shinyo ("sea quake") suicide boats, and fukuryu ("crouching dragons") suicide divers or human mines. Mashburn described the threat imposed by enemy swimmers to Allied ships while at anchor:

> We are in constant alert. Japs swim out and plant TNT on [ship's] hull or hawse pipes [openings in the hull that are used to "hawse" or store anchors].[8]

CONDITIONS IDEAL FOR ENEMY AIRCRAFT ATTACKS

Previous kamikaze attacks on fleet units in the Leyte Gulf and on assault and resupply echelons to Ormoc on Leyte and Mindoro Island had resulted in heavy losses of, or damage to destroyers, reducing the availability of these type ships for the Lingayen Gulf landing. An alternate route to proceeding to Lingayen Gulf via the Surigao Strait and Sulu Sea had been considered in order to decrease the vulnerability of convoys to enemy attack. The alternative was for ships to remain well off the eastern Philippine coast and then proceed through the Luzon Strait. Ultimately the route through Surigao Strait was selected—in spite of the disadvantages imposed by restricted waters and the likelihood of alerting the enemy of Allied intentions at an earlier date—because it allowed for the use of friendly land-based aircraft to provide cover for the convoys. However, despite these and other precautions, attacks by Japanese planes continued, and the conditions within Lingayen Gulf were favorable to both suicide and conventional aircraft.[9]

The foot or southern end of the gulf offered shallow sand beaches suitable for landing amphibious forces, backed by flat land, interspersed with marshes, extending into the central plain of Luzon. Conversely, hills and mountain ranges bordering the gulf to the east and west were ideal for helping shield approaching enemy planes from detection. A series of strikes by Allied land and carrier-based aircraft had caused substantial damage to Japanese facilities and aircraft in the Philippines area. Nevertheless, there remained over seventy fields in the islands from which enemy aircraft could operate, and the Japanese could stage planes from air bases in China—on the islands of Formosa (now Taiwan) and Hainan—and from the Netherlands East Indies. The Japanese would greatly increase the employment of kamikaze aircraft against ships during the Lingayen operation as a major part of their defense, and these attacks were numerous and more skillfully executed than those previously encountered.[10]

Sunset during the Lingayen Gulf landings was at 1740, and thirty percent of the suicide attacks occurred between the hours of 1700 and 1800. The preference of Japanese pilots was to attack one half-hour before sunset. This allowed them to use the sun's glare to help cover their approach, and there were fewer adversaries in the sky, as the American carriers recovered their daytime combat air patrols prior to the onset of darkness. The enemy reduced the effectiveness of shipboard radar by approaching low over nearby hills. Pilots typically flew near the surface to avoid detection until within about 10-15 miles of their target. They would then climb rapidly to 15,000-20,000 feet before beginning a shallow glide towards the target keeping a constant angle of elevation. Ships often detected aircraft climbing through radar beams, but then lost them and did not reacquire on radar until they were close aboard. Three-quarters of the attacks were made by groups of planes within a half-hour period against several ships. A formation of two to fifteen planes would appear, and then sometimes split into two or three attacking groups. The kamikaze pilots would pick out their targets, and all the planes would then attempt to crash into them simultaneously or in quick succession. This tactic split the collective anti-aircraft fire of convoy ships and reduced its effectiveness against any one plane. Sometimes a single plane would make a bombing run in one sector, to focus the attention of gun crews on it, before a formation of planes would attack in another. The Japanese were now employing coordinated tactics, and the use of suicide aircraft was becoming an organized effort rather than an individual one.[11]

Following the arrival of Echelon G-3 at Lingayen Gulf on 13 January, other resupply echelons appeared at regular intervals off beachheads as scheduled. The last convoy arrived on 27 January carrying army reinforcements made up of the 32nd Infantry Division, the 1st Cavalry Division and the 112th Regimental Combat teams from Leyte. The safe arrival at these troops was made possible by the collective efforts of the crews of Navy, Army, and merchant ships in preceding convoys in combating suicide plane attacks. On only two occasions were destroyers of the Luzon attack force called upon to engage enemy surface ships. In the first encounter the range was not closed to the Japanese destroyer *Momi* by the American destroyer *Bennion* (DD-662), and the Australian frigate *Gascoyne* (K354) and sloop *Warrego* (U73). In the subsequent engagement the Japanese destroyer *Hinoki* was sunk by 5-inch naval gunfire without damage to the destroyers *Braine* (DD-630), *Charles Ausburne* (DD-570), *Russell* (DD-414), and *Shaw* (DD-373).[12]

During the five days preceding the landing on 9 January, kamikaze aircraft struck thirty-one ships. Suicide planes crashed the carriers *Manila Bay* (CVE-61) and *Savo Island* (CVE-78), and destroyers *Helm* (DD-388) and *Stafford* (DE-411) off Mindoro; nearly all the other attacks were at Lingayen. There, three minesweepers—the *Hovey* (DMS-11), *Long* (DMS-12), and *Palmer* (DMS-5)—were sunk, ten of the other large ships received significant damage, and twelve assorted vessels received minor damage.[13]

ECHELON G-4 OF TASK GROUP 78.3

> *This echelon, proceeding at a speed of advance of four point five knots for eight days through the numerous enemy occupied islands of the Philippines, presented an attractive target. The fact that all units were delivered to the objective area without damage is difficult to explain.*
>
> The commanding officer of the destroyer escort USS *Day* (DE-225) describing in a report the transit of a "slow tow" group of Army and Navy tugs from Leyte to Lingayen Gulf on the large island of Luzon. No damage was incurred by the convoy, or two DEs escorting it, during three separate attacks by Japanese aircraft.[14]

Echelon G-4 of Task Group 78.3, a "slow tow" convoy of tugs escorted by the destroyer escorts *Day* (DE-225) and *Tinsman* (DE-589), left Leyte at 0800 on 6 January for Lingayen Gulf. It was composed of a former Navy minesweeper, the tug *Whippoorwill* (ATO-169), the Australian tug HMAS *Reserve*, an assortment of thirteen Army tugs, and the Army coastal tankers *Y-6* and *Y-21*. The commanding officer of the *Whippoorwill* was the convoy commander. In tow astern of his ship was one pontoon crane barge, one pontoon GSK barge, and one gasoline barge (*BK031*). Eleven of the Army tugs were towing barges and/or lighters; the other two unburdened vessels were assigned as "trouble shooters" with the duty of assisting the other ships if necessary. The convoy's sluggish 4.5 knot speed and composition—57 hulls in three columns stretching back six miles—precluded any tactical maneuvers except changes of course of twenty degrees or less. Since the convoy had no voice radio communications, all course and speed changes were effected with signal light by day and with bull horn at night. The *Day* was positioned ahead of the convoy and the *Tinsman* astern of it. The location of the two DEs was not optimal for anti-air defense of the formation flanks, but instead reflected concern about torpedo boat or midget submarine attacks on the deep draft gasoline barges under tow.[15]

The *Day* went to general quarters that evening to investigate an unknown surface craft, which proved to be a native Filipino outrigger banca boat. The following morning the *Tinsman* picked up a bogie on radar at 0616, only six miles distant and approaching from the starboard quarter of the convoy. The radar screen was degraded by land echoes and the plane's approach had been masked by Bohol Island, which lay southwest of Leyte Island and north of Mindanao. Moreover, visibility was poor; a heavy haze hung low over the water and sunrise was still forty minutes away. Before the identity of the aircraft could be resolved, it had passed overhead the *Day* and released two bombs that fell about 150 yards off her port bow. The plane, apparently conducting reconnaissance, had flown up the entire convoy at low altitude. After dropping its ordnance, it circled to the north before radar contact was lost eight miles away. No guns were able to get on target, but in any case no damage resulted.[16]

The next few days were uneventful as the ships proceeded first on a south-southwest course, and then west, northwest, and north, in a roughly circular route around islands of the Philippines. The group was about ninety miles west of Manila in the early afternoon of 12 January, when the *Day*—patrolling ahead of the formation—detected an inbound aircraft bearing 60 degrees relative off the starboard side of the convoy, range 18 miles. The other escort, the *Tinsman*, was then alongside the harbor tug *TP-129*, positioned at the rear of the starboard column, to transfer a pharmacist's mate aboard. The chief torpedoman on watch on the bridge of the DE sighted the enemy plane, a

Val, diving on the formation. It made a beam attack on the tug *Reserve*, angle of dive about 45 degrees, but overshot the target and crashed into the sea near the two lead ships in the center and port columns. The plane had apparently taken fire and was damaged, as it was emitting smoke as it bored into the water. The *Tinsman* had by then cleared the convoy and was turning with hard left rudder at twenty knots in an effort to "unmask her guns" (maneuvering to clear friendly ships from her line of fire). Two other Vals were sighted circling overhead, and at 1320 they began making a strafing and bombing attack on the convoy from the direction of the sun, the side opposite that of original attack. The *Tinsman* and the multitude of tugs, and the *Day* once she had a clear bearing, took the aircraft under fire. One plane dropped bombs that fell between two columns near the center of the convoy. Both aircraft disappeared into cloud cover overhead and retired towards Manila, tracked outward on radar by the *Day* for a distance of thirty miles.[17]

A single plane made an attack the following morning of 13 January. The unidentified Japanese single-engine fighter was sighted at 0751 off the starboard quarter of the convoy at a distance of six miles. Visibility was poor due to about eighty-five percent cloud cover and a low ceiling at approximately 2,000 feet. As the plane approached the convoy at an elevation of about 1,000 feet, it was identified as a "Hamp" (Mitsubishi A6M3 Navy Type 0 carrier fighter Model 32). The *Tinsman* took the enemy under fire with her 5-inch and 40mm batteries, and the plane immediately commenced a dive on a coastal tanker at the end of the center column. Several tugs opened fire with .50-caliber machine guns as the aircraft approached the oiler from just abaft its starboard beam and dove from a low altitude at an angle of about 25 to 30 degrees. The pilot overshot the target, likely due to damage—observers reported the plane was on fire—and crashed into the sea between the left and center columns.[18]

Echelon G-4 arrived at its destination in late morning the following day, where upon all Army tugs and tows were directed to "Blue Beach" and the American and Australian tugs and tows to the anchorage area. There is little information about the ships that were in the convoy. However, the periods for which three Army ships received battle stars—the large tug *LT-229* (7–14 January 1945), and the coastal tankers *Y-6* and *Y-21* (12–18 January 1945)—correlates with the movements of Echelon G-4.[19]

Chapter 17
ECHELON G-2 REINFORCEMENT GROUP (LUZON ATTACK FORCE)

At the time the enemy reconnaissance aircraft had dropped two bombs off the starboard bow of the *Day* (one of two destroyer-escorts shepherding Echelon G-4 to Lingayen Gulf on 7 January) there had been another large convoy seven miles astern. In fact the "snooper" had earlier closed to within one mile of an escort ship of Echelon G-2, the destroyer *McGowan* (DD-678), but had apparently failed to sight in the darkness either it or the formation it guarded. Accompanying the Luzon Attack Force reinforcement group of tank landing ships and merchant vessels were the freight-supply ships *FS-154*, *173*, *174*, and *364*. They along with *Liberty*-ship *Peter Lassen* had joined at Leyte. The mission of Echelon G-2 was to transport elements of the 158th Regimental Combat Team (Reinforced) from Noemfoor, a small island located off the coast of New Guinea, and miscellaneous I and XIV Corps and Sixth Army troops, equipment and supplies from south and southwest Pacific ports to Lingayen Gulf and land them on Lingayen and San Fabian assault beaches as directed by commander Task Force 78 and commander Task Force 79, respectively.[20]

The *FS-174* was then assigned to the U.S. Army, 4th - Engineer, Shore and Boat Regiment (4th ES&BR), responsible for directing the landing of troops and supplies on assault beaches. The duty of the freight-supply ship was to take necessary equipment, such as airstrip matting, 55-gallon drums of high octane gasoline, bulldozers, jeeps, and trucks in as close to the beach as possible for unloading into LCT and LCVP landing craft for movement ashore. Both the 180-foot *FS-174*, commanded by Lt. E. R. Sneeringer, USCG, and the slightly smaller also Coast Guard-manned 176-foot *FS-364* earned a battle star for the period 11-18 January 1945.[21]

The voyage to Lingayen Gulf was uneventful except for the usual difficulties experienced in keeping merchant ships in convoy closed up and closed in, particularly at night. Only three of the nine merchantmen had voice radios. To compensate for this communications deficiency, the task group commander assigned the commanding officer of the *Loeser* (DE-680) to oversee the merchant ships, issuing all orders to the formation, repeating all signals in MerSigs (Merchant Signals), and generally supervising the vessels. The formation performed well with flag signals by day but poorly at night. However, the destroyer captain was able to effectively maneuver the ships around corners in darkness through the use of a bull horn. The ordered convoy speed was reduced following discovery that the 9.5 knot LST-formation speed ran away from some of the Army FS ships. On 11 January, the task group entered the gulf and tank landing ships beached from Lingayen "Orange Beach" to San Fabian "Red Beach." Of the fifty LSTs, twenty-eight reported to Vice Admiral Barbey (CTF-78) and twenty-two to Vice Admiral Wilkinson (CTF-79).[22]

The unloading of ships was hampered the first night by Japanese artillery located in the hills to the east of San Fabian, as the guns bombarded White Beaches 1 and 2 and supply dump areas in the rear of them between the hours of 1945-2215 and 0150-0400. In the early morning darkness of 12 January, heavy fire, thought to be from five or six-inch guns, set supplies on the beach aflame, scored a direct hit on the port quarter of the *LST-270*, and caused numerous casualties among Army and Navy servicemen on the beach and aboard the beached ships. The task group commander ordered smoke pots lit on the beach to shield the ships from view of the enemy gunfire spotters, and LSTs to retract. However, because many of the ships had broached in deeper than normal water, and had accordingly constructed sand bag and sand ramps to assist in unloading, they were lodged on the beach. Only two tank landing ships were able to get off it, however, Army heavy artillery commenced counter-battery fire and silenced the enemy guns.[23]

The *FS-154* left Lingayen Gulf on 31 January as part of a slow convoy of LSTs, LCIs, and merchant ships (Task Unit 78.11.13) bound for Leyte. The large tugs *LT-1*, *129*, *225*, *231*, *352*, and *652* were also a part of this task unit. The *FS-364* arrived at Naval Base, Hollandia on 12 February, in company with the *FS-185* and large tugs *LT-135*, *229*, *454*, and *646* as part of a group of *Liberty* ships escorted by two patrol frigates and two destroyer escorts. That same day the *FS-174* left Lingayen Gulf in a slow tow convoy for Leyte (TU 78.11.23), and six days later, the *FS-173*, *FS-158*, *FS-163*, *FS-254*, and *LT-348* followed, on 18 February, as a part of another convoy (Task Unit 78.11.27).[24]

ECHELON G-5 OF TASK FORCE 78 (LUZON ATTACK FORCE)

The *APc-16* had been the first island hopper to sortie for Lingayen Gulf, as part of Task Group 78.1 which sailed from Aitape on the north coast of New Guinea on 28 December, en route to the Lingayen Gulf, via Leyte Gulf, Surigao Strait, Sulu Sea, and Mindoro Strait. Vice Admiral Barbey embarked in *Blue Ridge* (AGC-2) commanded the task group. Two escort carriers joined on 31 December. Five days later, a number of ships, including the *APc-16* and *APc-19*, detached from the formation on 4 January and proceeded to anchorage off Dulag, Leyte; awaiting formation of Echelon G-5 of the Luzon Attack Force. It comprised twenty-six tank landing craft (of LCT Groups 66 and 81) and the *APc-16*, escorted by the destroyer escorts *Daniel A. Joy* (DE-585) and *Lough* (DE-586). The convoy left the morning of 5 January for Mindoro, with the *Daniel A. Joy* positioned on the port bow and *Lough* on the starboard bow of the formation. The *APc-16* was centered behind the two combatant ships, assigned as the guide for the LCTs formed up in four columns behind her.[25]

Early the next morning, the *Lough* picked up an unidentified aircraft on radar during morning twilight, which dropped a single bomb near the port side of the formation. The plane was not sighted either before or after the attack, but caused no damage. The next appearance by the enemy occurred later that day, 6 January, during evening twilight, when a sighting was made aboard the *Lough* of a plane well astern, and so close to two friendly aircraft that it appeared to be a part of that group. Against a background of dark clouds and land which made it hard to distinguish, the plane then made an unopposed strafing run at 1853 on the convoy and the *Lough*. The aircraft—possibly a "Kate"—appeared briefly against the horizon after passing overhead, and the *Joy*'s 5-inch/38 gun mount got off four rounds but scored no hits. Neither DE could see the plane as it made a second strafing run several minutes later, but convoy guns opened and the enemy aircraft exploded in the air near the bridge of the *Lough*, and crashed into the water about fifty feet off her port bow. To witnesses aboard the *Daniel A. Joy*, it appeared the pilot had tried to "wing over" in an attempt to crash the *Lough*. However, whether due to damage or pilot error, there was one less enemy aircraft to worry about. Echelon G-5 reached Mangarin Bay, Mindoro Island in the evening of 8 January.[26]

Three days later Echelon G-5, formed as before less one LCT, stood out at 0845 on 11 January for Lingayen Gulf. Air coverage by P38s provide a measure of conform the first day, and there were friendly F4Us and F6Fs overhead the second day. The morning of 13 January, the commanding officer of the *Daniel A. Joy* set general quarters due to an unknown air contact eleven miles away. The plane circled over another nearby convoy, drew heavy anti-aircraft fire, and at 0820 crash-dove into what appeared from the destroyer to be a cargo ship, but which was actually the attack transport *Zeilin* (APA-3). Sightings of other convoys became more frequent and the following day, Echelon G-5 entered the Lingayen Gulf in early morning darkness on 14 January.²⁷

REMAINING "ISLAND HOPPERS" TO SEE ACTION IN THE LINGAYEN GULF

The *APc-12* left Hollandia for Leyte on 10 January 1944. Embarked aboard her was the commander of Tank Landing Craft Group 79 (of LCT Flotilla 27) with the group's landing craft—less the *LCT-695*, and the addition of LCTs *390* and *1151*—in company. The group reached Leyte on 15 January, and the small coastal transport thereafter made her way to the Lingayen Gulf, where she and three small Army ships, not previously discussed, earned battle stars. Little information exists about her activities and those of the freight-supply ship *FS-156* and large tugs *LT-231* and *454*. It is likely, however, that the stars earned and later affixed to Asiatic-Pacific theater ribbons on uniform blouses were linked to Japanese air raids.²⁸

18

Suicide Boat Attacks at Nasugbu, Luzon

> *The resupply of the Mike-Six Operation was a deviation from any previous resupply plan employed in this theater. Due to the scarcity of amphibious shipping, meager port facilities in the objective area, and the Navy's inability to provide a continuous protective screen for heavy shipping, it was necessary to send a block-loaded Liberty Ship [S.S. Wallace R. Farrington] to MINDORO and employ ten fast supply boats [freight-supply ships] and four landing ships (medium) in the shuttle run between MINDORO and the objective area.*
>
> Lt. Gen. Robert L. Eichelberger, commanding general 8th U.S. Army, describing frustrations associated with the movement over water of necessary materials and supplies to Nasugbu, Luzon Island[1]

> *Lack of protection and the proven danger of Japanese Q boat attacks made it necessary that echelons arriving at daylight be unloaded and sailed by dark or shortly thereafter. It cannot be said that the Army Shore Parties cooperated toward this end, either by furnishing adequate parties of their own, or by utilizing the abundant local sources of labor.*
>
> Rear Adm. William W. Fechteler, commander Amphibious Group Eight, Seventh Fleet, expressing similar displeasure about the length of time the Army expended to unload the freight-supply ships at Nasugbu[2]

MIKE-SIX AND MIKE-SEVEN OPERATIONS

The Sixth Army met little opposition on its landing at Lingayen Gulf, and during the thrust of infantry divisions into the central plains of Luzon, because the Japanese had expected a landing on Luzon in the

Damortis-San Fernando area to the south vice the Lingayen-Dagupan area to the north. However, enemy resistance had stiffened as American forces drove south towards Manila. Moreover, the Sixth Army had outrun its main supply route and was in great danger of a strong counterattack on its thinly held flanks that would sever the line of communication to Lingayen Gulf. To help prevent the massing of Japanese forces against Sixth Army troops, MacArthur ordered diversionary assaults, termed MIKE-SIX and MIKE-SEVEN, in the San Antonio-San Narciso and Nasugbu areas.[3]

The MIKE-SEVEN operation occurred first when on 29 January 1945, XI Corps under Eighth U.S. Army control landed on beaches in the San Antonio-San Narciso area on the west coast of Luzon without opposition. This landing completely surprised the Japanese and against only light opposition, the force captured Subic Town and Olongapo by 31 January. MacArthur had proposed the idea of MIKE-SIX, a raid in force led by Lt. Gen. Robert L. Eichelberger, the commanding general of the 8th U.S. Army, to him in November, at a conference on Leyte. The objective was to disrupt the Japanese lines of communication, create a diversion to support the planned landing at Lingayen Gulf, and, if possible, even occupy Manila. A series of planning conferences followed, but the original concept of the Eighth Army commander leading a raid in force remained. Subsequent reports by American reconnaissance parties and guerrillas of large numbers of Japanese in the target area ultimately resulted in a decision to land one regiment of the 11th Airborne Division at Nasugbu, on the southwest coast of Luzon below Manila Bay and forty-five miles from Manila. A second regimental combat team was to land later at Nasugbu as directed by Eichelberger. The 11th Airborne Division would then drive inland and join the 511th Parachute Infantry after its drop on Tagaytay Ridge to the east-northeast. The combined force was then to proceed northward as rapidly as the situation allowed.[4]

The MIKE-SIX assault was launched the morning of 31 January when, at 0715, air and naval units supporting the landing opened fire simultaneously on suspected enemy positions on Nasugbu and San Diego Points, which bracketed the opposite ends of the beachhead. It was a calm day and as the sun rose on a serene sea, it was easy to forget for a time that death waited ashore if the enemy was well entrenched on the landing beach. After aircraft—eighteen A20 Havocs and nine P38 Lightnings—gave the beach a raking over, bombardment from escort destroyers, and rocket ships (converted infantry landing craft) followed. This bombardment drew no return enemy fire, but as the first boat wave made the beach at 0830 it was met with light machine gun and 75mm artillery fire from Nasuabu Point. The remainder of the 187th Glider Regimental Combat Team followed, and by early afternoon the 188th Glider RCT and other division troops were all ashore. American artillery soon silenced the fire from Nasugbu Point, and the 11th Division moved inland and overran Nasugbu Town and its airfield without difficulty. By 1530 the Allied invasion force had reached and seized intact the strategic Palico River Bridge on the Nasugbu-Tagaytay road. The Japanese had cut stringers and uprights of the steel bridge and placed demolition charges to destroy the bridge, but were overrun and unable to do so. The bridge was of immense value as it permitted use of the road, enabling a short supply line. Eichelberger, aware of the value of surprise achieved through rapid movement, ordered the commander of the 11th Airborne Division to continue the advance during the night and to get as far forward as possible by daylight. That night, Japanese "Q" boats attacked a defensive screen of Navy ships in Nasugbu Bay sinking one submarine chaser before they were dispersed.[5]

JAPANESE EMPLOYMENT OF SUICIDE BOATS

> *Survivors from PC 1129 stated that these small craft seemed to surround them and then crash into their sides. It is believed these small craft carry armed bombs that go off as craft crashes into side of ship.*
>
> Destroyer USS *Tinsman* (DE-589) war diary entry describing an attack by Japanese "Shinyo" suicide boats that sank an American sub-chaser off Nasugbu, Philippine Islands on 31 January 1945

Despite the significant losses of Navy and merchant ships at Leyte and Lingayen Gulfs and off Mindoro, the necessary ships to carry assault troops to Nasugbu Bay were found and assembled on the southwest coast of Luzon. Totaling almost a hundred ships, the convoy was comprised of high-speed transports, and landing craft—LSMs, LSTs, and LCIs—escorted by destroyers. It sailed from Tarragona on the Leyte Gulf on 27 January, headed south through the Mindoro Sea, and then swung north through the Sulu Sea to Mindoro. The ships carrying the 511th Parachute Infantry Combat Team departed there, and the convoy continued on to Nasugbu Bay arriving on 31 January following an uneventful voyage. The assault troops were disembarked and that night, a special disposition was ordered to protect the ships and unloaded landing craft still present off the beachhead from enemy suicide craft reportedly based in the area. The infantry landing craft anchored to form a close protective screen around the beachhead stretching from Nasugbu Point to San Diego Point, with the LSTs beached inside them. Patrolling outside this defensive screen further offshore were destroyer escorts and submarine chasers, supported by two destroyers that were also available for fire support if requested.[6]

These measures proved prudent, as that night Japanese suicide boats launched attacks from seaward against the beachhead. The submarine chaser *PC-1129* reported at 2245 sighting several small craft, upon which the destroyer escort *Lough* (DE-586) closed her. At 2300, after sighting a line of small boats 1,000 yards ahead, the *Lough* turned to seaward to outflank them, and after doing so, opened fire. Between 2305 and 2337, the destroyer escort worked back and forth across the flank of the group, firing on enemy boats as sighted and maneuvering radically to avoid contact. As this search for Japanese craft took place, two or three of the suicide boats surrounded the *PC-1129* fifty minutes shy of midnight and depth-charged her, resulting in her loss. The commanding officer of the destroyer *Claxton* (DD-571) described the action:

> The *Lough*, who was patrolling off Talin Point to the south of the beaches, reported that numerous small unidentified boats were in her immediate vicinity and that she was taking them under fire. . . . Both the *Claxton* and *Flusser* [DD-368] illuminated the area with star shells in an attempt to afford the *Lough* an opportunity to see the boats and to try to identify them. It was strongly suspected that they were either or all of the following, enemy "Q" boats, midget submarines, or other small craft intent on suicide missions. The illumination was of little assistance in that the targets were so small and at such short range. At 2326 the *Lough* reported sinking one, there having been very little flame, no smoke, and no explosion. . . . The *Claxton* made contact on two small targets and opened fire with the 40mm battery, results were unobserved. The peculiar and definitely provoking thing about these boats was the inability to sight them visually.

At 0007 the Task Group Commander reported that the *PC 1129*, a ship of the Control Unit, had been seriously damaged and left in a sinking condition. Reports later received indicated that these small craft had encircled the *PC 1129* very close aboard and dropped explosive charges in or near her. No explosion was felt, but when discovered by the *Lough* her decks were practically awash. The *Lough* picked up survivors, later reports indicated that one man was lost.

In the darkness of night, total enemy losses were difficult to estimate, but included at least six boats. Late that morning, the task group commander directed that three LCI(R)s, landing craft fitted with rocket launchers, accompanied by two destroyers investigate and destroy a Japanese small boat hideout at Talin Bay.[7]

Termed Shinyo (meaning "Sea Quake") the motorboats were part of a wider Japanese Special Attack Units program. During the war approximately 6,200 Shinyo were produced for the Navy and 3,000 similar Maru-ni (coastal defense motorboats) for the Army. A majority of the Shinyo were stored along the coast in Japan for the ultimate defense against the expected invasion of the Home islands. The main use of the Shinyo boats that were employed took place during the Philippines Campaign. The first successful attack had occurred three weeks earlier in the Lingayen Gulf, when Shinyo crippled the auxiliary transport *War Hawk* (AP-168) and sank the landing craft *LCI(G)-365* and *LCI(M)-974*. A suicide boat laden with explosives and going full-throttle slammed into the port side of the *War Hawk*, blowing a 25-foot diameter hole in her hull, killing sixty-one, and knocking out power as the engine room flooded. Driven by a single man, the boats were typically equipped with a bow-mounted charge of up to 700 pounds of explosives which was detonated by either impact or from a manual switch in the driver's area. The Shinyo also carried two anti-ship rockets mounted on launchers located on either side behind the driver. The craft employed against the sub-chaser *PC-1129* were likely Maru-ni or Renraku-tei (liaison boats), based on a report they dropped explosive charges near the submarine chaser. These craft of the Imperial Japanese Army boasted two depth charges on racks behind the driver, and were not true suicide boats. In theory the driver of the boat approached the target at high speed, swerved at the last moment and dropped the depth charges alongside the ship. However, as the ordnance was set to detonate only three to four seconds after release, the attacking boat might or might not make it clear of the destructive force of the detonation. Moreover, boats that got clear were often sunk by gunfire from the vessel they had just attacked.[8]

FREIGHT-SUPPLY SHIPS MOVE FORWARD TO NASUGBU

Task Unit 78.2.11 left Magarin Bay, Mindoro at 0300 on 3 February for Nasugbu. Comprising the group were eight Army FS ships—*FS-163, FS-168, FS-187, FS-191, FS-352, FS-365, FS-387,* and *FS-389*—and twenty-one landing craft, screened by the destroyer escorts *Lough* and *Tinsman* and the submarine chasers *SC-514, SC-1052,* and *SC-1319.* The group arrived in the objective area about four hours later, but unloading of the freight-supply ships was exceedingly slow due to the small Army shore party on the beach, which necessitated the vessels remaining at Nasugbu overnight and at risk of attack from the suicide boats. After spending two long days and longer nights off the beach waiting to discharge their cargo, the ships were finally able to leave for Mindoro on the afternoon of 5 February. Seven of the Army ships—all except the *FS-187*—earned a battle star for 4 February 1945:

Ship	Length/Type Construction	Commanding Officer
FS-163	180-feet/steel	Lt. (jg) Donald K. Townsend, USCGR
FS-168	180-feet/steel	Lt. (jg) Joseph A. Kean, USCGR
FS-187	180-feet/steel	Lt. (jg) W. A. Skelton, Jr. USCGR
FS-191	180-feet/steel	Lt. (jg) E.R. Holden, USCGR
FS-352	176-feet/steel	Lt. (jg) E. B. Drinkwater, USCG
FS-365	176-feet/steel	Lt. Comdr. Benjamin Ayesa, USCGR
FS-387	176-feet/steel	Lt. J. L. Gray, USCG
FS-389	176-feet/steel	Lt. C. N. Brown, USCGR[9]

ARMY *FS-309* ATTACKED BY "Q" BOAT

Two other Coast Guard-manned freight-supply ships assigned to the operation, the *FS-184* and *FS-309*, had remained behind when the task group sortied from Leyte Gulf in the early evening of 27 January due to not having completed loading, but arrived later at Nasugbu. The *184* was taking on ammunition for the 11th Airborne Division, and the *309* bringing aboard materials to construct a dock, and other stuff for combat engineers. The two freight-supply ships arrived at Nasugbu on 7 February in company with four medium landing ships and two destroyer escorts, following which the LSMs beached at 1000. There were no vehicles to unload them, not even trucks, and the Army officer in charge was informed that the landing ships would retract from the beach and sail prior to nightfall due to the danger of enemy "Q" boat attacks, regardless of the condition of unloading. The work was was done by 2000, due largely to the "bluejackets" aboard the landing craft, with some Army personnel and Filipinos also working the cargo. The task unit reformed thirty minutes later and sailed, leaving both freight-supply ships in the area.[10]

A former crewman of the *FS-184*, Quartermaster First Hank Rodgers, Jr., later described having suffered the same lack of support and, due to the threat of attack by suicide boats, the *FS-309* anchoring well away from his explosives-laden freighter:

> We were supposed to have native labor waiting for us to unload the vessel, but as it turned out, that wasn't the case at all, and, of course, the troops which were engaged with the Japanese about two miles up the beach, they had their hands full. So, we unloaded our own cargo once we got there, but, of course, our biggest concern was the Japanese Q-boats . . . the waterborne brothers of the kamikaze. . . . When the *309* found out that the *184* had ammo on board, they hoisted their anchor and went over to the far side of the cove to get away from us so that in the event of an attack that they would have a little protection. Once we unloaded the cargo of ammo we had on board, to the tune of 60 tons, we got a new cargo put on board for transport—dead American paratroopers. We returned with these dead paratroopers to Tacloban, Leyte, for air transportation back to Finchaven, New Guinea for the [Army] graves people at that location. It wasn't very pleasant to do. But we got it done.[11]

The *FS-309* subsequently moored alongside the partially wrecked Wawa River Wharf at Nasugbu Bay where, nearly three years earlier, the Japanese had landed the last 300 defenders of Bataan and Corregidor and many of the prisoners had died for want of medical care. The *FS-309* was the first United States ship to remain overnight. To help safeguard his ship from waterborne attack, Lt. Oliver Rahle, USCG, ordered the construction of a raft extending out from the vessel. Five days later, the expected "Q" boat attack came when at a little over an hour past midnight on 14 February, a crewman on watch sighted three helmeted Japanese approaching in a motorboat. He gave the alarm and the searchlight was turned on them. Blinded, the driver ran the boat into the raft near the fantail. The explosion that followed propelled the "Q" boat into the air, and also lifted the stern of the *FS-309* out of the water. Harbor sand and water raining down filled a lifeboat on the ship's boat deck, crewmen hurrying to their battle stations were thrown violently to the deck, and water poured into berthing areas through weather doors and passageways. No one was hurt and the ship was comparatively undamaged thanks to the protective device around the hull. Rahle earned the Bronze Star for his foresight in rigging the raft about his ship, which prevented the deaths of crew members and likely the loss of the *FS-309*. A direct impact by the "Q" boat would almost certainly have sunk the Army ship, based on the damage caused by the explosives, whose force had been dissipated well away from the vessel's hull when the boat struck the barrier. The bodies of a Japanese captain and a lieutenant were found, indicating the importance of the mission, one of many such suicide boat attacks made in February 1945.[12]

In recognition of the danger that these type Japanese forces posed, the PT boats of Motor Torpedo Squadron 27, operating from Subic Bay, were conducting patrols of the Bataan, Cavite, Corregidor, and Manila Bay areas. During the course of these near-shore patrols they destroyed or damaged numerous craft and also recovered survivors of ships sunk by Japanese Q boats.[13]

LOSS OF ARMY *FS-255* TO ENEMY ACTION

For the Sixth Army, fighting associated with the campaign for the liberation of Luzon continued until 30 June 1945. During the interim period, MacArthur—far from satisfied with the liberation of Leyte and Luzon only—had pursued operations in the central and southern Philippines as well, with the goal of expelling the enemy from the entire Archipelago. Sarangani Bay on Mindanao was the scene of the last amphibious landing in the Philippines. On 12 July, a battalion landing team of the 21st Infantry Regiment landed at the head of the bay, and advanced rapidly inland. It was engaged until mid-August, when Japan surrendered, in tracking down the enemy.[14]

The most tragic event involving an island hopper in the Philippine Islands Campaign had occurred earlier on 11 May 1945. The *FS-255* commanded by Lt. George A. Tardif, USCG, was anchored in seventeen fathoms of water, 1,000 yards from the pier at the head of Taloma Bay, in Davao Gulf at Mindanao, on that day, having arrived at the island the previous day as part of the Davao Gulf First Re-Supply Echelon. Much of her cargo of 155mm ammunition for use by the 24th Infantry Division, Sixth Army had been unloaded, but there were still 80 tons on board and both No. 1 and No. 2 cargo hatches were open. At thirty minutes past midnight, she was struck by a torpedo on her port quarter in the after crew's compartment, killing four crewmen. Two of the men had been asleep in crew berthing, and the other two sleeping above deck in hammocks beneath the 40mm gun platform on the fantail. A search failed to located the bodies of these men; large quantities of blood were sighted on the deck, which had been distorted to a 90-degree angle.[15]

The force of the detonation buckled the ship between the No. 2 hatch and the bridge structure, with foot-high ridges in the deck plating extending down the sides of the ship into the water. On the boat deck, the lifeboat had been blasted out of its cradle and its stern blown off, and the gig, its stern rented and propeller and shaft bent double, was also out of the cradle and hanging over the side by the forward falls. The 40mm gun mount had been blasted overboard; one ready ammunition box was found on the fo'c'sle near the anchor winch, with 40mm shells strewed about. Below deck, water had poured into the engine room through a hole in the after bulkhead, flooding the engines and requiring evacuation of the space.[16]

With the wrecked ship settling fast, two life rafts were launched which, after the officers and men boarded, stood well off clear of the vessel. The *FS-255* healed over on her port side and sank three minutes later at 0050. The infantry landing craft *LCI-21*, which the ship had signaled earlier, thereafter retrived the survivors from the rafts; all four officers and twelve of the sixteen men that had comprised her crew.[17]

19

Assault and Occupation of Okinawa

> *The Americans had seen from April 1 to July 2 [1945] the damage that a cornered Japanese military—shorn of its navy, air force, and intermingled with civilians—could inflict on Americans. They clearly wanted no more Okinawas. Had the Americans not invaded Okinawa, it is more, not less, likely that they would have landed on the Japanese mainland in late summer and thereby suffered far greater casualties.*
>
> Victor Davis Hanson postulating in *Ripples of Battle* that because the Japanese on Okinawa were so fierce in their defense, and because casualties were so appalling, many American strategists looked for an alternative means to end the war other than a direct invasion of mainland Japan. This means presented itself in the use of atomic bombs.

The Battle of Okinawa was the largest amphibious assault of the Pacific campaigns of World War II. It lasted from 1 April 1945, when troops first went ashore, to 22 June 1945, when the island was declared secure. The Allied naval force that was assembled to conduct pre-assault bombardment and support the assault and occupation of Okinawa consisted of approximately 1,300 ships, including 40 carriers, 18 battleships, and 200 destroyers. The fighting ashore was conducted by the U.S. Tenth Army commanded by Lt. Gen. Simon Bolivar Buckner, Jr., USA. Comprising the assault force were the 3rd Marine Amphibious Corps and the 24th Army Corps; 172,000 combatant and 115,000 service troops. The Japanese 32nd Army—the 9th, 24th, and 62nd Divisions, as well as the 44th Independent Mixed Brigade, totaling some 77,000 soldiers—comprised the island defense forces.[1]

Because of extensive Japanese preparations to fortify defensive positions and tenacious fighting, the land battle was fierce and long.

American forces had to clear the Japanese out from each cave or hiding place of the outer defenses. Total U.S. casualties were over 12,500 dead and 38,000 wounded, while the Japanese who fought to the death lost over 110,000 men. By the end of May, Buckner had captured Conical Hill and Sugar Loaf Hill, key positions enveloping Shuri Castle on both sides. United States forces captured Shuri Castle, bastion of a large enemy force, on 29 May, and a little over three weeks later, the island was declared secure on 22 June. Some Japanese, however, continued fighting. The latter date coincided with the last organized enemy kamikaze attack of the campaign and ritual suicide of generals Mitsuru Ushijima and Isamu Cho, the commanding general and chief of staff, respectively, of the Japanese 32nd Army.[2]

The Japanese had used kamikaze tactics since the Battle of Leyte Gulf, but the Battle of Okinawa marked the first time they became a major part of the defense. While small groups of kamikazes struck the fleet on a nightly basis, the worst damage resulted from Operation TEN-GO, a series of concentrated kikusui attacks that occurred between 6 April and 22 June. (The term kikusui referred to a suicide air strike by a large massed group of kamikazes.) Much has been written about the bravery of ships' crews who fended off wave after wave of aircraft bent on their destruction. Despite these efforts, Japanese airmen piloting their planes into American ships resulted in 21 vessels sunk; 43 scrapped, decommissioned, or left unrepaired at war's end; and another 23 put out of action for over 30 days. At least 355 kamikazes and 341 additional aircraft (mostly conventional bombers) participated in the first kikusui attack, with decreasing numbers of planes committed to subsequent attacks due to attrition. The tenth and final massed attack on 22 June included 45 kamikazes and an estimated 40 additional aircraft. In the following days there were other attacks by planes against naval shipping.[3]

SMALL COASTAL TRANSPORTS DISPATCHED TO OKINAWA

Four small coastal transports, the *APc-23*, *26*, *28*, and *32*, received a battle star for the assault and occupation of Okinawa—the last earned by these types of ships during the war. The *APc-26* and *APc-32* reached Nakagusuku Wan, a bay on the southern coast of the island on 21 June, and were joined by the *APc-23* and *28* a week later. The first pair arrived off the island near the end of the kikusui attacks, and the other two small coastal transports in time for occasional air raids that continued into July. A summary of the award periods for these four ships and the identities of their commanding officers follow:

Ship	Period of Award	Commanding Officer
USS *APc-26*	21–30 Jun 1945	Lt. (jg) Arthur E. Koski, USNR
USS *APc-32*	21–30 Jun 1945	Lt. (jg) Thomas H. Keifer, USNR
USS *APc-23*	27–30 Jun 1945	Ens. E. R. Gordon, Jr., USNR
USS *APc-28*	27–30 Jun 1945	Lt. (jg) A. L. Toombs, USNR[4]

The *APc-26* and *APc-32* had departed Apra Harbor, Guam for Okinawa at noon on 14 June and joined the other six ships of the convoy of which there were a part: the minesweeper *Gladiator* (AM-319), yard minesweepers *YMS-371* and *YMS-430*, fleet tug *Bannock* (ATF-81) towing the dredge *Sacramento*, rescue tug *ATR-16* towing the barge *BC168*, and Coast Guard cutter *Balsam* (AGL-62). Arriving at Okinawa (a part of the 620-mile-long Ryukyu chain that extends southwest from Japan's main four islands to Taiwan) on 21 June the two small coastal transports proceeded into Nakagusuku Wan and anchored. Enemy aircraft made two raids that afternoon and evening, but no planes approached in the vicinity of the APcs. At 0929 the next morning, an enemy aircraft identified as a "Tony" (Kawasaki Ki-61 Hien Army Type 3 fighter aircraft) was sighted coming in low and taken under fire by ships within gun range. Following it were two "Zekes" (Mitsubishi Navy carrier fighter planes). The first crashed into a tank landing ship, the *LST-534*, at the far side of the anchorage. The second plane was driven off by gunfire from ships positioned in an anti-aircraft screen at the harbor entrance.[5]

Crewmen aboard the LST first detected the low-flying plane—approaching the ship at about 150 feet in altitude and 150 knots from dead astern—less than five miles away, leaving little time for guns to open. However, the ship's four 20mm mounts expended one hundred thirty rounds, and two slower 40mm mounts ten rounds during the 3-5 seconds between the first shot and when the Val impacted the ship. The enemy plane, aflame and out of control, had veered to the right, and then banked left into the starboard side of the tank landing ship near frame 20. The detonation of the large bomb it carried blasted a hole in the vessel's hull, and the bow immediately sank and grounded. Fortunately, the LST was anchored in shallow water near the beach. Fire also broke out in adjacent areas, and the explosion and subsequent conflagration resulted in buckled decks, a gutted tank deck and other areas, and thirty-two personnel casualties. Thereafter, salvage work necessary to refloat the ship commenced. However, despite successful makeshift repairs, the amphibious ship was later deemed beyond economical restoration, towed out to sea and sunk off Okinawa on 9 December 1945.[6]

On 23 June 1945, the *APc-26* and *32* in company with the medium landing ship *LSM-424* and the sub-chaser *PC-466* left Nakagusuku Wan for Hagushi anchorage, arriving there in the early evening. After reporting for duty, the *APc-26* was assigned as the mail, freight, and passenger ship between Ie Shima and Hagushi anchorage. The *APc-32* was dispatched to Kerama Rhetto ("Suicide Bay")—a body of water some twenty miles southwest of Okinawa which contained the Kerama Islands—which had been cleared by mine forces in late March for use as a staging area for U.S. forces prior to the assault on Okinawa. Six days before the invasion of Okinawa, the pilots of two Piper Cub reconnaissance planes sighted during a low flight over the islands many sets of railroad tracks leading from the water's edge to naturally formed caves that dotted the islands, which aroused suspicion. Not long after this finding, Navy ships sank three Q boats and captured a forth, and military brass quickly deduced that the caves were sanctuaries for the boats and the tracks were their launching ramps. Army troops (of the 77th Infantry) and Navy landing craft converted to gunboats were dispatched to eliminate the threat the boats presented by scuttling or destroying them. Navy gunner's mate Don Brockman described the operation:

> We went into the Keramas more than a week before the invasion and shot the hell out of these suicide boats. We had four 20-millimeter guns that were especially effective against them. It looked like the Japs had 1,000 boats stashed out there, and we sank all of them we saw—except for one boat that we took on board and used later as a mail boat.[7]

Following her arrival at Kerama Rhetto the *APc-32* took up duties similar to those of the *APc-26*, a regular schedule of carrying mail, freight, and passengers between the tank landing ship *LST-851* and attack transport *Natrona* (APA-214) at Kerama Rhetto and the *LST-795* and *Crescent City* (APA-21) at Hagushi and return to Kerama Rhetto. During the evenings of both 27 and 29 June, enemy planes made raids. One of the aircraft in the first raid was shot down in the vicinity of the *APc-26* near Ie Shima anchorage.[8]

The small coastal transports *APc-23* and *28* left Guam for Okinawa on 16 June. They were part of a convoy consisting of the fleet tug *Serrano* (ATF-112) towing three patrol boats, the fleet tug *Accokeek* (ATA-181) towing the barge *BCN-1107* and dump scow *3*, the minesweeper *Nimble* (AM-266), and yard minesweepers *YMS-390* and *YMS-443*. The group arrived at Nakagusuku anchorage in late morning of 28 June, and within a few days, the two APcs had joined their sister ships in hauling mail, freight and passengers as part of Task Unit 99.1.95, an inter-island ferry command.[9]

Typhoon evasion was ordered on 18 July, whereupon the *APc-26* proceeded that day from Hagushi anchorage to Naha Harbor to seek shelter. In the evening of the following day, two enemy planes passed over the harbor, undecernable despite their low level as they passed through a cloud bank. They were likely the two "Oscars" (Nakajima Ki-43 Hayabusa Army Type 1 fighters) which later dove out of heavy overcast hanging over a ridge located about 3,000 yards from where the destroyer *Thatcher* (DD-514) was riding at anchor in Buckner Bay. The second plane executed a wingover when astern of the destroyer and dove into her port side just above the waterline at about frame 71. The impact dished in the hull and caused two minor personnel casualties. The plane burned and sank about twenty feet off the *Thatcher*'s port bow, having left one of its wings, sheared off by contact with a life raft, lodged aboard. The aircraft's single bomb did not detonate due to the collision, but instead fractured, scattering what appeared to be picric acid—a pale yellow, crystalline solid used for military explosives—over the port side and decks of the destroyer.[10]

At the time of the attack, the center of the approaching typhoon was estimated to be one hundred miles distant. The barometer aboard the *Thatcher* had reached a low of 29.42 inches of mercury at 1700 and steadily increased thereafter as the storm moved slowly away. The *APc-26* returned to Hagushi on 21 July and relieved the *APc-23* of her mail run duties between Ie Shima and Hagushi. Six days later an explosion was heard aboard the *APc-26* around 2000 on 27 July, following which radio communication reported that the *Victory*-ship S.S. *Pratt Victory* had been torpedoed. After the dissipation of smoke generated in an attempt to screen shipping from the view of enemy pilots, it was possible to see the merchantman low in the water at the bow, and beside her the *LCT-1050* completely submerged except for about fifteen feet of bow protruding out of the water. A low flying aircraft had closed the anchorage at Ie Shima from the eastward and dropped a torpedo. The ordnance passed under the tank landing craft, which was alongside the *Pratt Victory* receiving cargo, and struck the merchant ship at the No. 2 hold. The resulting explosion ruptured her hull and severely damaged the tank landing craft as well.[11]

INTER-ISLAND FREIGHT DUTIES CONTINUE AND ANOTHER TYPHOON HITS

Throughout August, the *APc-23* and *28* carried mail between Hagushi anchorage and Buckner Bay. On the first day of the month following execution of Typhoon Plan William, the *APc-26* left Ie Shima for Unten Ko, Okinawa, to seek shelter, and *APc-32* got under way from Hagushi anchorage for Naha Harbor. The storm abated three days later, whereupon the *APc-26* resumed her regular mail run between Ie Shima and Hagushi. The *APc-32* proceeded to Buckner Bay, to resume mail duties for the fleet post office aboard the *LST-890*. She carried mail to ships in the bay there, and as necessary to the Hagushi anchorage. The typhoons that passed through or near the Okinawa area in July and August preceded dramatically more deadly ones in September and October, which would result in the loss or severe damage to scores of ships, including ten of the "Pacific Island hoppers" that are the subject of this book.[12]

ISLAND HOPPERS AMONG SHIPS LOST TO TYPHOONS

> *It was impossible to steer course because of violent sea; wind velocity estimated to be above 100 knots with even greater gusts. Sea became extremely rough and turbulent with waves estimated to be 40 feet high; wind blew off crest of waves; and at times the pilot house was completely enveloped in a solid wall of water. Several times it was necessary to stop engine; because sea suction was lost and lines had to be cleared of air in order to keep main engine cooling system functioning. During the periods when engine was stopped, the ship rolled up to estimated 60 [port]—60 [starboard] degrees and was carried indefinite distances with the sea. It was impossible to determine even an approximate position of the ship, for no identifiable markers were visible. . . . 1528, ran aground on reef; ship came to a sudden grinding stop.*
>
> Excerpts from an account of the loss of the USS *APc-103* at Okinawa due to damage sustained on 9 October 1945 during Typhoon LOUISE. The small coastal transport had been made up astern of the gasoline barge *YOG-111* with a 25 fathom, 7-inch hawser

and 35 fathoms of ¾-inch anchor chain veered. However, yawing caused both to part despite the use of the ships propulsion engine to relieve strain on them. Upon the ship being torn loose from her moor at 1330, her commanding officer, Lt. (jg) T. G. George, USNR, had ordered engine "ahead full" to keep the vessel from broaching and had attempted to steer a course that would keep her clear of reefs and headed towards good water.[13]

The subject of ships lost to typhoons at Okinawa in autumn 1945 is taken up here, before the final chapters devoted to the war's end, because it involves some units that participated in the invasion of Okinawa. Because the Empire of Japan had surrendered on 15 August, the loss or damage of American ships that had survived the lengthy, bloody war, so soon thereafter to the forces of nature, was particularly disheartening. Their loss highlights that many vessels did not immediately return home at war's end. They instead remained in Far East waters involved with supporting the landing of occupational forces, and recovering American and Allied POWs, or in the Solomon Islands engaged in duties unique to that area.

At midnight on 16–17 September, Typhoon IDA hit Buckner Bay moving on a course north-northwest at 16 knots. The wind force at the center of the storm, forty-nine miles away, was 14 (80-90 knots) and force 9 (41-47 knots) within 200 miles. The typhoon caused severe damage at Okinawa. Breakwaters (seawalls) and piers were badly damaged; at the Navy Supply Depot, 140 Mae West–type buildings collapsed but were repairable, and another 100 were destroyed. Preliminary report of damage to ships at Okinawa indicated twenty-three ships were aground, including the *APc-28*. Commander Service Squadron Ten noted about the *APc-28*, "Beached; severe structural damage; salvage doubtful." This appraisal proved accurate; she subsequently decommissioned at Okinawa on 28 November 1945.[14]

The *APc-32* under Ens. Harry E. Snyder, Jr.—who had taken over command of the ship only a few weeks earlier on 30 July—suffered damage as well, but survived the typhoon. The small coastal transport was at anchor on 16 September in Yonabaru Wan on the southern part of Buckner Bay. As the force of the wind and sea grew, her starboard anchor chain parted at 1130, and the port anchor chain at 1600, necessitating that she remain under way for the duration of the storm. The commanding officer described his ship being tossed about and

Map 19-1

The Allied invasion of Okinawa resulted in thousands of Americans dead and wounded, and greater numbers of Japanese casualties. On 9 October 1945, Typhoon LOUISE passed over the island, battering American fleet units and merchant ships present in Buckner Bay; 12 ships and craft were sunk, 222 grounded, and 32 severely damaged.
Source: http://www.ibiblio.org/hyperwar/USN/Building_Bases/maps/bases2-p398.jpg

the constant need for avoidance action during the ensuing twenty-four-hour period:

> When darkness came, visibility was limited to a few hundred feet and lessoned during violent rain squalls. Steering was almost impossible, full rudder and two-thirds speed being needed to turn the ship very slowly. Going ahead one-third into the wind the ship was blown backwards and two-thirds speed (usually 6.5 knots) was needed to make any headway. As there were many other ships that

had lost both anchors and were under way, the danger of collision was great. There were many objects floating in the water such as small boats, sections of pontoon barges, large logs and others which could not be identified. We were in constant danger of running into such objects or catching them in our screw. In the afternoon of 17 Sept[ember, the] storm had abated somewhat and we were able to tie astern of [the station tanker *Camel*] IX-113 using an 8 inch hawser.

The *APc-32* remained in Buckner Bay, moored astern or alongside larger ships, for the next few days. On 21 September, she received orders to report to the commanding officer of the destroyer *Ericsson* (DD-440) for duty escorting LCTs engaged in Northern Occupation Lift—the delivery of occupational forces ashore—and proceeded to the rendezvous at Unten Ko, Okinawa.[15]

The following month, an even more devastating typhoon struck Okinawa on 9 October. Five days after this horrific event, the commandant Naval Operating Base, Okinawa, identified ninety-one ships (eighteen were casualties of the 16 September typhoon) that were aground and for which salvage was considered unwarranted. Among the vessels lost were ten "Pacific island hoppers":

- Navy small coastal transports *APc-28* and *APc-103*
- Navy yard patrol craft *YP-239* (ex-*Challenger*), *YP-289* (ex-*Paramount*) and *YP-520* (ex-*Conte Grande*)—all former San Diego tuna boats
- Army freight-supply ships *FS-128*, *FS-290*, *FS-406*, and *FS-410*
- Army large tug *LT-358*

The forces of nature, and not the Japanese, would prevent the return of these small wooden-hulled ships—APcs and YPs—and small steel ships—the FSs and LT—to the United States.[16]

SMALL COASTAL TRANSPORTS CONTINUE THEIR TOIL

The *APc-32* received a dispatch from commander Task Force Fifty-five on 26 November 1945 ordering her to return to the United States and report to commandant Twelfth Naval District at San Francisco for disposal. The *APc-40* and *98* had received similar orders and in December were undergoing decommissioning in the San Francisco area; the *APc-98* moored to a buoy off Sausalito. Other small coastal transports were involved in the same process including the *APc-49*, which at year's end was at Pearl Harbor stripped for decommissioning. Some long-serving wooden ships were, however, still employed in the South or Southwest Pacific.¹⁷

Photo 19-1

USS *APc-42* moored at Guiuan, Samar, Philippine Islands, in April 1946. Her armament had been removed. Shortly thereafter, she sailed to San Diego for decommissioning. (Courtesy of Charles R. Perrin, Lt., USNR (Ret.), her last commanding officer, NavSource: www.navsource.org/archives/09/23/092304201.jpg)

The *APc-34* was, for example, operating on a Tulagi-Russells-Guadalcanal run in the Solomons—carrying passengers, freight, and mail between the islands—with her schedule subject to modification by port directors. On 3 December 1945, she embarked one hundred natives under the direction of an officer of the Solomon Islands Labor Corps, and left for Santa Isabel Island. After discharging her passegers at Naifaro, Sepi, Tanabuli, Haevo, and Maringe, the ship returned to Guadalcanal two days later. The APc received on board on 11 December a member of the Army Graves Registration Service and sailed for Sigana and Fulakora, on Santa Isabel, to recover two American bodies. She returned to Guadalcanal the following day. Less than a week later, she embarked one hundred six natives for return to Kira Kira, Wanoni Bay, Marunga, and Hawa, on Malaita Island. As 1946 broke, the *APc-34* was still employed making runs between the islands. A few other small coastal transports were also still carrying out operational duties, but few records exist as there was no longer any requirement to maintain war diaries.[18]

20

Borneo Campaign of 1945

> *On the eve of your departure I wish to express admiration and appreciation of the thorough efficient gallant and successful manner in which the naval force under your command carried out its vital role in both of the Borneo operations. Thank you for all your help and cooperation. Our best wishes for further successes and good luck to you always.*
>
> Message sent on 16 June 1945 by Lt. Gen. Leslie James Morshead, the general officer commanding I Australian Corps, to Rear Adm. Forrest B. Royal, U.S. Navy, following the first two of the three operations of the Borneo Campaign

The last battle stars earned by "Pacific Island hoppers" were for the Borneo Campaign of 1945, involving the amphibious landings of the final major Allied campaign in the Southwest Pacific area during World War II. The objectives of the campaign were to deny Japan the continued fruits of its conquests in the Netherlands East Indies, present-day Indonesia, and use of the approaches to those areas. To achieve these aims, an Australian-led assault force set out to in succession: capture Tarakan Island and its petroleum resources and airfields for support of an assault on Balikpapan; seize Brunei Bay for an advanced fleet base that could protect resources in the area; and occupy Balikpapan for its naval air and logistic facilities as well as its petroleum installations. The freight and passenger vessel *FP-47* serving as a Press Ship garnered two battle stars and three freight-supply ships—the *FS-164*, *FS-167*, and *FS-361*—one apiece, as also did the Navy yard patrol craft *YP-421*, a former Massachusetts fishing trawler.[1]

Chapter 20
INVASION OF TARAKAN ISLAND

The primary objective for the assault at Tarakan, code named OBOE 1, was to secure and improve the island's airstrip to provide air cover during subsequent amphibious landings at Brunei, Labuan, and Balikpapan. The secondary objective was to secure Tarakan's oilfields as a source of fuel for the Allied forces in the theater. Dotting the southwestern coast of the small marshy island, located off the northeast coast of Borneo, were pumps and tower rigs attesting to the Dutch-discovered rich oil reserves lying below; the impetus for Japan's invasion and seizure of the island in 1942. To soften up enemy fortifications in preparation for the landing, Allied forces bombed and shelled the Japanese garrison on Tarakan from 12 to 29 April 1945.[2]

The ships of the Tarakan Attack Group (Task Group 78.1), aboard which was embarked the 26th Infantry Brigade of the 9th Australian Division—"The Rats of Tobruk"—sailed from Morotai, Maluku Islands, in the late afternoon of 27 April. Leading the main body—comprised of twenty tank landing ships, the attack cargo ship *Titania* (AKA-13), the dock landing ship *Rushmore* (LSD-14), and the Australian infantry landing ships HMAS *Manoora* (C77) and HMAS *Westralia* (F95)—was the command ship *Rocky Mount* (AGC-3), flagship of the task group commander, Rear Adm. Forest B. Royal, USN. Positioned astern of these five columns were six columns comprised principally of fifteen infantry landing craft and three medium landing craft, as well as a fleet tug, a rescue tug, the patrol craft *PCE(R)-849*, and the *FP-47*. One of the landing craft, the specially configured *LCI(L)-635*, along with the *PCE(R)-849* and the *FP-47* formed the Press Unit. During the invasion of Leyte the 114-foot wooden freight and passenger vessel *FP-47* had served as a press ship for correspondents covering the return of MacArthur to the Philippines. Aboard the LCI were seventeen press relations officers and war correspondents whose job was to observe and report on the current operation. The duty of the Army officers and men aboard the *FP-47* was to censure and transmit to Manila, Philippine Islands, and to Sydney, Australia, press copy put out by correspondents, and of those aboard the *PCE(R)-849*, to pass information relative to the progress of the invasion to Army General Headquarters in Manila.[3]

The task group, screened by destroyers, patrol frigates, and subchasers, exited the Strait of Morotai in the early evening with weather conditions favorable for cruising, clear weather and very calm seas.

Map 20-1

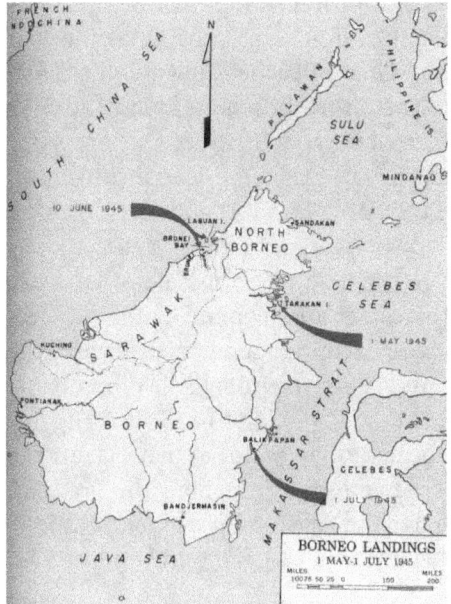

Movement of Australian assault forces en route to landings at Tarakan Island, at Labuan Island in Brunei Bay, and at Balikpapan during the 1945 Borneo Campaign.
Source: http://www.lib.utexas.edu/maps/historical/engineers_v1_1947/borneo_landings_1945.jpg

In the early evening of 28 April the task group proceeded through Siaoe Passage between what are today Indonesian islands and continued the passage. Two days later the group changed from a cruising to an approach formation, requiring the ships to operate in much closer proximity to one another. Approaching Tarakan in the early morning of 1 May, the group stood into Muara Batagau in a violent rain squall, and each vessel proceeded independently due to low visibility to their assigned anchorage. The *LCI(L)-635* requested a berth that would provide her correspondents a good view of the line of departure and landing beaches. There was in progress naval bombardment and aerial bombing of the beachhead by surface craft and Allied planes. At 0800, four LCVPs (Higgins boats) reported for duty to furnish transportation for press relations officers and war correspondents; one was dispatched to the *FP-47* for duty there.[4]

Tracked landing vehicles (LVTs or "Amtraks") launched from parent LSTs, formed boat waves and proceeded to the line of departure in preparation for the assault of Tarakan. At 0756, as the first wave proceeded towards Red and Green Beaches, four B24 bombers flew overhead to make an air strike on the beach area, and LCI(M)s opened mortar fire to cover the movement of the troops ashore. Four minutes later large support landing craft LCS(L)s opened with 40mm and 3-inch. Waves of LCMs, LCTs, and LCVPs continued to make the beach to discharge their troops or cargo, followed by tank landing ships. The only opposition to the landings consisted of Japanese small arms and mortar fire. There was an elaborate system of steel and concrete pillboxes banked with earth designed for defense of the beaches, but these were not manned after the initial Allied bombardment started. A party had left the *LCI(L)-635* at 0815 in a Higgins boat and proceeded along the beach to get pictorial material and to begin writing copy describing the action. Throughout the first day, correspondents made many trips to the flagship *Rocky Mount* and the beach, which was still being shelled by naval craft and being strafed by aircraft.[5]

Although the assault force of the 9th Australian Division met little resistance the first day, American minesweepers found plenty of it the second day. The sea area was heavily mined by both enemy and Allied mines and, as a result, mine clearance was required. In mid-afternoon a battery of camouflaged coastal guns at Cape Djoeata opened fire on four YMSs sweeping north of Tarakan. Direct hits set the wooden *YMS-481* aflame and the commanding officer ordered the crew to abandon ship. As the last of the men went over the side, a shell hit the depth charges and exploded, demolishing the after part of the minesweeper. The magazines aboard blew up at 1700 and, as a third explosion blasted the ship apart, she sank. Japanese gunfire also damaged YMSs *334* and *364* before the high-speed transport *Cofer* (APD-62) and the LCS(L)s *8* and *28* silenced the battery. The *LCS(L)-44*, *LCI(L)-1008*, and Higgins boats launched from the *Cofer* closed the shore to rescue survivors under direct fire from Japanese gunners on the beach. At 1543, shortly after the enemy batteries opened, four B25s strafed and bombed the Cape Djoeata area, and for good measure, the destroyer *Fletcher* (DD-445) bombarded the same area. The following morning, the light cruiser *Phoenix* (CL-46) fired on coastal batteries and other installations on the cape.[6]

On 4 May, the *PCE(R)-849*, one of the ships of the Press Unit, was straddled by shell fire from the beach, origin unknown. No particularly unusual activities or events followed until four days later in the early evening of 8 May, when a man was sighted in the water 300 yards distant. The patrol craft's motor whaleboat picked up the man, Quartermaster First Class Edwin Charles Englebrecht, who proved to be a survivor of the *YMS-481*. Despite being wounded, he had made his way ashore, and while evading the enemy had worked his way by night to the southeast side of the island. He then took to the sea in his lifejacket and was carried by the current towards the anchorage. Despite his wounds and having had nothing to eat for six days and little or no fresh water, Englebrecht was in fair condition. He was given clean clothes and treatment, and transferred to the tank landing ship *LST-667* for hospitalization. The *PCE(R)-849* left Tarakan on 9 May in company with four other Army ships—the *FT-230* (a 115-foot wood vessel), *FS-274*, *LT-134*, and *Y-109*—bound for Morotai.[7]

Ashore, there was fierce fighting as the Australians pushed inland to initially take the airfield and then the entire island. More than 200 troops were killed before the last Japanese positions fell on 20 June. The dead included one of the most famous Australian soldiers of the war, Lt. Thomas Currie "Diver" Derrick, 2/48th Battalion, awarded the Distinguished Conduct Medal for his bravery at Tel el Eisa in North Africa and the Victoria Cross at Sattleberg, New Guinea. Also killed was Corp. John Mackey, 2/3rd Pioneer Battalion, the sole recipient of the Victoria Cross for actions on Tarakan.[8]

BRUNEI BAY OPERATION

Rarely was such a prize obtained at such a low cost.
Gen. Douglas MacArthur in the book *Reminiscences*

The second operation, code named OBOE 6, was a landing on Labuan Island in Brunei Bay on northwest Borneo. The 9th Division had orders to secure the Brunei Bay area so it could be used as an advanced naval base. The secondary objective was to capture the area's oil fields and rubber plantations and production plants. On 10 June the Australians augmented by American troops stormed ashore with smaller landings made on nearby Muara Island and the Brunei Peninsula.

Naval bombardment and air attacks helped clear the way as the Allied troops advanced on each front. On Labuan Island, a force of several hundred Japanese made a determined stand in an area known as "the pocket," consisting of a number of ridges and spurs covered with heavy timber and dense undergrowth almost entirely surrounded by swamp. However, the enemy was subjected to concentrated fire from ship and shore—followed by infantry sent in to finish the job—and the battle for Labuan was as good as over. Sporadic fighting continued until the war's end, by which time more than 100 Australians had been killed.[9]

The freight-supply ship *FS-167*, under the command of Lt. Pardue Geren, U.S. Coast Guard Reserve, received a battle star for the period 4 to 15 July. She departed San Pedro Bay, Leyte, on 4 July in company with the motor torpedo boat tender *Jamestown* (AGP-3) bound for Mindoro. After taking on personnel and cargo the two ships set out for Brunei Bay on the 10th, rendezvousing with escort sub-chaser *SC-982* the following day. The group arrived off Muara Island, Brunei Bay, British North Borneo, on 12 July and the *FS-167* came alongside the motor torpedo boat tender *Willoughby* (AGP-9) to discharge dry provisions. She returned to her side the next day to take on some PT boat engines. The freight-supply vessel continued to provide logistic support for the tender serving the PT boats of Squadrons Thirteen and Sixteen until 22 July, when she stood out of the bay as a part of a convoy which included the *FS-317* for return passage to Leyte.[10]

BALIKPAPAN OPERATION

> *The Amphibious Operation for the capture of Balikpapan, Borneo, was notable primarily for the exceedingly heavy action and passive defenses of the enemy, his aggressive and desperate resistance, and the additional hazard of a thickly sown Allied mine field which necessitated extensive sweeping operations under the muzzles of enemy shore batteries.*
>
> Rear Adm. Albert G. Noble, USN, commander Amphibious Group Eight, 7th Fleet, and commander Task Group 78.2 (Balikpapan Attack Group)[11]

The final operation, code named OBOE 2, was at Balikpapan on southeast Borneo. It was the largest operation of the campaign with more than 33,000 army, air force, and navy personnel landed from 1 July 1945 in the largest ever amphibious assault by Australian forces. As with the other operations, the Australians were well supported with naval and air attacks and employment of tanks to attack Japanese pillboxes (fortified structures equipped with loopholes through which to fire weapons) reducing the numbers of casualties suffered. During the sixteen-day pre-assault period, operations focused on minesweeping, underwater demolition activities, and systematic reduction of enemy guns and defense positions by Allied ships and aircraft. The bombing and arrival of minesweepers in the objective area disclosed to the Japanese the Allies' intentions, and general locations of the landing beaches. This forewarning prompted a determined and sustained enemy effort to cause the abandonment of minesweeping operations. The shallow and mineable waters initially forced Allied combatant ships assigned as a covering force to remain at ranges of six to seven miles, where neutralization of enemy guns was difficult. The Japanese initiated the use of smoke from burning oil in an attempt to screen installations and activities ashore. Heavy anti-air defenses also forced Allied bombers and cruiser spotting planes to remain at an altitude that precluded the pin-point bombing and spotting for gunfire necessary for destructive effect.[12]

Between 16 and 23 June the *YMS-50* and *368* were damaged by mine detonations; *YMS-50* so seriously that after survivors had abandoned and Japanese artillery had inflicted additional damage to her, the light cruiser *Denver* (CL-58) sank her to keep the shamble of wreckage from drifting ashore. Three other YMSs—*10*, *335*, and *364*—were also damaged by enemy gunfire. With the entrance of destroyers into the sweep area on 24 June the situation greatly improved. Their presence caused the enemy to keep many of the gun batteries masked, and others which opened, were smothered by fire from cruisers and destroyers. Air strikes by approximately one hundred Allied aircraft a day also oppressed the Japanese as their defenses, barracks areas, and other strategic targets were receiving heavy and sustained bombing. From this time onward, minesweeping efforts were only slightly hampered by enemy activity, but mine detonations continued to take their toll; YMSs *39* and *365* were lost on 26 June and *YMS-47* damaged the following day. It was not the final minesweeper casualty. The last surface ship of the United States Navy to be sunk in the far corner of the Pacific, where the realm of the Golden Dragon sweeps down under the Southern Cross, was the *YMS-84*, sunk by a moored mine on 9 July.[13]

Underwater Demolition Teams Eleven and Eighteen carried out reconnaissance and demolition missions between 25 and 30 June under the fire of enemy shore batteries which ranged from heavy to light. Cover gunfire from cruisers, destroyers, and close support craft working in conjunction with air strikes kept casualties to a minimum; there were no fatalities. While frogmen were blasting gaps in underwater obstacles off the Klancasan, Manggar, and Manggar Ketjil beaches, the landing craft *LCS(L)-8* and *30* were hit by enemy 3-inch gunfire sustaining light casualties and minor damage.[14]

The Balikpapan Assault Group—composed of 121 ships under the command of Rear Adm. Alfred G. Noble, USN, in which were embarked the assault units of the 7th Australian Division—left Morotai for Balikpapan the afternoon of 26 June. Three days later a task unit arriving from Tawi Tawi, Philippine Islands, rendezvoused with the group. Among the twenty ships comprising it were the *LCI(L)-635* serving as Press Correspondent Ship and the *FP-47* as Press Relay Ship. The duty of the *FP-47*, under the control of Public Relations Officers of the U.S. Army General Headquarters, was to clear censored dispatches to Manila, Philippines, and Sydney and Melbourne, Australia. The weather was fair and sea calm during the passage to the objective area. Following the arrival of the Assault Group off Balikpapan at 0700 on 1 July, the two ships proceeded with the cutter *Spencer* (WPG-36) to their anchorage. Shore bombardment began about this time, and thereafter four LCVPs arrived and correspondents were dispatched to landing beaches. The heavy bombardment of the beaches continued until the first assault wave had landed. The landing craft of this and ensuing waves encountered relatively light resistance. Enemy counter-fire was fairly heavy during the first days of the assault but was not particularly effective; three Japanese aircraft were shot down in the area of the Press Unit.[15]

The *FS-164*, under the command of Lt. N. Hanson, Jr., USCG, arrived separately having left Tawi Tawi on 28 June in company with the fleet oiler *Chepachet* (AO-78) and the destroyer escort *Leland E. Thomas* (DE-420). Following arrival of the group at Balikpapan the morning of 30 June, the oiler moored alongside the light cruiser *Montpelier* (CL-57) which was then engaged in bombarding enemy beach positions, to discharge black oil to her. The *FS-164* thereafter joined the service unit which, although comprised primarily of large Navy service ships, also included the *FS-361* and the even more diminutive Navy *YP-421*.[16]

Two days after the assault of Balikpapan was launched on 1 July, the first reinforcement echelon for the landing arrived on 3 July from Morotai. Comprising it were tank landing ships, merchant ships, the landing craft repair ship *Creon* (ARL-11), the tanker *Banshee* (IX-178) and the *FS-361* commanded by Lt. C. C. Gerber, USCGR. Elements of the 7th Australian Division and supporting forces were embarked aboard the tank landing ships. The *Banshee* carried black fuel required by ships and the *Creon* the necessary shop equipment and skilled personnel to serve as a repair ship. The LSTs immediately began to discharge their troops and cargo; some beached at pontoon causeways while other unloaded to amphibious craft (LCMs, LCTs, and DUKWs) "in the stream." In the mid-afternoon that day, two war correspondents—John Elliott representing the Australian Broadcasting Commission, and William Smith the Australian Department of Information—were killed while accompanying a forward patrol through the native quarter of the Pandansari Refineries area.[17]

The following day, 4 July, the destroyer *Frazier* (DD-607) observed much Japanese gunfire in the area of Manggar Airport, which appeared to be 5-inch guns firing at houses on the edge of the airfield. Splashes in the water between the beach and the *Frazier* were determined to be "overs." At 1510, the light cruiser *Phoenix* (CL-46) dropped several gun salvos in the area of the enemy gun flashes, and the batteries ceased firing. On 5 July, a Japanese plane dropped two bombs in the town area killing one Australian soldier and wounding four. Despite these actions and some raids on Australian positions, there was never any doubt the operation would succeed and by 15 August, when the Empire of Japan surrendered, ending the war, all major objectives had been achieved. But there was a sad footnote to the victory with discovery of the previous deaths of 2,345 Allied prisoners of war held captive by the Japanese in the Sandakan and Ranau POW Camps. In 1942 and 1943 the Japanese had sent more than two thousand Australian and British POWs—who had been captured at the 1942 Battle of Singapore—to North Borneo to build a military airstrip and POW camp at Sandakan. By 1945 many had died of a combination of starvation, overwork, and disease. In January 1945, Allied aircraft bombed and destroyed the airstrip, after which the

Japanese initiated a series of forced marches to move the remaining prisoners westward to Ranau, a town on the eastern slope of Mt. Kinabalu approximately 160 miles away. During what would later become known as "The Sandakan Death Marches," any POWs who were not fit enough or collapsed from exhaustion were killed or left to die en route. Men too sick to attempt the march either died or were killed while still at Sandakan. By war's end, of all the Allied servicemen who had been incarcerated at Sandakan and Ranau, only six—all Australians whom escaped—survived. The last POWs were killed at Ranau on 27 August, well after the Japanese surrender, apparently to prevent them from being able to testify to the atrocities committed. The world learned of the slaughters due to eyewitness accounts given by survivors. The POW Camp commandant was found guilty of war crimes and hanged, and two other officers were hanged and shot, respectively.[18]

It is fair to say that the American Navy minesweepers and frogmen did heavy lifting at Balikpapan. The steel 184-foot *Scout* (AM-296), *Scuffle* (AM-298), and *Sentry* (AM-299), and smaller, 136-foot wooden-hulled sweeps—*YMS-9, 10, 39, 46, 47, 49, 50, 52, 53, 95, 196, 314, 315, 335, 336, 339, 364, 365, 366, 368,* and *392*—received the Presidential Unit Citation; the highest award a military unit may receive for heroism and the equivalent for an individual of the Navy Cross. Underwater Demolition Team Eleven received two "PUCs" during the campaign, the first one for the Brunei Bay landings and the second citation for the Balikpapan operation.

Gen. Douglas MacArthur observed in *Reminiscences* about the amphibious assault of Balikpapan launched on 1 July 1945, "Today I think we settled the score of that Makassar Strait affair of three and a half years ago." The reference was to the Naval Battle of Balikpapan on 24 January 1942, which is also sometimes referred to as the Battle of Makassar Strait. On that date the 59th U.S. Navy Destroyer Division attacked the escort ships screening an invasion force but the belated action failed to prevent the capture of Balikpapan by the Japanese.

21

Final U.S. Naval Battle of World War II

> *It is ironic that this fight of 20 August 1945, the final naval battle of a war in which aircraft, carriers, and a galaxy of new weapons were employed, should have been fought by sailing ships, and concluded by the classic tactics of boarding. Perhaps there is a subtle lesson in this incident to the world of ever-expanding wonders. After a war of annihilation, the sailing frigate, the cutlass and the boarding pike may stage a comeback. Sailors, never forget how to sail!*
>
> Samuel Eliot Morison in History of United States Naval Operations in World War II, The Liberation of the Philippines—Luzon, Mindanao, the Visayas, 1944–1945

The United States Navy's last surface engagement of the war was won off the China coast by a handful of Yanks aboard two Chinese sailing junks. The Navy's first battle under sail since the Civil War days took place on 20 August 1945, five days after the Japanese armistice, when one Army captain, two Marine Corps officers, one Navy lieutenant, and four Navy enlisted allocated between the two vessels bested a heavily armed Japanese army junk, killed forty-three Japanese and took thirty-nine prisoners, all but four of them wounded. Following the battle, the Japanese lieutenant who was in command surrendered his sword to Lt. Livingston "Swede" Swentzel, Jr., USN, and told him that he had believed the two junks to be Chinese pirates. Unfortunately, it was his bad luck to have engaged in battle a foe more deadly than Chinese pirates. One of the duties of the eight American servicemen—whom had been assigned to SACO Unit 8 based at Wenchow (now Wenzhou)—had been to train Chinese pirates to fight the Japanese.[1]

Map 21-1

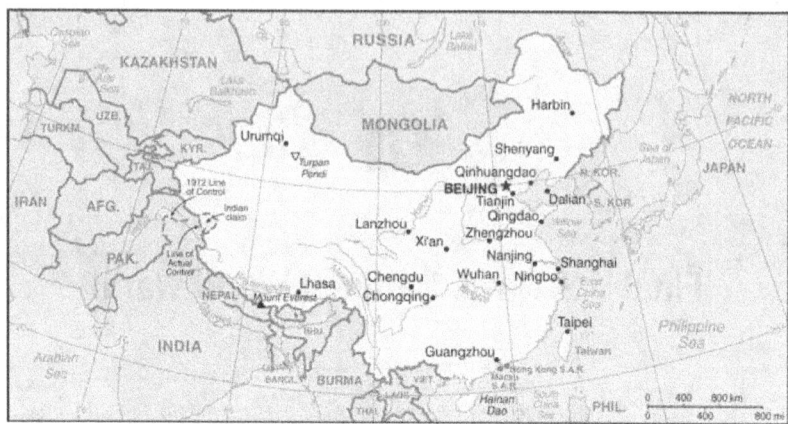

The last U.S. naval battle of World War II occurred on 20 August 1945 off Shanghai, China, between two commandeered Chinese fishing junks, aboard which were eight American servicemen, and a large Japanese junk.
Source: http://www.lib.utexas.edu/maps/cia13/china_sm_2013.gif

SINO-AMERICAN COOPERATIVE ASSOCIATION

The acronym SACO stood for Sino-American Cooperative Association, one of the best kept secrets of the war, a U.S. Naval Group whose members served in scores of units all over China. The organization's predecessor, the "Friendship Project," began in the first few weeks after Pearl Harbor when the Navy and the National Military Council of China, laying immediate foundations for offensive action against Japan, moved to establish a weather service in Japanese-held areas out of which the weather comes across China and Japan into the Pacific. Aided by the Chinese Government, the Fleet began getting regular weather reports from many occupied areas in the Far East by the end of 1942, and the weather project expanded into other areas. American observers then began to collect coastal intelligence, and China assigned substantial quantities of irregular forces to protect them. The Navy, aided by Marine Corps and Coast Guard personnel, gave these men training and equipment, and they became the best organized and most effective of all Chinese guerillas engaged in fighting the Japanese.[2]

Soon the joint activities had become so large as to need substantial and dependable logistic support, and resulted in early 1943 in the creation of the Sino-American Cooperative Organization—SACO—which integrated the common interests of the Chinese Government and the U.S. Navy in the war against Japan. Chinese and American personnel lived, worked, and fought side by side, knowing that they were the only source of essential intelligence in China for the ranging U.S. Fleet and for American submarines just off the coast. SACO units established weather, communications and intelligence stations that spanned from the borders of Indo-China to the northern reaches of the Gobi Desert, with a concentration of activity along the China Coast behind the Japanese lines. The SACO coast watchers played an important role in the American submarine and mining campaigns against Japanese shipping. They provided United States subs location information which enabled them to intercept enemy ships, and furnished intelligence to bombers that assisted in planting mines along coastal shipping routes, in Japanese-held harbors and on vital inland water routes of the Yangtze River. The sea mines forced Japanese shipping routes further out to sea where ships carrying material critical to the war effort and sustainment of the home islands were more vulnerable to American submarines.[3]

United States Navy personnel also trained and armed Chinese guerillas. Some formed demolition squads to kill Japanese, and destroy or disrupt trains, railroads, highways, and river traffic, and destroy or capture great quantities of enemy material and equipment. Others carried out ambushes, and raids on outposts, patrols, and small garrisons, and struck repeatedly against roving Japanese out on search for food in rural areas. American-trained Chinese saboteurs also conducted raids against anchored Japanese vessels and small craft, sinking many of the vessels and capturing others. In one of these raids a sabotage unit of Chinese and Americans attacked a freighter of 1,000 tons docked in Amoy, using delayed charges to kill or injure everyone aboard and destroy the freighter. Other sabotage units conducted operations against river and lake craft in the Yangtze River Lake area.[4]

SACO UNIT EIGHT

Following President Harry S. Truman's announcement of Japan's surrender on 15 August 1945, all SACO units in China were ordered to make their way to Hankow, Shanghai, or Chongqing, whichever was the nearest. All three were river or sea ports; Hankow was located just north of the junction of the Han and Yangtze Rivers, Shanghai at the mouth of the Yangtze River in the middle of China's east coast, and Chongqing—Chiang Kai-shek's provisional capital in the upper

Yangtze River basin—at the confluence of the Yangtze and Jialing rivers. Unit Eight, based at Yuhu—situated thirty-five miles west-southwest of the seaport of Wenchow—was ordered to break camp and proceed to Shanghai. Lieutenant Swentzel, with a party of seven set off for Wenchow on the coast. There he commandeered two Ningpo sailing junks and shoved off for Shanghai with thirty Chinese; the fishermen crews and some Chinese Army personnel armed with rifles and tommy guns. Swentzel wisely chose indigenous craft that could easily make the five-day, 344 nautical mile voyage north to Shanghai. These bluff-bowed junks regularly sailed long distances bringing iced catches purchased from estuary and ocean fishing fleets to markets from coastal Ningpo to Shanghai. When the vessels experienced pounding in heavy seas, two holes were opened in the bow to permit flooding and thereby reduce stresses in the forepeak. The junks could also heave to in rough weather, through the use of an eight-foot diameter, one-foot deep basket secured to a bridle that kept the vessel's head into the wind.[5]

Lieutenant Swentzel had commanded Unit 8 since 23 January 1945. The unit operated Coast Watcher Net No. 2 and its operating area extended from a point half-way between Foochow and Wenchow (now Wenzhou) to Hangchow Bay and the islands east of the bay, including the Saddle Island group. The officers and men under his command also taught guerrilla tactics and amphibious operations. An early task of the unit was to train Chang Kwei Fong's pirate group, the "Green Circle Brotherhood," which had no love for the Japanese invaders. The initial group of 458 pirates left the Shanghai area and had to pass through three different enemy-held areas to reach the unit; 59 pirates died on the way to school.[6]

The Unit Eight boys divided the weapons they had brought from camp between the two junks, one commanded by Swentzel and the other by Marine 2nd Lt. Stewart L. Pittman. These included one .50-caliber machine gun, two, or more, shorter-range drum firing .30-caliber Lewis guns, and two bazookas. Because bazooka ammunition was in very short supply, each junk got only five rounds apiece. Aboard Swentzel's junk (the "flagship") were Capt. Austin B. Cox, an army air-ground support officer, Capt. Patrick J. O'Neill, U.S. Marine Corps Reserve, and Gunner's Mate Third James R. Reid, Jr. With Pittman were three Navy enlisted; Gunner's Mate First William K. Barrett, Gunner's Mate Floyd Rose, and Motor Machinist's Mate Second

David A. Baker. With this "naval force," Swentzel set sail from Wenchow at dusk with Japanese-held Shanghai as his destination.[7]

THE SEA BATTLE

Five days into the voyage, the two junks were tacking north against a heavy wind when, at 0930 on 20 August, they sighted a large, black junk coming out from behind Chongming Island. This island lay against the northern shore of the Yangtze River mouth off the coastal town of Haimen on the opposite side of the river to Shanghai. Swentzel believed that the ominous looking 80-ton vessel—which was acting suspiciously and had a 75mm howitzer lashed on deck—was under Japanese control. The gun, a Japanese Army mountain "pack" field piece with a range of 8,000 meters, immediately opened fire. The first round sheared off the foremast of Swentzel's junk, and fragments killed a pair of Chinese tommy gunners, knocked out a third and wounded Captain Cox. Two machine guns raked the decks of the two junks, wounding other Chinese. In addition to the field piece, there were aboard the enemy sailing vessel both heavy and light machine guns, and one hundred rifles and grenades. Swentzel took over the helm, established contact by means of a handy talkie (hand-held AM SCR-536 radio) with the second junk and gave orders to close with the enemy. He also ordered the American flag run up. Meanwhile Gunner's Mate Third James Reid carried a bazooka to the bow of the damaged, but sailable Chinese junk. From this exposed position he scored four direct hits on the enemy junk. As Swentzel drew closer, Reid climbed upon the rail at the junk's bow—and by doing so, put himself at even greater risk—and hurled a grenade into the open hatch of the enemy junk inflicting heavy casualties and loss of life. The Japanese then surrendered via the use of a dirty white undershirt draped on a rifle bayonet.[8]

Aboard the second Chinese junk, Gunner's Mate First William Barratt manned the .50-caliber machine gun until they closed with the black junk, and then secured a Thompson sub-machine gun abandoned by a Chinese crewman and from an open and exposed position on the bow kept up a steady and harassing fire on the enemy. By this action he successfully covered Gunner's Mate Floyd Rose, who was then manning the .50-cal., and kept enemy riflemen under cover as Rose knocked out the 75mm gun crew, putting the howitzer out of action. The third Navyman, Motor Machinist's Mate Second David

Baker, meted out additional damage with bazooka and .30-caliber rounds, having taken over the machine gun after the Chinese gun crew alongside him was killed. With his ammunition spent and little but hand grenades left, Pittman ran alongside the battered Japanese junk intending to pitch some of the hand-thrown ordnance aboard. But nothing more was needed—the enemy had by then surrendered.[9]

Swentzel boarded the Japanese junk with a prize crew at 1015 and found a total of forty-three Japanese (3 officers, 40 enlisted men) killed and thirty-five wounded. The Japanese were likely assigned to the Special Naval Landing Force based at Shanghai. Special Landing Forces, the amphibious forces of the Japanese Navy, were comprised of sailors trained as light infantry and organized into battalion-size units led by naval officers. A prize crew sailed the enemy junk to Haimen and turned both it and the prisoners over to Colonel Lo of the Chinese Army. Aboard Swentzel's two ships, five Chinese were killed, five Chinese wounded, and one American, Captain Cox, wounded superficially in the leg. A brief account of the 30-minute long violent battle provided by Lieutenant Swentzel appeared in the newspaper *The Norwalk Hour*, on 8 October 1945:

> They fired on us first, with a 75-mm field piece they had amidships. The shell hit our foremast and knocked it down. It was a lucky shot, for they could not have been aiming at it.
>
> Then we opened up with our .30-caliber Lewis gun and a bazooka, plus a few tommy guns we had aboard. The Japanese were firing with heavy machine guns, four light ones and 80 rifles.
>
> It was a fast, savage battle, and one reason we won was that Gunner's Mate Floyd Rose, a North Carolina boy, knocked out their 75-mm crew quickly with his .50-caliber machine gun.
>
> We watched [at 200 yards away] Japs falling on the deck while we sprayed fire at them, and it finally ended when they hoisted a white shirt on a rifle.
>
> We were less than 50 yards away then, and had just tossed a hand grenade down their hatch.[10]

This battle was the last U.S. Naval battle of World War II, and the last between ships under sail. Swentzel and Reid, who were both aboard the first Chinese junk to close with and engage the larger Japanese junk—despite their vessel having lost its foremast to the opening fire of the Japanese Army 75mm field gun aboard the enemy ship—received the Navy Cross. Pittman, Baker, and Barratt aboard the second Chinese junk—which silenced the large gun's deadly fire—earned Silver Stars for their heroism. (Copies of their citations are provided in Appendix E.)

Postscript

> *Ship and crew ready to haul cargo or fight and not necessarily in that order.*
>
> Statement in a damage report submitted by the USS *Brule* (AKL-28), the former Army freight-supply ship *FS-370*, after sustaining seven rocket hits in 1968 during one of her normal supply runs in the inland waters of the Republic of Vietnam. Despite suffering extensive damage to her superstructure and electrical cabling, the *Brule* suppressed the enemy fire and proceeded on schedule.[1]

Two of the sixty 103-foot small coastal transports that served in the Pacific were lost during the war. The *APc-35* grounded off New Georgia in 1943 and was abandoned and the *APc-21* was lost to an air attack off New Britain later that same year. (Two others, the *APc-28* and *APc-103*, were lost to typhoons at Okinawa in autumn 1945.) Following the war, the small coastal transports still serving overseas returned home to the United States. Five—the *APc-4, 6, 12, 16,* and *22*—were transferred to foreign countries, and another three, worn out by war duty, were destroyed; *APc-17* and *102* in 1946 and *APc-89* in 1948. The Navy transferred the remaining wooden ships to the U.S. Maritime Administration in 1947–1948 for disposal via scrapping or private sale.[2]

Six Army freight-supply ships were lost, all in 1945 during the closing months of the war or immediately following it. The *FS-255* was torpedoed and sunk off Mindanao, Philippines; the *FS-163, FS-290, FS-406,* and *FS-410* were lost to typhoons; and the *FS-172* sank off Mugil Point on Cape Croisilles at New Guinea. The Navy acquired forty-five of the remaining small, rugged, and war-tested freighters between 1947 and 1966, taking possession of the initial thirteen ships in 1947, and another one in 1948. The vessels were originally commissioned Miscellaneous Auxiliary Ships, and a few years later were reclassified on 1 July 1950 as Light Cargo Ships. That same day, the U.S.

Photo Postscript-1

USS *APc-9* arriving at San Francisco Bay in late 1945 or early 1946. Early postwar modifications included the removal of armament and the addition of portholes in her deckhouse. (Official U.S. Navy photo # 81031, from the collections of the U.S. Naval History and Heritage Command, NavSource: www.navsource.org/archives/09/23/23009.htm)

Army Transportation Corps transferred twenty-two Army freight-supply ships to the Military Sea Transportation Service. The *T-AKL-15* through *T-AKL-30*, *T-AKL-32* and *33*, and *T-AKL-35* and *36* served as United States Naval Ships (USNS), the designation given to Navy owned non-commissioned ships. The Navy later acquired two additional ships—*T-AKL-31* and *34*—on 1 November 1950, and another five—*AKL-37* through *40* and *AKL-42*—on 12 December 1951. The latter vessels were transferred immediately to the Republic of Korea under the Mutual Defense Assistance Program. The final acquisition of ships occurred in 1966, when the U.S. Navy took possession of the *AKL-44* and *AKL-45*. These two ships, along with the *AKL-25*, served as the "Environmental Research Ships" (intelligence gathering ships) USS *Banner* (AGER-1), USS *Pueblo* (AGER-2), and USS *Palm Beach* (AGER-3). The *Pueblo* was captured by North Korean naval forces on 23 January 1968. She remains today a commissioned United States Navy Ship, despite still being held by the Communist country.[3]

Among the forty-five former freight-supply ships acquired by the Navy, nine received unit awards for combat duty in either the Korean War or Vietnam War, or for service gathering intelligence. The USS *Deal* (AKL-2), USS *Estero* (AKL-5), USS *Ryer* (AKL-9), USS *Sharps* (AKL-10), and USS *Hewell* (AKL-14) collectively earned thirty battle stars during the Korean War. (The *Hewell* was the fictitious Navy cargo ship *Reluctant* depicted in the 1955 American comedy-drama film *Mr. Roberts* which, filmed in Hawaii, stared Henry Fonda, James Cagney, William Powell, and Jack Lemmon.) Two others, the USS *Mark* (AKL-12) and the USS *Brule* (AKL-28), received four combat action ribbons, five Navy Unit Commendations and thirty-two other unit awards between them for Vietnam War service. USS *Pueblo* (AGER-2) garnered a combat action ribbon and she and the USS *Banner* (AGER-1) the Armed Forces Expeditionary Medal. A summary of these awards is provided below, with greater detail regarding qualifying dates and associated campaigns in Appendix F:

	Korean War				
	ex *FS-263* USS *Deal*	ex *FS-275* USS *Estero*	ex *FS-361* USS *Ryer*	ex *FS-385* USS *Sharps*	ex *FS-391* USS *Hewell*
Battle Stars	7	7	6	3	7
Vietnam War					
				ex *FS-370* USS *Brule*	ex *FS-214* USS *Mark*
Combat Action Ribbons				2	2
Navy Unit Commendations				2	3
Vietnam Service Medals				11	14
Republic of Vietnam Meritorious Unit Citations, Gallantry				3	4
Intelligence Gathering Missions					
				ex *FS-345* USS *Banner*	ex *FS-344* USS *Pueblo*
Combat Action Ribbon					1
Armed Forces Expeditionary Medal				1	1[4]

A description of the lengthy service of the five light cargo ships during the Korean War is not within the scope of this book, and that of the intelligence gathering ships has been covered in other works. Following their acquisition by the Navy the USS *Brule* and USS *Mark* were placed in commission as AKLs, and later from 1956 to 1965 placed "out of commission in service" and used to shuttle supplies and passengers between Subic Bay and Sangly Point, Philippines. The Navy re-commissioned the AKLs in 1965, and dispatched them to the Republic of Vietnam for service. Operating from Naval Support Activity, Saigon, the *Brule* hauled cargo, ammunition, petroleum, oil, and lubricants to ports all along the rivers and coastline of South Vietnam, including Vung Tau, Cat Lo, My Tho, Dong Tam, Chau Doc, Binh Thuy, and An Thoi. On an average run, the 176-foot ship could carry up to 225 tons of cargo, 38,000 gallons of water and 20,000 gallons of fuel oil.⁵

Photo Postscript-2

USS *Brule* (AKL-28) under way on the Bassac River, Republic of Vietnam, in 1968. (Courtesy of Jim Swank, *Harnett County* Gunnery Officer and 1st Lieutenant, 1967–68, NavSource: www.navsource.org/archives/09/14/09142808.jpg)

In Operation GIANT SLINGSHOT, a campaign initiated on 5 December 1968 to end uncontested Viet Cong control of the Mekong Delta southwest of Saigon, the *Brule* carried out high priority resupply despite harassment fire from enemy units. She also served as a mother ship for PBRs (river patrol boats), other type patrol boats, and Coast Guard patrol craft at U.S. Naval Support Activity An Thoi, an isolated base on the southern tip of Phu Quoc Island in the Gulf of Siam, and at U.S. Naval Support Activity Vung Tau, located on a peninsula on the South China Sea.⁶

Following her arrival in Vietnam, the *Mark* conducted a bottom survey of the shallow Dinh River and Dong Nia River to validate the feasibility of establishing a naval base for the maintenance of swift boats and Coast Guard patrol craft (WPBs) at Cat Lo, and the use of an anchorage at Cat Lai, near Saigon for deep draft ammunition ships. The *Mark* and the *Brule* were the first U.S. Navy support ships to transit the Mekong and Bassac rivers. Lt. Comdr. Leroy Davis, the commanding officer of the *Brule*, described in an article titled "Waiting at the Levee for the USS *Brule*" the hazards associated with traversing shallow un-buoyed and otherwise unmarked rivers in the Mekong Delta:

> We have to tip-toe out of one river and into another. I've been a deep-water sailor all my life and I've tried to learn from the Vietnamese. They live on the water and know how to use it. If you don't learn from the natives, you don't learn.[7]

In addition to the possibility of running aground, the ships periodically drew enemy small arms fire and infrequently rocket attacks as well while hauling food, spare parts, and ordnance to far flung Navy activities. Aboard the *Brule*, long hours spent at general quarters were followed by the necessity to off-load tons of cargo after the ship arrived at its destination. In addition to getting laborious tasks done, there were other benefits that accrued from workdays as long as 18 to 20 hours. The first lieutenant and cargo officer addressed this aspect:

> The long hours and hard work break down the outer shell a man builds around himself and everyone becomes much closer—working with more unity. Without being asked, men from other divisions pitch in and help load and unload cargo.[8]

Like the *Brule*, the *Mark* routinely faced perilous conditions ranging from the danger of running aground in shallow water to being shot at by enemy forces on the bank. In an attack on 20 February 1968, while on a resupply mission on the Mekong River, the *Mark* sustained a Viet Cong rocket hit amidships wounding twelve men, none critically. During the period 1 January 1968 to 1 July 1970, the *Mark* transited 80,000 miles of river and coastal waters of the Mekong River Delta while delivering over 21,230,000 pounds of vital cargo, and ammunition to United States and Allied Naval Forces.[9]

Following their Vietnam service, the *Mark* was transferred to Taiwan in 1971 as the *Yung Kang* and the *Brule* to Korea in 1974. Although the post-World War II service of the *Pueblo* is the most well-known, other former Army Freight-Supply ships had, and some continue to have today, interesting service. The civilian service of the *FS-263* after her naval stint as USS *Deal* (AG-131/AKL-2) included operation's off the coast of England as the M.V. *Olga Patricia* and M.V. *Laissez Faire* hosting a pirate radio station. As depicted in the 2009 motion picture *Pirate Radio*, from aboard the ex-*Deal* and other ships located in international waters off England's east coast, rebellious disc jockeys were broadcasting rock 'n' roll music which, although spreading like wildfire in the United States, was all but banned from the British airwaves. The BBC owned all but one commercial TV network, and the broadcasting corporation favored a bland fare of news and information, light entertainments, and children's programs. Swinging Radio England ("SRE") operated from 3 May to 13 November 1966 from the former *FS-263*, anchored in the North Sea three-and-a-half miles off the coastal community of Frinton-on-Sea, Essex, England. The studio and 50-kilowatt AM transmitter of Swinging Radio England occupied the two holds of the M.V. *Olga Patricia*, which it shared with a sister station. This other AM station, Britain Radio, was billed as the Hallmark of Quality and broadcast easy listening music. Most recently, the former freight-supply and "radio pirate" ship has been employed as the commercial fishing vessel F/V *Earl J. Conrad, Jr.*, operating out of Reedville, Virginia.[10]

Photo Postscript-3

M.V. *Olga Patricia* under way off the coast of England while operating as a pirate radio station in 1966. (Courtesy of Svenn Martinsen, NavSource: www.navsource.org/archives/09/49/094913102.jpg)

The environmental research ship USS *Pueblo* (AGER-2/ex *FS-344*) is still being held captive by North Korea, moored along the Taedong River near the capital city of Pyongyang and open to citizens as a "museum ship." It remains officially a "commissioned vessel" of the U.S. Navy. Sister ship USS *Banner* (AGER-1/ex *FS-345*) was struck from the Naval Register on 14 November 1969 and transferred to the Maritime Administration for disposal. The third similar type intelligence-gathering ship had a more ominous end. USS *Palm Beach* (AGER-3/ex *FS-217*) was decommissioned and struck from the Naval Register on 1 December 1969. She was sold to an owner in Bayou La Batre, Alabama, and later resold to a Panamanian Company and renamed M.V. *Oro Verde*. While involved in drug smuggling, she ran aground in the Cayman Islands and was sunk by the Cayman government for use as an artificial reef for scuba diving.[11]

Other former Army freight-supply ships are still in service under foreign or American ownership. One, the ex *FS-289*, first served the Navy as the USNS *New Bedford* (T-AKL-17), and later as a Torpedo Test Firing Vessel (IX-308) in the Puget Sound area. Sold by Defense Reutilization and Marketing Service in 1996, she thereafter plied ocean waters as the fishing vessel F/V *Sea Bird*, a tuna longliner out of San Diego, California.[12]

The Navy also acquired six Army Large Tugs and five Coastal Tankers after World War II. The Army tugs—*LT-60, 132, 156, 455,* and *532*—were put in service as Fleet Tugs USNS *T-ATA-239, T-ATA-240, T-ATA-241, T-ATA-242, T-ATA-243,* and *T-ATA-244*. The *T-ATA-244*'s previous war service as the 127-foot wooden-hulled large tug *LT-156* had included taking part in the Normandy invasion; departing Cardiff, Wales, for the Omaha beach on 6 August 1944 towing barges. Following her post-World War II naval service, she was sold to Towboat & Salvage Co., Long Beach, California, and later to Alaska Barge & Transport Company, Seattle, Washington. Named *Tyonek*, she was abandoned in Vietnam in 1970. The other five tugs were all of steel construction, and either 123 or 143 feet in length. The Navy acquired the tankers *Y-38, 39, 87, 88,* and *90* in 1946 and designated them Fuel Oil Barges *YO-237, 238, 242, 243,* and *244*. The 182-foot ships, ocean-going while under the stewardship of the Army, were considered by the Navy to be fit only for harbor craft duties. Likely, few sailors viewing these barges made up alongside their ships in port were aware of their valiant service during World War II.[13]

Little information exists today about what happened to the Army's World War II fleet of TP vessels. The TP designation, meaning "Small Freight and Passenger Vessels," was initially given to the privately-owned trawlers, tow boats, purse seiners, and sailing schooners which the Army acquired. It was later also used for a class of forty-three purposely built 96-foot, diesel-powered, wooden, harbor tugs constructed in American yards. There would have been great demand for these sturdy vessels following the war. Some were likely returned to their owners, and others obtained by private or commercial interests to serve in as variety of roles, including tug, fishing vessel, and perhaps private yacht as well.

Appendix A

Battle Stars Earned During World War II

Ship	Period of Award	Commanding Officer
\multicolumn{3}{c}{Consolidation of Southern Solomons (8 February–20 June 1943)}

Consolidation of Southern Solomons (8 February–20 June 1943)

Ship	Period of Award	Commanding Officer
USS *APc-23*	7 Apr 1943	Lt. Dennis Mann, USNR
USS *APc-25*	7 Apr 1943	Lt. John D. Cartano, USNR
USS *APc-29*	11 May 1943	Lt. (jg) Eugene H. George, USNR
USS *APc-33*	7 Apr 1943	Lt. James E. Locke, USNR
USS *APc-34*	16 Jun 1943	Lt. (jg) H. B. Palmer, USNR
USS *APc-35*	11 May 1943	Lt. Robert F. Ruben, USNR
USS *APc-36*	11 May 1943	Lt. (jg) Kermit L. Otto, USNR
USS *APc-37*	11 May 1943	Lt. Arthur W. Bergstrom, USNR

New Georgia Group operation: New Georgia-Rendova-Vangunu occupation (20 June–31 August 1943)

Ship	Period of Award	Commanding Officer
USS *APc-23*	30 Jun 1943	Lt. Dennis Mann, USNR
USS *APc-24*	30 Jun 1943	Lt. Bernard F. Seligman, USNR
USS *APc-26*	5 Jul 1943	Lt. (jg) James B. Dunigan, USNR
USS *APc-27*	1 Jul 1943	Lt. Paul C. Smith, USNR
USS *APc-35*	30 Jun–21 Jul 1943	Lt. Robert F. Ruben, USNR
USS *APc-36*	1 Jul 1943	Lt. (jg) Kermit L. Otto, USNR
USS *APc-38*	1 Jul 1943	Thomas Lee Ray, USNR

Eastern New Guinea operation: Lae occupation (4–22 September 1943)

Ship	Period of Award	Commanding Officer
USS *APc-4*	4–22 Sep 1943	Lt. (jg) Edwin R. Edwards Jr., USNR
USS *APc-6*	9 Sep 1943	Lt. C. R. Rosebro Jr., USNR
USS *APc-21*	8–12 Sep 1943	Lt. (jg) W. J. Bates, USNR

Eastern New Guinea operation: Finschaffen occupation (22 September 1943–17 February 1944)

Ship	Period of Award	Commanding Officer
USS *APc-16*	22 Sep 1943	Lt. W. W. Harris Jr., USNR
USS *APc-18*	25 Dec 43–17 Feb 44	Lt. R. O. Love, USNR
USS *APc-20*	5 Dec 43–30 Jan 44	Lt. (jg) S. P. Johnston Jr., USNR

Treasury-Bougainville operation: Treasury Island landing (27 October–6 November 1943)

Ship	Period of Award	Commanding Officer
USS *APc-33*	27 Oct 1943	Lt. James E. Locke, USNR
USS *APc-31*	1 Nov 1943	Lt. R. H. Loomis, USNR

Gilbert Islands operation (13 November–8 December 1943)

Ship	Period of Award	Commanding Officer
USS *APc-108*	13 Nov–8 Dec 1943	Lt. (jg) Keith L. Davey, USNR

Appendix A

Ship	Period of Award	Commanding Officer
USS APc-109	13 Nov–8 Dec 1943	Lt. J. S. Horton, USNR

Eastern New Guinea operation: 7th Fleet supporting operations (17 December 1942–24 July 1944)

Ship	Period of Award	Commanding Officer
USS APc-20	15 Oct–4 Dec 1943	Lt. (jg) S. P. Johnston Jr., USNR

Consolidation of Northern Solomons (27 October 1943–15 March 1945)

Ship	Period of Award	Commanding Officer
USS APc-30	15 Dec 43–12 Dec 44	Lt. John R. Shepard, USNR
USS APc-34	15 Dec 1943	Lt. (jg) R. P. Driscoll, USNR
USS APc-42	15 Oct 1943	Lt. (jg) C. E. Voyles, USNR

Bismarck Archipelago operation: Arawe, New Britain (15 December 1943–1 March 1944)

Ship	Period of Award	Commanding Officer
USS APc-2	20–21 Dec 1943	Lt. (jg) Porter L. Fortune Jr., USNR
USS APc-4	15–16 Dec 1943	Lt. (jg) Edwin R. Edwards Jr., USNR
USS APc-9	15–16 Dec 1943	Lt. W. V. French, USNR
USS APc-15	17–26 Dec 1943	Lt. (jg) Kemper Goffigon III, USNR
USS APc-21	16–17 Dec 1943	Lt. (jg) W. J. Bates, USNR
USS APc-22	19–20 Dec 1943	Lt. V. G. Martin Jr., USNR

Treasury-Bougainville operation: Supporting air actions (27 October–15 December 1943)

Ship	Period of Award	Commanding Officer
USS APc-30	15 Dec 1943	Lt. John R. Shepard, USNR
USS APc-37	27 Oct 1943	Lt. Arthur W. Bergstrom, USNR

Bismarck Archipelago operation: Cape Gloucester, New Britain (26 December 1943–1 March 1944)

Ship	Period of Award	Commanding Officer
USS APc-12	3–4 Feb 1944	Lt. (jg) W. O. Gay Jr. USNR

Bismarck Archipelago operation: Admiralty Island landings (29 February–17 April 1944)

Ship	Period of Award	Commanding Officer
USS APc-7	11–18 Mar 1944	Lt. W. T. Conlan, USNR

Hollandia operation: Aitape-Humbolt Bay-Tanahmerah Bay (21 April–1 June 1944)

Ship	Period of Award	Commanding Officer
USS APc-2	26 Apr 1944	Lt. (jg) Porter L. Fortune Jr., USNR
USS APc-4	22 May 44–1 Jun 44	Lt. (jg) Edwin R. Edwards Jr., USNR
USS APc-9	13 May 1944	Lt. W. V. French, USNR

Marianas operation: Capture and occupation of Guam (12 July–15 August 1944)

Ship	Period of Award	Commanding Officer
USS APc-46	21 Jul–15 Aug 1944	Lt. R. M. Ross, USNR

Western New Guinea operations: Duty in connection with motor torpedo boats (21 April–15 November 1944)

Ship	Period of Award	Commanding Officer
USA FS-167	13 Sep–15 Nov 1944	Lt. Pardue Geren, USCGR
USA FS-170	28 Sep–15 Nov 1944	

Western New Guinea operations: Morotai Landings (11 September 1944–9 January 1945)

Ship	Period of Award	Commanding Officer
USA LT-134	15 Sep 1944	
USA FS-255	1 Dec 44–9 Jan 45	Lt. Robert F. Maloney, USCGR or Lt. George A. Tardif, USCG

Leyte operation: Leyte landings (10 October–29 November 1944)

Ship	Period of Award	Commanding Officer
USS APc-18	12–29 Nov 1944	Lt. W. S. Fox, USNR
USA FS-167	23–29 Nov 1944	Lt. Pardue Geren, USCGR
USA FS-364	18–29 Nov 1944	

Ship	Period of Award	Commanding Officer
Leyte operation: Leyte landings (10 October–29 November 1944) (continued)		
USA FS-388	15 Oct 1944	Lt. Homer H. Freed, USGCR, or Lt. (jg) J. E. Emmett, USCGR
USA LT-20	10 Oct–10 Nov 1944	
USA LT-134	10 Oct–10 Nov 1944	
USA LT-229	24 Oct–4 Nov 1944	
USA LT-231	24 Oct–4 Nov 1944	
USA LT-454	2–9 Nov 1944	
USA Y-6	25 Oct–16 Dec 1944	
Leyte operation: Battle of Surigao Strait (24-26 October 1944)		
USA LT-637	24–26 Oct 1944	
Luzon Operation: Mindoro landings (12-18 December 1944)		
USA LT-1	12–18 Dec 1944	
USA ST-381	12–18 Dec 1944	
USA TP-113	12–18 Dec 1944	
USA TP-129	12–18 Dec 1944	
USA Y-14	12–18 Dec 1944	
Luzon operation: Lingayen Gulf landing (4–18 January 1945)		
USS APc-12	4–18 Jan 1945	Lt. (jg) W. O. Gay Jr., USNR
USS APc-16	4–18 Jan 1945	Lt. W. W. Harris Jr., USNR
USA FS-156	15–18 Jan 1945	Lt. (jg) William H. Burgess, USCG
USA FS-171	4–18 Jan 1945	Lt. (jg) Lemuel K. Hartsook, USCGR
USA FS-174	11–18 Jan 1945	Lt. E. R. Sneeringer
USA FS-254	9–18 Jan 1945	Lt. Robert A. Copeland Jr. USCGR
USA FS-364	11–18 Jan 1945	
USA FS-366	4–18 Jan 1945	Lt. (jg) Howard V. Reckhow, USCGR
USA LT-229	7–14 Jan 1945	
USA LT-231	14–18 Jan 1945	
USA LT-454	14–18 Jan 1945	
USA Y-6	12–18 Jan 1945	
USA Y-21	12–18 Jan 1945	
Manila Bay-Bicol operations: Zambales-Subic Bay (29–31 January 1945)		
USA FS-388	30 Jan 1945	Lt. Homer H. Freed, USCGR, or Lt. (jg) J. E. Emmett, USCGR
Manila Bay-Bicol operations: Nasugbu (31 January–10 February 1945)		
USA FS-163	4 Feb 1945	Lt. (jg) Don K. Townsend, USCGR
USA FS-168	4 Feb 1945	Lt. (jg) Joseph A. Kean, USCGR
USA FS-191	4 Feb 1945	Lt. (jg) E. R. Holden, USCGR
USA FS-352	4 Feb 1945	Lt. (jg) E. B. Drinkwater, USCG
USA FS-365	4 Feb 1945	Lt. Comdr. Benjamin Ayesa, USCGR
USA FS-387	4 Feb 1945	Lt. J. L. Gray, USCG
USA FS-389	4 Feb 1945	Lt. C. N. Brown, USCGR
Manila Bay-Bicol operations: Mariveles-Corregidor (14–28 February 1945)		
USA FS-388	15 Feb 1945	Lt. Homer H. Freed, USCGR, or Lt. (jg) J. E. Emmett, USCGR

Appendix A

Ship	Period of Award	Commanding Officer
Okinawa operation: Assault and occupation of Okinawa (24 March–30 June 1945)		
USS *APc-23*	27–30 Jun 1945	Ens. E. R. Gordon Jr., USNR
USS *APc-26*	21–30 Jun 1945	Lt. (jg) Arthur E. Koski, USNR
USS *APc-28*	27–30 Jun 1945	Lt. (jg) A. L. Toombs, USNR
USS *APc-32*	21–30 Jun 1945	Ens. Thomas H. Keifer, USNR
Borneo operations: Tarakan Island operation (27 April–29 May 1945)		
USA *FP-47*	27 Apr–5 May 1945	
Borneo operations: Brunei Bay operation (7 June–15 July 1945)		
USA *FS-167*	4–15 Jul 1945	Lt. Pardue Geren, USCGR
Borneo operations: Balikpapan operation (15 June–20 July 1945)		
USA *FP-47*	28 Jun–7 Jul 1945	
USA *FS-164*	28 Jun–7 Jul 1945	Lt. N. Hanson Jr. USCG
USA *FS-361*	28 Jun–7 Jul 1945	Lt. C. C. Gerber, USCGR

Appendix B

Army Freight (F) and Freight-Supply (FS) Ships

Ship	Design	Wood/Steel	Length Feet	Disp. Tons	Delivery	USCG Manned	Commanding Officer(s)
					Equitable Equipment, New Orleans, Louisiana		
F-1	216	S	99	180	11/42–12/42		
F-2	216	S	99	180	11/42–12/42		
F-3	216	S	99	180	11/42–12/42		
F-4	225	S	102	180	3/43		
					Sturgeon Bay Shipbuilding, Sturgeon Bay, Wisconsin		
F-5	216	S	99	180	5/43–9/43		
F-6	216	S	99	180	5/43–9/43		
F-7	216	S	99	180	5/43–9/43		
F-8	216	S	99	180	5/43–9/43		
F-9	216	S	99	180	5/43–9/43		
F-10	216	S	99	180	5/43–9/43		
F-11	216	S	99	180	5/43–9/43		
F-12	216	S	99	180	5/43–9/43		
F-13	216	S	99	180	5/43–9/43		
F-14	216	S	99	180	5/43–9/43		
					Kewaunee Shipbuilding, Kewaunee, Wisconsin		
F-15	216	S	99	189	7/43		1st Lt. Edwin T. Poster
F-16	216	S	99	189	7/43		
					Equitable Equipment, New Orleans, Louisiana		
F-17	225	S	102	189	4/43		
F-18	225	S	102	189	4/43		
					Converted Merchant Vessels		
FS-19							
FS-20							
FS-21							
FS-22							
FS-23							
FS-24							
FS-25							
FS-26							
FS-27							
FS-28							

Appendix B

Ship	Design	Wood/Steel	Length Feet	Disp. Tons	Delivery	USCG Manned	Commanding Officer(s)
	Petrich Shipbuilding, Tacoma, Washington
FS-29	277	W	114	270	4/43–8/43		
FS-30	277	W	114	270	4/43–8/43		
FS-31	277	W	114	270	4/43–8/43		
FS-32	277	W	114	270	4/43–8/43		
FS-33	277	W	114	270	4/43–8/43		
FS-34	277	W	114	270	4/43–8/43	x	
	Chilman Shipyard, Hoquiam, Washington
FS-35	277	W	114	270	5/43–7/43		
FS-36	277	W	114	270	5/43–7/43		
	Northwestern Shipbuilding, South Bellingham, Washington
FS-37	277	W	114	270	1/43		
FS-38	277	W	114	270	1/43		
FS-39	277	W	114	270	1/43		
FS-40	277	W	114	270	1/43		
FS-41	277	W	114	270	1/43		
	Davis & Sons, M. M., Solomons, Maryland
FS-42	277	W	114	270	6/43–7/43		
FS-43	277	W	114	270	6/43–7/43		
FS-44	277	W	114	270	6/43–7/43		
FS-45	277	W	114	270	6/43–7/43		
	Martinolich Repair, San Francisco, California
FS-46	277	W	114	270	5/43–8/43		
FS-47	277	W	114	270	5/43–8/43		
	Birchfield Boiler, Tacoma, Washington
F-48	216	S	99	180	9/43–11/43		
F-49	216	S	99	180	9/43–11/43		
F-50	216	S	99	180	9/43–11/43		
F-51	216	S	99	180	9/43–11/43		
F-52	216	S	99	180	9/43–11/43		
F-53	216	S	99	180	9/43–11/43		
F-54	216	S	99	180	9/43–11/43		
F-55	216	S	99	180	9/43–11/43		
	Casey Boatbuilding, Fairhaven, Massachusetts
FS-56	277	W	114	270	11/43		

FS-57 through FS-62 cancelled
FS-63 and FS-64 completed as other type vessels
FS-65 through FS-69 cancelled
FS-70 completed as another type vessel
FS-71 and FS-72 cancelled

	Kewaunee Shipbuilding, Kewaunee, Wisconsin
F-73	216	S	99	180	8/43–11/43		
F-74	216	S	99	180	8/43–11/43		
F-75	216	S	99	180	8/43–11/43		

Ship	Design	Wood/ Steel	Length Feet	Disp. Tons	Delivery	USCG Manned	Commanding Officer(s)
\multicolumn{8}{c}{**Kewaunee Shipbuilding, Kewaunee, Wisconsin (continued)**}
F-76	216	S	99	180	8/43–11/43		
F-77	216	S	99	180	8/43–11/43		
F-78	216	S	99	180	8/43–11/43		
F-79	216	S	99	180	8/43–11/43		
\multicolumn{8}{c}{**Converted Merchant Vessels**}
FS-80							
FS-81							
FS-82							
FS-83							
FS-84							

FS-85 through FS-88 cancelled

Ship	Design	Wood/ Steel	Length Feet	Disp. Tons	Delivery	USCG Manned	Commanding Officer(s)
\multicolumn{8}{c}{**Converted Merchant Vessels**}
FS-89							
FS-90							
\multicolumn{8}{c}{**Birchfield Boiler, Tacoma, Washington**}
F-91	216	S	99	180	9/43–11/43		
F-92	216	S	99	180	9/43–11/43		
F-93	216	S	99	180	9/43–11/43		
F-94	216	S	99	180	9/43–11/43		
F-95	216	S	99	180	9/43–11/43		
F-96	216	S	99	180	9/43–11/43		
\multicolumn{8}{c}{**Converted Merchant Vessels**}
FS-97							
FS-98							
FS-99							
FS-100							
FS-101							
\multicolumn{8}{c}{**Cambridge Shipbuilding, Cambridge, Maryland**}
FS-102	247	W	140	450	11/43–3/44		
FS-103	247	W	140	450	11/43–3/44		
FS-104	247	W	140	450	11/43–3/44		
FS-105	247	W	140	450	11/43–3/44		
FS-106	247	W	140	450	11/43–3/44		
\multicolumn{8}{c}{**Minneford Yacht Yard, City Island, New York**}
FS-107	247	W	140	450	10/43		
FS-108	247	W	140	450	3/44–4/44		
FS-109	247	W	140	450	3/44–4/44		
\multicolumn{8}{c}{**Grays Harbor Shipbuilding, Aberdeen, Washington**}
FS-110	247	W	140	150	6/43		
\multicolumn{8}{c}{**Stonington Yacht Basin, Stonington, Maine**}
FS-111	247	W	140	450	3/44		
FS-112	247	W	140	450	8/44		

Appendix B

Ship	Design	Wood/Steel	Length Feet	Disp. Tons	Delivery	USCG Manned	Commanding Officer(s)
Warren Fish, Pensacola, Florida							
FS-113	247	W	140	450	10/43		
FS-114	247	W	140	450	4/44		
Calumet Shipyard, Chicago, Illinois							
F-115	216	S	99	180	7/43–10–43		
F-116	216	S	99	180	7/43–10–43		
F-117	216	S	99	180	7/43–10–43		
F-118	216	S	99	180	7/43–10–43		
F-119	216	S	99	180	7/43–10–43		
F-120	216	S	99	180	7/43–10–43		
Kewaunee Shipbuilding, Kewaunee, Wisconsin							
F-121	216	S	99	180	11/43–1/44		
F-122	216	S	99	180	11/43–1/44		
Converted Merchant Vessels							
FS-123							
FS-124							
FS-125							
Sturgeon Bay Shipbuilding, Sturgeon Bay, Wisconsin							
F-126	216	S	99	180	9/43–11/43		
F-127	216	S	99	180	9/43–11/43		
F-128	216	S	99	180	9/43–11/43		
F-129	216	S	99	180	9/43–11/43		
F-130	216	S	99	180	9/43–11/43		
Converted Merchant Vessels							
FS-131							
FS-132							
FS-133							
FS-134 number not used							
Higgins Industries, New Orleans, Louisiana							
FS-135	330	S	170	512	9/43–3/44		
FS-136	330	S	170	512	9/43–3/44		
FS-137	330	S	170	512	9/43–3/44		
FS-138	330	S	170	512	9/43–3/44		
FS-139	330	S	170	512	9/43–3/44		
FS-140	330	S	170	512	9/43–3/44	x	
FS-141	330	S	170	512	9/43–3/44	x	Lt. W. J. Holbert
FS-142	330	S	170	512	9/43–3/44	x	
FS-143	330	S	170	512	9/43–3/44	x	
FS-144	330	S	170	512	9/43–3/44	x	
FS-145	330	S	170	512	9/43–3/44	x	Lt. (jg) H. H. Sandridge Jr., Lt. (jg) Jack Patterson, Lt. Lloyd C. Wilson

Appendix B {275}

Ship	Design	Wood/Steel	Length Feet	Disp. Tons	Delivery	USCG Manned	Commanding Officer(s)
	Higgins Industries, New Orleans, Louisiana, continued						
FS-146	330	S	170	512	9/43–3/44	x	Lt. Comdr. William Moss, Lt. (jg) Fred S. Pillsbury, Lt. (jg) Charles C. Sears
FS-147	330	S	170	512	9/43–3/44	x	Lt. Oscar Berg, Ens. Harry J. Kolebeck, Lt. (jg) John D. Massman
FS-148	330	S	170	512	9/43–3/44	x	Lt. (jg) John I. Moore, Ens. Chester B. Brach
FS-149	330	S	170	512	9/43–3/44	x	Lt. Jack V. Lum, Lt. Montford F. Gallagher, Lt. (jg) Richard A. Gall
FS-150	330	S	170	512	9/43–3/44	x	Lt. (jg) D. W. Ellis
FS-151	330	S	170	512	9/43–3/44	x	
FS-152	330	S	170	512	9/43–3/44	x	
FS-153	330	S	170	512	9/43–3/44	x	Lt. V. G. Beaudet, Lt. (jg) R. F. Horwath, Lt. Robert B. English, Jr.
FS-154	330	S	170	512	9/43–3/44	x	Lt.Comdr D. H. Williams, Lt. J. D. Lee, Lt. W. A. DeVine
FS-155	330	S	170	512	9/43–3/44	x	
FS-156	330	S	170	512	9/43–3/44	x	Lt. (jg) William H. Burgess
FS-157	330	S	170	512	9/43–3/44	x	Lt. Lester B. P. Dale
FS-158	330	S	170	512	9/43–3/44	x	Lt. Sloan Wilson, Lt. Wallace E. Cooke, Lt. (jg) Robert J. Pate, Jr.
FS-159	330	S	170	512	9/43–3/44	x	Lt. Oliver Pickford
FS-160	330	S	170	512	9/43–3/44	x	Lt. W. H. Seeman, Jr., Lt. (jg) William E. Thirkel
FS-161	330	S	170	512	9/43–3/44	x	
FS-162	330	S	180	573	4/44–5/44	x	Lt. F. Roebuck, Lt. K. L. Torrell, Lt. (jg) Harry F. Rice, Jr., Lt. L. O. Pressey
FS-163	330	S	180	573	4/44–5/44	x	Lt. (jg) Don K. Townsend, Lt. (jg) C. M. Fish
FS-164	330	S	180	573	4/44–5/44	x	Lt. N. Hanson, Jr.
FS-165	330	S	180	573	4/44–5/44	x	
FS-166	330	S	180	573	4/44–5/44	x	
FS-167	330	S	180	573	4/44–5/44	x	Lt. Pardue Geren, Lt. P. H. Ward
FS-168	330	S	180	573	4/44–5/44	x	Lt. (jg) Richard W. Jones, Lt. (jg) Joseph A. Kean
FS-169	330	S	180	573	4/44–5/44	x	Malcolm Bell, Jr.
FS-170	330	S	180	573	4/44–5/44	x	
FS-171	330	S	180	573	4/44–5/44	x	Lt. (jg) Lawrence O. Bragg, Lt. (jg) Lemuel K. Hartsook
FS-172	330	S	180	573	4/44–5/44	x	

Appendix B

Ship	Design	Wood/Steel	Length Feet	Disp. Tons	Delivery	USCG Manned	Commanding Officer(s)
	Higgins Industries, New Orleans, Louisiana, continued
FS-173	330	S	180	573	4/44–5/44	x	Lt. (jg) Lester F. Bain, Lt. (jg) Joseph L. Kelly
FS-174	330	S	180	573	4/44–5/44	x	Lt. E. R. Sneeringer
FS-175	330	S	180	573	4/44–5/44	x	Lt. (jg) H. W. Mueller
FS-176	330	S	180	573	4/44–5/44	x	
FS-177	330	S	180	573	4/44–5/44	x	
FS-178	330	S	180	573	4/44–5/44	x	
FS-179	330	S	180	573	4/44–5/44	x	
FS-180	330	S	180	573	5/44–7/44	x	
FS-181	330	S	180	573	5/44–7/44	x	Lt. K. M. Baker, Lt. (jg) L. Treatman, Lt. Martin S. Hanson, Jr.
FS-182	330	S	180	573	5/44–7/44	x	Lt. R. P. Anderson, Lt. (jg) Robert L. Mobley, Lt. Leon A. Danco, Jr.
FS-183	330	S	180	573	5/44–7/44	x	Lt. (jg) E. W. Owiazda, Lt. Clive V. Clark, Lt. (jg) Elliott Rubin
FS-184	330	S	180	573	5/44–7/44	x	Lt. E. G. Berdaw, Lt. Juan R. Root, Lt. (jg) Henry P. Hancock
FS-185	330	S	180	573	5/44–7/44	x	Lt. (jg) L. C. Rickert, Lt. (jg) L. W. Cotro
FS-186	330	S	180	573	5/44–7/44	x	Lt. F. D. Obrian, Lt. (jg) G. N. Paul, Lt. (jg) Ernest H. Thompson, Jr.
FS-187	330	S	180	573	5/44–7/44	x	Lt. (jg) W. A. Skelton, Jr.
FS-188	330	S	180	573	5/44–7/44	x	Lt. (jg) A. R. Freedy
FS-189	330	S	180	573	5/44–7/44	x	Lt. B. Spencer, Lt. (jg) William J. Barry
FS-190	330	S	180	573	7/44–10/44	x	Lt. (jg) A. Peterson
FS-191	330	S	180	573	7/44–10/44	x	Lt. (jg) E. R. Holden
FS-192	330	S	180	573	7/44–10/44	x	Lt. (jg) C. J. Stevenson, Lt. (jg) Charles W. Shannon
FS-193	330	S	180	573	7/44–10/44	x	Lt. (jg) G. W. Hayman
FS-194	330	S	180	573	7/44–10/44	x	Lt. (jg) C. J. Hanks, Lt. H. S. Squires
FS-195	330	S	180	573	7/44–10/44	x	Lt. J. P. McNabb
FS-196	330	S	180	573	7/44–10/44	x	Lt. (jg) F. B. Davis
FS-197	330	S	180	573	7/44–10/44	x	
FS-198	330	S	180	573	7/44–10/44	x	Lt. J. J. Grant, Lt. (jg) Charles W. Shannon
FS-199	330	S	180	573	7/44–10/44	x	Lt. (jg) L. E. Parsons
FS-200	330	S	180	573	7/44–10/44	x	Lt. (jg) F. J. Mahoney
FS-201	330	S	180	573	7/44–10/44	x	Lt. R. P. Champney, Jr.

Appendix B {277}

Ship	Design	Wood/Steel	Length Feet	Disp. Tons	Delivery	USCG Manned	Commanding Officer(s)
					Higgins Industries, New Orleans, Louisiana, continued		
FS-202	330	S	180	573	7/44–10/44	x	Lt. F. G. Markle, Lt. (jg) Kenneth D. Killman, Lt. (jg) Armand J.P. White
FS-203	330	S	180	573	7/44–10/44	x	Lt. (jg) F. S. Shine
FS-204	427	S	180	573	10/44–1/45		
FS-205	427	S	180	573	10/44–1/45		
FS-206	427	S	180	573	10/44–1/45		
FS-207	427	S	180	573	10/44–1/45		
FS-208	427	S	180	573	10/44–1/45		
FS-209	427	S	180	573	10/44–1/45		
FS-210	427	S	180	573	10/44–1/45		
FS-211	427	S	180	573	10/44–1/45		
FS-212	427	S	180	573	10/44–1/45		
FS-213	427	S	180	573	10/44–1/45		
FS-214	427	S	180	573	10/44–1/45		
FS-215	427	S	180	573	10/44–1/45		
FS-216	427	S	180	573	10/44–1/45		
FS-217	427	S	180	573	10/44–1/45		
FS-218	427	S	180	573	10/44–1/45		
FS-219	427	S	180	573	10/44–1/45		
FS-220	427	S	180	573	10/44–1/45		
FS-221	427	S	180	573	10/44–1/45		
FS-222	330	S	180	573	1/45–3/45	x	Lt. (jg) J. A. Sayre, Lt. J. V. Freeny, Lt. (jg) A. L. Lundberg
FS-223	330	S	180	573	1/45–3/45	x	Lt. E. G. Hamilton, Lt. (jg) J. W. Bingham
FS-224	330	S	180	573	1/45–3/45	x	Lt. V. A. Molstad, Lt. W. J. Barry
FS-225	330	S	180	573	1/45–3/45	x	Lt. F. A Maier, Lt. G. W. Pruitt
FS-226	330	S	180	573	1/45–3/45	x	V. S. Colomb, Lt. (jg) J. D. Peterson
FS-227	330	S	180	573	1/45–3/45	x	Lt. (jg) James C. Hale, Jr.
FS-228	330	S	180	573	1/45–3/45	x	Lt. Budd B. Bornhoft
FS-229	330	S	180	573	1/45–3/45	x	
FS-230	330	S	180	573	1/45–3/45	x	
FS-231	330	S	180	573	1/45–3/45	x	
FS-232	330	S	180	573	1/45–3/45	x	
FS-233	330	S	180	573	1/45–3/45	x	
FS-234	330	S	180	573	1/45–3/45	x	

Converted Merchant Vessel

FS-235

FS-236 number not used

Converted Merchant Vessel

FS-237

{278} Appendix B

Ship	Design	Wood/Steel	Length Feet	Disp. Tons	Delivery	USCG Manned	Commanding Officer(s)
				Martinolich Repair, San Francisco, California			
FS-238	342	W	148	540	3/44–12/44		
FS-239	342	W	148	540	3/44–12/44		
FS-240	342	W	148	540	3/44–12/44		
FS-241	342	W	148	540	3/44–12/44		
FS-242	342	W	148	540	3/44–12/44		
				Northwestern Shipbuilding, South Bellingham, Washington			
FS-243	342	W	148	540	3/44–8/44		
FS-244	342	W	148	540	3/44–8/44		
FS-245	342	W	148	540	3/44–8/44		
FS-246	342	W	148	540	3/44–8/44		
FS-247	342	W	148	540	3/44–8/44		
FS-248	342	W	148	540	3/44–8/44		
				Pacific Shipways, Anacortes, Washington			
FS-249	342	W	148	540	3/44–7/44		
FS-250	342	W	148	540	3/44–7/44		
FS-251	342	W	148	540	3/44–7/44		
FS-252	342	W	148	540	3/44–7/44		
				Wheeler Shipbuilding, Whitestone, New York			
FS-253	381	S	176	560	4/44–3/45	x	Lt. E. P. Jadro, Lt. L. S. Sadler
FS-254	381	S	176	560	4/44–3/45	x	Lt. Robert A. Copeland, Jr., Boatswain Peter Butler
FS-255	381	S	176	560	4/44–3/45	x	Lt. Ludwig Ehlers, Lt. George A. Tardif
FS-256	381	S	176	560	4/44–3/45	x	Lt. C. E. Thorsen, Lt. (jg) K. F. Erickson
FS-257	381	S	176	560	4/44–3/45	x	Lt. G. P. Hammond, Lt. (jg) S. N. Harstook, Lt. (jg) William F. Moffatt
FS-258	381	S	176	560	4/44–3/45	x	
FS-259	381	S	176	560	4/44–3/45	x	
FS-260	381	S	176	560	4/44–3/45	x	Lt. A. Smalley, Lt. (jg) L. F. Jones, Lt. (jg) William L. Barlow
FS-261	381	S	176	560	4/44–3/45	x	Lt. (jg) L. W. Conover
FS-262	381	S	176	560	4/44–3/45	x	Lt. (jg) B. Hribar
FS-263	381	S	176	560	4/44–3/45	x	Lt. (jg) W. G. Hill
FS-264	381	S	176	560	4/44–3/45	x	Lt. (jg) E. F. Warner
FS-265	381	S	176	560	4/44–3/45	x	Lt. H. E. Dennis, Lt. Walter R. Young
FS-266	381	S	176	560	4/44–3/45	x	Lt. (jg) J. D. Legon
FS-267	381	S	176	560	4/44–3/45	x	Lt. E. W. Stachle
FS-268	381	S	176	560	4/44–3/45	x	Lt. Johannes Larsen
FS-269	381	S	176	560	4/44–3/45	x	Lt. Jacob Bursey
FS-270	381	S	176	560	4/44–3/45	x	Lt. (jg) O. T. Fretz, Jr.

Appendix B {279}

Ship	Design	Wood/ Steel	Length Feet	Disp. Tons	Delivery	USCG Manned	Commanding Officer(s)
	Wheeler Shipbuilding, Whitestone, New York, continued
FS-271	381	S	176	560	4/44–3/45	x	Lt. Pettus Kaufman, Lt. (jg) N. S. Hobart
FS-272	381	S	176	560	4/44–3/45	x	Lt. E. Ayers
FS-273	381	S	176	560	4/44–3/45	x	Lt. W. P. Clark, Jr., Lt. Edward L. Ayers, Lt. (jg) Louis B. Adair, Lt. Juan E. Lacson
FS-274	381	S	176	560	4/44–3/45	x	Lt. R. S. Crampton, Lt. (jg) G. B. Dowley
FS-275	381	S	176	560	4/44–3/45	x	Lt. H. L. Sutcliffe
FS-276	381	S	176	560	4/44–3/45	x	Lt. Antonio N. S. Santa Cruz
FS-277	381	S	176	560	4/44–3/45	x	Lt. (jg) F. A. Grantham, Lt. Matthew L. Stansell
FS-278	381	S	176	560	4/44–3/45	x	Lt. (jg) Beverly L. Higgins, Lt. D. W. Engle
FS-279	381	S	176	560	4/44–3/45	x	Lt. (jg) George W. Litchfield
FS-280	381	S	176	560	4/44–3/45	x	Lt. (jg) Davis, Lt. John A. Waldron
FS-281	381	S	176	560	4/44–3/45	x	
FS-282	381	S	176	560	4/44–3/45	x	Lt. E. C. Sturgis, Lt. (jg) Joshua W. Reed
FS-283	381	S	176	560	4/44–3/45	x	Lt. (jg) A. H. Coane
FS-284	381	S	176	560	4/44–3/45	x	Lt. (jg) Byron G. Crawford
FS-285	381	S	176	560	4/44–3/45	x	Lt. (jg) Gordon E. Miniclier, Lt. (jg) Carl A. Haldenwanger, BMC U. L. Needles
FS-286	381	S	176	560	4/44–3/45	x	Lt. (jg) William J. Nolan, Lt. (jg) Bruce B. Davidson
FS-287	381	S	176	560	4/44–3/45	x	Lt. Walter A. Devine
FS-288	381	S	176	560	4/44–3/45	x	Lt. (jg) Paul A. Berg
FS-289	381	S	176	560	4/44–3/45	x	
FS-290	381	S	176	560	4/44–3/45	x	
FS-291	381	S	176	560	4/44–3/45		
FS-292	381	S	176	560	4/44–3/45		

FS-293 through FS-308 cancelled

Ship	Design	Wood/ Steel	Length Feet	Disp. Tons	Delivery	USCG Manned	Commanding Officer(s)
	John H. Mathis, Camden, New Jersey
FS-309	381	S	176	560	3/44–10/44	x	Lt. (jg) Richard H. Greenless, Lt. Oliver Rahle
FS-310	381	S	176	560	3/44–10/44	x	Lt. (jg) Orville E. Cummings
FS-311	381	S	176	560	3/44–10/44	x	Lt. (jg) Kenneth P. Howard
FS-312	381	S	176	560	3/44–10/44	x	Lt. E. L. Jennsen
FS-313	381	S	176	560	3/44–10/44	x	Lt. (jg) J. F. W. Anderson
FS-314	381	S	176	560	3/44–10/44	x	Lt. (jg) W. I. Mittendorf
FS-315	381	S	176	560	3/44–10/44	x	Lt. D. B. Oaksmith, Lt. (jg) S. N. Megos
FS-316	381	S	176	560	3/44–10/44	x	Lt. (jg) J. B. Funk, Jr., Lt. M.S. Hanson, Jr.

Appendix B

Ship	Design	Wood/Steel	Length Feet	Disp. Tons	Delivery	USCG Manned	Commanding Officer(s)
John H. Mathis, Camden, New Jersey, continued							
FS-317	381	S	176	560	3/44–10/44	x	Lt. C. B. Christiansson, Lt. (jg) T. B. Barron, Lt. (jg) J. V. Harrison
FS-318	381	S	176	560	3/44–10/44	x	Lt. R. S. Graves, Lt. (jg) Richard S. True
FS-319	381	S	176	560	3/44–10/44	x	Lt. (jg) Sterling M. Anderson
FS-320 through FS-342 cancelled							
Kewaunee Shipbuilding, Kewaunee, Wisconsin							
FS-343	381	S	176	560	6/44–10/44	x	
FS-344	381	S	176	560	6/44–10/44	x	Lt. (jg) J. R. Choate, Lt. (jg) Marvin B. Barker
FS-345	381	S	176	560	6/44–10/44	x	Lt. (jg) G. W. Oberst
FS-346	381	S	176	560	6/44–10/44	x	Lt. (jg) F. J. Bell
FS-347	381	S	176	560	6/44–10/44	x	Lt. F. N. Blake
FS-348	381	S	176	560	6/44–10/44	x	Lt. (jg) M. R. Cook
J. K. Welding, Brooklyn, New York							
FS-349	381	S	176	560	4/44–12/44	x	Lt. (jg) F. H. James, Lt. (jg) F. A. Ziemba, Lt. B. T. Bassford
FS-350	381	S	176	560	4/44–12/44	x	Lt. R. J. Hoenschel
FS-351	381	S	176	560	4/44–12/44	x	Lt. (jg) Frederick Sturges, III
FS-352	381	S	176	560	4/44–12/44	x	Lt. (jg) E. B. Drinkwater
FS-353	381	S	176	560	4/44–12/44	x	Lt. (jg) Robert H. Foster
FS-354	381	S	176	560	4/44–12/44	x	Lt. Ranger Rogers, Ens. Frank C. Anderson, Lt. George B. Schwartz
FS-355	381	S	176	560	4/44–12/44	x	Lt. R. W. Coe
FS-356	381	S	176	560	4/44–12/44	x	Lt. R. V. Flouton
FS-357 through FS-360 cancelled							
Sturgeon Bay Shipbuilding, Sturgeon Bay, Wisconsin							
FS-361	381	S	176	560	2/44–9/44	x	Lt. C.C. Gerber
FS-362	381	S	176	560	2/44–9/44	x	
FS-363	381	S	176	560	2/44–9/44	x	Lt. R. A. McCaffery
FS-364	381	S	176	560	2/44–9/44	x	
FS-365	381	S	176	560	2/44–9/44	x	Lt. Comdr. Benjamin Ayesa, Lt. (jg) Richard H. Greenless
FS-366	381	S	176	560	2/44–9/44	x	Lt. (jg) Howard V. Reckhow, Lt. (jg) Charles Mashburn
FS-367	381	S	176	560	2/44–9/44	x	Lt. (jg) R.H. Greenless
FS-368	381-A	S	176	560	7/44		
FS-369	381-A	S	176	560	7/44		
FS-370	381-A	S	176	560	7/44		
FS-371	381	S	176	560	2/44–9/44	x	Lt. H. E. Melton
FS-372	381	S	176	560	2/44–9/44	x	Lt. W. H. Bowden
FS-373	381	S	176	560	2/44–9/44	x	Lt. (jg) J. L. Barron, Lt. (jg) W. H. Bosworth

Appendix B {281}

Ship	Design	Wood/Steel	Length Feet	Disp. Tons	Delivery	USCG Manned	Commanding Officer(s)
	Sturgeon Bay Shipbuilding, Sturgeon Bay, Wisconsin, continued
FS-374	381	S	176	560	2/44–9/44	x	
	FS-375 through FS-382 cancelled
	Ingalls Shipbuilding, Decatur, Alabama
FS-383	381	S	176	560	7/44–2/45	x	Lt. (jg) G. P. Kretzschman, Lt. H. A. Mister, Lt. W. L. Stansell
FS-384	381	S	176	560	7/44–2/45	x	Lt. R. L. Young
FS-385	381	S	176	560	7/44–2/45	x	Lt. Peter Marcoux
FS-386	381	S	176	560	7/44–2/45	x	Lt. F. S. McVeigh
	United Concrete Pipe, Los Angeles, California
FS-387	381	S	176	560	4/44–12/44	x	Lt. J. L. Gray
FS-388	381	S	176	560	4/44–12/44	x	Lt. Homer H. Freed, Lt. (jg) J. E. Emmett, Lt. (jg) R. I. Cox, Lt. (jg) O. D. Springer
FS-389	381	S	176	560	4/44–12/44	x	Lt. C. N. Brown
FS-390	381	S	176	560	4/44–12/44	x	Lt. G. E. Oliver, Lt. (jg) John L. Murchison
FS-391	381	S	176	560	4/44–12/44	x	Lt. (jg) Ted C. Larsen, Lt. Thomas A. Buddy, Lt. (jg) Henry P. Mistrey, Lt. (jg) George W. Litchfield
FS-392	381	S	176	560	4/44–12/44	x	Lt. J. A. Small, Lt. Philip G. Adams, Lt. E. R. Holden
FS-393	381	S	176	560	4/44–12/44	x	Lt. R. H. H. Nichols
	Ingalls Shipbuilding, Decatur, Alabama
FS-394	381	S	176	560	7/44–2/45	x	Lt. H. J. Whitmore, Lt. Henry J. Sandlasse, Lt. (jg) Kenneth R. Keeler, Lt. (jg) C. F. Mashburn
FS-395	381	S	176	560	7/44–2/45	x	Lt. J. R. Baylis, Lt. (jg) Melvin A. Alvey
FS-396	381	S	176	560	7/44–2/45	x	Lt. (jg) E. H. Bowler, Lt. R. H. Johnson
FS-397	381	S	176	560	7/44–2/45	x	Lt. (jg) E. Roswell, Lt. (jg) Arthur N. Froedman
FS-398	381	S	176	560	7/44–2/45	x	
FS-399	381	S	176	560	7/44–2/45	x	
FS-400	381	S	176	560	7/44–2/45	x	
	FS-401 through FS-403 cancelled
	Hickinbotham Brothers, Stockton, California
FS-404	381	S	176	560	10/44–4/45	x	Lt. (jg) R. S. Hall
FS-405	381	S	176	560	10/44–4/45	x	Ens. F. D. Statts, Lt. (jg) David Mitter
FS-406	381	S	176	560	10/44–4/45	x	Lt. E. F. Chandler
FS-407	381	S	176	560	10/44–4/45	x	Lt. (jg) J. B. Rowell
FS-408	381	S	176	560	10/44–4/45	x	Lt. (jg) F. Roebuck
FS-409	381	S	176	560	10/44–4/45	x	

Appendix B

Ship	Design	Wood/Steel	Length Feet	Disp. Tons	Delivery	USCG Manned	Commanding Officer(s)
	Hickinbotham Brothers, Stockton, California, continued
FS-410	381	S	176	560	10/44–4/45	x	
FS-411	381	S	176	560	10/44–4/45	x	

FS-412 through FS-520 cancelled
FS-521 through FS-523 numbers not used

Calumet Shipyard, Chicago, Illinois

Ship	Design	W/S	Length	Disp.	Delivery	USCG	Commanding Officer(s)
FS-524	381	S	176	560	7/44–12/44	x	Lt. (jg) K. B. Kell
FS-525	381	S	176	560	7/44–12/44	x	Lt. (jg) George C. Steinemann
FS-526	381	S	176	560	7/44–12/44	x	Lt. Francis M. Holbrook
FS-527	381	S	176	560	7/44–12/44	x	Lt. Gil K. Phares
FS-528	381	S	176	560	7/44–12/44	x	Lt. W. E. Ehrman
FS-529	381	S	176	560	7/44–12/44	x	Lt. (jg) J. W. Harrison

FS-530 through FS-533 cancelled

Converted Merchant Vessels

FS-534
FS-535

United Concrete Pipe, Los Angeles, California

Ship	Design	W/S	Length	Disp.	Delivery	USCG	Commanding Officer(s)
FS-546	381	S	176	560	4/44–12/44	x	Lt. (jg) C. A. Brown, Lt. Charles L. King, Lt. (jg) Richard Herpers
FS-547	381	S	176	560	4/44–12/44	x	Lt. E. M. Harrison
FS-548	381	S	176	560	4/44–12/44	x	Lt. (jg) N. R. Samuelson, Lt. (jg) James E. Warren
FS-549	381	S	176	560	4/44–12/44	x	Lt. (jg) A. B. Freedy, Lt. Thomas D. Miller, Lt. Israel Trestman
FS-550	381	S	176	560	4/44–12/44	x	Lt. J. F. Anderson

Converted Merchant Vessel

FS-551

Brunswick Marine, Brunswick, Georgia

Ship	Design	W/S	Length	Disp.	Delivery
FS-552	381	S	176	560	10/44–1/45
FS-553	381	S	176	560	10/44–1/45
FS-554	381	S	176	560	10/44–1/45

Appendix C

Army Harbor Tugs (TP)—96 Feet, Diesel-powered, Wooden-hull

Builder's Yard	Ship	Delivery Dates
Clyde W. Wood, Stockton, California	TP-97, TP-98, TP-99, TP-100, TP-101, TP-102, TP-103, TP-104, TP-105, TP-106	Feb 1944–Jul 1944
Ackerman Boat, Newport Beach, California	TP-107, TP-108, TP-109, TP-110, TP-111, TP-112, TP-113, TP-114, TP-115, TP-116, TP-117, TP-118, TP-119, TP-120, TP-121	Mar 1944–Aug 1944
Peyton Co., Newport Beach, California	TP-122, TP-123, TP-124, TP-125	Mar 1944–Aug 1944
Wilmington Boat Works, Wilmington, California	TP-126, TP-127, TP-128, TP-129, TP-130, TP-131	Mar 1944–Aug 1944
Peterson Boatbuilding Co., Tacoma, Washington	TP-133, TP-134	Feb 1944–Apr 1944
Petrich Shipbuilding, Tacoma, Washington	TP-224, TP-225	Dec 1943–Jan 1944
Puget Sound Boatbuilding, Tacoma, Washington	TP-229, TP-230	1944
Pacific Boatbuilding, Tacoma, Washington	TP-231, TP-232	1944

Appendix D

Navy Small Coastal Transports—103 Feet, 47 Tons, Wooden-Hull

Ship	Shipyard Delivery	American Commanding Officer(s) or Foreign Navy Ship Designation	Postwar Disposition
Herreshoff Manufacturing, Bristol, Rhode Island			
APc-1	1942	Frank E. Shine, Jr.	To Maritime Administration (MARAD) 1947
APc-2	1942	Porter L. Fortune, Jr., P. S. Lewis	To MARAD 1947
APc-3	1942	P. C. Lindley, Jr., T. L. Baker, P. L. Verner, C. F. Monard, J. M. Abbott	To MARAD 1947
APc-4	1942	Edwin R. Edwards, Jr.	Transferred foreign
APc-5	1942	Claude E. Fike, Jr.	To MARAD 1947
APc-6	1942	C. R. Rosebro, Jr.	Transferred foreign
APc-7	1942	W. T. Conlan, F. W. Dailey, Archie C. Walker	To MARAD 1947
APc-8	1942	L. E. Hansen	To MARAD 1947
APc-9	1942	W. V. French	To MARAD 1947
APc-10	1942	R. T. Kelley	To MARAD 1947
Warren Boat, Warren, Rhode Island			
APc-11	1942	S. Touchet	To MARAD 1947
APc-12	1942	W. O. Gay, Jr.	Transferred foreign
Henry G. Marr, Damariscotta, Maine			
APc-13	1942	O. Knapp, R. A. Franatis	To MARAD 1947
APc-14	1942	B. H. Kowlkes	To MARAD 1947
Camden Shipbuilding, Camden, Maine			
APc-15	1942	Kemper Goffigon III, Matthew Weiner	Repaired following attack off New Britain
APc-16	1942	W. W. Harris, Jr.	Transferred foreign
APc-17	1942	C. O. Smith	Destroyed 1946
APc-18	1942	R. O. Love, W. S. Fox, G. S. Weigel, G. W. Larson	To MARAD 1947
Hodgdon Brothers, East Boothbay, Maine			
APc-19	1942	C. B. Link, Jr.	To MARAD 1947
APc-20	1942	J. Rodriquez, S. P. Johnston, Jr., H. T. S. "Hank" Heckman	To MARAD 1947
APc-21	1942	W. J. Bates	
APc-22	1942	V. G. Martin, Jr.	Transferred 1947

Appendix D

Ship	Shipyard Delivery	American Commanding Officer(s) or Foreign Navy Ship Designation	Postwar Disposition
	**Fulton Shipyard, Antioch, California**		
APc-23	1942	Dennis Mann, E. R. Gordon, Jr.	To MARAD 1947
APc-24	1942	Bernard F. Seligman, J. L. Stevenson, Miles Vukson	To MARAD 1947
APc-25	1942	John. D. Cartano, E. L. Burdick, C. R. McClarley, A. P. O'Kelly, J. E. Evans	To MARAD 1947
APc-26	1942	James B. Dunigan, Arthur E. Koski, Willis D. Witter, Jr., Donald L. Soboe	To MARAD 1947
APc-27	1942	Paul C. Smith, R. J. Olds, S. Slive, M. J. Richards, Jr.	To MARAD 1947
APc-28	1942	Austin D. Shean, J. N. Wall, A. L. Toombs	Damage in typhoon at Okinawa in 1945, and destroyed in 1946
APc-29	1942	Eugene H. George, H. Shapiro, H. F. Kendall III	To MARAD 1947
APc-30	1942	John R. Shepard, John Dockery McDonald, Joseph Ficenec, Lloyd M. Gerber, Clifton E. Shotwell	To MARAD 1947
APc-31	1942	R. H. Loomis, U. Valeri, R. O. Herreman	To MARAD 1947
APc-32	1942	Thomas M. Beers, A. M. Farrell, Jr., Thomas H. Keifer, Harry E. Snyder, Jr.	To MARAD 1947
	**Anderson & Cristofani, San Francisco, California**		
APc-33	1942	James E. Locke, L. C. Bartlett, J. R. Hersey, Lewis H. Earl	To MARAD 1947
APc-34	1942	H. B. Palmer, R. P. Driscoll, Arthur M. Smith, Alton S. Lee, R. D. Tobey, G. F. Smedley, Michael McClintock	To MARAD 1947
APc-35	1942	Robert F. Ruben, John Dockery McDonald	Grounded off New Georgia 1943 and abandoned
APc-36	1942	Kermit L. Otto, J. T. Wolfson	To MARAD 1947
APc-37	1942	Arthur W. Bergstrom, G. W. F. Simmons, Jr.	To MARAD 1947
APc-38	1942	Thomas Lee Ray, L. R. Lovett, H. P. Jancst	To MARAD 1947
APc-39	1942	Franklin L. Knox, Jr., David W. Warren, Jr., Walter Edward Pausemann	To MARAD 1947
APc-40	1942	A. H. Heitzler, J. T. Brown, Cletus A. Ratterman	To MARAD 1947
	**Cryer & Sons, Oakland, California**		
APc-41	1942	W. D. Higby, J. E. Fuld, Jr., J. D. Gray	To MARAD 1947
APc-42	1942	C. E. Voyles, Charles R. Perrin	To MARAD 1947
APc-43	1942	H. R. Swanson, Jr. R. W. Neilson, R. J. Sheridan	To MARAD 1947
APc-44	1942	Joseph M. Price, L. H. Bounds, R. C. Shortall, S. I. Nelson	To MARAD 1947
	**Lynch Shipbuilding, San Diego, California**		
APc-45	1942	Robinson D. Williams, G. R. Taweal, Vernon N. Crouch	To MARAD 1947
APc-46	1942	R. M. Ross, D. R. Adolphs, Justin S. Smith, J. R. Jackson	To MARAD 1947

Appendix D {287}

Ship	Shipyard Delivery	American Commanding Officer(s) or Foreign Navy Ship Designation	Postwar Disposition
		Lynch Shipbuilding, San Diego, California, continued	
APc-47	1942	W. E. Durin, R. O. Decleeney, R. N. Worden, B. O. Freeman	To MARAD 1947
APc-48	1942	Dwight D. Currie, W. H. D. Bush, Loyal L. McCormick, S. B. Davis	To MARAD 1947
APc-49	1942	Ross A. Cunningham, N. Weiss, Lee W. Landrum, Samuel G. Hopkins	Sold 1946
APc-50	1942	P. Keller, R. L. Linder, G. H. Taylor, Morrison C. Huston	To MARAD 1947
		Warren Boat, Warren, Rhode Island	
APc-51	1942	HMS *FT-1*	To Britain, returned, transferred foreign
APc-52	1942	HMS *FT-2*	To Britain, returned, transferred foreign
APc-53	1942	HMS *FT-3*	To Britain, returned, transferred foreign
APc-54	1942	HMS *FT-4*	To Britain, lost 1946
		Henry G. Marr, Damariscotta, Maine	
APc-55	1942	HMS *FT-5*	To Britain, returned, to MARAD 1947
APc-56	1942	HMS *FT-6*	To Britain, returned, transferred foreign
APc-57	1942	HMS *FT-20*	To Britain, not returned
		Camden Shipbuilding, Camden, Maine	
APc-58	1942	HMS *FT-7*	To Britain, returned, transferred foreign
APc-59	1942	HMS *FT-8*	To Britain, returned, transferred foreign
APc-60	1942	HMS *FT-9*	To Britain, returned, transferred foreign
APc-61	1942	HMS *FT-10*	To Britain, returned, transferred foreign
APc-62	1942	HMS *FT-21*	To Britain, returned, transferred foreign
APc-63	1942	HMS *FT-22*	To Britain, returned, transferred foreign
APc-64	1942	HMS *FT-23*	To Britain, returned, to MARAD 1947
		Hodgdon Brothers, East Boothbay, Maine	
APc-65	1942	HMS *FT-11*	To Britain, returned, to Greece
APc-66	1942	HMS *FT-12*	To Britain, returned, to Greece
APc-67	1942	RHS *Lechovon*	To Greece
APc-68	1942	HMS *FT-25*	To Britain, returned, to MARAD 1947
APc-69	1942	HMS *FT-26*	To Britain, not returned
APc-70	1942	HMS *FT-27*	To Britain, returned, transferred foreign

Appendix D

Ship	Shipyard Delivery	American Commanding Officer(s) or Foreign Navy Ship Designation	Postwar Disposition
		Bristol Yacht, Bristol, Maine	
APc-71	1942	HMS *FT-13*	To Britain, returned, to Greece
APc-72	1942	HMS *FT-14*	To Britain, returned, destroyed 1946
APc-73	1942	RHS *Anchialos*	To Greece
APc-74	1942	HMS *FT-29*	To Britain, returned, to MARAD 1947
		W. A. Robinson, Ipswich, Massachusetts	
APc-75	1942	RHS *Distomon*	To Greece
APc-76	1942	HMS *FT-16*	To Britain, returned, to MARAD 1947
APc-77	1942	HMS *FT-17*	To Britain, returned, transferred foreign
APc-78	1942	HMS *FT-18*	To Britain, returned, transferred foreign
APc-79	1942	HMS *FT-19*	To Britain, returned, to MARAD 1947
		Herreshoff Manufacturing, Bristol, Rhode Island	
APc-85	1942	BAE *Cinco De Junio*	To Ecuador 1943 as *Cinco de Junio*, later *El Oro*
APc-86	1942	Unknown	
APc-87	1942	J. P. Lillis	To MARAD 1948
APc-88	1942	J. J. Conlon, David I. Levine	
APc-89	1942	J. W. Martin	Destroyed 1948
APc-90	1942	W. G. Hayward	
APc-91	1942	John C. Barzen	
APc-92	1942	W. P. Croxton	To Haiti 1952 as *Vertieres*
APc-93	1942	Edward P. Shaw	Struck 1950
APc-94	1942	H. R. Hoyt	
APc-95	1942	Roswell B. Milligan, J. P. Hughes, R. C. Lindgren	To MARAD 1948
APc-96	1942	Richard A. Green	To MARAD 1948
		Noank Shipbuilding, Noank, Connecticut	
APc-97	1942	HMS *FT-30*	To Britain, returned, transferred foreign
APc-98	1942	Gordon D. Winsor, Lyle H. McDowell, J. D. Davis III	To MARAD 1948
		Fulton Shipyard, Antioch, California	
APc-101	1942	J. J. Snel, C. J. Glavin	To MARAD 1948
APc-102	1942	William F. Grandy, David I. Levine, Dale A. Isaacs, James A. Elmore	Destroyed 1946
APc-103	1942	R. J. Wissinger, J. W. McCloy, T. G. George, L. S. Fort	Damaged in typhoon at Okinawa in 1945, and destroyed in 1946
		Anderson & Cristofani, San Francisco, California	
APc-108	May-43	Keith L. Davey, R. E. Riordan, W. P. Brown, N. W. Preszler, H. J. Butler	To MARAD 1948

Ship	Shipyard Delivery	American Commanding Officer(s) or Foreign Navy Ship Designation	Postwar Disposition
APc-109	Jun-43	J. S. Horton, Donald D. F. Bphn, C. F. Keyser, Jr., L. B. Gould	To MARAD 1948
APc-110	Jul-43	R. M. Raffelson, Thomas B. De Mott, C. Klopsic, R. E. Ransom	Sold 1947 as *Surprise*, later *Capt. Jack*, grounded and burnt 2004 off Edna Bay, Alaska
APc-111	Aug-43	W. J. Jolly, M. L. Richardson, T. J. Kane, Jr.	To MARAD 1948

Appendix E

Award Citations for Final U.S. Naval Battle of World War II

Naval Group (China): 21 August 1945
NAVY CROSS—2

Lt. Comdr. Livingston Swentzel, Jr., USNR

The President of the United States of America takes pleasure in presenting the Navy Cross to Lieutenant Commander [then Lieutenant] Livingston Swentzel, Jr., United States Naval Reserve, for extraordinary heroism above and beyond the call of duty while serving with the Naval Group, China, when on 21 August 1945, he did so skillfully and relentlessly press the attack on a heavily armed Japanese junk against overwhelming odds that he captured the enemy vessel and inflicted great loss of life to the enemy. On 21 August 1945, Lieutenant Commander Swentzel was in command of two Chinese junks en route from Haimen to Shanghai, with seven Americans and a crew of twenty Chinese guerillas. At 0930 they were attacked by a heavily armed Japanese junk, i.e. one 75-mm pack howitzer, two heavy machine guns, four light machine guns, one hundred rifles and grenades, a crew of five officers and seventy-eight enlisted men. The first round from the 75-mm howitzer struck Lieutenant Commander Swentzel's junk shearing off the foremast. The Chinese crew left their posts and Lieutenant Commander Swentzel took over the helm. Meanwhile, he established contact by means of handy talkie with his second junk and gave orders to close with the enemy. He also ran up the American Flag. They engaged the enemy with two bazookas, one .50 caliber machine gun, one .30 caliber machine gun, and grenades. Lieutenant Commander Swentzel pressed the attack so skillfully and relentlessly against overwhelming odds that at 1015 he boarded the Japanese junk with a prize crew and found a total of forty-four Japanese (3 officers, 41 enlisted men) killed and thirty-five wounded. The prize crew sailed the junk back to Haimen and turned the craft and prisoners over to Colonel Lo of the Chinese Army. Of Lieutenant Commander Swentzel's crew, four Chinese were killed, five Chinese wounded, and one American wounded. His distinguished heroism and courageous actions were in accordance with the highest traditions of the Navy of the United States.

Gunner's Mate Third Class James R. Reid, Jr., USNR
The President of the United States of America takes pleasure in presenting the Navy Cross to Gunner's Mate Third Class James Ralph Reid, Jr., United States Naval Reserve, for extraordinary heroism and devotion to duty while serving with Naval Group (China) when, as a crew member of an Allied junk on 21 August 1945, they were attacked by a heavily-armed Japanese junk. Though his craft was under heavy fire, and the enemy's first round from a 75-mm pack howitzer carried away the foremast of Gunner's Mate Reid's junk, he coolly and deliberately carried a bazooka gun to the bow where in an extremely exposed position he scored four direct hits on the enemy vessel. He fired and reloaded his weapon in a highly skillful manner with utter disregard for his own personal safety. When his junk had closed to within 50 feet of the enemy, Gunner's Mate Reid further distinguished himself by climbing upon the rail and hurling a grenade into the hatch of the enemy craft inflicting heavy casualties and loss of life, whereupon the enemy ran up a white flag of surrender. Gunner's Mate Third Class Reid's coolness under heavy fire, his skillful handling of his weapons, extreme courage and distinguished heroism were highly commendable and were in keeping with the highest traditions of the United States Naval Service.

SILVER STAR MEDAL—3
First Lieutenant Stewart L. Pittman, USMC
The President of the United States of America takes pleasure in presenting the Silver Star to First Lieutenant Stewart L. Pittman, United States Marine Corps, for conspicuous gallantry and intrepidity as Commanding Officer of an Allied Junk when that vessel was attacked by a heavily armed enemy Japanese junk off the East China Coast on 21 August 1945. When the first round from a 75-mm pack howitzer killed his .30 caliber machine gun crew and helmsman, First Lieutenant Pittman promptly took over the helm and skillfully maneuvered

his craft alongside the hostile vessel. Bold and aggressive, he remained in his exposed position throughout a bitterly fought close range engagement to account for many Japanese dead and wounded and to aid in the subsequent surrender of the remainder. By his daring initiative, expert seamanship and cool courage maintained in the face of tremendous odds, First Lieutenant Pittman contributed materially to the success of this hazardous operation against the enemy in the China Theater and his inspiring devotion to duty throughout was in keeping with the highest traditions of the United States Naval Service.

Motor Machinist's Mate Second Class David A. Baker, USN
The President of the United States of America takes pleasure in presenting the Silver Star to Motor Machinist's Mate Second Class David Ambrose Baker, United States Navy, for conspicuous gallantry and intrepidity in action while serving as a crew member of an Allied junk under heavy fire along the China coast. Despite heavy fire and from an exposed position he operated a bazooka gun and skillfully fired his limited supply of ammunition. The crew of a .30 caliber machine gun alongside him were killed and Motor Machinist's Mate Second Class Baker took over the machine gun and skillfully pressed the attack until the enemy surrendered. His efforts under extremely hazardous conditions, utter disregard for his own personal safety and courageous actions were in accordance with the highest traditions of the United States Naval Service.

Gunner's Mate First Class William K. Barrett, USN
The President of the United States of America takes pleasure in presenting the Silver Star to Gunner's Mate First Class William Keith Barratt, United States Navy, for conspicuous gallantry and intrepidity in action as a crew member of an Allied junk when attacked by a heavily armed Japanese junk off Haimen on the East China Coast on 21 August 1945. He manned a .50 caliber machine gun until they closed with the enemy. He then secured a Thompson Sub-Machine gun abandoned by a Chinese guerilla crew member and from an open and exposed position on the bow he kept up a steady and harassing fire on the enemy successfully covering a shipmate who was manning a machine gun and keeping the enemy riflemen under cover. With disregard for his own safety he exposed himself to heavy fire from the enemy and materially assisted in the capture of the enemy vessel and inflicted heavy casualties on the enemy. His action throughout was in keeping with the highest traditions of the United States Naval Service.

Appendix F

Navy Unit Awards Received by Former Army Freight-Supply Ships

Ship	Period of Award	Commanding Officer
BATTLE STARS EARNED IN THE KOREAN WAR		
Inchon landing 1950 (13–17 September 1950)		
USS *Estero* (AKL-5) ex-USA *FS-275*/ex-USS *Estero* (AG-134)	14–17 Sep 1950	
USS *Hewell* (AKL-14) ex-USA *FS-391*/ex-USS *Hewell* (AG-145)	15–17 Sep 1950	Lt. Stanley Jaworski
USS *Ryer* (AKL-9) ex-USS *FS-361*/ex-USS *Ryer* (AG-138)	15–17 Sep 1950	
North Korean Aggression 1950 (27 June–2 November 1950)		
USS *Estero* (AKL-5)	18 Sep–5 Oct 1950	
USS *Hewell* (AKL-14)	18 Sep–2 Nov 1950	Lt. Stanley Jaworski
USS *Ryer* (AKL-9)	18 Sep–2 Nov 1950	
Communist China Aggression 1950–1951 (3 November 1950–24 January 1951)		
USS *Deal* (AKL-2) ex-USA *FS-263*/ex-USS *Deal* (AG-131)	13 Nov–29 Dec 1950	
USS *Hewell* (AKL-14)	6 Dec 50–7 Jan 51	Lt. Stanley Jaworski
USS *Ryer* (AKL-9)	3–22 Nov 1950	
First UN Counter Offensive 1951 (25 January–21 April 1951)		
USS *Deal* (AKL-2)	7 Feb–19 Apr 1951	
USS *Ryer* (AKL-9)	7 Feb–21 Apr 1951	
Communist China Spring Offensive 1951 (22 April–8 July 1951)		
USS *Deal* (AKL-2)	23 Apr–8 Jul 1951	
USS *Ryer* (AKL-9)	2 May–3 Jul 1951	
U.N. Summer-Fall Offensive 1951 (9 July–27 November 1951)		
USS *Deal* (AKL-2)	9 Jul–16 Nov 1951	
USS *Estero* (AKL-5)	21 Sep–13 Nov 1951	
USS *Ryer* (AKL-9)	29 Jul–20 Sep 1951	
USS *Sharps* (AKL-10) ex-USA *FS-385*/ex-USS *Sharps* (AG-139)	15–20 Nov 1951	Lt. R. E. Hoover

Appendix F

Ship	Period of Award	Commanding Officer
Second Korean Winter 1951–1952 (28 November 1951–30 April 1952)		
USS *Estero* (AKL-5)	22 Dec 51–30 Apr 52	
USS *Hewell* (AKL-14)	7 Dec 51–30 Apr 52	Lt. Dale E. Holland/ Lt. Quinnie B. Preston
USS *Sharps* (AKL-10)	1 Dec 51–27 Apr 52	Lt. R. E. Hoover/ Lt. Comdr. R. D. Sweet
Korean Defense, Summer–Fall 1952 (1 May–30 November 1952)		
USS *Deal* (AKL-2)	31 Jul–12 Nov 1952	
USS *Estero* (AKL-5)	1 May–2 Nov 1952	
USS *Hewell* (AKL-14)	1 May–25 Nov 1952	Lt. Quinnie B. Preston
USS *Sharps* (AKL-10)	2–7 May 1952	Lt. Comdr. R. D. Sweet
Third Korean Winter 1952–1953 (1 December 1952–30 April 1953)		
USS *Deal* (AKL-2)	23–24 Apr 1953	
USS *Estero* (AKL-5)	9–10 Mar 1953	
USS *Hewell* (AKL-14)	1 Dec 52–30 Mar 53	Lt. Quinnie B. Preston
Korea, Summer–Fall 1953 (1 May–27 July 1953)		
USS *Deal* (AKL-2)	2 May–10 Jun 1953	
USS *Estero* (AKL-5)	17 May–9 July 1953	
USS *Hewell* (AKL-14)	15 Jun–26 Jul 1953	Lt. Quinnie B. Preston

Ship	Award	Period of Award
UNIT AWARDS EARNED IN THE VIETNAM WAR		
Vietnam Counteroffensive		
USS *Brule* (AKL-28)	Vietnam Service Medal	7 Jan–28 Mar 1966
	Vietnam Service Medal	22 Apr–29 June 1966
USS *Brule* (AKL-28)	Navy Unit Commendation	16 Mar 1966–1 Jan 1969
USS *Mark* (AKL-12)	Vietnam Service Medal	29 Dec 1965–11 Jan 1966
	Vietnam Service Medal	21 Jan–5 Feb 1966
	Vietnam Service Medal	18 Feb–3 Mar 1966
	Vietnam Service Medal	18 Mar–5 Apr 1966
	Vietnam Service Medal	18 Apr–5 May 1966
	Vietnam Service Medal (1)	17 May–30 Jun 1966
USS *Mark* (AKL-12)	Navy Unit Commendation	16 Mar 1966–1 Jan 1969
Vietnam Counteroffensive—Phase II		
USS *Brule* (AKL-28)	Vietnam Service Medal	24 Jul–18 Aug 1966
	Vietnam Service Medal	29 Aug–28 Sep 1966
	Vietnam Service Medal	22 Oct–20 Nov 1966
	Vietnam Service Medal	28 Nov–15 Dec 1966
	Vietnam Service Medal (2)	9 Jan–31 May 1967
USS *Brule* (AKL-28)	Combat Action Ribbon	28 Jan 1967
USS *Mark* (AKL-12)	Combat Action Ribbon	15 Feb 1967
USS *Mark* (AKL-12)	Vietnam Service Medal (1)	1–27 Jul 1967
	Vietnam Service Medal	30 Aug–25 Oct 1966
	Vietnam Service Medal	15 Nov–16 Dec 1966
	Vietnam Service Medal (3)	1 Jan–31 May 1967
Vietnamese Counteroffensive—Phase III		
USS *Brule* (AKL-28)	Vietnam Service Medal (2)	1 Jun–30 Oct 1967
USS *Mark* (AKL-12)	Vietnam Service Medal (3)	
	Vietnam Service Medal	24 Oct 1967

Appendix F {297}

Ship	Award	Period of Award
	Vietnamese Counteroffensive—Phase IV	
USS *Brule* (AKL-28)	Vietnam Service Medal (4)	8 Apr–30 Jun 1968
USS *Brule* (AKL-28)	Republic of Vietnam Meritorious Unit Citation, Gallantry	8 Apr 1968–2 Feb 1969
USS *Mark* (AKL-12)	Republic of Vietnam Meritorious Unit Citation, Gallantry	28 Jan–4 Mar 1968
USS *Mark* (AKL-12)	Vietnam Service Medal (5)	30 Jun 1968
	Vietnamese Counteroffensive—Phase V	
USS *Brule* (AKL-28)	Vietnam Service Medal (4)	1 Jul–1 Nov 1968
USS *Brule* (AKL-28)	Combat Action Ribbon	24 Aug 1968
USS *Mark* (AKL-12)	Vietnam Service Medal (5)	1 Jul–31 Dec 1968
USS *Mark* (AKL-12)	Republic of Vietnam Meritorious Unit Citation, Gallantry	21 Nov–31 Dec 1968
	Vietnamese Counteroffensive—Phase VI	
USS *Brule* (AKL-28)	Vietnam Service Medal (4)	2 Nov 1968–2 Feb 1969
	Tet 69/Counteroffensive	
USS *Brule* (AKL-28)	Vietnam Service Medal (6)	2 Mar–8 Jun 1969
USS *Brule* (AKL-28)	Republic of Vietnam Meritorious Unit Citation, Gallantry	2 Mar–31 Dec 1969
USS *Mark* (AKL-12)	Vietnam Service Medal (7)	
USS *Mark* (AKL-12)	Republic of Vietnam Meritorious Unit Citation, Gallantry	1 Jun–31 Jul 1969
	Vietnam Summer–Fall 1969	
USS *Brule* (AKL-28)	Vietnam Service Medal (6)	9 Jun–31 Oct 1969
USS *Mark* (AKL-12)	Vietnam Service Medal (7)	9 Jun–21 Jul 1969
USS *Mark* (AKL-12)	Navy Unit Commendation	1–31 Jul 1969
	Vietnam Winter–Spring 1970	
USS *Brule* (AKL-28)	Vietnam Service Medal (6)	1 Nov–31 Dec 1969
USS *Mark* (AKL-12)	Combat Action Ribbon	19 Nov 1969
USS *Mark* (AKL-12)	Vietnam Service Medal (8)	1 Jan–30 Apr 1970
USS *Mark* (AKL-12)	Republic of Vietnam Meritorious Unit Citation, Gallantry	1 Jan–31 May 1970
	Sanctuary Counteroffensive	
USS *Brule* (AKL-28)	Vietnam Service Medal (9)	1–30 Jun 1970
USS *Brule* (AKL-28)	Republic of Vietnam Meritorious Unit Citation, Gallantry	1 Jun–21 Nov 1970
USS *Mark* (AKL-12)	Vietnam Service Medal (8)	1 May–30 Jun 1970
	Vietnamese Counteroffensive—Phase VII	
USS *Brule* (AKL-28)	Vietnam Service Medal (9)	1 Jul–1 Dec 1970
	Vietnam Service Medal (10)	28 Jan–30 Jun 1971
USS *Brule* (AKL-28)	Navy Unit Commendation	3 May–30 Jun 1971
USS *Mark* (AKL-12)	Vietnam Service Medal (8)	1 Jul–2 Aug 1970
	Vietnam Service Medal	31 Oct 1970–27 Mar 1971
USS *Mark* (AKL-12)	Navy Unit Commendation	16 Oct 1970–30 Jun 1971
	Consolidation I	
USS *Brule* (AKL-28)	Vietnam Service Medal (10)	1 Jul–10 Oct 1971

Note: The period of award for some Vietnam Service Medals spans more than one campaign. The numbers (1) through (10) associate the same medals listed under two or more campaigns.

Bibliography

BOOKS

Bruhn, David D. *Wooden Ships and Iron Men: the U.S. Navy's Coastal and Motor Minesweepers, 1941-1953*. Westminster, Maryland: Heritage Books, 2009.

Building the Navy's Bases in World War II: History of the Bureau of Yards and Docks and the Civil Engineer Corps 1940-1946, Vol. II. Washington, D.C.: U.S. Government Printing Office, 1947.

Bulkley, Robert J., Jr. *At Close Quarters: PT Boats in the United States Navy*. Washington, D.C.: Naval History Division, 1962.

The Capture of Makin. Washington, D.C.: Center of Military History, U.S. Army, 1990.

Carter, Worrall Reed. *Beans, Bullets, and Black Oil*. Washington, D.C.: U.S. Government Printing Office, 1953.

Christ, James E. *Mission Raise Hell*. Annapolis, Maryland: Naval Institute, 2006.

Crown, John A., and Frank O. Hough. *The Campaign on New Britain*. Washington, D.C.: Historical Branch, Headquarters, U.S. Marine Corps, 1952.

Cunningham, Chet. *The Frogmen of World War II: An Oral History of the U.S. Navy's Underwater Demolition Teams*. New York: Pocket Star, 2005.

Directory of American Naval Fighting Ships. Washington, D.C.: Naval History and Heritage Command (http://www.history.navy.mil/danfs).

DiStasi, Lawrence. *Una Storia Segreta: The Secret History of Italian American Evacuation and Internment during World War II*. Berkeley, Calif: Heyday Books, 2001.

Donovan, Robert J. *PT 109*. New York: Fawcett World Library, 1965.

Dyer, George Carroll. *The Amphibians Came to Conquer: The Story of Admiral Richmond Kelly Turner*. Washington, D.C.: U.S. Government Printing Office, 1972.

Johnston, Richard. *Follow Me! The Story of The Second Marine Division in World War II*. New York: Random House, 1948.

Kane, Douglas T., and Henry I. Shaw, Jr. *History of U.S. Marine Corps Operations in World War II*, Vol. II, *Isolation of Rabaul*. Washington, D.C.: Headquarters, U.S. Marine Corps, 1963.

Kerr, Robert. *A General History and Collection of Voyages and Travels*, Vol. 12. Project Gutenberg EBook, 2004.

Lott, Arnold. *Most Dangerous Sea*. Annapolis, Maryland: Naval Institute, 1959.

Lunney, Bill, and Ruth Lunney. *Forgotten Fleet 2*. Medowie, New South Wales: Forfleet Publishing, 2004.

MacArthur, Douglas. *Reports of General MacArthur, The Campaigns of MacArthur in the Pacific*, Vol I. Washington, D.C.: Center of Military History, U.S. Army, 1994.

McClurg, Robert W. *On Boyington's Wing*. Bowie, Maryland: Heritage Books, 2003.

Miles, M. E. *A Different Kind of War*. Garden City, New York: Doubleday, 1967.

Miller, John Jr. *Guadalcanal: The First Offensive*. Washington, D.C., Center of Military History, United States Army, 1995 (First Printed 1949-CMH Pub 5-3), 210, 215–216.

——*The War in the Pacific: CARTWHEEL: The Reduction of Rabaul*. Washington, D.C.: Department of the Army, 1959.

Morison, Samuel Eliot. *History of United States Naval Operations in World War II: Breaking the Bismarcks Barrier, 22 July 1942–1 May 1944*. Boston: Little, Brown, 1984.

——*History of United States Naval Operations in World War II: New Guinea and the Marianas*. Boston: Little, Brown, 1953.

——*History of United States Naval Operations in World War II: The Liberation of the Philippines Luzon, Mindanao, the Visayas 1944–1945*. Boston: Little, Brown, 1984.

——*History of United States Naval Operations in World War II: The Struggle for Guadalcanal, August 1942–February 1943*. Boston: Little, Brown, 1984.

——*The Two-Ocean War*. Boston: Little, Brown, 1963.

O'Donnell, Kenneth P., and David F. Powers. *Johnny, We Hardly Knew Ye: Memories of John Fitzgerald Kennedy*. Boston: Little, Brown, 1972.

Pub. 126 Sailing Direction (Enroute) Pacific Islands. Bethesda, Maryland, National Geospatial-Intelligence Agency, 2008.

Reed, A.W. *Place-Names of New South Wales: Their Origins and Meanings*. Sydney, Australia: A.H & A.W. Reed, 1969.

Rentz, John N. *Bougainville and the Northern Solomons*. Washington, D.C.: Historical Branch, Headquarters, U.S. Marine Corps, 1946.

Roscoe, Theodore. *United States Destroyer Operations in World War II*. Annapolis, Maryland: Naval Institute, 1953.

Rottman, Gordon. *U.S. Special Warfare Units in the Pacific Theater 1941–45: Scouts, Raiders, Rangers and Reconnaissance Units*. New York: Osprey, 2005.

Royce, Patrick M. *Royce's Sailing Illustrated*, Vol. I, *The Tall Ships*. Author and Publisher, 1997.

Sloan, Bill. *Brotherhood of Heroes: The Marines at Peleliu, 1944—The Bloodiest Battle of the Pacific War*. New York: Simon and Schuster, 2005.

United States Coast Guard Book of Valor: A Fact Book on Medals and Decorations. Washington, D.C.: Public Relations Division, 1945.

DOCUMENTS/REPORTS

"CincPac Report of Operations in Pacific Ocean Areas, July 1943."

"Combat Narratives, Solomon Islands Campaign: X Report of Operations in the New Georgia Area 6/21/43—8/5/43." Washington, D.C.: Office of Naval Intelligence, 1944.

"Combat Narratives, Solomon Islands Campaign: XI Kolombangara and Vella Lavella 6 August–7 October 1943." Washington, D.C.: Office of Naval Intelligence, 1944.

"Combat Narratives, Solomon Islands Campaign: XII The Bougainville Landing and the Battle of Express Augusta Bay 27 October—2 November 1943." Washington, D.C.: Office of Naval Intelligence, 1945.

Masterson, James R. *U.S. Army Transportation in the Southwest Pacific Area, 1941–1946*. Washington, D.C.: Transportation Unit, Historical Division, Special Staff, U.S. Army, 1949.

Seventh Amphibious Force Command History, 10 January 1943–23 December 1945.

Note: Numerous other unpublished reports, letters, and messages cited in book notes.

GLOSSARY OF ACRONYMS USED IN BIBLIOGRAPHY AND NOTES

1stMarParaRegt:	First Marine Parachute Regiment
2ndParaBn:	Second Parachute Battalion
CincLant:	Commander in Chief, U.S. Atlantic Fleet
CincPac:	Commander in Chief, U.S. Pacific Fleet
CincPac-CincPoa:	CincPac-Commander in Chief, Pacific Ocean Area
Com5thFlt:	Commander, Fifth Fleet
Com7thFlt:	Commander, Seventh Fleet
Com7thPhibFor:	Commander, Seventh Amphibious Force
ComAirPac:	Commander, Air Force, U.S. Pacific Fleet
ComAmpFor SoPacFor:	Commander, Amphibious Force, South Pacific Force
ComCortDiv:	Commander, Escort Division
ComDesDiv:	Commander, Destroyer Division
ComDesRon:	Commander, Destroyer Squadron
Com LST Flot 5:	Commander, Tank Landing Ship Flotilla Five

ComMTBRon: Commander, Motor Torpedo Boat Squadron
ComNavBase: Commander, Naval Base
ComPanSeaFron: Commander, Panama Sea Frontier
ComSerFor 7thFlt: Commander, Service Force Seventh Fleet
ComWestSeaFron: Commander, Western Sea Frontier
CTF: Commander, Task Force
CTG: Commander, Task Group
CTU: Commander, Task Unit
DANFS: Directory of American Naval Fighting Ships
ONI: Office of Naval Intelligence
SOPA: Senior Officer Present Afloat
VMF: Marine Fighting Squadron

SHIP WAR DIARIES

USCGC *Balsam* (AGL-62), USS *Achilles* (ARL-41), USS *APc-2*, USS *APc-5*, USS *APc-13*, USS *APc-23*, USS *APc-24*, USS *APc-25*, USS *APc-26*, USS *APc-27*, USS *APc-28*, USS *APc-30*, USS *APc-31*, USS *APc-32*, USS *APc-33*, USS *APc-34*, USS *APc-35*, USS *APc-36*, USS *APc-31*, USS *APc-37*, USS *APc-38*, USS *APc-40*, USS *APc-42*, USS *APc-46*, USS *APc-49*, USS *APc-95*, USS *APc-98*, USS *APc-103*, USS *APc-108*, USS *APc-109*, USS *Belfast* (PF-35), USS *Chepachet* (AO-78), USS *Daniel A. Joy* (DE-585), USS *Day* (DE-225), USS *Drayton* (DD-366), USS *Eichenberger* (DE-202), USS *Gillespie* (DD-609), USS *Gladiator* (AM-319), USS *Glendale* (PF-36), USS *Hidatsa* (AT-102), USS *Jamestown* (AGP-3), USS *Lark* (ATO-168), USS *LCI(L)-327*, USS *Lough* (DE-586), USS *LST-452*, USS *LST-456*, USS *Mackinac* (AVP-13), USS *Menominee* (AT-73), USS *Oceanographer* (AGS-3), USS *Ogden* (PF-39), USS *Ortolan* (ARS-5), USS *Oyster Bay* (AGP-6), USS *Pawnee* (AT-74), USS *PCE(R)-748*, USS *PCE(R)-749*, USS *PCE(R)-849*, USS *Reid* (DD-369), USS *Rochambeau* (AP-63), USS *Roe* (DD-418), USS *SC-703*, USS *Sioux* (AT-75), USS *Sonoma* (AT-12), USS *Rigel* (AR-11), USS *Tinsman* (DE-589), USS *Welles* (DD-628), USS Whippoorwill (AM-35), USS *Whitehurst* (DE-634), USS *Williamson* (AVP-15), and USS *Willoughby* (AGP-9).

WAR DIARIES OF NAVY OPERATIONAL/ADMINISTRATIVE COMMANDS

CincLant, CincPac, CincPac-CincPOA, Com5thFlt, Com7thFlt, ComAmpFor SoPacFor, Commander Amphibious Group 6, ComCortDiv 32, ComCortDiv 37, ComDesDiv 38, ComDesRon 14, ComDesRon 22, Commander LSM Group 5, Commander LST Flotilla 14, ComMTBRon 13, ComMTBRon 27, Commander Naval Advanced Base Bora Bora, Commander Naval Base Hollandia, Commander Naval Operating Base Navy 3256, ComPanSeaFron, ComSerFor 7thFlt, CTF 31, CTF 76, CTG 32.3, U.S. Naval Station Bora Bora. VMF-112, VMF-121, and VMF-122.

Notes

PREFACE NOTES:
1. U.S. Coast Guard History Program (www.uscg.mil/history/weboralhistory/ USARS_Duluth_Flynn_Memoir.pdf: accessed 23 June 2013).
2. "Lieutenant John F. Kennedy," Naval History and Heritage Command (USNhttp://www.history.navy.mil/faqs/faq60-2.htm: accessed 19 July 2013).

CHAPTER 1 NOTES:
1. "Our Navy at War," Official Report by Admiral Ernest J. King, Covering Combat Operations Up To March 1, 1944, p. 26, 38; Operation I-GO, *Wikipedia* (http://en.wikipedia.org/wiki/Operation_I-Go: accessed 2 December 2012).
2. Samuel Eliot Morison, *History of United States Naval Operations in World War II, Breaking the Bismarcks Barrier, 22 July 1942–1May 1944* (Boston: Little, Brown, 1984), p. 92–93, 117; Samuel Eliot Morison, *The Two-Ocean War* (Boston: Little, Brown, 1963), p. 264; Papuan Campaign, Center of Military History United States Army, Washington, D.C., 1990.
3. Morison, History of United States Naval Operations in World War II, Breaking the Bismarcks Barrier, p. 118, 120; ComAirPac Analysis of Air Ops, Solomons Area, April 1943.
4. Morison, *History of United States Naval Operations in World War II, VI, Breaking the Bismarcks Barrier*, p. 120–121; World War II Allied names for Japanese aircraft, *Wikipedia* (http://en.wikipedia.org/wiki/World_War_II_Allied_names_for_Japanese_aircraft#List_of_names: accessed 30 November 2012); USS *Niagara* (AGP-1), subject: USS *Niagara* Action April 7, 1943, report of, dated April 8, 1943.
5. *Ortolan* War Diary, 4/1/43 to 6/30/43.
6. USS *Niagara* (AGP-1), subject: USS *Niagara* Action April 7, 1943, report of; USS *Conflict* (AM-85) Anti-Aircraft Action Report; Morison, *History of United States Naval Operations in World War II, VI, Breaking the Bismarcks Barrier*, p. 121; ComNavBase Fold [Tulagi] letter of

April 12, 1943, NB223/A16-3 Serial 02, subject: Air Attack on April 7, 1943.
7. CincPac, Operations in Pacific Ocean Areas, April 1943; USS *Niagara* (AGP-1), subject: USS *Niagara* Action April 7, 1943, report of; USS *Rail* (AM-26) Enemy Dive Bombing Attack at Advanced Naval Base, Fold, on 7 April 1943; Report of Operations of USS *Rail* during and subsequent to.
8. USS *Niagara* (AGP-1), subject: USS *Niagara* Action April 7, 1943, report of; USS *Rail* (AM-26) Enemy Dive Bombing Attack at Advanced Naval Base, Fold, on 7 April 1943; Report of Operations of USS *Rail* during and subsequent to.
9. CincPac Pacific Ocean Area—Operations in Pacific Ocean Areas, April 1943; ComAmpFor SoPacFor War Diary, April 1943.
10. ComAmpFor SoPacFor War Diary, March 1943.
11. USS *APc-33* Action Report for April 7, 1943, Forwarding of, dated May 6, 1943; Aichi D3A Val 1938, Carrier-Borne Dive Bomber (www.aviastar.org/air/japan/aichi_d3a.php: accessed 1 December 2012).
12. CincPac, Pacific Ocean Area—Operations in Pacific Ocean Areas, April 1943.
13. ComNavBase Fold [Tulagi] letter of April 12, 1943, NB223/A16-3 Serial 02, Subject: Air Attack on April 7, 1943; USS *Rail* Enemy Dive Bombing Attack at Advanced Naval Base, Fold, on 7 April 1943; USS *Kanawha*, Report of Action—USS KANAWHA, dated April 12, 1943; *Menominee* War Diary, April 1943.
14. ComNavBase Fold [Tulagi] letter of April 12, 1943, NB223/A16-3 Serial 02, Subject: Air Attack on April 7, 1943; CincPac, Pacific Ocean Area—Operations in Pacific Ocean Areas, April 1943.
15. *Rochambeau, DANFS*; *Rochambeau* War Diary, March 1943; Commanding Officer, USS *Aaron Ward* (DD-483), Report of enemy action resulting in loss of *AARON WARD*, of April 16, 1943; "Lieutenant John F. Kennedy," Naval History and Heritage Command; Robert J. Donovan, *PT 109* (New York: Fawcett World Library, 1965), p. 11–14; Commanding Officer USS *LST 449*, Attack by enemy aircraft, report of, dated 14 April 1943.
16. Commanding Officer USS *LST 449*, Attack by enemy aircraft, report of, dated 14 April 1943.
17. Donovan, *PT 109*, p. 20; ComAmpFor SoPacFor War Diary, April 1943; Commanding Officer USS *LST-449*, Attack by enemy aircraft, report of, dated 14 April 1943.
18. Commander Landing Craft Flotillas, South Pacific Force, First Endorsement, FE25-2/A16-3(3), Serial 0018, of April 20, 1943.

19. ComNavBase Fold [Tulagi] letter of April 12, 1943, NB223/A16-3 Serial 02, Subject: Air Attack on April 7, 1943; CincPac, Pacific Ocean Area—Operations in Pacific Ocean Areas, April 1943; ComAirPac Analysis of Air Ops, Solomons Area, April 1943.
20. Morison, *History of United States Naval Operations in World War II, VI, Breaking the Bismarcks Barrier*, p. 129.
21. ComAirPac Analysis of Air Ops, Solomons Area, April 1943.
22. Morison, *History of United States Naval Operations in World War II, VI, Breaking the Bismarcks Barrier*, p. 128–129; Daring intercept over open water! "Who Shot Down Yamamoto?" An Interview with Colonel Rex Barber by Blaine Taylor, *Pearl Harbor's WWII Collector's Edition The Official 50th Anniversary Magazine—1991* (http://ussslcca25.com/who-shot.htm: accessed 1 December 2012); Operation Vengeance, *Wikipedia* (http://en.wikipedia.org/wiki/Operation_Vengeance: accessed 1 December 2012).
23. Ibid.

CHAPTER 2 NOTES:

1. Ernest A. Flint, "The Formation and Operation of the US Army Small Ships in World War II," U.S. Army Small Ships Association Incorporated (www.usarmysmallships.asn.au/html/form_doc.html: accessed 28 December 2012).
2. "The Official Chronology of the U.S. Navy in World War II—1941," Hyperwar (www.ibiblio.org/hyperwar/USN/USN-Chron/USN-Chron-1941.html: accessed 28 December 2012).
3. David Bruhn, *Wooden Ships and Iron Men: The U.S. Navy's Coastal and Motor Minesweepers, 1941–1953* (Westminster, Maryland: Heritage Books, 2009), p. 20–21; "The Official Chronology of the U.S. Navy in World War II—1941," Hyperwar.
4. Douglas MacArthur, *Reports of General MacArthur, The Campaigns of MacArthur in the Pacific, Vol I.,* (Washington, D.C.: Center of Military History, U.S. Army, 1994), p. 29–30.
5. MacArthur, *Reports of General MacArthur, The Campaigns of MacArthur in the Pacific, Vol I.*, p. 31, 34–35, 42–45, 55; James Brown, "Japan Captures Rabaul in Australia's Territory of New Guinea," The Battle for Australia 1942-43 (www.pacificwar.org.au/battaust/Japan-invadesNewGuinea.html: accessed 28 December 2012); "New-Guinea during World War II," (www.papuaerfgoed.org/en/New-Guinea_during_World_War_II: accessed 28 December 2012).
6. MacArthur, *Reports of General MacArthur, The Campaigns of MacArthur in the Pacific, Vol I.*, p. 42–43.

7. "Kokoda Track campaign," *Wikipedia* (http://en.wikipedia.org/wiki/Kokoda_Track_campaign: accessed 19 January 2013).
8. MacArthur, *Reports of General MacArthur, The Campaigns of MacArthur in the Pacific, Vol I.*, p. 45; "Kokoda Track campaign," *Wikipedia*.
9. Morison, *The Two-Ocean War: A Short History of the United States Navy in the Second World War* (Boston: Little, Brown, 1963), p. 140.
10. Ibid, p. 142, 144, 147; "Battle of the Coral Sea, 7–8 May 1942," Naval History and Heritage Command (www.history.navy.mil/photos/events/wwii-pac/coralsea/coralsea.htm: accessed 23 January 2013).
11. James R. Masterson, "U.S. Army Transportation in the Southwest Pacific Area, 1941–1946" (Washington, D.C.: Transportation Unit, Historical Division, Special Staff, U.S. Army, 1949), p. 586–587; MacArthur, *Reports of General MacArthur, The Campaigns of MacArthur in the Pacific, Vol I.*, p. 51.
12. Masterson, "U.S. Army Transportation in the Southwest Pacific Area, 1941–1946," p. 368–369, 588.
13. Ernest A. Flint, "The Formation and Operation of the US Army Small Ships in World War II," U.S. Army Small Ships Association Incorporated; Bill and Ruth Lunney, *Forgotten Fleet 2* (Medowie, New South Wales: Forfleet Publishing, 2004), book description; Masterson, "U.S. Army Transportation in the Southwest Pacific Area, 1941–1946," p. 588, 620, 622.
14. Masterson, "U.S. Army Transportation in the Southwest Pacific Area, 1941–1946," p. 587-588, 613, 617.
15. Masterson, "U.S. Army Transportation in the Southwest Pacific Area, 1941–1946," p. 370–371; Flint, "The Formation and Operation of the US Army Small Ships in World War II."
16. Masterson, "U.S. Army Transportation in the Southwest Pacific Area, 1941–1946," p. 371.
17. Ibid, p. 372, 376, 588, 592.

CHAPTER 3 NOTES:
1. "List of World War II vessel types of the United States," *Wikipedia* (http://en.wikipedia.org/wiki/List_of_World_War_II_vessel_types_of_the_United_States: accessed 10 December 2012); Ramon Jackson, "About Army Watercraft Designations" (http://patriot.net/~eastlnd2/armyhbsd.htm: accessed 10 December 2012).
2. Masterson, "U.S. Army Transportation in the Southwest Pacific Area, 1941–1946," p. 317.
3. "U.S. Army Small Ships Section, United States Army Services of Supply (USASOS) in Australian Waters during WWII" (http://home.st.net.au/~dunn/usarmy/usarmysmallships.htm: accessed 5 January 2013);

Lawrence DiStasi, *Una Storia Segreta: The Secret History of Italian American Evacuation and Internment during World War II* (Berkeley, Calif: Heyday Books, 2001), p. 79; Tim Colton, "U.S. Army Harbor Tugs (TP)" (http://shipbuildinghistory.com/history/smallships/armytpboats.htm: accessed 21 April 2013).
4. August Felando, 26 November 2012.
5. Masterson, "U.S. Army Transportation in the Southwest Pacific Area, 1941–1946," Appendices 37 and 38.
6. David Douglas, "The Splinter Fleet," *Invention and Technology Magazine*, (www.americanheritage.com/articles/magazine/it/2003/4/2003_4_26.shtml: accessed 8 July 2007).
7. Bruhn, *Wooden Ships and Iron Men: The U.S. Navy's Coastal and Motor Minesweepers, 1941–1953*, p. 25; Stephen S. Roberts, "Class: APC-1 (APC-1)," (www.shipscribe.com/usnaux/APC/APC01.html: accessed 29 November 2012)
8. Stephen S. Roberts, "Class: APC-1 (APC-1)."
9. Ibid.
10. Ibid.
11. Bruhn, *Wooden Ships and Iron Men: The U.S. Navy's Coastal and Motor Minesweepers, 1941–1953*, p. 54–55; Stephen S. Roberts, "Class: APC-1 (APC-1)."
12. Tim Colton, "Coastal Transports (APc, HST, HSV, JHSV)" (http://shipbuildinghistory.com/history/smallships/auxcoastal.htm: accessed 1 January 2013); "United States Pacific Fleet Organization 1 May 1945" (www.ibiblio.org/hyperwar/USN/OOB/PacFleet/Org-450501/index.html: accessed 11 November); Stephen S. Roberts, "Class: APC-1 (APC-1)."

CHAPTER 4 NOTES:

1. ComAmpFor SoPacFor letter, subject: Instruction for search for enemy spies in San Cristobal and adjacent islands, FE25/A16-3(6) Serial 00270 of 31 May 1943.
2. Morison, *The Two-Ocean War*, p. 164–165.
3. Morison, *The Struggle for Guadalcanal, August 1942-February 1943*, p. 15–16; *Guadalcanal: The U.S. Army Campaign of World War II*
4. Morison, *The Two-Ocean War*, p. 164; "Guadalcanal Campaign," *Wikipedia* (http://en.wikipedia.org/wiki/Guadalcanal_Campaign: accessed 30 January 2011). (www.history.army.mil/brochures/72-8/72-8.htm: accessed 19 February 2011).
5. John Miller, Jr., *Guadalcanal: The First Offensive* (Washington, D.C.: Center of Military History, United States Army, 1995, first printed 1949-CMH Pub 5-3), p. 210, 215–216.

6. Morison, *History of United States Naval Operations in World War II: Breaking the Bismarcks Barrier*, p. 89–90. 3/1/43 to 4/30/43; CincPac and ComAmpFor SoPacFor War Diary, April 1943.
7. ONI Combat Narratives, Solomon Island Campaign: X Report of Operations in the New Georgia Area 6/21/43—8/5/43; George Carroll Dyer, *The Amphibians Came to Conquer: The Story of Admiral Richmond Kelly Turner* (Washington, D.C., U.S. Government Printing Office), p. 488–489.
8. ComAmpFor SoPacFor War Diary, May 1943; *Sioux* War Diary, June 1943; CTG 32.3 War Diary, June 1943; Dyer, *The Amphibians Came to Conquer*, p. 509.
9. ComAmpFor SoPacFor War Diary, May 1943; *Sioux* War Diary, June 1943.
10. Dyer, *The Amphibians Came to Conquer*, p. 474, 476, 479, 501, 502, 504, 507; CTG 32.3 War Diary, June 1943; *APc-35* War Diary, June 1942; *APc-36* War Diary, 6/1/43 to 10/31/43.
11. *APc-35* War Diary, June 1942.
12. CTG 32.3 War Diary, June 1943; "Makira-Ulawa Province," *Wikipedia* (http://en.wikipedia.org/wiki/Makira-Ulawa_Province: accessed 4 January 2013).
13. CTG 32.3 and *APc-35* War Diary, June 1942;
14. CTG 32.3 and *APc-35* War Diary, June 1942; *APc-36* War Diary, 6/1/43 to 10/31/43.
15. *APc-35* War Diary, June 1943.
16. Ibid.
17. Ibid.
18. *APc-25* War Diary, 5/1/43 to 7/31/43; Bill Sloan, *Brotherhood of Heroes: The Marines at Peleliu, 1944—The Bloodiest Battle of the Pacific War* (New York: Simon and Schuster, 2005), p. 29; "Lieutenant John F. Kennedy," Naval History and Heritage Command; "Pavuvu," *Wikipedia* (http://en.wikipedia.org/wiki/Pavuvu: accessed 17 January 2013); Pub. 126 Sailing Direction (Enroute) Pacific Islands (Bethesda, Md.: National Geospatial-Intelligence Agency, 2008), p. 208.
19. *APc-25* War Diary, 5/1/43 to 7/31/43; VMF-112 War Diary, June 1943.
20. VMF-112 War Diary, June 1943.
21. VMF-112 War Diary, June 1943, Stephen Sherman, "Alphabetical List of WW2 Marine Aces 118 USMC pilots who shot down 5+ Japanese planes" (http://acepilots.com/usmc_aces_list.html: accessed 18 January 2013).

CHAPTER 5 NOTES:

1. Dyer, *The Amphibians Came to Conquer*, p. 533.

2. "New Georgia Campaign," *Wikipedia* (http://en.wikipedia.org/wiki/New_Georgia_Campaign: accessed 28 January 2013).
3. Dyer, *The Amphibians Came to Conquer*, p. 496–497, 499.
4. ONI Combat Narratives, Solomon Island Campaign: X Report of Operations in the New Georgia Area 6/21/43—8/5/43; Morison, *The Two-Ocean War*, p. 272; *Building the Navy's Bases in World War II: History of the Bureau of Yards and Docks and the Civil Engineer Corps 1940-1946, Vol. II* (Washington, D.C.: U.S. Government Printing Office), p. 241.
5. CTG 32.3 War Diary, June 1943; ONI Combat Narratives, Solomon Island Campaign: X Report of Operations in the New Georgia Area 6/21/43—8/5/43.
6. *APc-23* War Diary, 6/1/43 to 9/30/43, *APc-24* War Diary, June 1943; *APc-26* War Diary, 6/1/43 to 12/31/43; *APc-27* War Diary, 6/1/43 to 8/1/43; Aviation Radar Technician 1st Class Harold E. Ohanian, "Alameda Naval Air Museum" (http://www.alamedanavalairmuseum.org/Stories.aspx: accessed 15 January 2013).
7. Ibid.
8. *APc-26* War Diary, 6/1/43 to 12/31/4; Commanding Officer USS *Celeno* (AK-76), Report of Damage Sustained Through Enemy Aircraft Attack off Guadalcanal Island, June 16, 1943, dated June 27, 1943; Commanding Officer USS *O'Bannon* (DD-450), Action Report—Air Attack on Blue Shipping, Guadalcanal area by Japanese, 16 June 1943, dated June 18, 1943.
9. Commanding Officer USS *LST-340*, Action Report of USS *L.S.T. 340*, dated June 26, 1943.
10. *APc-23* War Diary, 6/1/43 to 9/30/43; *APc-26* War Diary, 6/1/43 to 12/31/43; *APc-24* War Diary, June 1943.
11. CTF 31 War Diary, 6/17-30/43; *LCI(L)(L)-327* War Diary, August 1943.
12. Commanding Officer USS *APc-34*, Action report—forwarding of, dated June 17, 1943; *APc-34* War Diary, June 1943.
13. Ibid.
14. *APc-31* War Diary, July 1943.
15. Ibid; "Canterbury Steam Shipping Company," New Zealand Coastal Shipping (www.nzcoastalshipping.com/canstem.html: accessed 16 January 2013); "HMNZS *Gale* (T04)," *Wikipedia* (http://en.wikipedia.org/wiki/HMNZS_Gale_%28T04%29: accessed 16 January 2013).
16. Dyer, *The Amphibians Came to Conquer*, p. 512, 514, 523–524.
17. Ibid, p. 524–525
18. Ibid, p. 525, 530.
19. Ibid, p. 530-531; ONI Combat Narratives, Solomon Island Campaign: X Report of Operations in the New Georgia Area 6/21/43–8/5/43; "The Solomons Campaign: Ground Action—The New Georgia Campaign,

June 20-November 3, 1943," *U.S. Naval Institute* (http://blog.usni.org/2009/10/15/the-solomons-campaign-ground-action-the-new-georgia-campaign-june-20-november-3-1943: accessed 31 January 2013).
20. ONI Combat Narratives, Solomon Island Campaign: X Report of Operations in the New Georgia Area 6/21/43—8/5/43; CTF 31 War Diary, June 1943.
21. CincPac Report of Operations in Pacific Ocean Areas, July 1943; ONI Combat Narratives, Solomon Island Campaign: X Report of Operations in the New Georgia Area 6/21/43—8/5/43; *Gwin*, *DANFS*.
22. ONI Combat Narratives, Solomon Island Campaign: X Report of Operations in the New Georgia Area 6/21/43—8/5/43; CTF 32.3 War Diary, June 1943; VMF-121 and VMF-122 War Diary, June 1943; Robert W. McClurg, *On Boyington's Wing* (Bowie, Md:, Heritage Books, 2003), p. 29.
23. VMF-221 Action Report of 6/30/43; ONI Combat Narratives, Solomon Island Campaign: X Report of Operations in the New Georgia Area 6/21/43—8/5/43.
24. CTF 32.3 War Diary, June 1943.
25. Ibid.
26. Ibid.
27. CTF 32.3 War Diary, June 1943; Commander Mine Squadron Two, Viru Occupation, Report of, dated July 10, 1943
28. Ibid.
29. *APc-27* War Diary, 6/1/43 to 8/1/43; *APc-36* War Diary, 6/1/43 to 10/31/43; *APc-38* War Diary, 7/1/43 to 8/31/43.
30. *APc-26* War Diary, 6/1/43 to 12/31/43; *APc-35* War Diary, July 1943.
31. *APc-38* War Diary, 7/1/43 to 8/31/43; Commanding Officer, USS *APc-25*, Report of Operations of USS *APc 25* and USS *APc 38*, dated 11 July 1943; "Battle of Enogai," *Wikipedia* (http://en.wikipedia.org/wiki/Battle_of_Enogai: accessed 28 January 2013); "Battle of Bairoko," *Wikipedia* (http://en.wikipedia.org/wiki/Battle_of_Bairoko: accessed 28 January 2013).
32. Commanding Officer, USS *APc-25*, Report of Operations of USS *APc 25* and USS *APc 38*.
33. *APc-38* War Diary, 7/1/43 to 8/31/43; Commanding Officer, USS *APc-25*, Report of Operations of USS *APc 25* and USS *APc 38*.
34. Commanding Officer, USS *APc-25*, Report of Operations of USS *APc 25* and USS *APc 38*.
35. Ibid.
36. Ibid.

37. "Battle of Bairoko," *Wikipedia* (http://en.wikipedia.org/wiki/Battle_of_Bairoko: accessed 28 January 2013).
38. *John Penn*, *DANFS*.
39. Commanding Officer, USS *APc-25*, Report of Action and Rescue Work, dated 15 August 1943.
40. Ibid.

CHAPTER 6 NOTES:
1. Com LST Flot 5, Report of Passage from New York to Noumea, NC, 3/9/43 to 5/14/43, CincPac War Diary, April and May 1943.
2. CincLant War Diary, February 1943; ComPanSeaFron War Diary, March 1943.
3. Commander Naval Advanced Base Bora Bora War Diary, 3/1/43 to 5/31/43; Dick Kirkham, "The War Diary of Dick Kirkham 1944–1946" (www.contractorsales.biz/gen/222/wardiary/?page_id=76: accessed 4 February 2013).
4. APc-5 War Diary, April 1943; *Building the Navy's Bases in World War II: History of the Bureau of Yards and Docks and the Civil Engineer Corps, 1940–1946, Vol. II*: p. 191–192.
5. *APc-5* War Diary, April 1943
6. CincPac, Com7thFlt, and CTF 76 War Diary, May 1943; Com 7th Fleet War Diary, August 1943; U.S. Naval Station Bora Bora War Diary, July 1943; Com LST Flot 5, Report of Passage from New York to Noumea, NC, 3/9/43 to 5/14/43.
7. CTF 76 War Diary, May through August 1943, and individual ships' war diaries.
8. CTF 76, Operation Chronicle—report upon, dated 1 October 1943.
9. Morison, *The Two-Ocean War*, p. 264, 272, 291; Edward J. Drea, *New Guinea: The U.S. Army Campaigns of World War II* (www.history.army.mil/brochures/new-guinea/ng.htm: accessed 9 February 2013).
10. CTF 76 War Diary, May and June 1943; A.W. Reed, *Place-Names of New South Wales: Their Origins and Meanings* (Sydney, Australia: A.H & A.W. Reed, 1969), p. 120; Robert Kerr, *A General History and Collection of Voyages and Travels*, Vol. 12, Project Gutenberg, 22 December 2004.
11. Commanding Officer USS *APc-3*, History of USS *APc-3*, dated 5 November 1945.
12. CTF 76, Operation Chronicle—report upon, dated 1 October 1943.
13. Ibid.
14. CTF 76, Operation Chronicle—report upon, dated 1 October 1943; CTF 76 War Diary, June 1943.

15. CTF 76, Operation Chronicle—report upon, dated 1 October 1943; CTF 76 War Diary, June 1943; "Walter Krueger," *Wikipedia* (http://en.wikipedia.org/wiki/Walter_Krueger: accessed 6 February 2013); "Alamo Scouts" (http://www.alamoscouts.org/index.htm: accessed 6 February 2013).
16. CTF 76 War Diary, July 1943.
17. CTF 76 War Diary, July 1943; "History of the 2nd Engineer Special Brigade, Chapter IV" (www.2esb.org/04_History/Book/Chapter_04.htm: accessed 6 February 2013) "LCVP (United States)," *Wikipedia* (http://en.wikipedia.org/wiki/LCVP_%28United_States%29: accessed 7 February 2013).
18. CTF 76 War Diary, July 1943.
19. CTF 76 War Diary, July and August 1943.
20. CTF 76 War Diary, August 1943; "Tufi," *Wikipedia* (http://en.wikipedia.org/wiki/Tufi: accessed 6 February 2013).
21. CTF 76 War Diary, August 1943; Com7thPhibFor, ARAWE Operation—report of, dated 10 January 1944.
22. CTF 76 War Diary, August 1943; Gordon Rottman, *U.S. Special Warfare Units in the Pacific Theater 1941-45: Scouts, Raiders, Rangers and Reconnaissance Units* (New York: Osprey Publishing Ltd., 2005), p. 37.
23. Chet Cunningham, *The Frogmen of World War II: An Oral History of the U.S. Navy's Underwater Demolition Teams* (New York, New York, Pocket Star, 2005), Chapter 1.
24. Rottman, *U.S. Special Warfare Units in the Pacific Theater 1941–45: Scouts, Raiders, Rangers and Reconnaissance Units*, p. 37.

CHAPTER 7 NOTES:
1. Commanding Officer, USS *Conyngham*, Action Report, 4 September 1943, dated 7 September 1943.
2. "Salamaua–Lae campaign," *Wikipedia* (http://en.wikipedia.org/wiki/Salamaua%E2%80%93Lae_campaign: accessed 16 February 2013).
3. CTF 76 War Diary, September 2013; "History of the 2nd Engineer Special Brigade, Chapter V;" William C. Baldwin, "Aviation and Amphibian Engineers in the Southwest Pacific" (http://140.194.76.129/publications/eng-pamphlets/EP_870-1-42_pfl/c-6-1.pdf: accessed 23 February 2013), p. 357; Samuel Eliot Morison, *History of United States Naval Operations in World War II, New Guinea and the Marianas* (Boston: Little, Brown, 1953), p. 54.
4. "History of the 2nd Engineer Special Brigade, Chapter V;" Com7thPhibFor, LAE Operation—Report upon, dated 23 October 1943.
5. Com7thPhibFor, LAE Operation—Report upon, dated 23 October 1943.

Notes {313}

6. Com7thPhibFor, LAE Operation—Report upon, dated 23 October 1943; Commanding Officer USS *L.S.T 471*, Report of battle, October 11, 1943.
7. Commanding Officer *YMS-49*, Action Report, dated 14 October 1943.
8. Masterson, "U.S. Army Transportation in the Southwest Pacific Area 1941–1947," p. 450; Commanding Officer USS SC-703 War Diaries and Action Reports—forwarding of, dated October 9, 1943.
9. "History of the 2nd Engineer Special Brigade, Chapter IV."
10. Com7thPhibFor, LAE Operation—Report upon, dated 23 October 1943; Seventh Amphibious Force Command History, 10 January 1943–23 December 1945; Carl White, "2nd Engineer Special Brigade" (http://corregidor.org/chs_2esb/lineage_esb.htm: accessed 21 February 2013); CTF Seventy-Eight, Report of the Lingayen Operation—San Fabian Attack Force, dated 12 February 1945.
11. Masterson, "U.S. Army Transportation in the Southwest Pacific Area 1941–1947," p. 450; Com7thPhibFor, LAE Operation—Report upon, dated 23 October 1943.
12. Com7thPhibFor, LAE Operation—Report upon, dated 23 October 1943.
13. Com7thPhibFor, LAE Operation—Report upon, dated 23 October 1943; Seventh Amphibious Force Command History, 10 January 1943–23 December 1945 (www.history.navy.mil/library/online/7thamphibcomdhist.htm: accessed 21 February 2013); Com7thPhibFor, FINSCHHAFEN Operation—Report upon, dated 23 October 1943; CTF 76 Operational Order No. NG 5-43.
14. Com7thPhibFor, FINSCHHAFEN Operation—Report upon, dated 23 October 1943.
15. Ibid.
16. CTF 76 War Diary, September 1943; *Ships of the U.S. Navy, 1940–1945* (www.ibiblio.org/hyperwar/USN/ships/ships-lcv.html: accessed 24 February 2012); Com7thPhibFor, FINSCHHAFEN Operation—Report upon, dated 23 October 1943; The Higgins Boat (www-cs-faculty.stanford.edu/~eroberts/courses/ww2/projects/fighting-vehicles/higgins-boat.htm: accessed 24 February 2013); Jared Bahr, "Higgins: The Forgotten Man: The LCVP (Landing Craft, Vehicle, Personnel): A Strategic Military Innovation with Impact" (http://andrewjacksonhiggins.weebly.com/wwii-impact.html: accessed 25 February 2013).
17. CTF 76 War Diary, September 1943; *Sonoma* War Diary, September 1943.
18. CTF 76 Operational Order No. NG 5-43; *Sonoma* War Diary, September 1943.

19. John Miller, Jr., *United States Army in World War II The War in the Pacific CARTWHEEL: The Reduction of Rabaul* (Washington, D.C.: Dept. of the Army, 1959), p. 219; *Sonoma* War Diary, September 1943.
20. Miller, Jr., *United States Army in World War II The War in the Pacific CARTWHEEL: The Reduction of Rabaul*, p. 219.
21. Robert J. Bulkley, Jr., *At Close Quarters PT Boats in the United States Navy*, Naval History Division, Washington, D.C., 1962, p. 198 (www.ibiblio.org/hyperwar/USN/CloseQuarters/index.html: accessed 25 February 2012).
22. Bulkley, Jr., *At Close Quarters PT Boats in the United States Navy*, p. 176, 178; *Building the Navy's Bases in World War II: History of the Bureau of Yards and Docks and the Civil Engineer Corps 1940–1946 Vol. II*, p. 286.
23. CTF 76 War Diary, November 1943; Bulkley, Jr., *At Close Quarters PT Boats in the United States Navy*, p. 211, 213.
24. Bulkley, Jr., *At Close Quarters PT Boats in the United States Navy*, p. 211, 213.

CHAPTER 8 NOTES:
1. Commanding Officer USS *SC-743*, Anti-Aircraft Action Report Letter, dated December 19, 1943.
2. Com7thPhibFor, ARAWE Operation—report of, dated 10 January 1944.
3. Ibid.
4. Com7thPhibFor, ARAWE Operation—report of, dated 10 January 1944; Seventh Amphibious Force Command History, 10 January 1943–23 December 1945; CTF 76 War Diary, September and December 1943.
5. Com7thPhibFor, ARAWE Operation—report of, dated 10 January 1944; Morison, *History of United States Naval Operations in World War II, New Guinea and the Marianas*, p. 54.
6. Commander LCT(5) Flotilla 7, Preliminary report on Operation [redacted], dated 10 January 1943.
7. Ibid.
8. Commanding Officer USS *SC-743*, Anti-Aircraft Action Report Letter, dated December 19, 1943.
9. Commanding Officer USS *SC-743*, Anti-Aircraft Action Report Letter, dated December 19, 1943; Commander LCT(5) Flotilla 7, Preliminary report on Operation [redacted], dated 10 January 1943; Commanding Officer, USS *APc-21*, Anti-aircraft Action Report—ARAWE, New Britain, 17 December 1943, and 16 December 1943, dated 24 December

Notes {315}

1943; Com7thPhibFor, ARAWE Operation—report of, dated 10 January 1944.
10. Commanding Officer USS *SC-743*, Anti-Aircraft Action Report Letter, dated December 19, 1943; Commander LCT(5) Flotilla 7, Preliminary report on Operation [redacted], dated 10 January 1943
11. Commanding Officer USS *SC-743*, Anti-Aircraft Action Report Letter, dated December 19, 1943.
12. Commanding Officer USS *SC-743*, Anti-Aircraft Action Report Letter, dated December 19, 1943; Com7thPhibFor, ARAWE Operation—report of, dated 10 January 1944; Commander LCT(5) Flotilla 7, Preliminary report on Operation [redacted], dated 10 January 1943.
13. Commander LCT(5) Flotilla 7, Preliminary report on Operation [redacted], dated 10 January 1943.
14. Commanding Officer USS *SC-743*, Anti-Aircraft Action Report Letter, dated December 19, 1943; CTF 76 War Diary, December 1943; Commander LCT(5) Flotilla 7, Preliminary report on Operation [redacted], dated 10 January 1943.
15. Commanding Officer USS *APc-2*, Anti-Aircraft action report—Arawe, New Britain operation, dated 23 December 1943.
16. Ibid; Commander LCT(5) Flotilla 7, Preliminary report on Operation [redacted], dated 10 January 1943.
17. Commanding Officer USS *APc-2*, Anti-Aircraft action report—Arawe, New Britain operation, dated 23 December 1943.
18. Ibid.
19. Ibid.
20. Ibid.
21. Ibid; Commander LCT(5) Flotilla 7, Preliminary report on Operation [redacted], dated 10 January 1943.
22. Commander LCT(5) Flotilla 7, Preliminary report on Operation [word redacted], dated 10 January 1944.
23. Commanding Officer, USS *APc-15*, General Report of Action, dated 29 December 1943; Commanding Officer, USS *SC-743*, Anti-Aircraft Action Report Letter, dated 28 December 1943; Commanding Officer, *PT-110*, Action Report, PTs *110* and *138*, Night of 25-26 December, 1943, dated 27 December 1943; Commander LCT(5) Flotilla 7, Preliminary report on Operation [word redacted], dated 10 January 1944; Kemper Goffigon, 14 February 2013.
24. Commanding Officer, USS *APc-15*, General Report of Action, dated 29 December 1943.
25. Ibid.
26. Ibid.

27. Commanding Officer, USS *APc-15*, General Report of Action, dated 29 December 1943; Kemper Goffigon, 14 February 2013.
28. Commanding Officer, USS *APc-15*, General Report of Action, dated 29 December 1943; Commanding Officer USS *APc-15*, Damage Report—submission of, dated 7 January 1944; Kemper Goffigon, 14 February 2013.
29. Commanding Officer, USS *APc-15*, General Report of Action, dated 29 December 1943.
30. Commanding Officer USS *APc-15*, Damage Report—submission of, dated 7 January 1944; Kemper Goffigon, 14 February 2013.
31. Commanding Officer, USS *APc-15*, General Report of Action, dated 29 December 1943; *Building the Navy's Bases in World War II: History of the Bureau of Yards and Docks and the Civil Engineer Corps 1940–1946 Vol. II*, p. 284.
32. John A. Crown and Frank O. Hough, *The Campaign on New Britain*, Historical Branch, Headquarters, U.S. Marine Corps, 1952, p. 140, 143.

CHAPTER 9 NOTES:

1. *APc-37* War Diary, 6/30/43 to 10/31/43.
2. United States Administration in World War II, CincPac, Motor Torpedo Squadrons, First Draft Narrative Prepared under the General Supervision of the Director of Naval History, p. 42; ONI Combat Narratives, Solomon Islands Campaign: XI Kolombangara and Vella Lavella 6 August–7 October 1943, p. 58; Bulkley, Jr., *At Close Quarters PT Boats in the United States Navy*, p. 34–36, 38; Morison, *History of United States Naval Operations in World War II, New Guinea and the Marianas*, p. 57.
3. Tactical and Technical Trends, No. 43, January 27, 1944, U.S. Military Intelligence Service (http://www.lonesentry.com/articles/ttt09/barges.html: accessed 1 March 2013).
4. "Daihatsu Class Japanese Landing Craft," *The Pacific War Online Encyclopedia* (http://pwencycl.kgbudge.com/D/a/Daihatsu_class.htm: accessed 1 March 2013); Daihatsu-class landing craft, *Wikipedia* (http://en.wikipedia.org/wiki/Daihatsu-class_landing_craft: accessed 1 March 2013).
5. ONI Combat Narratives, Solomon Islands Campaign: XI Kolombangara and Vella Lavella 6 August-7 October 1943, p. 36–37.
6. Ibid, p. 37.
7. ONI Combat Narratives, Solomon Islands Campaign: XI Kolombangara and Vella Lavella 6 August-7 October 1943, p. 38; CTF 31 War Diary, September 1943; Bulkley, Jr., *At Close Quarters PT Boats in the United States Navy*, p. 115, 117–118, 461; United States Administration

in World War II, CincPac, Motor Torpedo Squadrons, First Draft Narrative Prepared under the General Supervision of the Director of Naval History, p. 36.
8. Bulkley, Jr., *At Close Quarters PT Boats in the United States Navy*, p. 155–156.
9. Ibid, p. 156.
10. CTF 31 War Diary, September 1943, *Argonne, DANFS*.
11. *APc-31* War Diary, October 1943.
12. United States Administration in World War II, CincPac, Motor Torpedo Squadrons, First Draft Narrative Prepared under the General Supervision of the Director of Naval History, p. 38–39; CTG Thirty-One Point One, Report of occupation of the Treasury Islands, 27 October 1943, dated 10 November 1943.
13. CTF 31 Operation Order A16-43; *APc-33* War Diary, October-November 1943; *APc-37* War Diary, October 1943.
14. CTF 31 War Diary, October 1943; CTG Thirty-One Point One, Report of occupation of the Treasury Islands, 27 October 1943, dated 10 November 1943.
15. United States Administration in World War II, CincPac, Motor Torpedo Squadrons, First Draft Narrative Prepared under the General Supervision of the Director of Naval History, p. 38–39; CTG Thirty-One Point One, Report of occupation of the Treasury Islands, 27 October 1943, dated 10 November 1943.
16. *APc-34* War Diary, December 1943; *APc-42* War Diary, 7/1/43 to 10/31/43.
17. *Oceanographer* War Diary, December 1943; *APc-30* War Diary, December 1943 and January 1944.
18. *Oceanographer*, War Diary, February 1944.
19. *APc-35* War Diary, September 1943.
20. *Pawnee* War Diary, September 1943.

CHAPTER 10 NOTES:
1. "Combat Narratives Solomon Islands Campaign: XII The Bougainville Landing and the Battle of Express Augusta Bay 27 October—2 November 1943;" Kenny O'Donnell and Dave Powers, *Johnny, We Hardly Knew Ye: Memories of John Fitzgerald Kennedy* (Boston: Little, Brown, 1972), p. 438–439.
2. John N. Rentz, *Bougainville and the Northern Solomons* (Washington, D.C.: Historical Branch, Headquarters, U.S. Marine Corps, 1946) p. 106, 112; Greg Bradsher, "Operation Blissful How the Marines Lured the Japanese Away From a Key Target—and How 'the Brute' Got Some

Help from JFK," *Prologue*, Fall 2010, Vol. 42, No. 3; James E. Christ, *Mission Raise Hell* (Annapolis, Maryland: Naval Institute, 2006), p. xiv.
3. Rentz, *Bougainville and the Northern Solomons*, p. 106, 112; Bradsher, "Operation Blissful;" Christ, *Mission Raise Hell*, p. 180–181.
4. Bradsher, "Operation Blissful;" PT-BOAT OFFICER IN THE PACIFIC: Robert Ankers PT RONs 19, 23 Interview by Francis A. O'Brien for World War II, January 2003, 93rd Seabees Battalion (www.seabees93.net/GI%20PT%20RON%2019%20Ankers1.htm: accessed 29 March 2013).
5. Greg Bradsher, "John F. Kennedy and PT Boat 59," *Prologue*: Pieces of History (http://blogs.archives.gov/prologue/?p=10448: accessed 1 April 2013); Frank J. Andruss Sr., 7 April 2013.
6. PT-BOAT OFFICER IN THE PACIFIC: Robert Ankers PT RONs 19, 23 Interview by Francis A. O'Brien for World War II, January 2003, 93rd Seabees Battalion (www.seabees93.net/GI%20PT%20RON%2019%20Ankers1.htm: accessed 29 March 2013).
7. Rentz, *Bougainville and the Northern Solomons*, p. 111–113; Hq, 2ndParaBn, 1stMarParaRegt, 1MAC, in the Field, report dated 7 November 1943; Morison, *History of the United States Navy in World War II: Breaking the Bismarcks Barrier*, p. 308.
8. Rentz, *Bougainville and the Northern Solomons*, p. 111–113; Hq, 2ndParaBn, 1stMarParaRegt, 1MAC, in the Field, report dated 7 November 1943; Morison, *History of the United States Navy in World War II: Breaking the Bismarcks Barrier*, p. 308; Christ, *Mission Raise Hell*, p. 212.
9. Hq, 2ndParaBn, 1stMarParaRegt, 1MAC, in the Field, report dated 7 November 1943; Bradsher, "Operation Blissful;" Douglas T. Kane and Henry I. Shaw, Jr., *History of U.S. Marine Corps Operations in World War II Vol. II: Isolation of Rabaul* (Washington, D.C.: Headquarters, U.S. Marine Corps, 1963) p. 202–203; Donovan, *PT 109*, p. 149; Christ, *Mission Raise Hell*, p. 213–214; Frank J. Andruss Sr., 7 April 2013.
10. Bradsher, "Operation Blissful;" Kane and Shaw, Jr., *History of U.S. Marine Corps Operations in World War II Vol. II: Isolation of Rabaul*, p. 203; Donovan, *PT 109*, p. 148.
11. Bradsher, "Operation Blissful;" Kane and Shaw, Jr., *History of U.S. Marine Corps Operations in World War II Vol. II: Isolation of Rabaul*, p. 203; Donovan, *PT 109*, p. 148.
12. Bradsher, "Operation Blissful;" "Lieutenant John F. Kennedy," Naval History and Heritage Command; Donovan, *PT 109*, p. 153; John N. Mitchell (www.princeton.edu/~achaney/tmve/wiki100k/docs/John_N._Mitchell.html: accessed 2 April 2013); "John F. Kennedy" (www.historynet.com/john-f-kennedy: accessed 19 July 2013).

CHAPTER 11 NOTES:

1. Morison, *Two-Ocean War*, 296; "Battle of Tarawa," *Wikipedia* (http://en.wikipedia.org/wiki/Battle_of_Tarawa: accessed 15 October 2012).
2. Worrall Reed Carter, *Beans, Bullets, and Black Oil* (Washington, D.C.: U.S. Government Printing Office, 1953), 90-93.
3. The Capture of Makin (Washington, D.C.: Center of Military History, U.S. Army, 1990), 132; James R. Stockman, *The Battle for Tarawa*, Appendix B: "Marine Casualties" (www.ibiblio.org/hyperwar/USMC/USMC-M-Tarawa/USMC-M-Tarawa-B.html: accessed 15 October 2012); Richard Johnston, *Follow Me!: The Story of The Second Marine Division in World War II* (New York: Random House, 1948), p. 111.
4. *APc-108* and *APc-109* War Diary, December 1943; *Building the Navy's Bases in World War II: History of the Bureau of Yards and Docks and the Civil Engineer Corps 1940–1946 Vol. II*, p. 314.
5. *APc-108* and *APc-109* War Diary, December 1943; *Terror*, DANFS.
6. *APc-109* War Diary, December 1943.
7. Ibid.
8. *APc-108* War Diary, December 1943; *Building the Navy's Bases in World War II: History of the Bureau of Yards and Docks and the Civil Engineer Corps 1940–1946 Vol. II*, p. 316.
9. *APc-108* War Diary, December 1943.
10. *APc-108* and *APc-109* War Diary, December 1943.
11. Ibid.

CHAPTER 12 NOTES:

1. Loreen Brehaut, "The Scow Echo" (http://www.theprow.org.nz/the-scow-echo/#.UTjOl1e3lJI: accessed 7 March 2013).
2. *MacKinac* War Diary, March and May 1943; W. C. O'Ferrall, "Melanesia Santa Cruz and the Reef Islands" (http://anglicanhistory.org/oceania/oferrall_santacruz1908/: accessed 8 March 2013); Alan Powell, "Boye-Jones, Ruby Olive (1891–1990)" (http://adb.anu.edu.au/biography/boye-jones-ruby-olive-12242: accessed 8 March 2013); J. C. H. Gill, "Feldt, Eric Augustas (1899–1968)" (http://adb.anu.edu.au/biography/feldt-eric-augustas-10163: accessed 9 March 2013).
3. Brendan Nicholson, "Aussie mum who reported Japanese air and sea movements from Solomon Islands honoured," *The Australian*, April 25, 2011; Alan Powell, "Boye-Jones, Ruby Olive (1891–1990)" (http://adb.anu.edu.au/biography/boye-jones-ruby-olive-12242: accessed 8 March 2013).
4. Brendan Nicholson, "Aussie mum who reported Japanese air and sea movements from Solomon Islands honoured," *The Australian*, April 25, 2011; Alan Powell, "Boye-Jones, Ruby Olive (1891–1990)".

5. *APc-95* War Diary, 12/1/43 to 1/31/44
6. NZ Historic Ships A database of historic New Zealand Ships and Boats (http://maanz.wellington.net.nz/nzhistoricships/directory/Echo.html: accessed 6 March 2013); Brehaut, "The Scow Echo;" *Rigel* War Diary, November 1943.
7. NZ Historic Ships A database of historic New Zealand Ships and Boats (http://maanz.wellington.net.nz/nzhistoricships/directory/Echo.html: accessed 6 March 2013); "Cafe Food Drink business for sale Picton New Zealand" (www.bizoptions.com/10544.htm: accessed 6 March 2013); Brehaut, "The Scow Echo."
8. *APc-95* War Diary, February, March, and April 1944.

CHAPTER 13 NOTES:

1. Morison, *The Two-Ocean War*, p. 292; Bernard C. Nalty, Cape Gloucester: The Green Inferno (www.ibiblio.org/hyperwar/USMC/USMC-C-Gloucester/index.html: accessed 11 March 2013); Morison, *History of United States Naval Operation in World War II: Breaking the Bismarcks Barrier*, p. 370, 378–379, 386, 388.
2. Theodore Roscoe, *United States Destroyer Operations in World War II* (Annapolis, Maryland: Naval Institute Press, 1953), p. 404–405; Morison, History of United States Naval Operation in World War II: Breaking the Bismarcks Barrier, p. 384.
3. CTF 76 War Diary, February 1944; Commanding Officer *LST 463*, Anti-Aircraft Action Report-Echelon B-21, dated 10 February 1944.
4. *APc-13* War Diary, April 1944.
5. Commander Attack Group, Admiralty Islands Operation, 29 February 1944—Report on, dated 16 March 1944; Morison, *History of United States Naval Operation in World War II: Breaking the Bismarcks Barrier*, p. 435.
6. Morison, *The Two-Ocean War*, p. 293–294; Morison, *History of United States Naval Operation in World War II: Breaking the Bismarcks Barrier*, p. 432–433.
7. Commander Attack Group, Admiralty Islands Operation, 29 February 1944—Report on; Morison, *History of United States Naval Operation in World War II: Breaking the Bismarcks Barrier*, p. 436–437.
8. Commander Attack Group, Admiralty Islands Operation, 29 February 1944—Report on.
9. Ibid.
10. Commander Attack Group, Admiralty Islands Operation, 29 February 1944—Report on; Arnold Lott, *Most Dangerous Sea* (Annapolis, Md: Naval Institute, 1959), p. 138.

11. CTF 76 War Diary, March 1944; *Gillespie* War Diary, March 1944; *Reid* War Diary, March 1944; ComDesDiv 38 War Diary, March 1944; *LST-456* War Diary, 2/1/44 to 3/31/44; *LST-452* War Diary, March 1944.
12. *Drayton, Reid, Roe,* and *Welles* War Diary for March 1944; Morison, *History of United States Naval Operation in World War II: Breaking the Bismarcks Barrier,* p. 445–446.
13. Morison, *The Two-Ocean War,* p. 318–319.
14. ComCortDiv 37 War Diary, April 1943.
15. Commander Attack Force (CTF 77), Report of TANAHMERAH BAY-HUMBOLDT BAY-AITAPE Operation, dated 6 May 1944; Morison, *History of United States Naval Operations in World War II, New Guinea and the Marianas,* p. 60.
16. Commander Attack Force (CTF 77), Report of TANAHMERAH BAY-HUMBOLDT BAY-AITAPE Operation, dated 6 May 1944.
17. ComCortDiv 32 War Diary, April and May 1943; *Eichenberger* War Diary, April 1944.
18. CincPac Report of Operations in Pacific Areas, May 1944.
19. Ibid.
20. CincPac Report of Operations in Pacific Areas, May 1944; *APc-108* War Diary, 12/1/43 to 6/30/44.
21. Peter Dunn, "US Army Small Ships Section, United States Army Services of Supply (USASOS) in Australian Waters during WWII" (www.ozatwar.com/usarmy/usarmysmallships.htm: accessed 10 March 2013); ComWestSeaFron War Diary, December 1943.
22. Morison, *History of United States Naval Operations in World War II, New Guinea and the Marianas,* p. 83–87; *APc-2* War Diary, 2/1/44 to 7/31/44; *Oyster Bay, DANFS.*
23. *APc-2* War Diary, 2/1/44 to 7/31/44; Bulkley, Jr., *At Close Quarters PT Boats in the United States Navy,* p. 193, 213, 248.
24. Bulkley, Jr., *At Close Quarters PT Boats in the United States Navy,* p. 222, 236.
25. Morison, *History of United States Naval Operations in World War II, New Guinea and the Marianas,* p. 46, 50, 61, 141.

CHAPTER 14 NOTES:
1. Cyril J. O'Brien, "Liberation: Marines in the Recapture of Guam (www.ibiblio.org/hyperwar/USMC/USMC-C-Guam: accessed 25 March 2013).
2. Morison, *The Two-Ocean War,* p. 339, 342–343.
3. CTF Fifty-Three, Report of Amphibious Operations for the Capture of Guam, dated 10 August 1944.

{322} Notes

4. CTF Fifty-Three, Report of Amphibious Operations for the Capture of Guam, dated 10 August 1944; National Park Service War in the Pacific, Agat Beach Unit and Ga'an Point (www.nps.gov/wapa/planyourvisit/gaan-point.htm: accessed 19 March 2013)
5. National Park Service War in the Pacific, Agat Beach Unit and Ga'an Point (www.nps.gov/wapa/planyourvisit/gaan-point.htm: accessed 19 March 2013)
6. *Williamson, DANFS*; Pacific Aviation Museum Pearl Harbor, U.S. Scout/Observation Floatplanes in World War II (www.pacificaviationmuseum.org/pearl-harbor-blog/u-s-scoutobservation-floatplanes-in-world-war-ii: accessed 13 March 2013).
7. *APc-46* War Diary, July 1944.
8. *APc-46* War Diary, July 1944; *Williamson* War Diary, July 1943; CTF 53, Report of Amphibious Operations for the Capture of Guam, dated 10 August 1944.
9. *Williamson* War Diary, August 1943; *APc-46* War Diary for August and September 1943; CTF Fifty-Three, Transfer of the duties as SOPA-Guam to CTF Fifty-Seven (Deputy Forward Area, Central Pacific), dated 20 August 1944.
10. "Battle of Peleliu" (http://en.wikipedia.org/wiki/Battle_of_Peleliu: accessed 8 April 2013).

CHAPTER 15 NOTES:

1. Bulkley, Jr., *At Close Quarters PT Boats in the United States Navy*, p. 415–416.
2. Ibid, p. 415–416.
3. Ibid, p. 248, 418.
4. Ibid, p. 248, 418.
5. "Battle of Morotai," *Wikipedia* (http://en.wikipedia.org/wiki/Battle_of_Morotai: accessed 24 April 2013).
6. Bulkley, Jr., *At Close Quarters PT Boats in the United States Navy*, p. 259.

CHAPTER 16 NOTES:

1. United States Strategic Bombing Survey, Interrogation of Japanese Officials, OpNav P-03-100, Naval Analysis Division, 13-14 November 1945 (http://www.ibiblio.org/hyperwar/AAF/USSBS/IJO/IJO-75.html: accessed 9 November 2011).
2. Morison, *The Two-Ocean War*, p. 330–345.
3. Aerology and Amphibious Warfare The Assault Landings on Leyte Island NAVAER 50-30T-6, Chief of Naval Operations, Aerology Section,

Washington, D.C. (www.history.navy.mil/library/online/assault_leyte.htm: accessed 24 April 2013).
4. Morison, *The Two-Ocean War*, p. 432–435; CTF Seventy-Eight, Leyte Operation—report on, dated 10 November 1944.
5. *PCE(R)-848* and *PCE(R)-849* War Diary, October 1944; Masterson, "U.S. Army Transportation in the Southwest Pacific Area 1941–1947," p. 422.
6. Morison, *The Two-Ocean War*, p. 432–436; CTF Seventy-Eight, Leyte Operation—report on, dated 10 November 1944.
7. Morison, *The Two-Ocean War*, p. 432–436.
8. Commanding Officer USS *Coronado* (PF-38), Action Report—Central Philippines Operation, 8 Oct.—4 Nov. 44, dated 5 November 1944.
9. Ibid; *Hidatsa* War Diary, October 1944.
10. Commanding Officer USS *Coronado* (PF-38), Action Report—Central Philippines Operation, 8 Oct.—4 Nov. 44, dated 5 November 1944.
11. Ibid.
12. Ibid; *Hidatsa* War Diary, October 1944.
13. Morison, *The Two-Ocean War*, p. 441–451.
14. Morison, *The Two-Ocean War*, p. 441–451; "Japanese cruiser *Mogami* (1934)," *Wikipedia*, http://en.wikipedia.org/wiki/Japanese_cruiser_Mogami_%281934%29 (accessed: 13 May 2013).
15. Commanding Officer USS *Coronado* (PF-38), Action Report—Central Philippines Operation, 8 Oct.—4 Nov. 44, dated 5 November 1944; *Hidatsa* and *Lark* War Diary, October 1944.
16. *Ogden* War Diary, October and November 1944; ComSerFor 7th Fleet War Diary, 10/1/44 to 11/30/44; "Appendix VII Small Ships Section," 2nd Engineer Special Brigade.org (www.2esb.org/04_History/Book/Chapter_24.htm: accessed May 15, 2013).
17. *Ogden* War Diary, October and November 1944.
18. *Belfast* and *Glendale* War Diary, November 1944.
19. Samuel Eliot Morison, *History of United States Naval Operations in World War II: The Liberation of the Philippines—Luzon, Mindanao, the Visayas, 1944–1945* (Boston: Little, Brown , 1984), p. 98–99; Morison, *The Two-Ocean War*, p. 479–480.
20. Morison, *The Two-Ocean War*, p. 432–436; "Battle of Leyte Gulf," *Wikipedia* (http://en.wikipedia.org/wiki/Battle_of_Leyte_Gulf: accessed 9 November 2011).
21. *Whitehurst* War Diary, October 1944.
22. *The Coast Guard at War The Pacific Landings*, Historical Section Public Information Division U.S. Coast Guard Headquarters March 15, 1946, p. 157 (www.ibiblio.org/hyperwar/USCG/VI-Pacific/USCG-VI-21.

html: accessed 24 April 2013); "The Official Chronology of the U.S. Navy in World War II—1944," Hyperwar.
23. Commander LST Flotilla 14 War Diary, November 1944.
24. Ibid.
25. "Journal of Charles E. Mashburn, USCGR, Commanding Officer *FS-366*, 1944-1945," U.S. Coast Guard History Program (www.uscg.mil/history/weboralhistory/MashburnCharlesFSJournal1944.pdf: accessed 10 April 2013); *FS-366*, World War II Coast Guard-Manned U.S. Army Freight and Supply Ship Histories (www.uscg.mil/history/webcutters/FS_Vessels.asp: accessed 10 April 2013).
26. Journal of Charles E. Mashburn.
27. Ibid.
28. Journal of Charles E. Mashburn; *FS-366*, World War II Coast Guard-Manned U.S. Army Freight and Supply Ship Histories.
29. CTU 76.4.7, Action Report, Task Unit 76.4.7, dated 7 December 1944; Commanding Officer, *FS-170*, Action of December 5, 1944, report of, dated 23 December 1944; *Gilliam* War Diary, December 1944.
30. CTU 76.4.7, Action Report, Task Unit 76.4.7, dated 7 December 1944.
31. Ibid.
32. Harold Larson, "The Army's Cargo Fleet in World War II," Office of the Chief of Transportation, Army Service Forces, 1945, p. 14–16.
33. CTU 76.4.7, Action Report, Task Unit 76.4.7, dated 7 December 1944.
34. CTU 76.4.7, Action Report, Task Unit 76.4.7, dated 7 December 1944; "The Official Chronology of the U.S. Navy in World War II—1944," Hyperwar; "SS *Antoine Saugrain*," *Wikipedia* (http://en.wikipedia.org/wiki/SS_Antoine_Saugrain: accessed 29 April 2013); Commanding Officer, *FS-170*, Action of December 5, 1944, report of.
35. CTU 76.4.7, Action Report, Task Unit 76.4.7, dated 7 December 1944; "The Official Chronology of the U.S. Navy in World War II—1944," Hyperwar; "SS Antoine Saugrain," *Wikipedia*; Commanding Officer, *FS-170*, Action of December 5, 1944, report of; *United States Coast Guard Book of Valor* (Washington, D.C., 1945).
36. CTU 76.4.7, Action Report, Task Unit 76.4.7, dated 7 December 1944; Commanding Officer, *FS-170*, Action of December 5, 1944, report of.
37. CTU 76.4.7, Action Report, Task Unit 76.4.7, dated 7 December 1944; "History of the Armed Guard Afloat, World War II" (Washington, D.C.: 1946) p. 237–251 (www.history.navy.mil/faqs/faq104-10.htm: accessed 29 April 2013); *FS-170*, Action of December 5, 1944, report of.
38. Handwritten note titled Certification of destruction, dated 16 December 1944 and signed by Clifton H. Linville, Commanding Officer *F-120*.

39. CTU 76.4.7, Action Report, Task Unit 76.4.7, dated 7 December 1944; Ray Thompson, "Mactan Memoirs: Stories of Three Survivors of the Attack on Clark Field, p. I. and Their Evacuation on the Red Cross Ship, MACTAN" (www.ww2f.com/topic/21361-the-fighting-mactan: accessed 29 April 2013); "Hospital Ships (AH)," *The Pacific War Online Encyclopedia* (http://pwencycl.kgbudge.com/H/o/Hospital_Ships.htm: accessed 29 April 2013).
40. Ray Thompson, "Mactan Memoirs: Stories of Three Survivors of the Attack on Clark Field, p. I. and Their Evacuation on the Red Cross Ship, MACTAN"
41. CTU 76.4.7, Action Report, Task Unit 76.4.7, dated 7 December 1944.
42. Ibid.
43. CTU 78.3.12 (CDD48), Report of Slow Tow Convoy, Love Three Phase of the Mike One Operation, dated 25 December 1944.
44. Morison, *History of United States Naval Operations in World War II: The Liberation of the Philippines—Luzon, Mindanao, the Visayas 1944–1945*, p. 16.
45. Morison, *History of United States Naval Operations in World War II: The Liberation of the Philippines—Luzon, Mindanao, the Visayas 1944–1945*, p. 22; Masterson, "U.S. Army Transportation in the Southwest Pacific Area 1941–1947," p. 380; Tim Colton, "U.S. Army Harbor Tugs (TP)."
46. Report of Slow Tow Convoy dated 25 December 1944; Royal Australian Navy Ship/Unit Approved Battle Honours, March 2010 (http://web.archive.org/web/20110614064156/http://www.navy.gov.au/w/images/Units_entitlement_list.pdf: accessed 2 May 2013).
47. Harold Larson, "The Army's Cargo Fleet in World War II," Office of the Chief of Transportation, Army Service Forces, 1945, p. 119–122; Tim Colton, "U.S. Army Coastal Tankers (Y)" (http://shipbuildinghistory.com/history/smallships/armytankers.htm: accessed 4 May 2013).
48. Report of Slow Tow Convoy dated December 1944; USS *Whippoorwill* (ATO-169), Action Reports of the Mindoro Island, Philippine Islands Operations, dated 25 December 1944.
49. Letter from Master, *S.T. 381* to Gen. William F. Heavey, Headquarters, 2nd ESB, dated 21 December 1944.
50. Report of Slow Tow Convoy dated 25 December 1944; USS *Whippoorwill* (ATO-169), Action Reports of the Mindoro Island, Philippine Islands Operations, dated 25 December 1944.
51. USS *Whippoorwill* (ATO-169), Action Reports of the Mindoro Island, Philippine Islands Operations, dated 25 December 1944; USS *Holt* (DE-706), Action Report, 12 to 19 December 1944, dated 19 December 1944; USS *Jobb* (DE-707), Action Report, dated 21 December 1944;

Report of Slow Tow Convoy dated 25 December 1944; Letter from Master, *S.T. 381* to Gen. William F. Heavey dated 21 December 1944.
52. USS *Whippoorwill* (ATO-169), Action Reports of the Mindoro Island, Philippine Islands Operations, dated 25 December 1944; USS *Holt* (DE-706), Action Report, 12 to 19 December 1944, dated 19 December 1944; USS *Jobb* (DE-707), Action Report, dated 21 December 1944; Report of Slow Tow Convoy dated 25 December 1944; Letter from Master, *S.T. 381* to Gen. William F. Heavey dated 21 December 1944.
53. USS *Whippoorwill* (ATO-169), Action Reports of the Mindoro Island, Philippine Islands Operations, dated 25 December 1944; USS *Holt* (DE-706), Action Report, 12 to 19 December 1944, dated 19 December 1944; USS *Jobb* (DE-707), Action Report, dated 21 December 1944.
54. USS *Whippoorwill* (ATO 169), Action Reports of the Mindoro Island, Philippine Islands Operations, dated 25 December 1944; USS *Holt* (DE-706), Action Report, 12 to 19 December 1944, dated 19 December 1944; USS *Jobb* (DE-707), Action Report, dated 21 December 1944; Letter from Master, *S.T. 381* to Gen. William F. Heavey dated 21 December 1944.
55. Ibid.
56. Report of Slow Tow Convoy dated 25 December 1944.
57. Ibid.
58. Ibid.
59. Letter from Master, *S.T. 381* to Gen. William F. Heavey dated 21 December 1944.
60. CTG 77.11, Action Report, 27 December to 31 December 1944; Leyte-Mindoro, p. I., dated 4 January 1945; Commanding Officer, USS *Philip* (DD-498), Action Report for the Period From 27 December 1944 to 1 January 1945, U Plus 15 Mindoro Resupply Echelon, dated 3 January 1945.
61. Ibid.
62. CTG 77.11, Action Report, 27 December to 31 December 1944; Leyte-Mindoro, p. I., dated 4 January 1945.
63. CTG 77.11, Action Report, 27 December to 31 December 1944; Leyte-Mindoro, p. I., dated 4 January 1945; "The Official Chronology of the U.S. Navy in World War II—1944," Hyperwar; Bulkley, Jr., *At Close Quarters PT Boats in the United States Navy*, p. 409; War Shipping Administration Washington, Advance Release: for Sunday Papers October 14, 1945 (www.usmm.org/wsa/shipspacific.html: accessed 14 April 2013); Commanding Officer, USS *Philip* (DD-498), Action Report for the Period From 27 December 1944 to 1 January 1945, U Plus 15 Mindoro Resupply Echelon, dated 3 January 1945.

64. USS *Grapple* Memorandum of Salvage Operations, Subject: SS *William Sharon*—Recovery of, document not dated.
65. *FS-309*, World War II Coast Guard-Manned U.S. Army Freight and Supply Ship Histories; *United States Coast Guard Book of Valor* (Washington, D.C., 1945). The cited history of the *FS-309* incorrectly identifies the ammunition-laden ship that blew up on 28 December as the *Porcupine* vice the *John Burke*. The citation for the Bronze Star received by Francis Owens cites he was a crewman of the *FS-209*, which is also apparently an error as the *FS-309* history identifies him as a crewman of that ship.
66. CTG 77.11, Action Report, 27 December to 31 December 1944; Leyte-Mindoro, p. I., dated 4 January 1945; "The Official Chronology of the U.S. Navy in World War II—1944," Hyperwar; Commanding Officer, USS *Philip* (DD-498), Action Report for the Period From 27 December 1944 to 1 January 1945, U Plus 15 Mindoro Resupply Echelon, dated 3 January 1945.
67. CTG 77.11, Action Report, 27 December to 31 December 1944; Leyte-Mindoro, p. I., dated 4 January 1945; *FS-349*, World War II Coast Guard-Manned U.S. Army Freight and Supply Ship Histories.
68. CTG 77.11, Action Report, 27 December to 31 December 1944; Leyte-Mindoro, p. I., dated 4 January 1945; *FS-349*, World War II Coast Guard-Manned U.S. Army Freight and Supply Ship Histories.
69. CTG 77.11, Action Report, 27 December to 31 December 1944; Leyte-Mindoro, p. I., dated 4 January 1945.
70. Ibid.
71. *Gansevoort*, *DANFS*; *FS-367*, World War II Coast Guard-Manned U.S. Army Freight and Supply Ship Histories.
72. CTG 77.11, Action Report, 27 December to 31 December 1944; Leyte-Mindoro, p. I., dated 4 January 1945.
73. CTG 77.11, Action Report, 27 December to 31 December 1944; Leyte-Mindoro, p. I., dated 4 January 1945; War Shipping Administration Washington, Advance Release: for Sunday Papers October 14, 1945 (www.usmm.org/wsa/shipspacific.html: accessed 14 April 2013); Bruhn, *Wooden Ships and Iron Men: The U.S. Navy's Coastal and Motor Minesweepers, 1941–1953*, p. 84. CTG 77.11 cited one Army FS Ship immediately astern of the *John Burke* being sunk by the explosion of the *Liberty*-ship and of two survivors found. Accounts of other ships in the convoy make no such reference; two men rescued by the *FS-309*, which had been blown overboard from the shock wave, were from a Navy ship near the *Liberty*-ship. The ship reported lost may have been an Army crash boat. The vessels of the convoy were disposed over three square miles, making it difficult in some cases to visually ascertain

aboard particular ships exactly what had transpired elsewhere in the convoy.

CHAPTER 17 NOTES:
1. Commander Luzon Attack Force, Action Report—Luzon Attack Force, Lingayen Gulf—Musketeer Mike One Operation, dated 15 May 1945.
2. Commander Luzon Attack Force, Action Report—Luzon Attack Force, Lingayen Gulf—Musketeer Mike One Operation, dated 15 May 1945; Morison, *History of United States Naval Operations in World War II, The Liberation of the Philippines—Luzon, Mindanao, the Visayas, 1944-1945*, p. 128-132.
3. Commander Luzon Attack Force, Action Report—Luzon Attack Force, Lingayen Gulf—Musketeer Mike One Operation, dated 15 May 1945; Com7thFlt War Diary, January 1945.
4. Commander Luzon Attack Force, Action Report—Luzon Attack Force, Lingayen Gulf—Musketeer Mike One Operation, dated 15 May 1945.
5. Journal of Charles E. Mashburn; *FS-366*, World War II Coast Guard-Manned U.S. Army Freight and Supply Ship Histories.
6. Commander Luzon Attack Force, Action Report—Luzon Attack Force, Lingayen Gulf—Musketeer Mike One Operation, dated 15 May 1945; CTG 78.9, Action Report, dated 18 January 1945; Journal of Charles E. Mashburn; *FS-366*, World War II Coast Guard-Manned U.S. Army Freight and Supply Ship Histories.
7. CTG 78.9, Action Report, dated 18 January 1945.
8. Journal of Charles E. Mashburn; "Shinyo-class suicide motorboat," *Wikipedia* (http://en.wikipedia.org/wiki/Shinyo-class_suicide_motorboat: accessed 11 April 2013).
9. CTG 78.9, Action Report, dated 18 January 1945; Commander Luzon Attack Force, Action Report—Luzon Attack Force, Lingayen Gulf—Musketeer Mike One Operation, dated 15 May 1945.
10. Commander Luzon Attack Force, Action Report—Luzon Attack Force, Lingayen Gulf—Musketeer Mike One Operation, dated 15 May 1945.
11. Ibid.
12. Commander Luzon Attack Force, Action Report—Luzon Attack Force, Lingayen Gulf—Musketeer Mike One Operation, dated 15 May 1945; Morison, *History of United States Naval Operations in World War II, The Liberation of the Philippines—Luzon, Mindanao, the Visayas, 1944-1945*, p. 102, 116.
13. Commander Luzon Attack Force, Action Report—Luzon Attack Force, Lingayen Gulf—Musketeer Mike One Operation, dated 15 May 1945; Com7thFlt War Diary, January 1945.

14. Commanding Officer USS *Day* (DE 225), Action Report—Luzon Operation, dated 20 January 1945.
15. USS *Day* (DE 225), USS *Tinsman* (DE 589), USS *Whippoorwill* (ATO 169) and CTF 76 War Diary, January 1945; Commanding Officer USS *Day* (DE 225), Action Report—Luzon Operation, dated 20 January 1945.
16. Commanding Officer USS *Day* (DE-225), Action Report—Luzon Operation, dated 20 January 1945.
17. Commanding Officer USS *Tinsman* (DE-589), Action Report—Luzon Operation, dated 20 January 1945; *Day*, *Tinsman*, and *Whippoorwill* War Diary, January 1945.
18. *Day* and *Tinsman* War Diary, January 1945; Commanding Officer USS *Day* (DE-225), Action Report—Luzon Operation, dated 20 January 1945; Commanding Officer USS *Tinsman* (DE-589), Action Report—Luzon Operation, dated 20 January 1945.
19. *Day* War Diary, January 1945.
20. Commander Reinforcement Group, Luzon Attack Force, Report of Reinforcement Group participating in Amphibious Operations for the capture of Luzon, p. I., dated 20 January 1945; Commander LST Flotilla Three, Action Report, Lingayen Gulf Operation, Philippine Islands, dated 6 February 1945.
21. Cliff Beasley, "Damn the Torpedoes—Japanese Corrosion Saved a Ship" (www.uscg.mil/history/WEBORALHISTORY/WWII_Beasley_Stories.asp: accessed 23 April 2013).
22. Commander LST Flotilla Three, Action Report, Lingayen Gulf Operation, Philippine Islands, dated 6 February 1945.
23. Ibid.
24. Commander Amphibious Group Six War Diary, January and February 1945; ComNavBase Hollandia War Diary, February 1945.
25. Commander Transport Squadron Fourteen, Action Report, Amphibious Assault Operations on Luzon (Lingayen Gulf), 9-10 January 1945, dated 24 January 1945; *Lough* and *Daniel A. Joy* War Diary, January 1945.
26. *Lough* and *Daniel A. Joy* War Diary, January 1945.
27. *Daniel A. Joy* War Diary, January 1945.
28. CTF 76 War Diary, January 1945.

CHAPTER 18 NOTES:

1. Report of the Commanding General Eight Army on the Nasugu and Bataan Operations Mike Six and Mike Seven, compilation of After Action Reports dated 31 January 1946.

2. CTG 78.2, Action Report—Nasugbu, Luzon Operation—Report on, dated 8 March 1945.
3. Isaac Hoppenstein, The Operations of the 187th Glider Infantry Regiment (11th Airborne Division) in the Landing at Nasugbu, Luzon, Philippine Islands 31 January—3 February 1945 (The Luzon Campaign), The Infantry School Fort Benning, Georgia, Advanced Infantry Officers Course 1947–1948 (www.benning.army.mil/library/content/virtual/donovanpapers/wwii/STUP2/HoppensteinIssac%20%20MAJ.pdf: accessed 17 April 2013).
4. Report of the Commanding General Eight Army on the Nasugu and Bataan Operations Mike Six and Mike Seven, compilation of After Action Reports dated 31 January 1946; Isaac Hoppenstein, The Operations of the 187th Glider Infantry Regiment (11th Airborne Division) in the Landing at Nasugbu, Luzon, Philippine Islands 31 January—3 February 1945 (The Luzon Campaign), The Infantry School Fort Benning, Georgia, Advanced Infantry Officers Course 1947–1948 (www.benning.army.mil/library/content/virtual/donovanpapers/wwii/STUP2/HoppensteinIssac%20%20MAJ.pdf: accessed 17 April 2013).
5. Report of the Commanding General Eight Army on the Nasugu and Bataan Operations Mike Six and Mike Seven, compilation of After Action Reports dated 31 January 1946.
6. CTG 78.2, Action Report—Nasugbu, Luzon Operation—Report on, dated 8 March 1945; Isaac Hoppenstein, The Operations of the 187th Glider Infantry Regiment (11th Airborne Division) in the Landing at Nasugbu, Luzon, Philippine Islands 31 January—3 February 1945 (The Luzon Campaign), The Infantry School Fort Benning, Georgia, Advanced Infantry Officers Course 1947–1948 (www.benning.army.mil/library/content/virtual/donovanpapers/wwii/STUP2/Hoppenstein-Issac%20%20MAJ.pdf: accessed 17 April 2013).
7. *Tinsman* War Diary, February 1945; "Shinyo-class suicide motorboat," *Wikipedia* (http://en.wikipedia.org/wiki/Shinyo-class_suicide_motorboat: accessed 17 April 2013); *War Hawk, DANFS*; Robin L. Rielly, *Kamikaze Attacks of World War II: A Complete History of Japanese Suicide Strikes on American Ships, by Aircraft and Other Means* (Jefferson, North Carolina, McFarland & Company, Inc.,2010), p. 73.
8. *Lough* and *Tinsman* War Diary, February 1945; CTG 78.2, Action Report—Nasugbu, Luzon Operation—Report on, dated 8 March 1945.
9. CTG 78.2, Action Report—Nasugbu, Luzon Operation—Report on, dated 8 March 1945.
10. Commander LSM Group Five War Diary, February 1945.
11. "Coast Guard-manned U.S. Army *FS-184* Pacific Theater, World War II," Interview of Hank Rodgers, Jr. QM1, USCG, Retired, on 23 May

1995, U.S. Coast Guard Oral History Program (www.uscg.mil/history/weboralhistory/ArmyFSHankRogers.asp: accessed 9 July 2013).
12. *FS-309*, World War II Coast Guard-Manned U.S. Army Freight and Supply Ship Histories; *United States Coast Guard Book of Valor.*
13. ComMTBRon 27 War Diary, February 1945.
14. Morison, *History of United States Naval Operations, The Liberation of the Philippines—Luzon, Mindanao, the Visayas, 1944–1945*, p. 210, 214, 250.
15. "*FS-255*," World War II Coast Guard-Manned U.S. Army Freight and Supply Ship Histories.
16. Ibid.
17. Ibid.

CHAPTER 19 NOTES:
1. Morison, *The Two-Ocean War*, p. 528; "Battle of Okinawa," AnimEigo (http://www.animeigo.com/liner/out-print/battle-okinawa: accessed 28 June 2013).
2. "Battle of Okinawa," AnimEigo (www.animeigo.com/liner/out-print/battle-okinawa: accessed 28 June 2013).
3. Bruhn, *Wooden Ships and Iron Men: The U.S. Navy's Coastal and Motor Minesweepers, 1941–1953*, p. 36–37.
4. Commander Mine Squadron Four, General Action Report of CTG 32.4—22 June to 25 July 1945—Submission of, dated 27 August 1945.
5. *APc-26, APc-32, Gladiator,* and *Balsam* War Diary, June 1945.
6. USS *LST-534*, Action Report; submission of, dated 25 June 1945, *LST-534, DANFS.*
7. *APc-26* and *APc-32* War Diary, June 1945; Bruhn, *Wooden Ships and Iron Men: The U.S. Navy's Coastal and Motor Minesweepers, 1941–1953*, p. 36; Bill Sloan, *The Ultimate Battle: Okinawa 1945—The Last Epic Struggle of World War II* (Simon and Schuster, 2008) p. 104–105.
8. *APc-26* and *APc-32* War Diary, June 1945.
9. *APc-23* and *APc-28* War Diary, June 1945.
10. *APc-23* and *APc-28* War Diary, June 1945; Commanding Officer USS *Thatcher*, Action Report, USS *Thatcher* (DD-514), Okinawa, 19 July 1945, dated 24 July 1945.
11. *APc-23, APc-26,* and *APc-32* War Diary, June 1945; Commanding Officer USS *Thatcher*, Action Report, USS *Thatcher* (DD-514), Okinawa, 19 July 1945, dated 24 July 1945; Commander Naval Forces Navy 3256 (Okinawa) War Diary, July 1945.
12. *APc-23, APc-26, APc-28,* and *APc-32* War Diary, August 1945.
13. *APc-103* War Diary, October 1945.
14. Com5thFlt War Diary, September 1945.

15. Commander Service Squadron Ten, Memorandum: Ships Suffering Storm Damage and Extent of Damage in Cases Where Known. This information from Maint. CSD 104 as of 19 September. More reports of damage are expected, dated 19 September 1945; *APc-28* War Diary, September 1945, *APc-32* War Diary, July and September 1945.
16. CincPac-CincPoa War Diary, September 1945; Commandant Naval Operating Base Navy 3256 (Okinawa) War Diary, November 1945.
17. *APc-32* War Diary, November 1945; *APc-40*, *APc-49*, and *APc-98* War Diary, December 1945.
18. *APc-34* War Diary, December 1945.

CHAPTER 20 NOTES:
1. Bruhn, *Wooden Ships and Iron Men: The U.S. Navy's Coastal and Motor Minesweepers, 1941–1953*, p. 103–104.
2. Ibid, p. 105–106.
3. ComDesRon 22 War Diary, April 1945; Commanding Officer USS *LCI(L)-635*, Action Report of Task Group 78.1 on Oboe 1 Operation, dated 4 May 1945; CTG 78.1, Action Report, CTG 78.1 (ComPhibGruSix)—Tarakan, Borneo, Operation (1-3 May 1945), dated 5 May 1945; *PCE(R)-849* War Diary, May 1945.
4. Commanding Officer LCI(L) 635, Action Report of Task Group 78.1 on Oboe 1 Operation, dated 4 May 1945; *PCE(R)-849* War Diary, May 1945.
5. Commanding Officer USS *LCI(L)-635*, Action Report of Task Group 78.1 on Oboe 1 Operation, dated 4 May 1945.
6. Commanding Officer USS *LCI(L)-635*, Action Report of Task Group 78.1 on Oboe 1 Operation, dated 4 May 1945; Lott, *Most Dangerous Sea*, p. 159.
7. *PCE(R)-849* War Diary, May 1945.
8. "Australia's War 1939–1945" (www.ww2australia.gov.au/lastbattles/landings.html: accessed 29 May 2013).
9. "Australia's War 1939–1945;" Mervyn Towers, "Memoirs of a World War II Veteran" (www.mervyntowers.id.au/memoirs/assault_and_landing_on_labuan_islandi.html: accessed 29 May 2013).
10. *Jamestown, Willoughby*, ComMTBRon 13 War Diary, July 1945; *Achilles* War Diary, 7/18-31/1945.
11. CTG 78.2, Action Report—Balikpapan-Manggar-Borneo June 15—July 6, 1945, dated 14 August 1945.
12. "Australia's War 1939–1945;" CTG 78.2, Action Report—Balikpapan-Manggar-Borneo June 15—July 6, 1945, dated 14 August 1945.
13. CTG 78.2, Action Report—Balikpapan-Manggar-Borneo June 15—July 6, 1945, dated 14 August 1945; Lott, *Most Dangerous Sea*, p. 161, 163.

14. CTG 78.2, Action Report—Balikpapan-Manggar-Borneo June 15—July 6, 1945, dated 14 August 1945.
15. CTU 78.2.16 (Commander Press Unit), Action Report of Task Unit 78.2.16 on Assault Landing and Operation of Balikpapan, Borneo, 1 July 1945 to 6 July 1945, dated 6 July 1945; Commanding Officer USS *LCI(L)-1071*, Action report, USS LCI(L) 1071—BALIKPAPAN Operation, 1 July 1945, dated 4 July 1945.
16. *Chepachet* War Diary, June 1945; CTG 78.2, Action Report—Balikpapan-Manggar-Borneo June 15—July 6, 1945, dated 14 August 1945.
17. CTU 78.2.35, Action Report, Task Unit 78.2.35, BALIKPAPAN Operation, 3 July 1945, dated 6 July 1945; CTU 78.2.16 (Commander Press Unit), Action Report of Task Unit 78.2.16 on Assault Landing and Operation of Balikpapan, Borneo, 1 July 1945 to 6 July 1945, dated 6 July 1945.
18. ComDesRon 14 War Diary, July 1945; CTU 78.2.16 (Commander Press Unit), Action Report of Task Unit 78.2.16 on Assault Landing and Operation of Balikpapan, Borneo, 1 July 1945 to 6 July 1945, dated 6 July 1945; "Australia's War 1939-1945" (www.ww2australia.gov.au/lastbattles/landings.html: accessed 29 May 2013); "Sandakan Death Marches," *Wikipedia* (http://en.wikipedia.org/wiki/Sandakan_Death_Marches: accessed 14 June 2013).

CHAPTER 21 NOTES:

1. *The Stars and Stripes China Edition*, a compilation of the Sept. 29, Oct. 2, 6, and 10, 1945 issues (http://cbi-theater-10.home.comcast.net/~cbi-theater-10/starsnstripes/starsnstripes.html: accessed 11 July 2013). Accounts vary regarding the crew complement of the Japanese junk; I have used figures cited by Lt. Livingston Swentzel in an interview published in the newspaper *The Norwalk Hour* on October 8, 1945.
2. "Now it can be Told! American Naval Group and Chinese Guerillas Obtained Valuable Data while Operating Among Japanese Forces in China," Vertical file, SACO 1942-1945, Navy Department Library, Naval History and Heritage Command (www.history.navy.mil/library/online/saco_press.htm: accessed 10 July 2013).
3. Ibid.
4. Ibid.
5. Morison, *History of United States Naval Operations in World War II, The Liberation of the Philippines—Luzon, Mindanao, the Visayas, 1944-1945*, p. 300-302; *Royce's Sailing Illustrated, Vol. I: The Tall Ships*, author and publisher, 1997, p. 280; "Sea Fight Won by L.I. City Man Lieut. Swentzel Leads Junk Navy to Victor," *Long Island Star-Journal*,

October 5, 1945; "Last Naval Battle of War between Two Sailing Ships," *The Norwalk Hour*, October 8, 1945.
6. M. E. Miles, *A Different Kind of War* (Garden City, New York: Doubleday, 1967), p. 529.
7. *The Stars and Stripes China Edition*, a compilation of the Sept. 29, Oct. 2, 6, and 10, 1945 issues (http://cbi-theater-10.home.comcast.net/~cbi-theater-10/starsnstripes/starsnstripes.html: accessed 11 July 2013); "Last Naval Battle of War between Two Sailing Ships," *The Norwalk Hour*, October 8, 1945.
8. *The Stars and Stripes China Edition*, a compilation of the Sept. 29, Oct. 2, 6, and 10, 1945 issues (http://cbi-theater-10.home.comcast.net/~cbi-theater-10/starsnstripes/starsnstripes.html: accessed 11 July 2013); "Last Naval Battle of War between Two Sailing Ships," *The Norwalk Hour*, October 8, 1945; Lt. Livingston Swentzel's Navy Cross citation; GM3 James R. Reid's Navy Cross citation; Morison, *History of United States Naval Operations in World War II, The Liberation of the Philippines—Luzon, Mindanao, the Visayas, 1944–1945*, p. 300–302; Miles, *A Different Kind of War*, p. 529; "Sea Fight Won by L.I. City Man Lieut. Swentzel Leads Junk Navy to Victor," *Long Island Star-Journal*, October 5, 1945.
9. GMG1 William Barratt Miles Silver Star citation; Miles, *A Different Kind of War*, p. 529.
10. Lt. Livingston Swentzel's Navy Cross citation; "Last Naval Battle of War between Two Sailing Ships," *The Norwalk Hour*, October 8, 1945; "Special Naval Landing Forces," *The Pacific War Online Encyclopedia* (http://pwencycl.kgbudge.com/S/p/Special_Naval_Landing_Forces.htm: accessed 16 July 2013).

POSTSCRIPT NOTES:
1. "History of The USS *Brule* (AKL-28)," Mobile Riverine Force Association (www.mrfa.org/akl28.htm: accessed 20 June 2013).
2. Tim Colton, "Coastal Transports (APc, HST, HSV, JHSV)."
3. "Light Cargo Ship (AKL) Index," NavSource (www.navsource.org/archives/09/14/14idx.htm: accessed 18 June 2013); "World War II Coast Guard-Manned U.S. Army Freight and Supply Ship Histories;" Tim Colton, "U.S. Army Coastal Freighters (F, FS)" (http://shipbuildinghistory.com/history/smallships/armyfreighters.htm: accessed 21 June 2013).
4. U.S. Navy Awards (https://awards.navy.mil/awards/webbas01.nsf/%28vwWebPage%29/home.htm?OpenDocument: accessed 17 June 2013); Derek Burroughs, Jr., "The Radio Rose of Texas" (http://stellamaris.no/chapter10.htm: accessed 23 June 2013).

5. "History of The USS *Brule* (AKL-28)," Mobile Riverine Force Association; "Waitin At the Levee for the USS *Brule*," *Stars and Stripes*, July 26, 1970; "History of The USS *Mark* (AKL-12)," Mobile Riverine Force Association (http://www.mrfa.org/akl12.htm: accessed 21 June 2013).
6. "History of The USS *Brule* (AKL-28)," Mobile Riverine Force Association; "Waitin At the Levee for the USS *Brule*."
7. "History of The USS *Brule* (AKL-28)," Mobile Riverine Force Association; "Waitin At the Levee for the USS *Brule*;" "History of The USS *Mark* (AKL-12)," Mobile Riverine Force Association.
8. "Waitin At the Levee for the USS *Brule*."
9. "History of The USS *Mark* (AKL-12)," Mobile Riverine Force Association.
10. Tim Colton, "U.S. Army Coastal Freighters (F, FS);" USS *Deal* (AKL-2), NavSource (www.navsource.org/archives/09/49/49131.htm: accessed 16 June 2013); Vicki Barker, "The Real Story Behind Britain's Rock 'N' Roll Pirates," NPR, November 13, 2009 (www.npr.org/templates/story/story.php?storyId=120358447: accessed 19 June 2013); "Radio in the Water," The Dipole (http://mnarc.org/news/2013/03/radio-in-the-water/: accessed 23 June 2013).
11. USS *Palm Beach* (AGER-3), NavSource (www.navsource.org/archives/09/61/6103.htm: accessed 17 June 2013); *FS-289*, NavSource (www.navsource.org/archives/09/14/1417.htm: accessed 17 June 2013); Al Grobmeier, "The "Special Project Fleet 1961-69, 1985-89" (http://coldwar-c4i.net/SpecialProjectFleet/history.html: accessed 23 June 2013).
12. Tim Colton, "U.S. Army Coastal Freighters (F, FS)."
13. Tim Colton, "U.S. Army Ocean Tugs (LT, ST) Built During WWII" (http://shipbuildinghistory.com/history/smallships/armytugs.htm: accessed 16 June 2013); Tim Colton, "U.S. Army Coastal Tankers (Y);" "Auxiliary Fleet Tug (ATA) Index," NavSource (www.navsource.org/archives/09/38/38idx.htm: accessed 19 June 2013); "Thames Tugs" (www.thamestugs.co.uk/MULBERRY-TUGS-%5BUS%5D%5B1%5D.php: accessed 19 June 2013).

Index

Akin, Spencer B., 167
Anderson (Storekeeper Second), 104
Allen, Jr., B. C., 102
Australia(n), xiv, xviii, 2, 15–19, 37, 41, 67–69, 71, 73, 185, 187
    Army, xxv, 2–3, 16–18, 72, 76, 78, 163, 175, 243
        I Corps, 241
        2/4th Field Regiment, 81
        6th Rifleman Division, 73
        7th Infantry Division, 81, 248–249
        8th Infantry Brigade, 154
        9th Infantry Division, 77–78, 81–83, 87, 90–91, 242, 244
        16th Infantry Brigade, 76
        Australian and British POWs/Sandakan Death Marches, 249–250
    Borneo (Tarakan/Brunei Bay/Balikpapan) Campaign, xxvi, 242–250, 270
    Brisbane, xiv, 17, 21, 67, 69, 72, 74–75, 149, 154, 188
    Cairns, xiv, 75, 79, 91, 108
    Cape York Peninsula, 2
    Catboat Flotilla/Australian-built craft, xviii, 15, 20–23, 26, 28, 151, 184
    Coast watcher(s), xxi, xxiii, 3, 137–139, 143
    Port Stephens (Philip Stephens), 72
    Royal Australian
        Air Force (RAAF), 17, 52, 76, 148
        Navy (RAN), 21, 87, 138–139
    Sydney, 21–22, 67–69, 72, 74, 242, 248
    Townsville, 21, 72, 74
Ayesa, Benjamin, 224, 269, 280
Barbey, Daniel E., 67, 70–72, 74–75, 78–79, 81, 85–86, 96, 111, 150, 205, 215
Baily (Lt. Comdr.), 43–44
Baker, David A., xxvii, 255–257, 293
Baron, W. A., 59
Barrett, William K., xxvii, 254, 293
Bates, W. J., 70, 98, 267–268, 285
Battle of
    Bismarck Sea, xxiii, 137

Index

 Buna-Gona, 20, 71
 Coral Sea, 19
 Empress Augusta Bay, 128
 Final American naval battle of World War II, 251–257, 291–293
 Guadalcanal, 38
 Leyte Gulf, xxv, 165–166, 174–175, 230
 Makassar Strait (Naval Battle of Balikpapan), 250
 New Georgia, 58
 Okinawa, 229–230
 Philippine Sea, xxv, 155–156, 165, 175
 Saipan, 155
 Singapore, 249
 Surigao Strait, 162, 172, 269
Beers, Thomas M., 42, 286
Bergstrom, Arthur W., 42, 51, 267–268, 286
Bigger, Warner T., 123, 125–127
Bismarck Archipelago,
 Admiralty Islands, xxiv, 73, 146–149, 164, 268
 Cape Gloucester, 95, 102, 109, 143–144, 268
 New Britain, xiv, xix, xx, xxiv, xxix, 39–40, 72, 87, 92, 94–109, 143–145, 164–165, 259, 268, 285
 Pilelo Island, 96–99, 102
Bligh, William, 115
Borneman, Warren C., 108
Bowling, Selman S., 153, 162
Boye, Ruby and Skov, 138–139
Boyington, Gregory, 59
Bradshaw, Frederick W., 75
Brett, George H., 17
British, xxvii, 21, 33–35, 41, 45, 131, 135, 139, 182, 246, 264
 Royal Navy, xxi, 35, 72
Brockman, Don, 232
Brockway, C. W., 8
Brown, C. N., 224, 269, 281–282
Buckner, Jr., Simon Bolivar, 229–230
Bulkeley, John D., 16
Cagney, James, xxvii, 261
Carpender, Arthur S., 39, 70, 72
Carpenter, R. E., 189
Cartano, John D., 11, 42, 64–66, 267, 286
Carter, Grayson, B, 67
Carteret, Philip, 138

China/Chinese, xxvi, 210, 251–254
    Friendship Project/National Military Council, 252
    Guerillas/Pirates, xxvi–xxvii, 251–256, 291–293
    Junks, xxvi, 112, 251–252, 255–257, 291–293
    Sino-American Cooperative (SACO), 252–253
Cho, Isamu, 230
Christoph, Karl J., 148–149
Churchill, Winston, xx
Cilly (Motor Machinist's Mate Second), 105
Clifford (Lt. Col.), 48
Conlan, W. T., 70, 268, 285
Conolly, Richard L., 155, 205
Cook, James, 72
Cox, Austin B., 254–256
Crawford, William F., xxix, 125
Cunningham, Ross A., and Currie, Dwight D., 42, 287
Dailey, Jr., Robert, 59
Davey, Keith L., 130, 267, 288
Davis, Alan W., 182, 205
Davis, Leroy, 262
DeRosset, Richard W., xxix, 94, 122
Derrick, Thomas Currie, 245
Doebler, H. J., 180
Donahue (Capt.), 47
Dowd, Lt. (jg), 104
Drinkwater, E. B., 224, 269, 280
Dunigan, James B., 11, 42, 267, 286
Durin, W. E., 42
Echols, (Capt.), 138
Edwards, Jr., Edwin R., 70, 267–268, 286
Eichelberger, Robert L., 71, 219–221
Eisenhower, Dwight D., 87
Ekford, Charles, 140
Elliott, John, 249
Ellis, James D., 199
Englebrecht, Edwin Charles, 245
Fairfield, William, 185
Fechteler, William M., 147, 150, 219
French, W. V., 70, 268, 285
Fike, Jr., Claude E., 70, 285
Fitzgerald, Thomas G., 101
Flint, Ernest A., 15

Fonda, Henry, xxvii, 261
Fort, George H., 6, 10, 37, 40, 42–43, 51, 57, 60, 118–119, 121
Fortune, Jr., Porter L., 70, 100–101, 268, 285
Fowlkes, B. H., 70, 285
Fox, W. S., 176, 268, 285
Fraser, Roger B., 47–48
French, W. V., 70, 268, 285
Fukudome, Shigeru, 12
Fuld, Jr., J. E., 42, 286
Garner, David, 182
Gay, Jr., W. O., 70, 204, 268–269, 285
George, Eugene H., 42, 267, 286
George, T. G., 235, 288
Gerber, C. C., 249, 270, 280
Geren, Pardue, 246, 268, 270, 275
Goffigon, III, Kemper, xv, xix, xx, xxix, 70, 94, 103–108, 268, 285
Gordon, Jr., E. R., 231, 270, 286
Grandy, William F., 130, 288
Gray, J. L., 224, 269, 281
Green, Richard A., 130, 288
Griswold, Oscar W., 41
Hagen, Paul E., 182
Halsey, Jr., William F., xxiv, 6, 13, 20, 38–39, 49–50, 56, 116, 137, 139, 165
Hansen, Jr., Herman, 59
Hansen, L. E., 70, 285
Hanson, Jr., N., 248, 270, 275–276, 279
Harper (Lt.), 43
Harris, Jr., W. W., 70, 205, 267, 269, 285
Hart, Thomas, 16
Harter (Lt.), 47
Heavey, William F., 81
Heitzler, A. H., 42, 286
Herrich (RNZAF), 48
Herring, Edmund F., 76
Higgins, Andrew, 77, 82, 87–88
Holden, E. R., 224, 269, 276, 281
Horii, Tomitaro, 18
Horton, J. S., 130, 268, 289
Inouye, Shigeyoshi, 19
Jannotta, A. Vernon, 194
Japan(ese)
    Armistice (surrender), xxvi, 226, 235, 249, 250–251, 253

Index   {341}

Coast watcher(s), 41
Imperial Japanese Army
    14th Army, 15
    20th Division, 154
    32nd Army, 229–230
    38th Regiment, 157
    44th Independent Mixed Brigade, 229
    320th Independent Infantry Battalion, 157
    Maru-ni (coastal defense motorboat)/Renraku-tei (liaison boat), 223
    Ranau and Sandakan POW Camps, 249–250
    Southern Detachment, 58
Imperial Japanese Navy
    air fields and/or bases
        Bairoko Harbor, New Georgia, 62, 64–65
        Ballale Island, Shortlands/Buka Island, Bougainville Islands, 3, 38, 40
        Enogai, New Georgia, 62–65
        Faisi, Bougainville, 49
        Kahili, Bougainville, 3, 12, 38
        Munda, New Georgia, 12, 38–40, 49–52, 56–59, 62, 65, 120
        Rabaul, New Britain, xxix, 2, 12, 17, 19–20, 38–40, 49, 51, 81, 84, 89, 94, 99, 103, 128, 144–146, 149–150
        Rekata Bay, 38
        Truk, 52, 146
        Vila, New Georgia, 12, 38–39, 49–51, 56, 58, 139–141
    fleets, flotillas, forces, and detachments
        1st Mobile Fleet, 165
        3rd Fleet, 2
        8th Fleet, 50
        11th Air Fleet, 2, 89
        11th and 26th Air Flotillas, 13
        Combined Fleet, 1, 12–13, 19, 155, 169
        South Seas Detachment, 17
        Southern Force, 172
        Special Naval Landing Force/Special Base Force, 256
    Operation/Battle Plan
        I-GO, xxii, 1–2, 12, 41
        SHO-1 and SHO-GO, 169
        TEN-GO, 230
Military aircraft
    "Betty" (Mitsubishi G4M medium bomber or Type 96 torpedo plane), 12, 59, 89, 102–104, 191, 194, 197

"Hamp" (Mitsubishi A6M3 Navy type 0 carrier fighter), 213
"Helen" (Nakajima Ki-49 Donryu Army type 100 heavy bomber), 198
"Jill" (Nakajima B6N Tenzan torpedo bomber), 182, 185
Kamikaze (various type aircraft)/attacks, xxv, 6, 166, 168, 170, 175–176, 178, 185, 195, 197, 199, 203–204, 207–211, 230
"Kate" (Nakajima B5N Navy Type 97 attack bomber), 182, 185, 216
"Oscar" (Nakajima Ki-43 Army type 1 fighter), 98, 182, 184, 207, 233
"Rufe" (Nakajima A6M2-N Navy type 2 interceptor/fighter-bomber), 99
"Sally" (Mitsubishi Ki-21 Army type 97 heavy bomber), 191–192
"Tony" (Kawasaki Ki-61 Hien Army type 3 fighter), 231
"Val" (Aichi D3A dive bomber), 3, 7, 9, 53, 60, 83–84, 89, 98–101, 103–104, 195–197, 213, 231
"Zeke" (Mitsubishi A6M Zero fighter), 3, 12, 47–48, 59, 83, 89–90, 98–101, 103, 181–183
Special Attack Units Program (Kamikaze, Kaiten, Shinyo, and Fukuryu), 209, 223
Q-boats, xxv, 209, 219, 226, 232
Johnson (Lt.), 47
Johnston, Jr., S. P., 70, 92, 267–268, 285
Jolly, W. J., 130, 289
Kean, Joseph A., 224, 269, 275
Keifer, Thomas H., 231, 270, 286
Kelley, R. T., 70, 285
Kelley, Robert B., 118
Kennedy, Donald, 57–58
Kennedy, John F., xxi, xxii, xxix, 9–10, 46, 122–128
Keresey, Jr., Richard E., 127
King, Ernest J., 25
Knapp, O, 70, 285
Knox, Frank, 13
Knox, Jr., Franklin L., 42, 286
Koski, Arthur, E., 231, 270, 286
Krohn, Abraham, 182
Krueger, Walter, 75, 203–204
Krulak, Victor H., 123
Kuper (Mr.), 45
Kurita, Takeo, 165
Leary, Herbert F., 17
Leckie, Robert, 143

Leith, Stanley, 61
Lemmon, Jack, xxiii, xxvii, 137, 261
Linder, R. L., 42, 287
Lindley, Jr., P, C., and Link, Jr., C. B., 70, 285
Linville, Clifton H., 184
Livingston, Carlton S., 9–10
Locke, James E., 7, 11, 42, 267, 286
Logan (Lt.), 48
Loomis, R. H., 42, 267, 286
Love, R. O., 70, 267, 285
Lowery, George A., 183
MacArthur, Douglas, xvii, xviii, xxiv, xxvi, 2–3, 15, 20, 26, 39, 49, 58, 71–72, 75, 82, 91, 95, 131, 145, 149, 151, 154–155, 161, 163, 165, 167, 185, 200, 203–204, 220, 226, 242, 245, 250
Mackey, John, 245
Macklin, Edward E., 183
Mahoney, Jr., G. T., 180
Mann, Dennis, 11, 42, 51, 267, 286
Marshall, George C., 25
Martin, Jr., V. G., 70, 268, 285
Mashburn, Charles E., 178–179, 205–206, 209, 280–281
McLean, John B., 186, 193, 207
Milligan, Roswell, B., 130, 288
Mitchell, John N., xxii, 128
Morshead, Leslie James, 241
Mumma Jr., Morton, C., 91–92, 151, 153, 162
Nelson, Ricky, xxiii, 137
New Guinea/Papua (Papua, New Guinea)
    Biak, 20, 146, 177, 180, 206
    Buna, 2, 20–21, 71, 76–78, 83, 85–87, 89, 96, 108
    Cape Cretin, 96–97, 102, 145, 148
    Dampier and Vitiaz Straits, xxiv, 39–40, 95, 143–144, 154
    Fergusson Island, 75, 79, 96
    Finschhafen, 71, 77–79, 85, 92, 96
    Goodenough Island, 75, 96
    Gona, 2, 20–21, 71, 76
    Green Island, 52
    Hollandia, xxiv, 149–154, 162, 170, 173–178, 180–181, 206, 215, 217, 268
    Huon Gulf/Peninsula, 39, 71, 78, 82, 87, 91, 154
    Kiriwina and Woodlark Islands, 58, 71, 74–75, 96
    Kokoda Trail, 18
    Lae, 18, 58, 71, 76–78, 81, 85–87, 90–92, 267

Madang, 154
Milne Bay, xix, xx, 3, 15, 18–21, 41, 58, 71–79, 91, 96, 100, 108, 145
Oro Bay, 20, 76–78
Owen Stanley Mountain Range, 17, 19–20
Papuan Campaign, 2
Port Moresby, 2–3, 15, 17–21, 37
Saidor, 92, 153–154
Salamaua, 18, 58, 71, 76–78, 86, 91
Sanananda, 2, 71, 76
New Zealand, xviii, 20, 22–23, 140
    9th Auxiliary Minesweeping Group, 56
    Army, 43, 117
Nimitz, Chester W., xviii, 13, 16, 129, 131, 155, 165
Nishimura, Shoji, 172
Nixon, Richard M., xxii, 128
Nobel, Albert G., 150
North Korea(n), xxvii, 260, 265, 295
Oldendorf, Jesse, 172–173, 205
O'Neill, Patrick J., 254
Operation
    BLISSFUL, 123–124
    CARTWHEEL, 49, 51, 72, 75
    CHRONICLE, 71, 74
    FORAGER, 155–160
    GALVANIC, 129
    GIANT SLINGSHOT, 262
    MUSKETEER (MIKE-ONE, MIKE-SIX, and MIKE-SEVEN), 203, 219–221
    OBOE (1, 2, and 6), 242–250
    POSTERN, 78, 81, 86
    TOENAILS, 41, 51
    WATCHTOWER, 145
Osmena, Sergio, 168
Otto, Kermit L., 42, 267, 286
Owen, Robert W., 183
Owens, Francis L., 196–197
Palmer, H. B., 11, 42, 54–55, 267, 286
Pacific Island(s)/Atoll(s)
    Aleutian, 19
    Bora Bora (Tearanui Harbor), xiv, 68
    Canton, 152
    Cook Islands, 68

Index {345}

Ellice (Funa Futi), xix, xxii, 41, 129–131, 133, 151
Fiji/Fijian troops, xiv, xxi, 11, 19, 41, 43–45, 68–69, 135, 151
Gilberts (Apamama, Makin, Tabiteuea, Tarawa), xxii, xxiii, 19, 129–131, 134–136, 152, 155, 165, 267
Malukus (Halmahera, Morotai), 20, 163–164, 177, 242, 245, 248–249, 268
Marianas (Guam, Saipan, Tinian), xxi, xxii, 15, 131, 155–160, 165, 231, 233, 268
Marshalls (Eniwetok, Kwajalein), 19, 131, 155–156, 159, 165
Midway, 1, 18
New Caledonia (Noumea), xiv, xix, xxii, xxiii, 11, 19, 40–41, 50, 68–69, 71, 116, 129–130, 139–140
New Hebrides (Efate, Espiritu Santo), xix, xxii–xxiii, 9–11, 41, 140–141
Palau (Angaur, Peleliu), 146, 155, 160, 165
Tonga, 68
Tutuila, Samoa (Pago Pago Harbor), xiv, 11, 19, 68–69
Wake, 15, 19
Percy (Lt.), 47
Peters, Sidney, 32
Philippines,
    Camiguin Island; and Aparri, Vigan, and Gonzaga, Luzon Island, 15–16
    Batan Island, 15
    Bataan Peninsula, 15–16, 168, 185, 225–226
    Cabanatuan POW Camp on Luzon, 76
    Corregidor Island, 16, 168, 225–226, 269
    Leyte Island/Leyte Gulf, xxiv, xxv, 76, 149, 154, 161–180, 183–190, 193–196, 204–206, 209–230, 242, 246, 268–269
    Lingayen Gulf, xxv, 86, 162, 168, 183, 186–187, 203–217, 219–221, 223, 269
    Luzon Island, xxv, 15–17, 27, 76, 86, 168, 176, 186–187, 203–227, 269
    Mindoro Island, xxv, 27, 162, 165, 168, 172, 175–176, 186–201, 206–224, 246, 269
    Nasugbu Bay/Nasugbu Town, xxv, 219–227, 269
Pittman, Stewart L., xxvii, 254, 256–257, 292–293
Powell, William, xxvii, 261
Price, J. M., 42, 286
Quezon, Manuel, 168
Quigley, William M., 41
Raffelson, R. M., 130, 289
Rafferty, Chips, xxiii, 137
Rahle, Oliver, 225–226, 279
Ray, Thomas Lee, 42, 267, 286
Reid, Jr., James R, xxvii, 254–256, 292

Rockwell, Francis W., 16
Rodgers, Jr., Hank, 225
Romalo (Col.), 185
Roosevelt, Franklin D., 13, 16, 31, 34
Rose, Floyd, 254–256
Rosebro, Jr., C. R., 70, 267, 285
Ross, R. M., 42, 268, 286
Royal, Forrest B., 241–242
Rua, Louis, 183
Ruben, Robert F., 42, 44–45, 267, 286
Sasaki, Minoru, 58
Schnell, Edward James, 126–127
Seligman, Bernard F., 11, 42, 267, 286
Shean, Austin D., 42, 286
Shepard, John R., 42, 268, 286
Shine, Jr., Frank E., 70, 77, 285
Ships and Craft
    Allied or Foreign
        Australian
            Benalla, 75
            Gascoyne and *Warrego*, 211
            James Cook, 173
            Mactan, 184–185
            Manoora and *Westralia*, 242
            Potrero, 92
            Reserve, 187, 189, 193, 211, 213
            Warramunga, 148
        British
            Dart, 115
            FT-1 through *FT-14*, *FT-16* through *FT-23*, *FT-25* through *FT-27*, and *FT-29*, 35, 287–288
            FT-30, 35, 288
            John Williams, 152
            Swallow, 138
        Ecuadorian
            Cinco de Junio, 35, 288
        Greek
            RHS *Anchialos*, RHS *Distomon*, and RHS *Lechovon*, 35, 287–288
        Japanese
            Amagiri, xxii, 125
            Asagumo, *Fuso*, *Michishio*, *Shigure*, *Yamagumo*, and *Yamashiro*, 172
            Daihatsu-class landing barges, 112–113

Hijo, 165
Hinoki and *Momi*, 211
Hiyo, Junyo, Zuiho, and *Zuikaku*, 2
midget submarine(s), 8, 212, 222
Mogami, 172–173
Shoho, 19
Shokaku and *Taiho*, 156, 165
New Zealand,
    Breeze, Gale, and *Matai*, 56
    Echo, 140
    Moa, 4–5, 10
Panamanian
    Oro Verde, 265
Taiwanese
    Yung Kang, 263
U.S. Army
    Apache, 167
    F-1 through *F-3, F-5* through *F-12, F-15, F-16, F-74* through *F-76, F-92* through *F-94, F-115, F-116, F-121, F-122, F-126*, and *F-128*, 29
    F-14, xxiii, 29, 130, 151–152, 271
    F-15, 170–171, 271
    F-55, 151, 272
    F-73, 29, 151, 272
    F-78 and *F-93*, 151, 273
    F-95 and *F-96*, 29, 273
    F-117 and *F-126*, 29, 151, 274
    F-119, F-122, F-129, and *F-130*, 29, 274
    F-120, 180, 184, 274
    F-127 and *F-128*, 151, 274
    FP-47 (FS-47), xxvi, 29, 167–168, 241–243, 248, 270
    FS-1, FS-27, FS-195, FS-253, FS-256 through *FS-258, FS-260* through *FS-262, FS-264* through *FS-273, FS-276* through *FS-280, FS-282* through *FS-287, FS-311, FS-312, FS-314* through *FS-316, FS-318, FS-319, FS-343, FS-346* through *FS-348, FS-350, FS-351, FS-353* through *FS-356, FS-362, FS-363, FS-371* through *FS-374, FS-383, FS-384, FS-386, FS-390, FS-392* through *FS-397, FS-404, FS-405, FS-407, FS-408, FS-524* through *FS-529*, and *FS-546* through *FS-550*, 29
    FS-128 and *FS-290*, 237
    FS-141 through *FS-160*, 29
    FS-145, 180, 186

Index

FS-154, 214-215
FS-156, xxv, 204–205, 217, 269
FS-158, 180, 215
FS-162, FS-165, FS-166, FS-169, FS-176 through *FS-179, FS-180* through *FS-183, FS-186, FS-190, FS-192* through *FS-194, FS-196* through *FS-203*, and *FS-222* through *FS-226*, 30
FS-163, xxvi, 30, 180, 215, 224, 259, 269
FS-164, 30, 241, 248, 270
FS-167, xxv, 30, 162-163, 177, 241, 246, 268, 270
FS-168, xxvi, 30, 224, 269
FS-170, 30, 162-163, 180, 182-184, 268
FS-171, xxv, 30, 180, 204-206, 269
FS-172, 29, 30 259
FS-173, 30, 214-215
FS-174, xxv, 30, 204, 214-215, 269
FS-175, 30, 163
FS-184, 30, 224-225
FS-185, 30, 215
FS-187, 30, 224
FS-191, 30, xxvi, 224, 269
FS-214, 261
FS-217 and *FS-289*, 265
FS-254, xxv, 204-206, 215, 269
FS-255, 163, 226-227, 259, 268
FS-263, xxvii, 261, 263–264
FS-274, 245
FS-275 and *FS-385*, 261
FS-309, xxv, 196-197, 224–226
FS-310, 180
FS-317, 246
FS-344, xxvii, 261, 265
FS-345, 261, 265
FS-349, 197-198
FS-352, xxvi, 224, 269
FS-361, 241, 249, 261, 270
FS-364, xxv, 204, 214–215, 263, 268–269
FS-365, xxvi, 224, 269
FS-366, xxv, 178, 204–208, 269
FS-367, 199–200
FS-370, 259, 261
FS-387, xxvi, 224, 269
FS-388, xxv, xxvi, 269

FS-389, 224, 269
FS-391, xxvii, 261
FS-399, xxvi
FS-406 and *FS-410*, 237, 259
FT-230, 245
LT-1, xxv, 170–171, 189, 194, 215, 269
LT-20, xxv, 29, 173, 194, 269
LT-60, *LT-132*, *LT-156*, and *LT-532*, 265
LT-108, *LT-113*, *LT-116*, and *LT-529*, 174
LT-125, *LT-133*, *LT-140*, *LT-219*, *LT-226*, *LT-451*, *LT-530*, *LT-644*, *LT-645*, and *LT-784*, 29
LT-129, 29, 170–171, 215
LT-131, 170–171
LT-134, xxv, 170–171, 173, 194, 245, 268–269
LT-135, *LT-352*, *LT-646*, and *LT-652*, 215
LT-225, 170-171, 215
LT-229, xxv, 170–171, 173, 194, 204–205, 213, 215, 269
LT-231, xxv, 170–171, 173, 194, 204–205, 215, 217, 269
LT-348, 29, 174, 215
LT-358, 237
LT-454, xxv, 173–174, 180–183, 194, 204–205, 215, 217, 269
LT-455, 170–171, 181, 265
LT-633, *LT-634*, and *LT-635*, 170–171
LT-637, xxv, 170–171, 173, 194, 269
ST-18, 174
ST-381, xxv, xxvi, 30, 151, 189–194, 269
TP-1, *TP-124*, *TP-128*, and *TP-381*, 170–171
TP-92 (ex-*Lone Wolf*), 28
TP-97, *TP-101* through *TP-106*, *TP-108* through *TP-110*, *TP-112* through *TP-121*, *TP-124*, *TP-125*, and *TP-128* through *TP-131*, 29
TP-97 through *TP-131*, *TP-133*, *TP-134*, *TP-224*, *TP-225*, and *TP-229* through *TP-232*, 283
TP-102, *TP-112*, *TP-117*, *TP-119*, *TP-121*, *TP-130*, *TP-140*, *TP-242* (ex-*San Jose*), *TP-243* (ex-*Bennehaven*), *TP-244* (ex-*Ardito*), and *TP-245* (ex-*San Giovanni*), 27
TP-109, 27, 174
TP-113, xxv, 27, 187, 269
TP-124, 171
TP-129, xxv, 27, 187, 212, 269
TP-246 (ex-*Sea Tern*), 27, 151–152
WT-1, *WT-33*, *WT-36*, and *WT-63*, 151

Index

    Y-3, Y-4, Y-7, Y-11, Y-13, Y-15, Y-18, and *Y-19,* 29–30
    Y-5, 29-30, 188
    Y-6, xxv, 30, 170–171, 173, 204–205, 211, 213, 269
    Y-14, Y-18, Y-19, Y-21, Y-35, Y-44 through *Y-46, Y-53, Y-56, Y-58,*
        Y-59, Y-93, Y-100, Y-101, Y-103, Y-108, and *Y-109,* 30
    Y-14, xxv, 30, 170–171, 188, 192–193, 269
    Y-20, 29–30, 170–171
    Y-21, xxv, 29–30, 204–205, 211, 213, 269
    Y-38 and *Y-39,* 265
    Y-87, 188, 265
    Y-88 and *Y-90,* 265
    Y-109, 30, 245
U.S. Coast Guard
    Balsam, 231
    Spencer, 248
U.S. Merchant Marine Ships, Fishing Vessels and other Small Craft
    Alrita, Bergen, Ethel S., and *Tacoma,* 28–29
    Antone Saugrain, 182–183
    Ardito, San Giovanni, and *San Jose,* 27, 29
    Bennehaven, 29
    David Dudley Field, Edward N. Westcott, Kyle V. Johnson, and *Otis*
        Skinner, 207
    Earl J. Conrad, Jr., xxvii, 264
    Francisco Morozan, 196
    John Burke, 196, 200
    John Evans, 183
    Marcus Daly, 181–182, 184–185
    Olga Patricia (later *Laissez Faire*), xxvii, 263–264
    Peter Lassen, 214
    Pratt Victory, 233–234
    Sea Bird, 265
    Sea Tern (*TP-246*), 27, 29, 152
    Wallace R. Farrington, 219
    William Sharon, 196, 200
U.S. Navy
    Amphibious
        Blue Ridge, 215
        Brooks and *Humphreys,* 88, 147
        Cofer, 177, 244
        Crescent City, 232
        Crosby and *Kilty,* 61, 118, 123
        Dent, 58, 118

Index   {351}

Gilliam, 180
Gilmer, 72, 88
Kephart, 177
LCI(G)-365 and *LCI(M)-974*, 223
LCI(L)-24 and *LCI(L)-334*, 60, 188
LCI(L)-62, LCI(L)-67, LCI(L)-69, LCI(L)-222, and *LCI(L)-330,* 118 *LCI(L)-224* and *LCI(L)-226,* 79
LCI(L)-233, 60
LCI(L)-327 and *LCI(L)-328*, 54
LCI(L)-329, 54, 67, 69
LCI(L)-332, LCI(L)-333, and *LCI(L)-335,* 60
LCI(L)-336, 54, 60, 118
LCI(L)-339 and *LCI(L)-341*, 83
LCI(L)-624, 196–198
LCI(L)-635, 242–244, 248
LCI(L)-984, 180
LCI(L)-1000, LCI(L)-1001, LCI(L)-1005, and *LCI(L)-1006,* 197
LCI(L)-1008, 244
LCI(L)-1076, 194–195
LCP(R) (Christ Craft-built Higgins-designed boat), 81–82, 88, 126–127, 147
LCS(L)-8, 244, 248
LCS(L)-28, 244
LCS(L)-30, 248
LCS(L)-44, 245
LCT-58 and *LCT-62*, 4, 62
LCT-60, 61-62
LCT-61, 75, 78
LCT-63, 4, 60–61
LCT-64, LCT-65, LCT-66, LCT-129, and *LCT-375*, 62
LCT-67 and *LCT-180*, 52
LCT-69, 120
LCT-72, 96
LCT-82 and *LCT-396*, 109
LCT-83, 75-76
LCT-85, 75, 100
LCT-87 and *LCT-184*, 78
LCT-88, 98
LCT-127, LCT-132, LCT-144, LCT-145, LCT-367, and *LCT-481*, 61
LCT-133 and *LCT-482*, 60
LCT-134, 61–62
LCT-156, LCT-182, and *LCT-322*, 4

LCT-171, 100, 102
LCT-172, *LCT-176*, *LCT-374*, and *LCT-381*, 97, 100
LCT-173 and *LCT-183*, 75–77
LCT-174, 78, 97
LCT-177, *LCT-179*, *LCT-368*, *LCT-371*, *LCT-372*, and *LCT-373*, 75
LCT-178, 75, 78
LCT-259, *LCT-260*, *LCT-298*, and *LCT-400*, 102
LCT-321, 118
LCT-323, 4, 62
LCT-325, 61, 65, 118
LCT-327, 65
LCT-330, 61-62, 118
LCT-369, 4, 61-62
LCT-382, *LCT-384*, and *LCT-386*, 98, 109
LCT-387, 78, 98, 109
LCT-388, 98, 100
LCT-389 and *LCT-675*, 189
LCT-390, *LCT-695*, and *LCT-1151*, 217
LCT-1050, 233
LCVP (Higgins Boat), xiii, 64, 66, 77, 81–82, 87–89, 112, 126–127, 177, 243–244
Liddle and *Lloyd*, 177
LSM-424, 232
LST-66, *LST-204*, *LST-206*, and *LST-463*, 144
LST-180, 54
LST-201, 151
LST-270, 215
LST-339 and *LST-485*, 118
LST-340, 53, 69
LST-398, 53
LST-446, 9
LST-449, xxii, 4, 9–10
LST-452, 83, 148
LST-453, 85, 106, 108
LST-454, *LST-457*, *LST-459*, and *LST-465*, 148
LST-455, 85
LST-456, 72, 148
LST-458, 72, 83
LST-460, *LST-735*, *LST-911*, and *LST-1018*, 180
LST-464, 86
LST-471 and *LST-473*, 83
LST-534, 231

LST-605, 193
LST-667, 245
LST-741, 180
LST-750, 197, 200
LST-778, 207
LST-795 and *LST-851*, 232
LST-890, 234
LVT (Amtrak), 96, 156, 159, 244
McCawley, 58, 60
McKean, 60, 118, 123
Natrona, 232
President Jackson, 52
Rochambeau, xxii, 9
Rocky Mount, 242, 244
Rushmore and *Titania*, 242
Sands, 72, 88, 147
Schley, 60
Stringham and *Talbot*, 118
Ward, 118, 123
War Hawk, 223
Waters, 58, 118
Zeilin, 217
auxiliary/service/support
Accokeek, 233
Adhara, 10
ARD-7, 108
Argonne, 116
Amycus, 108
ATR-16 and *Bannock*, 231
Banner, 260-261, 265
Banshee and *Creon*, 249
Boots, 180
Brule, 259, 261-263, 296-297
Butternut, 8
Camel, 237
Cascade, 131
Celeno, 53, 55
Chepachet, 248
Deal, xxvii, 260–261, 263, 295–296
Deimos, 55
Echo, xxiii, 137–140
Erskine M. Phelps, 4, 10

Estero, 260–261, 295–296
Etamin and *Goldstar*, 145
Grapple, 196
Half Moon and *San Pablo*, 195
Hewell, xxvii, 260–261, 295–296
Hidatsa, 170–173
IX-308, 265
Jamestown and *Willoughby*, 246
Kanawha, 4–8, 10
Lark (ex-AM 21), 170–171, 173
Mackinac, 137–138
Mark, 261–263, 296–297
Menominee, 8
Mobjack, 163
New Bedford (T-AKL-17), 265
Niagara (ex-yacht *Hi-Esmaro*), 5
Oceanographer, 119
Orestes, 195, 198–200
Ortolan, 4, 8–9
Oyster Bay, 152, 163
Palm Beach, 260, 265
Pastores and *Triangulum*, 176
Pawnee, 120
Phaon and *Vestal*, 131
Porcupine, 180, 195–197, 199–200
Pueblo, xxvii, 260–261, 263, 265
Quapaw, 183
Rigel, 72, 140
Ryer, 260–261
Sepulga, 67
Serrano, 233
Sharps, 260–261, 295–296
Sioux, 41
Sonoma, 87, 89–90, 151
Tappahannock, 6
Thornton, 137
Tyonek, 265
Vireo (ex-AM 52), 8, 170–171
Wachopreague, 206
Williamson, 157, 159
Whippoorwill (ex-AM 35), 173, 186–187, 189–190, 193, 211
YO-237, *YO-238*, *YO-242*, *YO-243*, and *YO-244*, 267

YOG-41 and *YP-418* (ex-fishing trawler *Crest*), 41
YOG-111, 234
YP-61 (ex-USCGC *Dallas*), xix
YP-239 (ex-tuna boat *Challenger*) and *YP-289* (ex-tuna boat *Paramount*), 237
YP-421 (ex-fishing trawler *Surf*), 52, 241, 249
YP-520 (ex-tuna boat *Conte Grande*), 237
Transport (small coastal)
    APc-1, xix, 33, 41, 67, 69–70, 72, 75–78, 285
    APc-2, xix, 41, 67, 69–70, 78–79, 96, 100–102, 108–109, 151–154, 268, 285
    APc-3, xix, 41, 67, 69–70, 72, 285
    APc-4, xix, 41, 67, 69–70, 78, 84, 86, 95, 97, 109, 154, 259, 267–268, 285
    APc-5, xix, 41, 67, 69–70, 72, 75, 78, 285
    APc-6, xix, 41, 69–70, 78, 86, 259, 267, 285
    APc-7, xix, 41, 69–70, 148–149, 268, 285
    APc-8, xix, 41, 70, 285
    APc-9, xix, 41, 70, 78, 95, 109, 154, 260, 268, 285
    APc-10, xix, 41, 70, 285
    APc-11, xix, 41, 69–70, 285
    APc-12, xix, 41, 70, 96, 100, 144–145, 204, 217, 259, 268–269, 285
    APc-13, xix, 41, 67–70, 145, 285
    APc-14, xix, 41, 70, 285
    APc-15, xiii, xiv, xv, xix, xx, xxix, 41, 67, 69–70, 72, 75, 77–79, 94–95, 102–109, 268, 285
    APc-16, xix, xxv, 41, 70, 78, 89, 91–92, 204–205, 215–216, 259, 267, 269, 285
    APc-17, xix, 41, 67–70, 259, 285
    APc-18, xix, xxv, 41, 70, 78, 92, 176, 267–268, 285
    APc-19, xix, 41, 67, 69–70, 72, 75, 216, 285
    APc-20, xix, 41, 70, 78, 91–92, 153, 267–268, 285
    APc-21, xix, 41, 70, 78–79, 86, 95, 98–100, 102, 109, 259, 267–268, 285
    APc-22, xix, 41, 70, 78, 95, 108–109, 259, 268, 285
    APc-23, xix, 6, 11, 41–42, 51–52, 54, 59, 65, 119, 230–231, 233–234, 267, 270, 286
    APc-24, xix, 6, 11, 41–42, 51–52, 54–55, 59, 61–62, 114, 267, 286
    APc-25, xix, 6, 11, 41–42, 45, 47–48, 51, 63–66, 116, 267, 286
    APc-26, xix, 6, 11, 41–42, 51–53, 62, 230–234, 267, 270, 286
    APc-27, xix, 41–42, 51–52, 62, 267, 286
    APc-28, xix, 41–44, 51, 114, 230–231, 233–235, 237, 259, 270, 286

Index

APc-29, xix, 41–45, 51, 267, 286
APc-30, xix, 41–42, 119, 268, 286
APc-31, xix, 41–42, 55–56, 116–119, 267, 286
APc-32, xix, 41–42, 51, 68, 230–237, 270, 286
APc-33, xix, 6–8, 11, 41–42, 51, 116, 118–119, 267, 286
APc-34, xix, 6, 11, 41–42, 45, 51, 54–55, 117, 119, 238–239, 267–268, 286
APc-35, xix, 41–44, 51, 60–62, 120–121, 259, 267, 286
APc-36, xix, 41–44, 51, 61–62, 111, 267, 286
APc-37, xix, 41–42, 51, 61, 118–119, 267–268, 286
APc-38, xix, 41–42, 51, 62–64, 267, 286
APc-39, xix, 42, 51, 286
APc-40, xix, 42, 237, 286
APc-41, APc-43, APc-44, and APc-45, xix, 42, 286
APc-42, xix, 42, 238, 268, 286
APc-46, xix, xxi, 42, 157–160, 268, 286
APc-47 and APc-50, xix, 42, 287
APc-48, xix, 42, 119, 287
APc-49, xix, 42, 237, 287
APc-50, xix, 42, 287
APc-51 through APc-79, APc-85, and APc-97, 35, 287–288
APc-86 through APc-88, and APc-90 through APc-94, 34, 288
APc-89, 34, 259, 288
APc-95, xix, 130, 137, 139–140, 288
APc-96, xix, 130, 288
APc-98, xix, 130, 237, 288
APc-101, xix, 130, 288
APc-102, xix, 130, 259, 288
APc-103, xix, 130, 234, 237, 259, 288
APc-108, xix, xxiii, 129–131, 133, 135–136, 152, 267, 288
APc-109, xix, 129–130, 133–136, 268, 289
APc-110 and APc-111, xix, 130, 289
combatants
  aircraft carrier
    Cabot, *Essex*, *Hancock*, and *Intrepid*, 177
    Lexington and *Yorktown*, 19
    Manila Bay and *Savo Island*, 211
    Ommaney Bay, 204
    Santee and *Suwannee*, 175
  battleship
    California, *Colorado*, *Idaho*, *New Mexico*, *Pennsylvania*, and *Tennessee*, 156

cruiser
  Birmingham, Cleveland, Honolulu, Indianapolis, Montpelier, and *St. Louis,* 156
  Boise, 204
  Denver, 247
  Nashville, 145–146, 167
  Phoenix, 146–147, 244, 249
destroyer/destroyer escort
  Aaron Ward, 4, 8–10
  Braine and *Charles Ausburne,* 211
  Buchanan, 58–59
  Bush, 190, 192, 194–195
  Claxton, 175, 222
  Cony, 118
  Converse, 196
  Conyngham, 81, 83, 87
  Daniel A. Joy, 216
  Drayton, 75, 81, 83, 88, 149
  Edwards, 195, 197
  Eichenberger, 151
  Ericsson, 237
  Eugene, 176
  Farenholt, 6, 59–60
  Fletcher, 244
  Flusser, 75, 88, 144, 148, 222
  Frazier, 249
  Gavsevoort, 195
  Gillespie, 148
  Gwin, 58–59
  Halford, 190–191
  Helm, 211
  Hobby, 148
  Holt, 190, 193
  James E. Craig, 51, 177
  Jobb, 190
  Kalk, 148
  Lamson, 81, 83, 88
  Leland E. Thomas, 248
  Loeser, 214
  Lough, 216, 222–224
  Lovelace, 176
  Mahan, 75, 144

Manning, 177
McGowan, 214
Mugford, 81, 83, 88
Neuendorf, 151
Nicholson, 148
Perkins, 75
Philip, 118
Pringle, 195
Radford, 190
Reid, 148–149, 175
Roe, 149
Russell, *Shaw*, and *Stafford*, 211
Saufley, 118
Selfridge, 116
Stanley, 196
Sterett and *Stevens*, 195
Thatcher, 233
Tinsman, 211–213, 221, 224
Welles, 149
Whitehurst, 151, 176
Wilson, 195–196
Woodworth, 6
gunboats *Asheville* and *Tulsa*, 173
patrol craft
  PCE(R)-848 and *PCE(R)-850*, 167
  PCE(R)-849, 167, 242, 245
patrol frigate
  Belfast, 175, 181
  Coronado, 170–171, 176, 181–183
  El Paso, 151, 177
  Glendale, 175, 181, 183, 185
  Hutchison, 175
  Ogden, 151, 174, 181, 183, 185
  San Pedro, 181–182
  Van Buren, 151, 177
PT (Motor Torpedo) boat,
  PT-32, *PT-34*, *PT-35*, and *PT-41*, 16
  PT-59, xxii, xxix, 122, 125–128
  PT-109, xxii, 10, 46, 125
  PT-110 and *PT-138*, 103
  PT-121 and *PT-122*, 164
  PT-236, xxii, xxix, 122, 125, 127

PT-332, 196
PT-352, 197
submarine chaser (PC/SC)
  PC-466, 232
  PC-1129, 222–223
  PC-1131, 145
  SC-514, *SC-1052*, and *SC-1319*, 224
  SC-521, 10
  SC-637, 79
  SC-648, 79, 89
  SC-698 and *SC-734*, 89
  SC-699, 97, 89
  SC-703, 67, 84, 89, 102, 176
  SC-736, 89, 145
  SC-738, 100
  SC-742, 67, 89
  SC-743, 95, 98–100, 102, 105–106, 176
  SC-982, 246
mine warfare
  coastal minesweeper *Kingbird* (ex-*Governor Saltonstall*), xiv
  destroyer-minesweeper
    Hamilton, 148, 195
    Hopkins, 61
    Hovey, *Long*, and *Palmer*, 204, 211
  minelayer *Terror*, 134
  minesweeper
    Advent, 69
    Conflict, 1, 4, 8
    Gladiator, 231
    Nimble, 233
    Rail, 5, 8
    Scout, *Scuffle*, and *Sentry*, 250
    Trever, 60
  yard minesweeper
    YMS-8 and *YMS-48*, 148
    YMSs 9, *53*, *95*, *196*, *314*, *315*, *336*, *339*, *366*, and *392*, 250
    YMS-10, 148, 247, 250
    YMS-39, *YMS-365*, and *YMS-368*, 247, 250
    YMS-46, 148, 250
    YMS-47, 148, 247, 250
    YMS-49, 84, 144, 250
    YMS-50, 98, 247, 250

YMS-51, 84, 148
YMS-52, 144, 250
YMS-70, 97, 102
YMS-72, 67
YMS-84, 248
YMS-237, 41, 67
YMS-238, 67
YMS-334, 244
YMS-335, 247, 250
YMS-364, 244, 247, 250
YMS-371 and *YMS-430*, 231
YMS-390 and *YMS-443*, 233
YMS-481, 244-245
Siek (Motor Machinist's Mate Second), 104
Skelton, Jr., W. A., 224, 276
Smart, Ned E., 183
Smith, C. O., 70, 285
Smith, Craig C., 114
Smith, Paul C., 42, 267, 286
Smith, William, 249
Snel, J. J., 130, 288
Snyder, Jr., Harry E., 235, 286
Solomon Islands
    Bougainville, 3, 12, 39-40, 49-50, 109, 116, 119, 123-124, 128, 146, 267-268
    Choiseul, xxii, xxix, 115-116, 119, 122-128
    Guadalcanal area
        Camp Crocodile, 40
        Florida Island, 3-5, 9, 37, 54, 116
        Henderson Field, 1, 3-4, 12, 18, 38-39
        New Georgia Sound/"The Slot"/"Iron Bottom Sound," xxii, 3-4, 10, 37, 47, 54, 123, 127
        Savo Island, 3, 6
        Tulagi Island, xxii, 1, 3-8, 10-12, 19, 37-39, 41, 44, 53-56, 62, 116, 125, 128, 138, 238
    Malaita, 55-56, 238
    New Georgia
        Baanga Island and Lokuloku Reef, 58
        Rendova Island, 50, 54, 56-60, 62, 113-117, 267
        Segi, 50, 56-58, 61-64, 120
        Viru Harbor, 50, 57, 61-62

Index {361}

Russell Islands Group (Banika and Pavuvu), xxi, 38, 40, 45–48, 50, 52, 57–61, 119–121, 238
San Cristobal, 37, 41–44
Santa Cruz Island(s), 1, 137–138
Santa Isabel, 238
Treasury Islands (Mono and Stirling), 52, 111, 116–119, 123, 267–268
Ugi Island, 43–44
Vella Lavella, 39, 113–116, 123, 125, 127–128
Sooy, Jr., Benjamin H., 194
Spruance, Raymond A., 156
Swanson, Jr., H. R., 42, 286
Swentzel, Jr., Livingston, xxvii, 251–257
Synar (Lt.), 47
Tardif, George A., 226, 268, 278
Taylor, Leroy T., 114–115
Toombs, A. L., 231, 270, 286
Touchet, S., 70, 285
Townsend, Donald K., 224, 269, 275
Toyoda, Soemu, 165, 169
Truman, Harry S., 253
Turner, Richmond K., 37, 41–42, 49, 56–60, 111
Typhoon, IDA, LOUISE, and WILLIAM, 234–236
United States
    Army
        1st Cavalry Division, 73, 145, 147–148, 211
        2nd Engineer Special Brigade, xxvi, 81, 85, 87, 163, 170, 174, 189–190, 194
        4th Engineer, Shore, and Boat Regiment, 214
        5th Cavalry and 12th Cavalry, 149
        6th Army, 27–28, 75, 153, 162, 165–169, 175, 189, 203–204, 208, 214, 219–220, 226
        6th Ranger Battalion, 76
        8th Army, 219–220
        11th Corps/11th Airborne Division, 220
        14th Corps, 41, 214
        21st Infantry Regiment, 226
        24th Corps, 229
        24th Infantry Division, 187, 226
        27th Infantry Division, 131, 155
        32nd Infantry Division, 22, 153, 210
        41st Infantry Division, 22, 76–77
        43rd Infantry Division, 50, 58

{362} Index

 54th Evacuation Hospital, 106
 77th Infantry Division, 157, 232
 81st Infantry Division, 160
 103rd Infantry Division, 61
 112th U.S. Cavalry Regiment, 96, 211
 158th Regimental Combat Team, 214
 187th and 188th Glider Regimental Combat Team, 221
 503rd Parachute Infantry Regiment, 81, 187
 511th Parachute Infantry Regiment, 220–221
 Alamo Force/Scouts, 75, 143
 Graves Registration Service, 225, 238
 Transportation Corps/Service, and Transport Service, xxiv, 20–21, 28–29, 171, 181, 194, 204, 260
Army Air Force/Corps
 5th Air Force, 83, 196
 67th Fighter Squadron, 74
 Air Transport Service, 181, 225
 Sea Rescue Group, Army Air Force, Alaska Division, 28
Coast Guard, xiii, xvii, xxiv, 26, 30, 36, 171, 178, 180, 182, 204, 214, 224, 252, 262
Marine Corps
 1st Marine Division, 37, 73, 95, 109, 123, 143–144, 160
 1st Provisional Marine Brigade, 157, 159
 2nd Marine Division, 133, 155
 2nd Marine Parachute Division and 3rd Marine Division, 123, 128
 3rd Amphibious Corps, 229
 3rd Marine Raider Battalion and 10th Marine Defense Battalion, 50
 3rd Marine Regiment, 9th Marine Division, and 21st Marine Division, 157
 4th Marine Division, 155
 4th Marine Raider Battalion, 58, 60–62
 Marine Air Group 21, 48
 Marine Fighting Squadron (VMF)
  112, 48
  121, 122, 213, 214, and 221, 59
Merchant Marine/Mariners, xiii, xxiii, xxiv, 30, 152, 184, 196, 200–201, 204
Military aircraft
 A20 Havoc, 220
 B24 Liberator, 244
 B25 Mitchell, 52, 147, 244
 C47 Skytrain, 181
 Curtis-Wright SOC Seagull and Vought OS2U Kingfisher, 158

"Dumbo" rescue plane, 152
F4F Wildcat, 3, 52
F4U Corsair, 3, 52, 181, 191, 216
F6F Hellcat, 52, 216
J2F5 Duck, 48
P38 Lightning, 3, 12, 52, 89–90, 101–102, 178–179, 196, 198, 216, 220
P39 Airacobra, 3, 52, 74
P40 Warhawk, 3, 47–48, 52
P47 Thunderbolt, 96. 98, 101–102, 105
P61 Black Widow, 198
Piper J3 Cub, 232
SBD Dauntless and TBF Avenger, 52

Navy/Naval
    Armed Guard aboard merchant ships, 184, 196
    base
        Cavite Naval Base, 16, 226
        Motor Torpedo Boat Advance Base
          Five (Tinaogan Point), 161
          Six (Kana Kopa) and Dreger, 91
          Seventeen (Bobon Point), 161–162
          Twenty-one (Mios Woendi), 164
          Lambu Lambu, 113–114, 116–117, 123, 125, 127
          Lever Harbor, 113
          Mangarin Bay, 193, 198, 200, 216
          Mocambo, 116
          Morobe, 76
          Morotai, 163
          Rendova, 113, 117
          Russell Islands, 50
          Saidor, 153
          Stirling, Treasury Islands, 116, 118
          Tufi, 78
    battalion
        Construction (Seabees), xxiii, 148, 161
          Thirty-third, 50
          Fifty-fifth, 91
          Seventy-fourth, Ninety-fifth, and Ninety-eighth, 135
    Beach Jumper Units No. 6 and No. 7, 195
    division
        Battleship Division Two, 177
        Cruiser Division Twelve, 128
        Destroyer Division

Forty-five and Forty-six, 128
Forty-eight, 186
Fifty-nine, 250
Escort Division Thirty-seven, 150, 152
Transport Division
   Sixteen, 88
   One hundred three, 177
fleet
   3rd (former South Pacific Force), 26, 37, 39, 41–42, 49, 56, 116, 166
   5th, 156, 165
   7th (former Naval Forces Southwest Pacific), 26, 39, 67, 70, 72, 74, 91–92, 151, 162, 166, 219, 246, 268
   Asiatic, 16, 173
flotilla
   APc Flotilla Five, xx, xxiv, 42, 51, 69, 129
   APc Flotilla Seven, xx, xxiv, 67, 70, 78, 92, 129
   LCI(L) Flotilla Twenty-four, 162, 194–195
   LCT(5) Flotilla Seven, 102, 105–106
   LCT Flotilla Twenty-three, 205
   LCT Flotilla Twenty-seven, 216
   LST Flotilla Sixteen, 159
force
   3rd Amphibious Force, 37, 41-42, 111, 166
   7th Amphibious Force, 67, 70, 72, 74, 81, 85–86, 96, 111, 143, 219, 246
   Amphibious Force Pacific Fleet, 111
   Service Force, Seventh Fleet, 162
Naval Group, China/SACO/Coast Watcher Net #2, 251–257, 291–293
Special Service Unit No. 1 (Amphibious Scouts), xxi, 75, 79, 82, 87, 96
Squadron
   Destroyer Squadron Twenty-four and Fifty-six, 172
   Mine Squadron
      One, 134
      Two, 62
   Motor Torpedo Boat Squadron
      Two, 10, 111
      Three, 16, 111
      Five, 111, 114
      Six, Nineteen, Twenty, Twenty-three, and Twenty-seven, 111
      Nine, 11, 114, 118, 163

  Ten, 111, 114, 153, 163
  Eleven, 114
  Twelve, 92, 170
  Eighteen and Thirty-three, 163
  Twenty-one, 92, 153
  Twenty-four, 153
  Twenty-eight, 111, 206
  Thirty-six, 206
 Service Squadron
  Two, Four, and South Pacific Force, xxii, xxiii, 129–131
  Ten, 235
 Support Activity An Thoi, Saigon, and Vung Tau, 261–262
 task force
  Eighteen, 12
  Thirty-one, 54, 56–57
  Thirty-two, 6, 56
  Thirty-nine, 128
  Fifty-three, 155
  Fifty-five, 237
  Seventy-four, 148
  Seventy-six, 72
  Seventy-seven (Luzon Attack Force), 169, 205
  Seventy-eight (San Fabian Attack Force), 148, 205–206, 208, 214–215
  Seventy-nine (Lingayen Attack Force), 203, 205, 214
 Underwater Demolition Team
  Three, Four, and Six, 156
  Eleven, 248
  Eighteen, 248, 250
Ushijima, Mitsuru, 230
Voyles, C. E., 42, 268, 286
Vietnam, xxvii, 259–265, 296–297
Wainwright, Jonathon M., 16
Washington, George, xvii
Weiner, Mathew, 104–105, 285
Wilkinson, Theodore S., 111, 205, 215
Williams, R. D., 42
Williams, Wilbert, 183
Wilson, Thomas B., 20
Winsor, Gordon, D. and Wissinger, R. J., 130, 288
Wootten, George Frederick, 91
Yamamoto, Isoroku, xxii, 1, 12–13, 41

About the Author

Commander David D. Bruhn, U.S. Navy (Retired) served twenty-two years on active duty and two in the Naval Reserve, as both an enlisted man and as an officer, between 1977 and 2001.

Following completion of basic training, he served as a sonar technician aboard USS *Miller* (FF 1091) and USS *Leftwich* (DD 984). He was commissioned in 1983 following graduation from California State University at Chico. His initial assignment was to USS *Excel* (MSO 439), serving as supply officer, damage control assistant, and chief engineer. He then served in USS *Thach* (FFG 43) as chief engineer and Destroyer Squadron Thirteen as material officer.

After graduation from the Naval Postgraduate School, Commander Bruhn was assigned to Secretary of the Navy and Chief of Naval Operation staffs as a budget analyst and resources planner before attending the Naval War College in 1996, following which he commanded the mine countermeasures ships USS *Gladiator* (MCM 11) and USS *Dextrous* (MCM 13) in the Persian Gulf.

Commander Bruhn's final assignment was executive assistant to a senior (SES 4) government service executive at the Ballistic Missile Defense Organization in Washington, D.C.

Following military service, he was a high school teacher and track coach for ten years, and is now a USA Track & Field official. He lives in northern California with his wife Nancy and has two sons, David and Michael.

www.ingramcontent.com/pod-product-compliance
Lightning Source LLC
Chambersburg PA
CBHW051624230426
43669CB00013B/2178